Alexander Mc Ghee

KERYGMA AND MYTH

KERYGMA AND MYTH

A THEOLOGICAL DEBATE

VOLUME II

With contributions by Hans-Werner Bartsch,
Karl Barth, Gustav Brøndsted, Rudolf Bultmann,
Karl Jaspers, Heinrich Ott, and
Rudolf Schnackenburg

EDITED BY
HANS-WERNER BARTSCH

TRANSLATED BY
REGINALD H. FULLER

LONDON
S·P·C·K
1962

English translation first published in 1962
by S.P.C.K.
Holy Trinity Church
Marylebone Road
London N.W.1
Printed in Great Britain by
Billing and Sons Ltd., Guildford and London

CONTENTS

TRANSLATOR'S PREFACE

THE first volume of *Kerygma and Myth*, which included selections from *Kerygma und Mythos*, I and II, edited by H.-W. Bartsch (1948 and 1952), was published in 1953. Since then, three further volumes of *Kerygma und Mythos* have appeared, together with a supplement to volumes I and II.

By about 1952 the demythologizing debate had crystallized round three related, though distinct, issues: the "objective factualness" of the redemptive events, the problem of hermeneutics (the legitimacy of existentialist exegesis of the New Testament), and the problem of the relation between kerygma and history. The first of these issues has already become familiar to English-speaking readers through the appearance of Friedrich Gogarten's *Demythologizing and History* (1955). The supplemental volume to *Kerygma und Mythos*, I–II, reports the debate on all three issues, and forms the first chapter of the present translation.

The debate was threatening to become sterile by the consolidation of the Bultmannians on the one hand and of the official Lutheran theologians on the other, and as a welcome voice from the outside the contribution of Karl Jaspers from a secular philosophical standpoint formed the central essay in *Kerygma und Mythos*, III, 1954 (*Das Gespräch mit der Philosophie*). This essay, together with the reply of Bultmann and his defence by Bartsch are included for translation here.

From about 1950 the debate spread far beyond the confines of Lutheranism and the German-speaking countries, and in 1955 *Kerygma und Mythos*, IV, appeared with contributions from the Swiss, Scandinavian, and Anglo-Saxon worlds. Since the latter are already available in the original, the present volume confines itself to the essays by Heinrich Ott of Switzerland, who broaches here the important subject to which he has since devoted much further thought, namely, the quest for a new ontological language for theological statement, and by Gustav Brøndsted (d. 1959) of Denmark, who writes from the point of view of a disciple of Grundtvig rather than of Kierkegaard.

Finally, there have been important criticisms from continental Roman Catholic scholars, one of whom, L. Malevez, *The Christian Message and Myth* (1958), has already become known to English-speaking readers. Volume V of *Kerygma und Mythos* is devoted entirely to such Roman Catholic contributions. Since the Chalcedonian formula is of particular concern to Anglicans, and since Bultmann's existentialist Christology raises important questions with regard to that formula, we have selected Rudolf Schnackenburg's essay, "Christology and Myth", for inclusion here, though without thereby implying that this is the definitive answer to Bultmann in the area of Christology.

In addition, the essay of Barth, "Rudolf Bultmann, an Attempt to Understand him" (the title is humorous, since "understanding" is a central concept in Bultmann's theology), is included here, though it does not form one of the essays in any of the volumes of *Kerygma und Mythos*. This has been done to make it available to English-speaking readers both for its own intrinsic value, and also because a knowledge of it is necessary for the understanding of the essay by Heinrich Ott.

Essays 1, 5, 7, and 8 are translated wholly by myself. No. 2 is the revision of a translation of Barth's *Attempt* which had been prepared for the S.C.M. Press, but was not used by them. Nos. 3 and 4 are taken from the translation in *Myth and Christianity*, published by the Noonday Press of New York, revised and edited to conform to the present series. No. 7 has been translated from the original Danish by my colleague, the Reverend Professor Carmeno de Catanzaro, PH.D.

REGINALD H. FULLER.

SEABURY-WESTERN THEOLOGICAL SEMINARY,
EVANSTON, ILLINOIS.

September 1960.

HANS-WERNER BARTSCH

THE PRESENT STATE OF THE DEBATE

(1954)

UNQUESTIONABLY, the outstanding event in the Bultmann controversy has been the pronouncement of the Bishops of the United Evangelical-Lutheran Church of Germany, which was drawn up at the bishops' conference in 1953, and read out from the pulpits of the constituent churches of that body on the Sunday next before Advent. Here is the pronouncement:

> Fear not! "I am the first and the last, and the living one; I died, and behold I am alive for evermore, and I have the keys of Death and Hades" (Rev. 1. 17f).
>
> That is the message of this Sunday. It is a potent message, a message of death and resurrection.
>
> The Christian Church is a waiting community, waiting for the return of the Lord Jesus Christ. As he rose from the dead, so likewise he will return in glory "to judge the living and the dead" (II Tim. 4. 1). Mindful of the transitoriness of human life, we wait for him who will raise us above this fallen world, where tribulation and suffering is our lot. "According to his promise we wait for new heavens and a new earth in which righteousness dwells" (II Pet. 3. 13).
>
> Here is the heart of our faith, and the centre of the Church's message. It is founded on fact, the fact that Jesus lives. The Church's mission is to bear constant witness to this message, preaching it to all nations and to every age in its own language, and in its own patterns of thought.
>
> In recent years a new anxiety has arisen within the Church, and with good reason. Some theologians in our universities, eager to find new ways to commend the gospel message to the modern world, have set about "demythologizing" the New Testament, as they call it. In

so doing, they are in danger of reducing parts of the New Testament, and even of abandoning it altogether. They rightly perceive that the New Testament is couched in the language and thought forms of the age in which it was written. But we are bound to ask whether this movement is not leading to a denial of the facts to which Scripture bears witness.

There is a pressing need for the Church to engage in debate with these theologians. That is why churchmen from our own administrative bodies, and from the theological faculties and seminaries are in continual discussion with representatives of this school of thought. Their purpose is to uphold the purity of Christian doctrine.

This, however, is not enough. We appeal to the congregations to hold fast to the confession of Jesus Christ, the incarnate, crucified and risen Lord, who lives and reigns at the right hand of the Father, and who will come again in glory. In the words of the Apostles' Creed the Church has borne witness to the mighty acts of God in history from century to century. Sunday by Sunday she has for all the world to hear confessed her faith in prayer. The creed will strengthen and encourage us to live our lives amid toil and tribulation. It will fortify us to believe that our labour is not vain in the Lord. With this creed on our lips we place ourselves in God's hands in this hour of crisis. "If we live, we live to the Lord, and if we die, we die to the Lord; so then, whether we live or whether we die, we are the Lord's. For to this end Christ died and lived again, that he might be Lord both of the dead and of the living" (Rom. 14. 8f.).

The importance of this pronouncement lies in the evidence it gives that the churches are no longer willing to discuss matters with Bultmann (for the pronouncement is really aimed at him, although he is not mentioned by name). Instead, they are bent on controversy with him as a teacher of theology. When they speak of the mighty acts of God to which the Church has borne witness from century to century, and of the fact on which the Church is founded, then, in asking whether Bultmann and his followers deny these facts, they are no longer asking a question, but implying a negative answer. Their appeal to the congregations to uphold the creed makes it look as though Bultmann is undermining it. This is to blur the issue and overlook a theological distinction which must be drawn between first-hand historical evidence and confession of faith in prayer. It is the failure to observe this distinction that creates the impression that Bultmann's theology is undermining the creed. By jumping to the conclusion that he is attacking it, they conclude that it is the Church's task "to be in continuous theological discussion with representatives of this school of thought" with the purpose of upholding "the purity of Christian doctrine".

But the worst feature of this document is its failure to offer any constructive alternative for the solution of the hermeneutic problem. It does indeed mention the problem: "The Church's mission is to bear constant witness to this message, preaching it to all nations and to every age in its own language, and in its own thought forms." But all it does is to express anxiety that demythologizing may lead to a reduction or abandonment of parts of the kerygma. No suggestion is offered as to how the task of interpretation is to be carried out. Since the document does mention the hermeneutic task, what it goes on to say inevitably gives the impression of helplessness in face of it.

If we are to arrive at some estimate about the importance of this pronouncement, we must recall how the debate began. At first it was essentially a discussion within the Church, and indeed, a discussion within the confessing Church, to which Bultmann himself belonged, and of which he was recognized as a spokesman, even by his critics.

Thus, for example, Sauter's essay in the second (German) volume of *Kerygma und Mythos* (pp. 41ff.) was a memorandum commissioned by and discussed in the confessing Church in the Electorate of Hesse. Similarly, Thielicke's essay (*Kerygma and Myth*, I, E.T., pp. 138ff.) was produced at the instigation of the Bishop of Wurtemberg, who was himself a member of the confessing Church. This essay quotes Sauter repeatedly, a sign that the debate was then being carried on within the Church. Thielicke openly admits that his differences with Bultmann concerned the method rather than the objective, on which they were both agreed. That is why he stressed their common bond in their membership of the Church: "How far can the theologian go without incurring the penalty of excommunication for unorthodoxy?

The criterion is never, or very rarely, whether we are travelling on the same road, but whether, as we travel along our different roads, we all look towards the same goal'' (op. cit., p. 174). The importance of what Thielicke says is all the more enhanced when we recall that it was written at a time of acute tension between Lutherans and Reformed churchmen over the question of intercommunion, and when the whole subject was bedevilled by the problem of the German Christians.

That the challenge of demythologizing was being taken seriously within the confessing Church all along the line is shown lastly by the list of participants to the discussion. They were the same theologians who were so anxious at that time about the whole fabric of the Church, an anxiety they all shared in spite of the tensions between the provisional governing body and the so-called Lutheran council.

The important thing to remember is that Bultmann's programme arose out of the Church struggle. It was not an accident that it began just then. Nor is it accidental that Bultmann's essay first appeared in the *Beiträge zur Evangelischen Theologie*, a series planned to carry on the work of the prohibited journal *Evangelische Theologie*. The policy of the *Beiträge* was to stimulate theological study in the confessing Church and thus provide a basis for the confession which the times demanded. There was no time then for risky ventures in academic scholarship.

Why it was so necessary for the debate to be carried on *within* the Church is made abundantly clear by Julius Schniewind in his first thesis: ''Bultmann's desire to emancipate the gospel message from mythology is something which he shares with every preacher who is worth his salt'' (*Kerygma and Myth*, I, E.T., p. 45). There is no polite take it or leave it about this thesis, as has often been the case with other replies to Bultmann. He takes up the same point again in his final thesis, No. VIII: ''Bultmann's challenge still stands. The world view and language of the Bible must be translated into our own'' (op. cit., p. 87).

The importance of Bultmann's challenge for the Church can be seen from this. That Schniewind's essay was written when it was is not only something we can well understand: it was an urgent necessity at the time of the Church struggle. We could put it like this: what Bultmann was trying to do was to interpret the first thesis of the Barmen declaration: "Jesus Christ is the *one* word of God which we must hear . . ." It will be for history to decide what effect the Barmen declaration had on the whole theological enterprise of our age. But the fact that Bultmann's programme was part and parcel of Barmen movement is to my mind undeniable. This must be insisted on in view of the Lutheran bishops' pronouncement. We might even claim that Bultmann was trying to prevent the Barmen declaration from hardening into a doctrinal proposition, so that all that was necessary was to give it formal assent. Bultmann was trying to keep it alive as a real confession of faith, as Martin Niemöller understands that word. If that is our purpose, we are bound to ask what relevance the declaration has for daily life. How can we put it across in our preaching and commend it to the hearts of men?

That is the very question Bultmann was asking. That is just the problem he was trying to solve. And that is why the discussion must still be carried on within the Church, unless of course we are ready to abandon what we recognized in 1934 to be its very foundation. It was for the same reason that Schniewind and Bultmann were agreed that the discussion as carried on within the Church is essentially the same as that between the Church and the outside world (*Kerygma and Myth*, I, E.T., pp. 102 and 123), "because it concerns the present task of the kerygma". Just think how important this agreement is. It means that Bultmann is regarded as one engaged in an enterprise which is a legitimate task of the Church, a programme which he is pursuing with the Church's commission. He is regarded as a theologian and doctor of the Church, even though his proposed solutions do not commend themselves to everybody. All this, let us remind ourselves, was being said when there were other professors of theology who were definitely *not* accepted as doctors of the Church, and when the Church felt obliged to organize alternative courses of lectures where professors of theology had actually withdrawn from the Church. This gives all the more weight to the prevailing view that Bultmann *was* a doctor of the Church. And it may well be asked what has changed since then, that Bultmann should no longer be counted as a churchman.

It was not until after the war that people began asking whether Bultmann's position was tenable. Quite likely the trouble began with the ill-advised activities of some of Bultmann's younger pupils, who as pastors or assistant clergy in Wurtemberg parishes were alleged to be teaching in the day schools and from their pulpits that Jesus never did any miracles or rose from the dead. Unfortunately, I have this information only by hearsay, though it would seem to explain the Bishop of Wurtemberg's charge, and the Church struggle which flared up in that province in the early fifties. Hermann Sasse had produced a parody of the creed à la Bultmann, which ran like this:

> . . . not conceived by the Holy Ghost,
> Not born of the Virgin Mary:
> Suffered, indeed, under Pontius Pilate,
> Was crucified, dead, and buried:
> He did not descend into hell;
> The third day he rose not from the dead:
> He ascended not into heaven,
> And therefore sitteth not at the right hand of God
> the Father Almighty:
> From whence therefore he shall not come to judge
> the quick and the dead.[1]

It was said that some of these young Bultmannians had taken up the parody and used it seriously. F. Reinecker published a pamphlet entitled *Entmythologisierung* (Wuppertal, 1951) in which he attacked this alleged reduction of the Creed (p. 68). Since Reinecker is a spokesman for the pietists, and since the opposition to Bultmann in Wurtemberg comes from the same quarter, the connection seems obvious.

It was this that led the Bishop of Wurtemberg (Dr Haug) to speak out so strongly in a charge to his diocese: "Resist this attempt to interpret the gospel as a myth, and to translate it into existentialist terms. Such a translation is supposed to get rid of the mythical elements in the gospel, but it ends by eliminating

[1] *Flucht vor dem Dogma, Luthertum*, 1942, pp. 161ff.

some of its essential parts. No one will come to your defence if you offer your congregations the truth of Christ with so many subtractions." The Bishop of Baden, Dr Bender, took a similar stand at his provincial synod in the autumn of 1950. So did a memorandum put forth by the Church in the Rhineland, which effectively prevented the appointment of Dr Ernst Fuchs, one of Bultmann's pupils, to a chair in Bonn.

Of course these official pronouncements of the Church spring from a genuine pastoral concern for the laity, who were bewildered by the preaching of Bultmann's followers. But the question, we must insist, is how far the preaching in question was true to Bultmann himself. As the case of Sasse shows, it is apparently very difficult to distinguish between the contention that the propositions like those in the Creed no longer have the same meaning for modern man as they once had, and the assertion that these propositions are no longer valid, but must be rejected. It should hardly be necessary to prove that Sasse's parody says the exact opposite of what Bultmann intends when he keeps repeating: "It is impossible to believe." This certainly does not mean "*not* born of the Virgin Mary". Putting it positively, we might say that Bultmann's interpretation of the Creed lays emphasis on the "credo"—"I *believe*", as Karl Barth taught us to do. The articles of the Creed are to be taken strictly as statements of faith, which means by implication that they are not propositions of objective knowledge.

If the younger Bultmannian clergy ignore this distinction, they should be brought to heel. Something must have been wrong with their training in practical theology. They should be told that they are saying something very different from the teacher to whom they appeal. They should remember what Schniewind said in his second thesis: "The Christian answer is, in W. Herrmann's phrase, 'God is Jesus' (Col. 1. 15; John 14. 9). Bultmann would agree in principle" (*Kerygma and Myth*, I, E.T., p. 47). Our own reason for going into all this is to explain the anxieties which led to the official pronouncements of the Church[1] and to

[1] To the pronouncements already mentioned should be added *Erklärung zur Bultmannischen Theologie*, a statement of the Evangelical Confessional Fellowship in Wurtemberg, published in *Für Arbeit und Besinnung*, 1952, pp. 18ff.

show their lack of any real concern for him whom they criticize. They do not really hit the mark at all, and are merely caricatures of his theology. The real reason is that by this time the demythologizing debate was no longer being conducted as a discussion within the Church. No attention was paid to Bultmann's later contributions to the discussion, nor was he ever challenged to speak for himself. It may be doubted whether there would have been any chance of talking with Eberhard Stauffer at the German Clergy Conference at Neustadt-on-Hardt in 1949, or if so, whether anything would have come of it. But the German clergy had a right to hear what Bultmann would have said in reply to Stauffer, and they should have been given a chance to make up their minds for themselves. But Neustadt was not the only place where Bultmann or his followers were given no chance to speak for themselves.

We are therefore driven to conclude that people no longer felt on speaking terms with Bultmann after the war. All the pronouncements, official and otherwise, simply ignore him. They make no attempt to hear what the other side has to say. This is all the more regrettable when we see how much came out of the discussion between Schniewind and Bultmann. Neither confined himself to stating his own position and then refusing to budge an inch. It was not only in the first and last theses that they expressed their basic agreement. Bultmann welcomed what Schniewind had to say even where he was critical of his own position. There was a clearing of the air and to some extent a rapprochement. There is something wrong with the Church when such discussions are no longer possible.

In April 1952 the General Synod of the United Evangelical-Lutheran Church in Germany showed that the strict Lutherans were firmly entrenched in the attitude they had chosen. True, their resolution avoids coming down clearly on one side or the other, and confines itself to a report of the three lectures that were delivered during the synod. At the same time, the line taken in the lectures was abundantly clear, and the publicity they were given (they were delivered in the principal church at Flensburg) made the whole procedure look like a public condemnation of

Bultmann. "Bultmann's Reply to his critics"[1] was already out by then. His aim was to point out the parallel between his own theology and Luther's. A discussion on that level would surely have been profitable for the Lutheran Church, and the fact that neither Bultmann nor anyone who could have spoken for him was invited only goes to show that nobody wanted to talk with him. It was said that there were no actual *Lutheran* theologians who could represent Bultmann. But that excuse won't hold water. Surely it would not have been out of place to invite a non-Lutheran to speak at such a gathering, assuming that Bultmann himself is not a Lutheran! And then Götz Harbsmeier, one of his pupils, was a pastor in the Church of Hanover at that time. It all goes to show that they were toeing the same line as the bishops did later, and had shifted from discussion to controversy. The anthology of essays circulated among various Lutheran provincial churches by the Bavarian Society for Evangelical Publications, edited by Ernst Kinder and made available to the bench of bishops, was almost given an official imprimatur by their pronouncement. This was hardly affected by the rider they added, that they assumed that the pertinent essays of Professor Bultmann were being carefully studied, and their reference to the two anthologies, *Entmythologisierung* (Stuttgart, 1949) and *Kerygma und Mythos*, Vols. I and II (Hamburg, 1952). The ordinary pastor knew that this was the official verdict of the Lutheran theologians, and that the authors were being officially recognized by the Lutheran Church as their spokesmen in the Bultmann controversy. All this adds weight to the statement in the Kinder volume, which says: "We have no alternative but to condemn Bultmann for false doctrine, much as we shrink from a heresy hunt" (op. cit., p. 96). This remark undercuts Bishop Meiser's explanation of the bishops' pronouncement: "Once more, let us make it crystal clear that there is no question of our condemning anyone for heresy. We are only seeking to promote scholarly discussion."[2] Apparently false doctrine is not the same thing as heresy! And despite Bishop Meiser's reassurances, the warning of the bishops

[1] *Kerygma und Mythos*, II, pp. 179ff. Cf. E.T., Vol. I, pp. 191ff.

[2] *Evangelische-Lutherische Kirchenzeitung*, 1953, p. 362.

against Bultmann's theology still seems to imply a condemnation of Bultmann for false doctrine. One thing at least is clear: the Bultmann controversy had long ceased to be a discussion within the Church. Everyone was too anxious to controvert Bultmann to listen to him or to promote a public discussion between both sides. Only one gain has come from the bishops' pronouncement and its associated publications. It has made it clear that this is no longer a discussion within the Church, but a controversy between the Lutheran Church allied with pietism on the one hand, and a cross section of theologians on the other, who owe a great debt to Bultmann and his theology as preachers of the Word of God.

It only remains to ask what is the outcome of all this. First, it means driving out of the Church all who cannot subscribe to the notion of objective "facts" of salvation, in the sense in which that term has become customary on the Lutheran side. Are the bishops ready to bear the burden of this responsibility? They cannot get out of it by telling us there won't be any heresy trials. (It is indeed unfortunate that they should have spoken in that ironical way of condemning Bultmann's theology as false doctrine.) On the other hand, Bultmann's disciples will now have to ask themselves whether they are prepared to alter their preaching, retract what they have written, and submit to the bishops. Whether they will have to do so will depend on the theological authority attaching to the bishops' pronouncement and the other publications connected with it (more will be said on that score later) or whether they will have no alternative but to defy them. In other words, they may find themselves in a *status confessionis*, ranged against their ecclesiastical authorities. But the reason for this state of affairs is that the Bultmann debate has ceased to be a discussion within the Church, and has taken on the form of a controversy between the Church and men whom it no longer regards as churchmen. Only a return to a genuine dialogue will avert a Church struggle and keep Bultmann's positive concern, which Bishop Meiser still recognizes, from going by the board.

It may be assumed that the ecclesiastical authorities, the bishops included, never dreamt what effect their policy might have on those clergy and theological teachers who are sensitive of their incalculable debt to Bultmann and his theology. Perhaps they feel it is still a discussion within the Church, despite their long-standing reluctance to let Bultmann speak for himself, i.e. to engage with him in a genuine dialogue. Instead, they talk about an academic debate. The trouble was, they failed to realize how important the issues Bultmann was raising were for the life of the Church, and its positive bearing on her message. Perhaps it was expecting too much that they should. After all, Bultmann's programme has been misinterpreted in many other quarters as springing from a concern for academic integrity. The ecclesiastical authorities were not the only ones to fall into that trap. The latest casualty is Karl Jaspers: "Now Bultmann, we feel, speaks from a sense of scientific responsibility."[1] What Jaspers really misses, as he goes on to show, is the sense that "the true man of faith speaks out of Encompassing Reality" (ibid.). There is no awareness that "theology grounds its understanding in the Holy Ghost". This is a serious criticism, all the more so since Jaspers is one with whom Bultmann is most anxious to engage in conversation, one to whom he hopes to communicate the gospel and help to understand where the decision of faith really lies. We cannot therefore blame the ecclesiastical authorities for regarding Bultmann as the scholar, merely concerned with academic integrity. Naturally, they are loathe to permit a scholar to decide what should be preached and what should not!

How are we to account for this misunderstanding? The reason for it is that Bultmann's original essay starts with the modern world view, and the consequent difficulty of believing the Christian message. He did not bring out clearly enough in that lecture his concern for the message of the New Testament and for the dilemma of the contemporary preacher, who has to pass on that message to the man in the pew in such a way that it makes sense to him. Only a man like Julius Schniewind could see that this was the real point of what Bultmann was driving at, although he was not happy with Bultmann's conclusions. It was a tragedy that the Bultmann-Schniewind debate fell into oblivion, and the cause they both shared went by the board.

[1] See below, pp. 33ff.

Instead, a new antithesis came to the foreground, and was still a determining factor in the bishops' pronouncement. The issue at stake, it was alleged, was whether demythologizing involves a denial of the "facts" which Scripture testifies. Such a denial was stigmatized as a subtraction from the kerygma. Those who follow Bultmann in their understanding of the preacher's task cannot possibly talk about "facts" in this vein. The kerygma does not contain any "facts". They find it impossible to go along with the bishops when they say that our faith "is founded on fact" (above, p. 1), that this is what inspires us to preach the gospel message, or that this is its centre. At all events, this is the case if the bishops were talking about "facts" in the same sense as the Lutheran theologians are. Bultmann's adherents must insist that there are no facts accessible to knowledge and prior to faith. They will appeal to Bultmann's oft-quoted statement: "Our radical attempt to demythologize the New Testament is in fact a perfect parallel to St Paul's and Luther's doctrine of justification by faith alone apart from the works of the Law. Or rather, it carries this doctrine to its logical conclusion in the field of epistemology."[1] But not enough attention has been paid to the reason Bultmann gives for this statement: "The man who wishes to believe in God as his God must realize that he has nothing in his hand on which to base his faith. He is suspended in mid-air, and *cannot demand a proof of the Word which addresses him*."[2] In reply to the bishops we must therefore insist that our faith is founded solely on the Word of God as it speaks to us, and that in saying this we are already making a very definite confession of faith by speaking of the Word of *God*.

There would seem however to be no real need for this disagreement. It is the result of a wrong turning which the debate took when it ceased to be a discussion within the Church. This is well illustrated by Schniewind's position. He shows that the pericopes can still be treated as historical narratives even when the historian is doubtful about them. Anyone familiar with Schniewind knows how much more cautious and sceptical he was in this respect in his academic work in seminar and lecture than his commentaries

[1] *Kerygma and Myth*, E.T., Vol. I, pp. 210ff. [2] Ibid. Italics, H.-W.B.

in the *Neues Testament Deutsch* suggest. Similarly, it has already been pointed out that in *Jesus and the Word* Bultmann made use of a considerable amount of material which he questioned as to its historicity in *Geschichte der Synoptischen Tradition*. The only conclusion we need draw from this is that the antithesis between kerygma and factual evidence is neither exclusive nor inevitable. (In a volume of sermons entitled *Die Anrede Gottes*[1] I have myself endeavoured to refute the mistaken notion that an absolute emphasis on the kerygmatic character of the New Testament message renders the pericopes useless for preaching purposes.) So long as we are agreed that the primary and sole intention of the New Testament message is proclamation, proclamation of the Word of God, we are entirely free to treat the individual pericopes either as historical narratives or as myths with no historical value. It is merely a practical consideration how best to bring home to others the actual message of the New Testament.

Once however this antithesis has been removed, we are bound to insist that to talk about "facts" in the way the bishops are suspected of doing (and with much excuse, considering what the Lutheran theologians had already said on the subject) cannot fail to suggest a misrepresentation of the New Testament message.

At least, so it would seem to anyone who understands that message as kerygma, and has learnt from Bultmann that everything else in the New Testament is only ancillary to the kerygma.

The bishops' pronouncement and the Lutheran theologians can ostensibly put up a good case. No one can deny that the New Testament speaks of facts, or witnesses to the mighty acts of God. But the facts are mixed up with the kerygma itself, and no distinction is drawn between them. But there is no going back to that situation to-day. We are compelled to draw the distinction between the facts themselves and the delivery of the message to-day. We are bound to acknowledge that the primary element here is the contemporary delivery of the message. It must also be added that the New Testament message does not bear witness to a series of facts, but to the eschatological act of God in the proclamation of the Christ. This is the crux of the dispute between

[1] Hamburg, 1953.

the Church authorities and the disciples of Bultmann. Let it be once more emphasized that there is no real necessity for this *status confessionis*. These matters could still be discussed within the Church. There is still room for debate about the significance and function of "facts" in the kerygma, of the "transubjective" element, or whatever we like to call it, which the Lutheran theologians are so worried about. This is especially so since there is still apparently some recognition of Bultmann's "positive concern".

This is not the place to assess the theological weight of the various opinions which have been expressed in the debate. Our initial task is merely to show the importance of the debate in the life of the Church, of both the various statements from the orthodox Lutheran side, and the inevitable reaction these have produced from the friends and pupils of Bultmann. We have tried to show what a serious issue Bultmann has raised in his positive concern, a matter which appears to have been widely overlooked. We must bear testimony to the debt we owe to Bultmann for what he has taught us and for the joy we have found in preaching the gospel. We are ready even to endure the condemnation of the bishops, and to defy it in confessing our faith. We may still ask however whether it is really necessary for things to come to this pass, and whether the discussion might not be resumed as one within the Church.

The Hermeneutical Problem

We hope, then, that the Bultmann controversy will return to its original character, and become a discussion within the Church. We hope it will become a genuine dialogue in which the parties are not so much concerned to define their own position against the other side as to reach a real mutual understanding. If this is to happen, we must consider the status of the problem of hermeneutics for the Church and its preaching. Was Schniewind right in his description of the situation facing the Church? The only reason why the debate lost its original character as a discussion within the Church was that people forgot the evangelistic urgency behind the challenge of Bultmann's original essay. They forgot that he was dealing with a problem whose seriousness, as Schniewind said, no preacher could ignore.[1] Schniewind's thesis must be taken seriously all along the line. It is not just a problem of the fringe doctrines, such as the Ascension. It dogs the preacher's footsteps in every sermon he preaches. In the *Lübecker Nachrichten*, a daily newspaper, the leading article on Ascension Day 1952 was entitled "The Ascension without Heaven". It bluntly asked the Church what it had to say on this day now that nobody believed in a heaven up in the sky. Schniewind gives a similar example.[2] But these are only the most glaring instances of a difficulty we face in every sermon we preach. It faces us not only on Good Friday, but even when the Sunday gospel is one of the parables. For every sermon is meant to be a proclamation of Jesus the Christ and Son of God, and the preacher must somehow or other make that message intelligible to his hearers. That is to say, he must confront them with the challenge to accept or reject this message. They cannot help misunderstanding it if it is presented to them as a series of facts or propositions which they have to accept as true.

The message of the pericopes is not brought home to people simply by repeating them as they stand, or when they are treated as narratives of fact. Such a treatment would only be in order if there was no problem whatever about their factual character. In this case the message would not be smothered by the reluctance of the hearer to accept the narrative as literally true, or impeded by his frantic attempt to bring himself to believe it. Yet the difficulty can be just as real when the hearer indicates his readiness to accept the literal truth of the narrative. For in this case his decision is not the answer to the real challenge of the pericope. The real kerygma behind it has never been brought out.

There is no doubt that Bultmann is right about this, and right about the reasons he gives for it. The situation is every whit as serious as Bultmann sees it. It confronts us in every pericope.

It is not only the pietists and Hermann Sasse who have contended that there was no real problem here at all. A recent and

[1] *Kerygma and Myth*, E.T., Vol. I, pp. 45f. [2] Op. cit., pp. 46f.

quite unsparing effort in this direction has come from the pen of Hans Beckmann,[1] an article which received the warm-hearted approval of the *Deutsches Pfarrerblatt*. Beckmann criticizes demythologizing (though he does not mention it by name) for showing too much deference to modern man. He condemns such things as the Priest-Worker movement for similar reasons, and even the use of such modern inventions as the radio to spread the gospel. On the other hand, he sees the church as a haven of refuge where man can satisfy his spiritual needs, a place of peace and quiet. If that is what the church is for, then there is certainly no point in Bultmann's challenge. That challenge is equally called in question where it is recognized as true only to a partial extent, i.e. where myth is regarded as one among other forms of expression in the New Testament. That suggestion was made quite early on by Helmut Thielicke, with his distinction between purely mythological statements and those which "though they appear to be mythical, are to be taken as literal history".[2] Admittedly, Thielicke only throws this out as a suggestion, without indicating whether this is a true picture of the situation.

This brings us to another and perhaps more promising feature of the debate. There seems to be general agreement that Bultmann has put his finger on a real problem. But is "myth", as Bultmann defines it, an acceptable term? What we need to begin with is to clarify the presuppositions from which Bultmann embarks upon his hermeneutic venture. Unless this is done first, it is impossible to discuss whether or not we agree with Bultmann's solution. Unless we agree about our presuppositions we shall be talking over one another's heads. This is one of the greatest difficulties which has dogged the whole discussion. It springs from a failure to distinguish between two entirely different questions. The first is, Bultmann's initial presuppositions and his description of the situation confronting the preacher (including his definition of "myth"). The other is the way he carries out his hermeneutics. Our judgement of Bultmann's results will vary

[1] "*Mitläufer des 20. Jahrhunderts*" ("Fellow travellers of the Twentieth Century") in *Zeitwende*, 1, 1954.

[2] *Kerygma and Myth*, E.T., Vol. I, p. 162.

with our hermeneutic principles. It is not at all surprising that the complaint about Bultmann's solution comes from those who have a different set of hermeneutic principles.

From the orthodox Lutheran side Ernst Kinder has made several attempts to work out a *via media* which will accept Bultmann's challenge and do justice to his concern, yet confine his criticism of Bultmann to the way he carries out his hermeneutics. In the process, however, Kinder inadvertently gets involved in a criticism of the terms in which Bultmann frames his challenge. As Kinder himself admits, "the existentialist interpretation of the New Testament message constitutes a fresh challenge to theology. But it can only fulfil its promise and prove its adequacy if it is prepared for a frank acceptance of the objective facts to which the New Testament bears witness, which the Church *confesses*, and which *faith apprehends*, though never at the cost of surrendering their objectivity."[1] If the italicized words are taken seriously, there is nothing wrong with this. The facts attested in the New Testament are certainly to be understood as testimonies to faith, and in this sense they must never be allowed to go by the board. But when Kinder comes to work out his thesis, it becomes as obvious here as in the bishops' pronouncement that the term "objective facts" is misleading in this context. For he goes on to distinguish between "objectively factual" and "kerygmaticly potent".[2] Thus he makes it clear that in speaking of objective facts he is not thinking of their apprehension in faith, but of a cognition which precedes faith and provides a foundation for it. He fails to see that he begins to disagree with Bultmann from the very moment he speaks of "facts", for facts conceived thus cannot be susceptible of existential interpretation. This can only be done independently of the facticity of what is alleged in the particular statement. Thus Kinder's contrast between "objectively factual" on the one hand, and "kerygmaticly potent" or "of existentialist (he should have said 'existential') significance" on the other is a construction of his own. The only importance which Bultmann attaches to objective factualness is that it is entirely devoid of im-

[1] *Ein Wort lutherischer Theologie zur Entmythologisierung.* Italics, H.-W.B.
[2] Op. cit., p. 55.

portance. And the only reason why he takes for granted this non-recognition of this objective factualness is that it is a given fact. In spite of this he insists that the New Testament kerygma can be presented in intelligible terms. For the same reason the "theology of demythologizing" as Kinder presents it[1] is a construction of his own, bearing little or no relation to Bultmann's programme.[2]

We turn now to a contribution by Walter Künneth. Künneth rejects Bultmann more definitely than Kinder does, and lacks his sympathetic approach, which does try to understand what Bultmann is aiming at, even if it ends up by insisting that it is a case of "both-and" rather than "either-or". Künneth rejects outright Bultmann's description of the preacher's dilemma, and his own as a theologian. Admittedly, he qualifies this to some extent: "Bultmann's concern appears to be justified in principle. The duty of the theologian as he sees it, the duty of producing a relevant translation of the kerygma is of course the primary task of every theologian and preacher."[3] This sounds almost like Schniewind in his first thesis. Nor does it matter so very much that Künneth mistakenly regards Bultmann as the "residuary legatee of the historico-critical method" (ibid.). Surely, Künneth ought to know that form-criticism, a movement in which Bultmann was one of the pioneers, and which he used as a tool for exegesis, is not the same thing as historical criticism. Historical criticism enquires into the literary motifs behind the text, form-criticism into the historical matrix in which the narratives took shape. The very fact that Bultmann has ceased to be concerned about the historical reliability of the tradition[4] means that he has moved away from historical criticism. Künneth's preoccupation with historical reliability goes a long way to explain why he cannot see the point of demythologizing. So, too, does his argument

[1] Op. cit., p. 33.

[2] Kinder's contention that Bultmann's theology represents a recrudescence of the older liberalism was refuted quite early on by Herbert Braun in his review of Bultmann's *Theology of the New Testament* in *Verkündigung und Forschung*, 1951, entitled "*Die Ueberwindung des Liberalismus auf der Ebene des Kritizismus*" ("The transcendence of liberalism on the level of criticism").

[3] *Ein Wort lutherischer Theologie*, p. 65.

[4] Ibid., p. 69.

for the possibility of miracle from the fact that even scientists are prepared to accept the miraculous to-day. Quite apart from the fact that this is simply repeating a mistake which is very common nowadays, it means that Künneth is deliberately shutting his eyes to the problem Bultmann has raised. His apologetic for the miraculous deprives them of their kerygmatic significance. The kerygma is to be sought in the miracle stories themselves, not in their alleged historicity which is accepted as possible even by modern science. In other words, Künneth bypasses the real intent of the stories, which is to report a *miracle*, nothing else. Künneth is thus open to the same charge he has so often levelled against Bultmann. He is following the path of traditional rationalism and trying to offer a rational explanation of the miracles. Such indeed is the trend of his argument.

There is yet another angle from which Künneth seeks to elude Bultmann's challenge. He speaks of "the modern revival of interest in mythical forces".[1] In saying this he at once betrays his misunderstanding of what Bultmann means by myth. In any case there is no question of any revival of the mythical world view. Künneth's essay in apologetics raises a very serious theological question: What is his real estimate of "the resurgence of love for the irrational and the transcendent" (ibid.), the flood of superstition, the fascination of spiritism, etc.? Does he really think that such phenomena make people "welcome statements of faith and predisposed to accept their truth"? (ibid.). Is it not a radical perversion of faith to confuse it with belief in the miraculous? In any case, Bultmann cannot help finding fault with him for this. And in any case, it is clear that Künneth is here avoiding Bultmann's challenge, and thus nullifying his initial acceptance of it.

The most outspoken rejection of Bultmann's challenge comes from Wilhelm Mundle.[2] He dismisses demythologizing as a recrudescence of liberalism. It represents a "preoccupation with subjective religious experience". Mundle completely ignores its

[1] Ibid., p. 77.

[2] *Der Glaube an Christus und der historische Zweifel* ("Faith in Christ and Historical Scepticism"), 1950.

implications for hermeneutics. Hence he contents himself by exposing Bultmann's rationalist presuppositions, and completely ignores his real concern, which is to communicate the New Testament message to those whose lives are governed by those presuppositions, in such a way that its challenge is brought home to them. He is blissfully unaware, like Künneth, that it is *he* who is bogged down by rationalist arguments, as for example, when he resorts to psychological explanations for the miracles (p. 164).

Much more attention is paid to the hermeneutic implications of demythologizing by Hans Loof in his essay *Symbol und Transcendenz mit besonderer Berzcksichtigung der Entmythologisierung der christlichen Religion*.[1] He approaches the question more from the point of view of the philosophy of religion, and makes the mistake of confusing demythologizing with "the separation of the kernel from the husk, of the essential content from its temporary garb". In other words, it means subtraction and elimination rather than an interpretation which preserves what it interprets. As a result, he regards it as a "discriminating and selective reduction". Bultmann, for him, is very much like Karl Jaspers except that he does not go so far. Even so, demythologizing involves a "monstrous reduction of the Christian faith". He might have contributed something by introducing the term "symbol" into the discussion had he not mistakenly insisted, and indeed taken for granted, that to demythologize means to eliminate symbolism.

In his essay *Entmythologisierung des Christentums*[2] A. Oepke begins by explicitly accepting Bultmann's challenge. Yet he too runs away from it by insisting that it is no new problem at all. "We did not need Bultmann to tell us about it, though we did not know of it before" (p. 333). This means that he fails to recognize the seriousness and urgency of its hermeneutic implications. He too bypasses the real question. On the one hand he offers too broad a definition of myth as an omnibus term for "the immanent, transcendent, internal, external, etc." (p. 335). On the other hand he claims that demythologizing leaves no room for a

[1] "Symbol and Transcendence, with special reference to the demythologizing of the Christian Religion", *Studium Generale*, 1953, pp. 324ff.

[2] "The Demythologizing of Christianity", *Studium Generale*, 1953, pp. 332ff.

revelation in history (p. 336). Even Oepke should have noticed that Bultmann shelved the question as to whether it is mythological to speak of an act of God[1] only to answer it on page 43. Of course, had he noticed it, it would have made his argument more difficult, but it might have called his attention to the real issue at stake. He would then have seen that the issue was not that of a revelation in history, but of the testimony to and apprehension of that revelation. As so often, the noetic question has been confused with an ontological one. Once again, this confusion has had a disturbing effect on the debate.

Unlike the *Wort lutherischer Theologie*, which received its imprimatur at the bishops' conference, Gerhard Gloege[2] expressly agrees with Bultmann's statement of the problem: "We have scrutinized the point of departure in Bultmann's programmatic essay, and find it accords with the Lutheran confession. Underlying it is a hermeneutic principle which is not only admissible, but vital. Perhaps only a theology founded on Luther's hermeneutics, a theology truly scriptural in its orientation, can fully appreciate the specific nature of Bultmann's concern, and may even understand it better than Bultmann does himself. At all events, those critics who reject his challenge out of hand must ask themselves whether they still share the concerns which animated Luther himself" (p. 90). This positive appreciation springs from Gloege's awareness that Bultmann's point of departure "is closely akin to the basic quest of the Reformation, the Lutheran distinction between law and gospel" (p. 57). Bultmann's distinction between mythology and kerygma is on all fours with the distinction between law and gospel (p. 37). Gloege underlines his point by describing demythologizing in these terms: "It is impossible to understand the intention of a text without regard to the language in which it is expressed. But the language must be interpreted in the light of its intention." This dialectic, which is inherent in demythologizing, is the mainspring of the Lutheran distinction between law and gospel (p. 41). Gloege maintains his point even in face of the possible ob-

[1] *Kerygma and Myth*, E.T., Vol. I, pp. 33f.

[2] *Mythologie und Luthertum*. No. 5 in the series *Luthertum*.

jection that Bultmann is poles apart from Luther in the penetration of his theological reflection and in the radical nature of his historical criticism. He sees what hardly anyone else has seen, that despite the undeniable differences between Bultmann and Luther "these are differences of degree rather than of kind" (p. 42). Both are asking the same question: "*Was Christum treibt?*"

Gloege later returned to the subject, clearly dissociating himself from the official theologians of the Lutheran Church. Their rejection of Bultmann's challenge, he says, springs from non-theological factors, from a particular "ideology". The Lutheran theologians—and they hardly deserve the name—are incapable of taking seriously the questions which form Bultmann's point of departure.

On this basis Gloege continues his discussion with Bultmann. The real question is whether it is really possible to carry through the intention Bultmann has set himself. There are certain obscurities in Bultmann's methodology. He does not draw a clear enough distinction between the hermeneutic, homiletical, and apologetic aspects of the problem. He lumps together the quite different problems which confront the exegete, the Christian believer and modern man. Although there is a connection between them, they must be kept apart (p. 44) for purposes of discussion. Bultmann is sometimes hazy in his terminology, e.g. uses myth and mythology almost as synonyms. Schniewind had made the same point. Again, for all his good intentions, Bultmann ends up by eliminating some of the mythological elements. Nor again is he clear about the relation between mythology and science. The connection between world view and ideology needs as much attention as he pays to that between world view and mythology (p. 50). Nor is he sufficiently clear about what he means by science and nature (pp. 52ff.). The same criticism was made by Jaspers.[1] All these points are well taken, but they are not the main point of Gloege's reaction. This comes in his discussion of the "limitations of the existentialist interpretation" (p. 71). After this must come a theological interpretation (of which he offers an outline), based on the distinction between law and

[1] See below, p. 136.

gospel (pp. 94ff.). The existentialist interpretation offers one hermeneutic possibility among others, but it is illegitimate because it claims to be the only one (p. 73). Again, the point is well taken. There is no need to make such exclusive claims for the existentialist interpretation, nor could they be substantiated. But it may still be asked whether Gloege's gravamen against the existentialist interpretation is a relevant one, and above all, whether it is theologically decisive. His chief complaint is that it leaves no room for the being and action of God outside my own direct experience. What about the doctrine of the Trinity for instance? Gloege has a point here. The existentialist interpretation can do nothing with such doctrines as that: it is bound to bracket them as mythological. But there is more to be said than Gloege allows, and the importance of his criticism should not be exaggerated. For instance, the main areas in which God's action extends to "that which is not God" always have a significance for my existence. I never know what things, forces, or persons, I shall be confronted with, and that is why it is important that God's action should cover this entire range of possible encounters. *Per contra*, we may wonder where Gloege would draw the line against mere speculation. Of course, the New Testament contains statements about God as he is in himself, e.g. about the Trinity. But this does not mean that they are not mere speculation. Gloege thinks that the fact that such statements are not susceptible of existential interpretation does fatal damage to Bultmann's case. It means that there is no longer any theological basis for soteriology. It makes it impossible to interpret "the action of God as *God's* work" (p. 73). This does not however seem necessarily to follow, for it concerns *me* directly that God's action should really be *his*. Redemption is only redemption in the proper sense of the word when it is *God's* work in this sense. Contrary to Gloege, we should argue that more doctrinal propositions are susceptible of existentialist interpretation than he supposes. On the other hand, we are still left wondering how he guards against mere speculation. It cannot be denied that the translation of soteriological affirmations into ontological propositions has led to speculation, as, for example, in the Trinitarian and Christological dogmas of the ancient Catholic Church. The quest for an existentialist interpretation would seem to be a protection against this danger without actually eliminating the ontological aspect.

This criticism, and the further point Gloege makes about the way Bultmann carries out his programme will be intelligible in the light of what he offers as the outcome of his critique (pp. 90ff.). He complains that Bultmann does not press his programme to its logical conclusion, for the object of knowledge, the kerygma, prevents him from doing so. To Bultmann's question, whether he still leaves a vestige of mythology in his restatement, Gloege answers with a definite "Yes". The kerygma itself is a mythological phenomenon (p. 91). Then there are two further mythological categories, the canon and the Church. Bultmann also sees the connection between these three facts. It is in them that the act of God is wrought. Here Gloege takes a similar line to Fritz Buri, who uses it to justify his own "dekerygmatizing" of theology.[1] Of course Gloege draws a different conclusion. What we need, he says, is a process of remythologizing; we must recover the mythological understanding of human life (p. 93). These are really two different things. The first is open to discussion. It concentrates attention on what the mythology is really saying, and thus seeks to preserve the kerygma. The second point is a very different matter. We are bound to ask what he really means by the mythological understanding of human life. Here is a point that requires further discussion. Does he mean the understanding of Being disclosed in the mythological statements? Hardly, for that is just what Bultmann is looking for. Gloege seems to want more than this. How he envisages the task of demythologizing can be seen by the way he sums it up under three heads. "First, the purpose of mythology is to convey the kerygma. Second, the mythology is transcended in the kerygma. Third, the mythology is retained in the kerygma" (p. 100). He is perfectly right when he observes that Bultmann accepts the first and second points, but not the third. We could perhaps improve Gloege's formulation, and do more justice to his concern: First, the pur-

[1] *Kerygma und Mythos*, II, pp. 85f.

pose of the mythological statements in the New Testament is to convey the kerygma. Second, the mythology they contain is transcended in the kerygma. Third, the kerygma is offered in mythological statements.

This revised form of Gloege's propositions removes the dialectic in the original form. There is place for this dialectic only when the term myth is given the sense Gloege ascribes to it. Only when thus defined does it acquire a dialectical relation to the kerygma. But this is just the question. Does the dialectic between law and gospel really apply to the relation between the kerygma and mythology? Does it help us to a theological interpretation? Certainly not, if we use myth in Bultmann's sense.

All the same, there is a valuable suggestion in Gloege's third point. What he really means is that we cannot get away from mythology because all our language about God can never be anything but "inauthentic". While we can certainly reflect upon the meaning of the resurrection message, we cannot pass it on except by repeating the apostles' witness to it, though always as a testimony of *faith*. This would make demythologizing the task of hermeneutics and remythologizing the task of homiletics. In other words, the last word rests with the practical theologian, and is made necessary by the kind of age we live in. Mythology is just a tool, without any intrinsic interest of its own. The danger here is that revelation loses its directness and immediacy. We can no longer say: "To *you* has been given the secret of the kingdom of God" (Mark 4.11). Any direct statement about God's action is excluded on principle. Mythological language is an inescapable necessity. Karl Jaspers would heartily agree, but that is because he rejects the claims of revelation.[1] The truth of the matter, however, is that mythological language is necessary as a tool but not on principle; it is necessary, that is, for the age in which we live.[2] This concession is necessary because everything we say about the action of God can never be anything else but a confession of faith, just as knowledge of it can only be knowledge in faith.

[1] See below, pp. 145f.

[2] See my arguments against Jaspers, below, pp. 195ff.

Thus it would seem that this question of the necessity of mythological language is one for further discussion. To continue it along these lines should prove fruitful, since it acknowledges the problem here. Friedrich Schumann's suggestions in this connection are worth listening to. Speaking of mythological language, he says: "What myth intends to say can never be said in any other way. Yet it needs to be interpreted."[1] Schumann goes on to speak of the suitability of mythological language: "It can express in narrative form what ordinary language is incapable of reproducing" (p. 41). It calls attention to the impossibility of using direct, descriptive language about what God does.[2] It reminds us that the language in which affirmatives are expressed "is quite different from concepts and judgements derived from the real world".[3]

Hans Iwand takes a completely different line from the orthodox Lutheran theologians and from Gloege in a very brief, though all the more significant, contribution to the discussion.[4] This article is an attack on an attempted explanation of the purpose of demythologizing by Hannelis Schultze, in a letter to a schoolgirl.[5] The heart of Bultmann's concern, in Miss Schultze's eyes, is to extract the existential meaning of the pericopes. She illustrates this from a number of examples. We must admit this is a very one-sided interpretation of Bultmann, but it does seize upon the most essential aim of his programme, and its onesidedness was inevitable, considering the purpose of the letter. In a page or so it was hardly possible to say any more. Unfortunately, Iwand completely misunderstands the character of this contribution, and his irritated language seems to have been provoked by the

[1] *Wort und Wirklichkeit* ("Word and Reality"), Berlin-Spandau, 1951.

[2] Schumann's use of the term, mythological language, is identical with Gloege's definition of myth and mythology (op. cit., p. 46). It is true to the extent that mythological language is not only an interpretation of reality, but is intended to be the kind of language whose vitality depends on that reality.

[3] This is not the main theme of Schumann's essay: we shall come to that in the proper context under the problem of Kerygma and History, cf. below, pp. 47ff. We shall also return to Gloege in that context.

[4] *Die Stimme der Gemeinde*, 1953, Nos. 7 and 11, "*Wider den Misbrauch des 'pro me' als methodisches Prinzip in der Grundlegung theologischer Erkenntnis*".

[5] "*Was will Rudolf Bultmann?*," *Die Stimme der Gemeinde*, No. 5, 1953.

debate as a whole, rather than by this particular letter. Miss Schultze could hardly have wished to suggest that demythologizing was the only exegetical aid which was of any use in education. But given the immediate purpose of her letter, any reference to further matters would only have obscured her explanation of Bultmann. Iwand complains that she said nothing of Karl Barth. But why should she? That would hardly have been relevant. Finally, Iwand simply shows his own ignorance when he says he does not know where she got "that pretentious notion" of the parallel between demythologizing and the Lutheran doctrine of justification. Apparently, he had never read "Bultmann Replies to His Critics", where the whole thing is explained. His misunderstanding of Miss Schultze's letter and his general ignorance of the debate make his language as annoying as Karl Steck's[1] (whose earlier contributions in the same magazine were particularly illuminating and commendable). Steck is replying to a layman who could not make any sense of Miss Schultze's letter, but found Iwand easy to follow. Now while it is true that rationalism could often be lucid and easy to understand, it does not follow, as Steck suggests, that an author who is lucid and intelligible is *ipso facto* to be suspected of rationalism. And it is for the layman, rather than the theologian, to say whether Iwand is guilty of technical jargon (what about the title of his article?), and his judgement will depend on the degree to which he understands what the author is saying. The editor of *Die Stimme der Zeit* hopes that the correspondence will continue. But if the reader has to wait four months for the second instalment of an article, he can hardly be blamed for not rushing prematurely into print. For the rest, Steck's distinction between what the laity say and what the theologians say is unfortunately all too true, and it has the effect of silencing "the voice of the congregation", which Schumann represents. It is this that makes the whole article seem so unfair, and makes it look like "irritated language". The whole debate shows how hard it is to explain what demythologizing means to the man in the pew, how easily it leads the theologian into dogmatism, and how difficult it is to

[1] *Die Stimme der Gemeinde*, No. 11, 1953.

remain *sine ira et studio* over such a matter. It almost looks as though the risk which *Die Stimme der Gemeinde* took in opening its columns to the subject was too great.

Iwand denies that there is any problem at all. We have got bogged down, and the problem is no problem. It is time we gave up being preoccupied with it. It is making us more and more oblivious of the real task of theology (col. 355). As he sees it, both sides are proceeding from the same assumption. Both recognize the traditional order of law and gospel. If this order were reversed, theology would recover its foundation on the *one* Word of God: it would no longer go to pieces under the dialectic between them (col. 336). At the conference of theologians in Berlin in January 1954 Iwand read a short paper in which he gave a clearer account of his position and his reasons for it. He distinguishes between the *pro me* of the Reformers and its misuse since Kant. *Pro me* has been erected into a methodological principle. A man can now say, "It is my decision that God should exist, for by postulating his existence my own being is vindicated as part of a higher, rational order".[1] Iwand complains that the New Testament is accepted only in so far as it concerns me, and this opens up the danger of its misuse. It means that it is my decision which makes it what it was not before, the truth, and apart from my decision it is probably not true at all. This is, of course, a very real danger. But it rests on a misunderstanding, as was clearly pointed out in a discussion between Günther Bornkamm, Friedrich Schumann, and Rudolf Bultmann on the Bavarian radio:

Bornkamm : As you have put it, the future possibility which the Christ event opens up depends on a decision made here and now. It only happens when I hear the word.

Bultmann : That would be a misunderstanding. The meaning of the Christ event, as a thing of the past, doesn't depend on my decision. My decision means that I hear and open myself to the claim which is latent in this event.[2]

[1] *Evangelische Theologie*, 1954, p. 122.

[2] *Die Christliche Hoffnung und das Problem der Entmythologisierung*, Stuttgart, 1954.

It is not difficult to extend this so as to cover the New Testament as a whole. The other point that he was so anxious about Iwand meets by restricting the application of *pro me* as a hermeneutic principle to election and justification. "The ego addressed here is not the same ego as in the sphere of the practical reason. It is the ego which is the subject of the divine election, the ego hidden in the history of Jesus Christ, the ego which seeks to be apprehended by me and made the centre of my selfhood in faith."[1] In other words, it is a question of the primacy of the divine action over my decision, a concern which Bultmann fully shares, as we saw just now in his broadcast discussion. Yet both Iwand and Bornkamm have voiced this fear, and we may well ask whether this fear is not chiefly responsible for the misunderstandings which have arisen over Bultmann's programme.

The whole atmosphere has been cleared by the reasons Iwand has given for his own position. It also helps us to understand Karl Barth's "Attempt to understand Bultmann".[2] We may well expect to learn here what the reversal of law and gospel implies for hermeneutics. For Iwand it clearly means that every effort to understand the New Testament is primarily an effort to understand the word of God as the word of *God*. This is what makes him so suspicious of all attempts to commend the gospel to modern man. Bultmann, for instance, "seems to think the preacher can know beforehand the direction God's arrow will fly, where it will land and become a thorn in the flesh".[3] Iwand thus refuses to draw any distinction between a purely historical understanding of the New Testament, and an understanding which proceeds from faith in its as the Word of God. Here is the hermeneutic consequence of his reversal of law and gospel. It is the same point which has so much worried Karl Barth (and H. Traub), the question of prior understanding.

Karl Barth obviously agrees with Iwand over the primacy of gospel and law. In fact, this is the key to his essay, "Rudolf Bultmann, an Attempt to Understand him". Take for instance what he says right at the beginning about the understanding of

[1] *Evangelische Theologie*, 1954, p. 121.

[2] See below, pp. 83ff.

[3] *Die Stimme der Gemeinde*, 1953, col. 344.

the New Testament message: "To understand them (sc. the statements of the New Testament) is at the same time to believe them, and to expound them is to preach."[1] Here, Barth thinks, he is following Bultmann. But very soon he begins to wonder whether he ought to go along with Bultmann any further, when Bultmann deduces that "the understanding of this sharing is an act of my understanding of myself".[2] Barth contends that the understanding of any passage does not contain any implications about my own self-understanding: "How can that be when in actual fact I am engaged in taking my eyes off myself and looking in the direction indicated by the message?" (ibid., p. 86). Here Barth is already showing his anxiety lest we attach more importance to the form of the New Testament (expressions of self-understanding) than to what it expresses (the word of God), his anxiety lest it is not treated properly as the word of *God*, and given absolute primacy in the hermeneutic process. This anxiety comes out into the open when Barth recognizes the necessity of translating the New Testament message. He wonders where he could introduce "within the framework of Bultmann's concern, something else that seems to (him) to be even more important" (ibid., p. 87). This "something else", which he contrasts with the cradle of the New Testament language, is the message itself.

We find in Barth the same antithesis between law and gospel as we found in Gloege, but in the reverse order. Gloege's acceptance of Bultmann's challenge was based on his recognition in him of the traditional Lutheran distinction between law and gospel (above, p. 21). But this is what makes Barth so anxious about it. Indeed, it is this that lies at the back of all Barth's other criticisms of Bultmann. That is why, for instance, he asks: "Can we in our exposition of the New Testament relegate the saving act of God, which provides the basis for Christian existence, to a secondary place, or understand his saving act only as reflected in the mirror of that existence?" (ibid., p. 94). The Barth-Bultmann controversy reaches its climax when Barth asks: "That *Christ* is the kerygma certainly seems to be what the New Testament says, but not *vice versa*, that Christ is the *kerygma*" (ibid., p. 96).

[1] See below, p. 85. [2] See below, p. 86.

Here we could reply to Barth by his own words in *Church Dogmatics*: "We come to it (sc. the knowability of God) from 'the knowledge of God in its fulfilment'. It is from there that we go to ask about the knowability of God. The type of thinking which wants to begin with the question of the knowability of God and then to pass on from that point to the question of the fulfilment of the knowledge of God is not grateful but grasping, not obedient but self-autonomous. It is not theological thinking. It does not arise from the Church, or rather, from the Church's basis, and it does not serve the Church."[1] Here Barth seems to be motivated by the same concern as Bultmann. This is, that theology should be understood as man's response to the word of God experienced as God's address to him. It is never, never a word proceeding from man. But then does it not follow that Christ encounters us only in the kerygma and that the saving act of God is visible to us only in the mirror of our own existence? Does it not follow that we can only begin by speaking of Christian existence, and only then make statements about the act of God or Christ itself? The kerygma is what we get to know about first, and in getting to know the kerygma we get to know Christ. Barth notes (below, p. 89) that Bultmann professed to have thrown in his lot with the Barthians in the nineteen twenties, and believed (with Tillich) that he could welcome him (Barth) as one of themselves. Was this a mistake, or was there more to it than that? We would like to know what Barth thinks about it. Here is the crucial point in the Barth-Bultmann controversy. Reduced to its simplest terms, in Gloege's words, "the whole obscurity arises from the confusion between the ontic and noetic approaches, and the respective points of view they imply. There is no question that Bultmann is right: in the problem of understanding (i.e. hermeneutics) the question of knowledge comes before the question of the object known. That, however, does not rule out, in fact it assumes that the question of the object known provides the basis and structure of the question of knowledge" (op. cit., p. 89). No wonder this is the point where Iwand finds common ground with his opposite number.

[1] *Church Dogmatics*, II, 1, p. 63.

Here, too, is the clue to the controversy about the prior understanding (*Vorverständnis*). Like Barth, H. Traub thinks that the right questions can only be asked by those who know that they are primarily the ones to whom the question is addressed, and whose questions are therefore always a reaction and a response.[1] He repudiates the suggestion that the asking of the question arises from the common concern of the questioner and the one who gives the answer, since this also presumes that man is the presupposition of everything else (ibid.). It is for this same reason that Barth, too, will have nothing to do with the kind of prior understanding Bultmann requires. Undoubtedly he is wrong when he says that one can only talk with Bultmann if he is prepared to accept a prior understanding based on the earlier philosophy of Heidegger (below, p. 114). Karl Jaspers, on the other hand, has accused Bultmann of working with inadequate philosophical presuppositions and complained that his ideas on science are popular rather than strictly scientific.[2] This agrees with Barth's own admission: "There is a bit of existentialism in all of us nowadays, in everything we think or say" (below, p. 115). But is that the only point? Every time a man opens his mouth he says something about himself, and what he says is universally intelligible, though not necessarily in the form in which he says it. Yet our only concern here is to find Barth's motive in rejecting Bultmann's prior understanding. Traub shows more clearly what this motive is. It is because they both want to uphold the priority of the message over man's understanding of it. As Barth himself admits: "There is one thing, and only one thing, which does not come from Heidegger: the transition is called the 'Christ event' and an 'act of God'." There is no prior understanding for this. This is the point at which Bultmann the theologian is speaking independently. Once again we must press upon Barth the question whether this is the end of the matter. It was Barth himself who taught us that the word of God encounters us vertically from above: like the mathe-

[1] *Anmerkungen und Fragen zur neutestamentlichen Hermeneutik und zum Problem der Entmythologisierung*, Neukirchen, 1952, p. 11.

[2] See below, pp. 134ff.

matical point, it is not susceptible of proof.[1] The discussion in *Church Dogmatics*, II, 1, pp. 634ff., suggests that to-day Barth would regard such statements as one-sided, provoking from him the comment, "Well roared, lion": "The sentences I then uttered were not hazardous (in the sense of precarious) on account of their content. They were hazardous because to be a legitimate exposition of the Bible they needed others no less sharp and direct to compensate and therefore genuinely to substantiate their total claim" (ibid., p. 635). True, the context here is the glory of God; yet it would seem to imply equally to other places where he is one-sided. But, we ask, is not Barth exaggerating here? At least, it seems pointless to refer to the example of Albert Schweitzer in this connection. For it was not one-sidedness that led Schweitzer astray in his theology, so that he ended up with the mysticism of "reverence for life" and nothing else (cf. ibid., p. 636). Rather, it was the false solution he attempted. Schweitzer failed to see, as the Swiss liberals of Berne still fail to see, that the delay in the parousia was not such a serious problem for the early Church as he and his disciples think it was. This is because the early Church had long since demythologized its apocalyptic into genuine eschatology. In the same vein, we must ask Barth whether his total rejection of any prior understanding (especially in the exaggerated form of that rejection by H. Traub, with the express approval of his master) is not equally one-sided, and whether this one-sidedness does not lead him into positive error. It can hardly be denied that everyone needs a prior understanding of the language and terminology of the Bible if he is to understand the Word of God. It was that need that added strength to Barth's attack on infant baptism. For the real question is not whether a candidate for baptism ought to have faith, but whether he ought not to be capable of some degree of prior understanding. The only reason why infant baptism is meaningless, or at least obscures the meaning of the rite, is that the assent required of the candidate requires a recipient who can hear and understand the requirement, i.e. a recipient who

[1] The Tübingen Memorandum, *Für und wider die Theologie Bultmanns*, Tübingen, 1952, p. 28, sees Bultmann's programme in this context.

approaches the rite with the prior understanding of which Bultmann speaks. To abandon the requirement of prior understanding would be to reduce the proclamation to a species of sacramental magic. This is just what Barth is protesting against in the case of infant baptism. If, however, the proclamation is sacramental magic then hermeneutics is not, to say the least, anywhere near as important as Bultmann and Schniewind think it is. The question is not whether there is such a thing as prior understanding, but what are its limits. Bultmann offers a suggestion here by confining "myth" to the purely formal sphere. The real ground of Barth's objection to this is that he refuses to recognize such a limitation. The whole idea of a prior understanding raises at once, he thinks, the dangers of natural theology. It is to be hoped that Bultmann's discussion with Fritz Buri, and still more that with Karl Jaspers[1] will make clear where this danger really lies. It lies where it is taken for granted that the use of mythological language is inescapable. This assumption is dangerous because it leads inevitably to a natural theology. Such a danger, however, is absent where, with Bultmann, we hold on to the formal conception of myth.

From all this it would seem that despite the emphasis Barth places on this point of disagreement with Bultmann, it is not one of basic principle. In fact there is really no need for it at all. It arises only where prior understanding is confused with the understanding of faith, as is the case when Traub says: "Understanding is the result of faith, not *vice versa*" (op. cit., p. 18). If it is true that only faith can understand scripture, some understanding must still precede it to allow scripture to be understood as a communication of something relevant to me. Traub goes on to say: "If I become the object of an encounter—and that is what I first experience—I am placed in a passive situation" (op. cit., p. 13). If this is so, it means that it is only after I have experienced this encounter that I start to reflect upon it. Bultmann, however, is concerned about what happens prior to the encounter. Traub's notion of understanding is just as limited, and in exactly the same way. He says: "Understanding begins when I allow

[1] See below, pp. 181ff.

myself to be addressed" (ibid.). This is no real objection against Bultmann, for both hermeneutics and homiletics operate with a broader conception of understanding, which concerns itself with what goes on before the person is addressed.

It would seem therefore that the disagreement between Barth and Bultmann arises from their very different conceptions of understanding. Incidentally, Barth's conception borders on the magical. One would expect to find it rather in *Catholic* theology! Hence, no doubt, the Catholic reaction to the debate.

On the one hand, Bultmann's Catholic critics give him credit for securing his base in Luther's doctrine of justification and his theology of the cross. That, they maintain, is why no Protestant has any real right to criticize him.[1] On the other hand they have criticized Bultmann for going too far in trying to make the Church's message congenial to the modern world. He makes modern man the final arbiter of the Biblical message.[2] This criticism, which is often found on the Protestant side too, is just what we might expect where the Barth-Traub conception of understanding is taken for granted. It is because he shares this assumption that Hamer can go on to say: "When Bultmann, with his secularist upbringing, proceeds to make modern man the sole arbiter of truth, he fails to do justice to the sovereignty and freedom of the divine word *vis à vis* all particular forms of human thought" (op. cit., p. 142). Hamer fails to see that the real issue is not the criterion of truth, but a criterion of the purely secular understanding. The sovereignty of the divine Word, so far from releasing us from the duty of aiming at such an understanding, actually imposes that duty upon us. Their recognition that the Biblical message needs to be translated is welcome, but does not go far enough. They must also take note of the thought of man within the limitations of his world view. The presuppositions which form part and parcel of our human existence, and which

[1] *Herder Korrespondenz*, VI, 354 and V, 324.

[2] P. Jerome Hamer: "*Zur Entmythologisierung Bultmanns*", *Catholica*, p. 140. Cf. also "*Une orientation de la pensee protestante: Rudolf Bultmann*" in *La Revue Nouvelle*, 1953, pp. 639ff.

we bring along with us when we hear the gospel, are more numerous than is generally assumed—and not only among Catholic theologians. Any attempt to translate the Bible, into the languages of Africa for instance, shows how difficult it is to reproduce particular terms which lie at the heart of the Biblical message, and how much the translator must reckon with a prior understanding.

This rejection of any prior understanding whatever is accompanied by an inability to distinguish between factual evidence and testimony of faith. Only so can we account for Hamer's statement that "it is characteristic of Bultmann's thought that in the last resort he has no place for the Church" (op. cit., p. 144). Bultmann, of course, does include the Church among the eschatological acts of God to which testimony has to be borne.[1] Hamer, however, ignores this because he is blind to the distinction between fact and witness. It also explains why Karl Thieme[2] does not begin with a discussion of the problems to which Bultmann has called attention, but proceeds at once to contest Bultmann's claim that Christian faith is indifferent to the question of historicity. He does not perceive that his quotation from the Catholic Biblical Lexicon really takes the same view as Bultmann: "The resurrection of Jesus is a mystery of faith. It cannot be proven by historical criticism." Fries narrows down the scope of the problems involved as a result of the traditional exposition which distinguishes between "what the Bible says and the terms in which it says it, between the truth of faith and the terminology or imagery in which it is clothed".[3] But although they are blind to the problem as it affects their own Church, they are quite convinced that the problem is a real one for Protestants. Bultmann and his disciples are "the successors of Luther, who carry his position to its logical conclusion" (p. 120).

Karl Adam, Professor of Systematics in the Catholic faculty of

[1] *Kerygma and Myth*, Vol. I, pp. 43ff. Cf. G. Gloege, op. cit., p. 92.

[2] *Entmythologisierung, Die Lehre Bultmanns in katholischer Sicht*, Frankfurter Hefte, 1953, pp. 112ff. Cf. also H. Fries, "*Zur Theologie der Entmythologisierung, Hochland*", 1952, pp. 354ff.

[3] Op. cit., p. 118, quoted from *Lexikon des katholischen Lebens*, col. 832, s.v. *Mythus*.

Theology at Tübingen, finds in Bultmann stronger traces of Calvinism; in fact these are the constitutive elements in his position.[1] He also thinks that the use of existentialism and the insistence on radical demythologizing spring "from certain exaggerations of the Calvinistic doctrine of faith and of God" (p. 389). In connection with this, Adam demonstrates the affinity between Bultmann's demythologizing and dialectical theology. Demythologizing implies a particular, exclusive conception of justifying faith as "an act of God in his sovereign freedom and an act of unqualified predestination". It does not require anything from man's side, no knowledge of experience. It comes to him "without any psychological point of contact, as a miracle, 'perpendicularly from above', strictly transcendental and beyond the range of observation. It is not a psychic, but a metaphysical event, a paradox, whose essence is not so much its irrationality, as its anti-rational character" (ibid.). Finally, Adam traces the source of all this in Bultmann's rejection of the *analogia entis*, which Karl Barth once denounced as "the invention of antichrist".[2] The question for Catholic theology, as Adam sees it, "is whether the supernatural can come within range of man's observation, or whether there can be any certainty of it" (p. 391). This is what it claims. For it believes that "the whole cosmos in all its breadth and depth is open to the operation of God and to responsive impressions of Being in a manner appropriate to its creaturely nature" (p. 392). While it is true that the knowledge of the supernatural is called "faith knowledge", nevertheless "such knowledge always presumes that the supernatural element is co-inherent in the historical, and can be clearly discerned in it" (p. 393). Thus for Karl Adam the faith of Paul is not grounded upon his experience on the Damascus road, but on the testimony of eyewitnesses to the resurrection. This overlooks Paul's own clear statement on the matter. And, of course, it contradicts the Vatican decree that "in matters of faith there is no proof such as would *compel* the understanding and

[1] "*Das Problem der Entmythologisierung und die Auferstehung des Christus*", *Theologische Quartalsschrift*, 1952, pp. 385ff.

[2] *Church Dogmatics*, I, 1.

would be universally binding".[1] Hence Adam finds himself obliged to restate what the Vatican Council said about the possibility of experiencing a saving event which leads to faith. For the Vatican constitution faith is "man's existential answer to God's call of grace" (ibid.). But for Karl Adam this peculiar quality of faith is bound up with its primary and essential character, which is the "firm acceptance of the truth of an objective fact, the existence of the Risen Christ". This truth, however, is "inaccessible to natural knowledge, and is only vouchsafed by supernatural impressions of its reality". Confronted with it, "all human thought must remain silent" (p. 404). It is a miracle, to be grasped intuitively with the *ésprit de finesse* of a Pascal. "Intuition is the 'sixth sense' which affords a new approach to reality" (ibid.). Adam then concludes with this assertion: "Belief in a miracle does not rest upon conclusive evidence which compels understanding and conviction, but it does rest upon the evidence of its credibility" (p. 404). Thus the Catholic gravamen against Bultmann rests essentially on the doctrine of the *analogia entis*. Hence their insistence on the "objective" nature of miracle, and their ambivalent conception of faith. Faith is at once the existential response to a divine appeal and the acceptance of a miracle as an objective datum.

The essays by Karl Adam's colleagues at Tübingen take a similar line. Two contributions from the pen of J. R. Geiselmann[2] level the same criticisms against Bultmann which were made against Strauss by their predecessors in the Catholic faculty at Tübingen, as represented by J. E. Kuhn. Like Kuhn in reference to Strauss, Geiselmann maintains that the supra-historical element in the original apostolic preaching is not detached from history, but rooted in it. The proclamation stands or falls with the claim that the incidents in the life of Jesus were the fulfilment of scripture. This is what makes secular history *Heilsgeschichte*. The fundamental difference between this interpretation of the

[1] P. 400. Cf. *Vaticanum*, sess. III, const. iv. 1.

[2] "Jesus Christus. *Der Urform des apostolischen Kerygmas als Norm unserer Verkündigung und Theologie von Jesus Christus*", *Katholisches Bibelwerk*, Stuttgart, 1951: "*Der Glaube an Jesus Christus, Mythus oder Geschichte?*" *Theologische Quartalsschrift*, 1949, pp. 257ff. and 418ff.

apostolic kerygma and a New Testament theology based on form-criticism is obvious. In the Catholic view the kerygma is based on definite facts and the way they fit in with the Old Testament promises. For us the narratives of these incidents are themselves kerygmatic in character. They are the witness borne by the Church to its own faith. It is this faith which causes the Church to accommodate the factual incidents in the kerygma to the Old Testament promises.

This Catholic interest in demythologizing is further illustrated in an article by A. Kolping in *Theologische Revue*, a publication of the Catholic faculty of Theology in Münster. This article bears the significant title, *Sola Fide*. The same interest is apparent in another article by Rudolf Schnackenburg in the *Münchner Theologische Zeitschrift*.[1] Schnackenburg traces the development of Bultmann's theology from form-criticism to demythologizing, and analyses its exegetical and systematic presuppositions. Both these articles make it clear that the reason behind this interest in the subject is that it enables Catholic scholars to rediscover the point at which the Reformation theology departed from that of Catholicism. Here, indeed, is the cardinal issue in Catholic-Protestant polemics. Hence Schnackenburg's conclusion: "Here—right at the beginning—is where Catholic exegesis comes to the parting of the ways" (p. 357). Catholic theologians invariably link up demythologizing with the starting-point of the Reformation. This should stimulate Protestant theologians to pay more attention to this connection than they—Bultmann's Protestant critics—have done hitherto.

The memoranda of the Theological School at Bethel (commissioned by the Church in Westphalia) and of the Theological Faculty of Tübingen (commissioned by the Church Assembly of the Church in Wurtemberg) are both inconclusive. This was inevitable, since both faculties represent varying points of view. The Tübingen memorandum, however, is particularly useful not only for its own theological discussion, but for the clear way in which it places the different points of view side by side. Some

[1] "*Von der Formgeschichte zur Entmythologisierung des Neuen Testaments*". 1951, pp. 345ff.

members of the faculty regard demythologizing as an extreme form of liberalism. Others think that it must be viewed as "a parallel to that great process of contraction in which all that was left was the mathematical point of the individual's existence before God, the point at which the true nature of faith becomes apparent". Faith, according to this view, is directed, not towards propositions, even propositions of a Biblical character but, as Luther says, towards the *nuda vox dei* (op. cit., p. 28). In this sense the faculty regards demythologizing as genuine exposition. The salient contribution of this memorandum is its frank recognition that both interpretations are tenable. Both are equally recognized, and the faculty promises to do everything in its power to guide developments in the second of these two directions.

The Bethel memorandum is of a very different character. The faculty there is a much more closely-knit body, offering greater opportunity for a common point of view. Yet in the very process of working out their standpoint they show how this can be done in a genuine dialogue with an opponent whom they still recognize as a fellow member of the Church, and with whom they share a common responsibility towards the Word of scripture. They register their complete agreement with Bultmann that the issue in demythologizing is a real one. "There is no way to faith which bypasses the proclamation of the Word" (p. 152). It is only at a later stage that they begin to take issue with Bultmann, i.e. with his particular views on Christian origins and on the relation between history and the kerygma.

We turn now to the English-speaking world. First, there is Austin Farrer's essay in *Kerygma and Myth*, I, pp. 212–23. For him the whole debate demonstrates how foreign the German religious attitude is to that of the Englishman. It is a good illustration of "German profundity". The practical-minded Englishman does not feel at home with it, however much he may wonder at it. All the same, the preacher in England is faced with the difficulty that the mythical language of the gospel is unintelligible to modern man. There may be various reasons for this. It may be due to dogmatic materialism. In this case, his stumbling at the gospel is real and deliberate. If, however, it is due to a lack of sense for poetical expression, we must sustain and augment whatever rudiments of poetical sense remain. If it is because the Biblical imagery draws on unfamiliar fields of experience, they must be replaced by images drawn from familiar fields. Demythologizing only becomes necessary when a real conflict breaks out between the Biblical story and modern man's mode of thought. All of us are subject to that mode of thought, whether we are Christians or not. This is the point where the question of truth arises, and that question cannot be baulked.

It is typical of the English-speaking world that it always sees demythologizing as a practical concern, which means too that it is generally recognized as a real problem. The various nuances given to the concept of myth, for instance, are generally determined by practical considerations. Some mythological images must be taken as symbols and nothing more. Over these there need be no dispute. The point at which the shoe begins to pinch is when we come to miracles and the idea of transcendence. Farrer attempts to explain Bultmann's existentialist interpretation to the reader who cannot go along with contemporary existentialism, even in Heidegger's brand. Lohmeyer, says Farrer, puts his finger on the real difficulty when he says that God and his action lie beyond the scope of human observation except insofar as he makes himself known to us by means of symbols or parables which he evokes in our minds. He does not allow himself to be expressed in the words for which these symbols and parables stand, but only in further figures. This is certainly a paradox, but at least it shows a grasp of the difficulty. Bultmann solves the paradox by means of his existentialist interpretation. What he does is to deprive the images of their objective character and reduce them to metaphors or ciphers. In such metaphors, Farrer believes, it is not only possible but necessary to speak of transcendental realities. Transcendence, he contends, is like a two-sided medal. We can only infer something about its hidden, invisible side insofar as it reveals to us its visible side. He then uses these metaphors to elucidate the meaning and interpretation of myth. It, too, must be interpreted "visibly". It must be interpreted to mean something which "plays a real part in our existence, like the part played by the friendship of an absent friend when we orientate our life and everything we do towards him and his friendship for us" (p. 218). Thus Farrer agrees all along the line with Bultmann's aim, which is to interpret what the New Testament says in such a way as to bring out its meaning for our existence. Most of the Anglo-Saxon contributors to the debate seem to agree with this. Among the essays which have come to my notice, I would mention Amos N. Wilder, "Mythology and the New Testament" (*Journal of Biblical Literature*, 1950, pp. 113ff.) and Kendrick Grobel, "Bultmann's Problem of New Testament Mythology", ibid., 1951, pp. 99ff. Bultmann takes note of both of these essays in *Kerygma und Mythos*, II. Further, we would mention John A. T. Robinson, *In the End God*, 1950, pp. 25ff.; G. Ernest Wright, *God Who Acts*, 1952, pp. 116ff.; J. H. Ottwell, "Neo-Orthodoxy and Biblical Research" (*Harvard Theological Review*, 1950, pp. 145ff.); Sherman E. Johnson, "Two Great New Testament Interpreters" (*Religion and Life*, 1952, pp. 288ff.), as well as Ian Henderson's *Myth in the New Testament* (Studies in Biblical Theology, No. 7, London, 1952). Amos N. Wilder's *Eschatology and Ethics in the Teaching of Jesus*, although not a direct contribution to the debate, deals indirectly with the subject, as does William Manson's *Jesus the Messiah* (London, 1943). The latter is less concerned with demythologizing, than with a critical treatment of the whole work of form-criticism. It places more confidence in the tradition, and emphasizes more strongly the Old Testament roots of the earliest Christian preaching.

Sherman Johnson begins his article on "Bultmann and the Mythology of the New Testament"[1] by recognizing the problems Bultmann has raised. "Every theologian, neo-orthodox, liberal, or conservative, has inevitably engaged in this (sc. demythologizing)" (p. 33). He asks: "Is it, as he (Bultmann) and some of his defenders suggest, in no way different from the task that theology, preaching and worship always undertake?" (p. 35). The difficulty and danger involved in this task, which Bultmann's

[1] *Anglican Theological Review*, 1954, pp. 29ff.

critics have not been slow to point out, are not of his making. They are due to the Greek thought-world "which Christian theologians, from Origen through Augustine, Anselm and Aquinas, down to the present, have learned to analyse and ask questions" (ibid.). But while he recognizes the inevitable combination of theological propositions with ideas drawn from philosophy, Johnson avoids the mistake of so many of Bultmann's critics, who conclude that he is completely subservient to Heidegger: "His essay is a Christian answer to Heidegger, and it is only fair to say that he is not trying to make Christian faith easy for secularists." Johnson begins to criticize Bultmann over the use of the term myth. His insistence that myth is fundamentally anthropological in nature is narrow and incorrect (p. 36). Johnson then goes on to make a valuable contribution by summarizing the recent discussions over the place of myth in religion, which have been going on quite independently of our debate. First, he speaks of Irwin Erdman's *Arts and the Man: A Short Introduction to Aesthetics*.[1] This book emphasizes the metaphorical nature of all language, especially that of poetry. And myth is certainly akin to poetry. Henri Frankfort's essay, *The Intellectual Adventure of Ancient Man* defines myth as "a form of poetry which transcends poetry in that it proclaims a truth; a form of reasoning which transcends reasoning in that it wants to bring about the truth it proclaims; a form of action, of ritual behaviour, which does not find its fulfilment in the act but must proclaim and elaborate a poetic form of truth. Myth is to be taken seriously, because it reveals a significant, if unverifiable truth—we might say a metaphysical truth. But myth has not the universality and the lucidity of theoretical statement. It is concrete, though it claims to be inassailable in its validity. It claims recognition by the faithful; it does not pretend to justification before the critical."[2] This definition, to which we may add that of Ernst Cassirer,[3] which is equally familiar to us in Germany, as well as

[1] New York, 1952.

[2] Op. cit., pp. 7f., quoted by Johnson, pp. 39f.

[3] *Philosophie der symbolischen Formen II: Das mythische Denken* (Berlin, 1925); *An Essay on Man* (Garden City, 1953).

Susanna Hare, *The Great King*[1] permits us to conclude that the literal or objective interpretation of myth is not true to ancient thought. Thus demythologizing, properly understood—and Johnson himself sanctions the use of the word in this sense—aims at bringing out the true meaning of the myth by means of interpretation. But there are limits to this: "language is not sufficient to describe the reality, and the only language that begins to be adequate is pictorial" (p. 42). Even the sacraments need to be demythologized. Two things need to be done: to "recapture the spirit of early Christianity and also (to) make the acts relevant to man's present life" (p. 44). The ritual action of the early Church includes not only the sacraments but also the proclamation of the gospel. In this connection "it is the duty of the theologian to carry over into the new language as much of the essence of the myth as possible; a reduced or truncated translation will not do" (p. 46).

These quotations from Anglo-Saxon contributions show more interest in the practical, homiletic side of the problem than in its theological aspect. Hence the frequent ease with which they accept the parallel between the mythological language of the New Testament and non-Christian myths.

Nor are the English-speaking theologians at all shocked by the philosophical background of Bultmann's thought. Ian Henderson gives a very penetrating analysis of that background, demonstrating Bultmann's debt to Heidegger, and raising the question of the relation between the ontological approach of philosophy and the ontic affirmations of theology. This brings him quite close to Gogarten's position in his defence of Bultmann (*Demythologizing and History*, London, 1955). The problem Bultmann raises, Henderson concludes, is a legitimate one. It must be raised again and again by anyone who wants to expound the New Testament message in its relevance for to-day: "Insofar as his philosophy sticks to the ontological he is not concerned with God but only with the abstract question of the nature of being as such. On the other hand, the New Testament interpreter has to keep in

[1] *The Great King: King of Assyria: Assyrian Reliefs in the Metropolitan Museum of Art*, New York, 1945.

touch with him because only he can tell what the real possibilities of *Dasein* are, and we do not summon men to a real decision unless we present them with real possibilities to choose from."[1] Yet Henderson recognizes the possible rejoinder that the Holy Spirit discloses new possibilities of being which do not intrinsically belong to man, and which therefore go beyond the philosopher's terms of reference. In this case the theologian would have nothing whatever to learn from the philosopher. On the other hand, Henderson justifiably asks: "How many Christian preachers have deluded themselves into believing that they have preached challenging sermons when only their ignorance of life has kept them from seeing that what they set before their hearers was not a real possibility for the latter?" (ibid.). Thus the Anglo-Saxon contributors not only agree that Bultmann has raised some real problems, but they also approve of the terms in which he seeks their solution.

This survey of the various contributions and the way they recognize the need for a hermeneutic would not be complete without a reference to the remarks made by Dietrich Bonhoeffer in his *Letters and Papers from Prison*.[2] Their importance lies in their origin in a particular concrete situation of encounter with the "world" in its alienation from God, a fact which explains why Bonhoeffer thinks that Bultmann did not go far enough in his demythologizing. Bonhoeffer would like to go farther at the very point where such critics of Bultmann as Gloege and Buri find vestiges of mythology. He will have no truck with the kind of argument which, e.g., H. Loof brings against Bultmann in the name of religion: "You cannot, as Bultmann imagines, separate God and miracles, but you do have to be able to interpret and proclaim *both* of them in a 'non-religious' sense" (p. 125). Bonhoeffer came to realize this from his experiences in prison, where he was thrown into close association with his fellow prisoners and came face to face with out-and-out Nazis. Hence his question: "The thing that keeps coming back to me is, what *is* Christianity, and, indeed, what is Christ for us to-day? The time when men could be told everything by means of words, whether theological

[1] Op. cit., p. 38. [2] American edition entitled *Prisoner for God*, 1953.

or simply pious, is over, and so is the time of inwardness and conscience, which is to say, the time of religion as such'' (p. 122). Hence, too, his haunting anxiety: ''If we had finally to put down the western pattern of Christianity as a mere preliminary stage to doing without religion altogether, what situation would result for us, for the Church?'' (ibid.). Barth had touched upon the problem, but he did not pursue it to the bitter end. Instead, he ended up in a ''positivism of revelation'' (pp. 122 and 148f.). Bonhoeffer points to where an answer might be found when he sees he would rather not find room for God where modern man in his maturity has not yet been able to squeeze him out: ''I should like to speak of God not on the borders of life but at its centre, not in weakness but in strength, not, therefore, in man's suffering and death but in his life and prosperity. On the borders it seems to me better to hold our peace and leave the problem unsolved. Belief in the Resurrection is not the solution of the problem of death. The 'beyond' of God is not the beyond of our perceptive faculties. Epistemological theory has nothing to do with the transcendence of God. God is the 'beyond' in the midst of our life'' (p. 124). He concedes that Bultmann has somehow sensed Barth's limitations in this regard, but thinks he is too much of a liberal. Yet when he comes to suggesting his own solution he really comes closer to Bultmann than any of his other critics: ''I am of the view that the full content, including the mythological concepts, must be maintained. The New Testament is not a mythological garbing of the universal truth; this mythology (resurrection and so on) is the thing itself—but the concepts must be interpreted in such a way as not to make religion a pre-condition of faith (cf. circumcision in St Paul). Not until that is achieved will, in my opinion, liberal theology be overcome (and even Barth is still dominated by it, though negatively), and at the same time, the question it raises be genuinely taken up and answered—which is not the case in the positivism of revelation maintained by the Confessing Church'' (p. 149). This would seem to suggest that the debate ought now to take quite a different course, a course suggested by what Bonhoeffer says about a Christianity without religion. In this sense he may well be right when he says that Bultmann does not go far enough. If so, we should then be taking the problems Bultmann raises with ultimate seriousness.

Kerygma and History

The relation between kerygma and history became a live issue the moment New Testament scholars took over the Greek word kerygma as a technical term in theology. This choice of a foreign word suggests that there are many problems lurking beneath the surface. There were plenty of other German words which might have been used such as *Botschaft* ("message"), or *Verkündigung* ("proclamation"). But such terms had already fixed connotations of their own, which made them useless to convey precisely what was meant by kerygma. The choice of the Greek word kerygma was due to more than a pedantic love for scientific jargon. It was rather the symbol of a whole range of new problems that came to light when the kerygmatic character of the gospels was discovered. Just as Dibelius introduced the term paradigm for one of the distinctively Christian literary forms, albeit a minute literary form, which has no parallel in any other ancient literature, so the introduction of the word kerygma suggested that there was something here which could not be exhaustively defined by any of the terms in previous use. True, the relation of the kerygma to history is only one of its distinctive characteristics, though it was one which was in the foreground right from the start.

As far as I can discover, it was Martin Kähler who first gave currency to the word in his famous lecture on "The so-called Historical Jesus and the Historic, Biblical Christ".[1] In introducing the word Kähler immediately offers a definition: "It is as *kerygma*, as the carrying out of the commission God has given to his heralds and ambassadors, that the ancient word of scripture becomes meaningful in the Church." We[2] must recall the context

[1] *Der sogannante historische Jesus und der geschichtliche, biblische Christus* (reprinted Leipsic, 1928, re-edited by E. Wolf, Munich, 1953, 1956[2]).

[2] 2nd Ed., p. 26. In what follows I would like at the same time to justify my appeal to Martin Kähler and Julius Schniewind, which I made in my defence of demythologizing, and which has been disallowed especially by Otto Michel.

in which Kähler delivered his lecture. This is revealed both in the lecture itself and in the debate that followed. The parallels between the Kähler and Bultmann debates are unmistakable. Kähler was fighting on two fronts at once. On the one side were the Lutheran theologians, whose organ was the *Neue Lutherische Zeitung*. They were scholastic rationalists, who were impugning Kähler for not subscribing to the doctrine of verbal inspiration.[1] On the other side were the liberals, with their quest for the historical Jesus and their theology of compromise. Kähler insists against both parties that it is both impossible and unnecessary to reconstruct a life of Jesus based on documentary evidence. On the positive side his argument culminates at the point where he says: "We have therefore two classes of document in the New Testament (sc. the gospels and the epistles). They are both documents to use as a basis for the preaching which is the foundation of the Church."[2] It is useless to try and get back behind this preaching in order to recover first-hand evidence for the history of Jesus: "All we find there is memorials which are inherently confessional in character" (ibid.).

What then is the historical basis for the kerygma? Kähler had already devoted some attention to this in his *Wissenschaft christlicher Lehre* ("The science of Christian doctrine"). This is an indication that his choice of the word kerygma was deliberate. It suggests the problem that was exercising his mind, and that is already touched upon in the introductory chapter which forms the prolegomena to his systematic theology. There he had posed the question whether theology was an exact science, and what its data were. The data, he insists, are not historical facts, but confessions of faith. He then gives his reasons: "In the first place, faith does not spring from the bare report of historical facts. There must be an additional element, testimony to their suprahistorical significance. And the testimony becomes effective only by believing participation in the facts. This is what makes them a confession of faith" (p. 21). But this is only to state the problem, not to answer it. A provisional answer immediately follows: "The original confession which is the foundation of the Church grew

[1] Op. cit., p. vi. [2] Op. cit., p. 22.

up under the impact of a revelatory history. This is what we find in Holy Scripture, and this is what the Church knows and preserves in the reciprocal relation in which she stands thereto" (p. 22).

The first point to be made here is that for Kähler the event on which the Church is founded is the preaching or the confession. Both originated from a revelatory history. Once again, this is merely to state the original problem in somewhat different terms. It does not solve it. We may perhaps infer from what he has said thus far that there is a coincidence between the occurrence and the testimony which accompanies it. A little further on he defines the relation between occurrence and testimony more precisely: "It (viz. the science of Christian doctrine) is, like all theology, a 'positive science'. It deals with material provided by history." But this material is not the history of primitive Christianity, the economy of salvation, or anything of that nature. Rather, it is the content of the continuous preaching in which the historical element is expounded in its direct relevance to each successive present. Without wishing to draw a parallel between Kähler and Bultmann, or to argue for any dependence of one on the other, we cannot help noticing the similarity between the solutions they each propose. To Kähler the relation between the kerygma and history is that the kerygma is always bringing out the meaning of the event for each succeeding present. Bultmann speaks of "significantness" (*Bedeutsamkeit*), the elevation of the event to cosmic dimensions. They are both moving in the same direction, even if Kähler understands history somewhat differently from Bultmann.

Kähler returns to the problem when he discusses the canon of scripture. For this we have to depend on the judgement of the Church: "The accreditation of the canon is not sufficient to make good the deficiency of scripture in regard to the redemptive facts.[1] Religious faith needs no historical evidence, even if such

[1] In the copy of Kähler's work in my possession the words "redemptive facts" are corrected by hand to "Biblical facts" by one who heard Kähler deliver the lecture. This is significant, for it bears out Schniewind's reluctance to speak of redemptive facts. The reasons for this change of wording are explained in terms which may equally go back to the lecture: "The fact that a thing

evidence could be furnished. All we need is the assurance that the Bible contains the continuously effective documentation of the preaching on which the Church is founded'' (p. 51). This is a negative definition. The kerygma, it says, does not depend upon the history from which it sprang. This negative definition acquires added importance when we realize the rôle which Christian experience plays in Kähler's thought in connection with the kerygma. Here again he reminds us very much of Bultmann. ''This material confronts us as the expression of a particular religious experience, i.e. as a confession of faith. And this inherent quality of the material is recognized and becomes effective when it is emphasized that it should be regarded as the content of the specifically Christian experience'' (p. 54). It should be obvious that by ''experience'' Kähler means something very different from Schleiermacher's ''self-consciousness''. It is much more like Bultmann's ''self-understanding''. In fact both terms are used in conscious opposition to Schleiermacher. It is equally obvious that for Kähler there is no direct relation between kerygma and history. On the positive side, Kähler repeatedly tries to define the relationship by using the term ''supra-historical''. He calls Jesus the supra-historical Saviour. He ''is more than a mere man, more in nature, more in his mission, more in his present status'' (p. 48). ''Supra-historical'', he continues, ''means something that would certainly not be true apart from history, but whose significance is not exhausted by it. It is not one of the series of links in the chain of cause and effect, for it combines general truth with historical occurrence in such a way as to make it effective in the present''.[1] This should make it clear that Kähler does not mean the same thing by ''supra-historical'' as Dibelius did in an essay[2] reviewed by Bultmann.[3] Kähler lays all

---

occurred historically is not sufficient to prove that it is really the act of God.'' In other words, when Kähler speaks of redemptive facts he means a testimony of faith. But to introduce the latter term is not to solve the problem, but merely to define it in other terms.

[1] Ibid. Cf. *Wissenschaft der christlichen Lehre*, XIII, 8f., 365, etc.

[2] *Geschichtliche und übergeschichtliche Religion im Christentum.*

[3] This review is reprinted in *Glauben und Verstehen*, I.

the emphasis on the present effectiveness, the significant historicity (*Geschichtlichkeit*) of what he calls supra-historical.

This brings us to the important distinction between "historic" (*geschichtlich*) and "past-historical" (*historisch*). It was Kähler who invented this distinction which we still use to-day. He gives us a concise definition of what he means by "historic": "Even from a purely historical point of view the truly 'historic' in an important figure is the personal effect which he leaves behind and which posterity can feel" (p. 63). This leads Kähler to identify the "historic" with the "Biblical" Christ. When we ask what lasting effect Jesus had there can only be one answer: "The effect Jesus had, according to the Bible and Church history, was to create faith in his disciples, a conviction which has been summed up in the acknowledgement of Christ as Lord" (ibid.).

Here we have the clue to Kähler's identification of "biblical" with "historic". He is not thinking of persuasive preaching, but of the "result of meticulous examination of the relevant facts" (op. cit., p. 66). But it is essential to realize what he means by "facts"—particularly in view of our present concern. For in speaking of facts Kähler is implying a particular definition of the relation between kerygma and history. The kerygma has a direct relation to *Geschichte*, significant history, but not to *Historie*, the dead past. The kerygma is not related to an event which can be reconstructed by scientific historical criticism out of the gospels. The "historic" Christ is the Christ of the proclamation (ibid.). As the object of faith, he is the foundation of the kerygma. So when Kähler speaks of facts he does not mean "the separate episodes in the life of Jesus. . . . Those facts which lead to this judgement concern the nature of the tradition which we have at our disposal. We mean particularly the two comprehensive facts. First, the impossibility of deducing from the sources any insight into the genesis of the Messiah Jesus. Secondly, the explanation of what Christ has always been to his Church, and still is to-day for all who believe in him" (p. 67). Since Kähler finds the foundation of the kerygma in the earliest Christian preaching, in the faith and in the initial proclamation of the earliest Christian community, he feels quite free to submit the documents to critical examination. Such examination cannot have any effect on the Christ of Christian preaching. It is this serenity which accounts for the particular pathos of his lecture, and his insensitivity to the charge of excessive scepticism. He is perfectly sure of his position in face of the life-of-Jesus theology.

Thus for Kähler the foundation of the kerygma, which is just as accessible to the scientific historian as it is to the simple reader of the Bible, is the preaching which brought the Church into being. Kähler never seeks to go back behind that preaching. This explains what he means by facts. The earliest preaching is the foundation of the kerygma, but not as an objective fact to which I can adopt the neutral attitude of an observer. Rather, preaching is an "historic" fact in the sense that its effects are still at work in history right down to the present day. It is not open to objective knowledge, but acquires significance only as a result of our decision to accept (or reject) it.

There is one important point, however, at which Kähler would appear to have gone beyond his self-imposed restriction of refusing to go back behind the earliest preaching. This is when he traces the effect of Jesus in history to the revelation contained in the resurrection. Thus he speaks of "the one great fact which God has made immune from all human error, the resurrection of Christ" (p. 197). This arises from the particular meaning he attaches to "historic personality". The first effect of the historic Christ is the faith and proclamation of the disciples. And the foundation of that faith and proclamation is the resurrection: "For this very reason there can be no doubt that the 'historic' effects of Jesus are to be attributed to the post-resurrection revelation" (p. 106). This revelation enabled the disciples to see the life of Jesus as it really was for the first time. "Hence his dying and rising again acquire in the New Testament the status of a new beginning instead of being merely the dignified conclusion to his earthly sojourn" (ibid.). Thus Kähler does not try to distinguish between the crucifixion as a fact of past history and the resurrection as something of quite a different character. Both events, he thinks, are of the same character. They are both "historic" events with effects in the proclamation right down to the present day. If this is what he means by the "historic" character of the resurrection, any statement about it must be a confession of faith, not a statement of objective fact. Hence Kähler's equally emphatic refusal to speak of these facts as "brute facts" (p. 106). When he speaks of the cross and resurrection as "foundation facts" he only means to stress the character of these events as the ground of faith. They never cease to be objects of faith. His emphasis on the certainty of faith must not mislead us into thinking that they are certainties apart from faith. When he speaks of the "foundation fact" of the resurrection, he means to suggest that the disciples' faith is not based upon itself. At the same time this does not dispose completely of the problem of the relation between kerygma and history.

This same problem crops up again in another form when Kähler discusses the use of the narrative sections of the gospels in the service of the kerygma. He felt obliged to answer the charge of excessive scepticism in his attitude to the historical value of these sections. He insists that he is not really concerned to impugn their historicity. The occasion of this charge was his assessment of them "in the light of their avowed purpose. . . . I deny that it is the purpose of the gospels to serve as documents for the scientific reconstruction of a biography of Jesus" (p. 23). Yet he goes on at once to qualify this in no uncertain terms: "A credible portrait of the Saviour for believers is quite a different matter" (p. 49). For a credible portrait of that kind the gospel narratives are beyond question serviceable. We need only compare his argument here with what he says in his *Kommet und Sehet: Der Prophet in Galiläa nach Markus*,[1] in order to see how innocent Kähler is of any sceptical attitude towards the gospels. To look for a scientific biography in the gospels is quite a different matter from reading them to find the kerygma and to see how their narrative material can be used in the service of the kerygma. While rejecting the former procedure, he pursues the latter as the original kerygma did. "The gospels are the quarry for Christian preaching and the source of its renewal" (p. 25). And they are this quite apart from their value for the historian. We

[1] "*Come and See*", *The Prophet of Galilee according to Mark*, Stuttgart, 1912.

can hardly claim that Kähler really faces the problem square in the face or provides an explicit answer, yet his use of the gospel narratives together with his denial of their value as historical evidence clearly implies such an answer. And it is all the more weighty since it is aimed at the confusion between historical value and value for preaching which was usual in his day. He frankly admits that it was this tendency and its inevitable though lamentable result of making faith dependent on historical criticism which led him to thinking out his fresh approach. That is why he begins his lecture with these preliminary considerations.

To sum up, two conclusions may be drawn:

First, Kähler finds the historical foundation of the kerygma in its earliest use as the foundation of the Church. His recourse to the historical fact of the resurrection is not to be taken to imply that he regards the resurrection as a historical datum independent of faith. He agrees that the only discernible fact is the faith it evoked in the disciples and their subsequent proclamation. Yet this does not make the resurrection any less historical. Our problem to-day has not as yet come to the surface in Kähler's lecture. But in speaking of the resurrection as a brute fact he is inconsistent with his own recognition that the New Testament from cover to cover is primarily and exclusively the earliest Church's witness to its own faith.

Secondly, the value of the gospel narratives does not lie in the historical evidence they furnish. It lies in their witness to the Church's faith. That is what makes them the source of renewal for the Church's preaching to-day. Hence their value or otherwise as historical documents does not affect their use as material for preaching. It should at once be apparent that Kähler here anticipates not only form-criticism but also demythologizing. While we can hardly claim that he offers any solution, he certainly points the way we must look for one. We cannot afford to neglect his insights—his insistence on the kerygmatic character of the gospels and his consequent indifference to their historicity.

At first there was a lively discussion of Kähler's lecture, and it appeared in a second edition, which gives us some idea of the course the discussion took. But it soon died down. Kähler is not even mentioned in Albert Schweitzer's *Quest of the Historical Jesus*, although he makes the same point as Kähler, that the gospels are not sources for a biography of Jesus. However, for the time being the old quest was continued, with Bousset, Jülicher and Wernle using the, by now, traditional methods of historical criticism, and Johannes Weiss doing the same thing with the apologetic aim of establishing confidence in what can be known of the teaching as well as the life of Jesus, and deliberately rejecting Schweitzer's conclusions. Yet there are traces to be found in Weiss of the newer view about the nature of the gospels and the purpose of the evangelists. Mark is not a chronicler, but a witness to the Gospel of Christ, the Son of God.[1] But this merely states the problem, and the solution he offers is a one-sided one. Recognizing as he does the character of the gospels as testimony, he nevertheless claims for them a direct relation to history, thus avoiding the radical implications of his initial insight. The central concern of all the critics, including Adolf von Harnack and Wilhelm Heitmüller, is the historical continuity between the Jesus they hope to recover from the gospels and the Church's proclamation. They cannot reconcile themselves to the idea of a radical breach in that continuity, a breach occasioned by what happened on Good Friday. Hence they cannot see that the origin of the Church's proclamation is to be sought in the first Easter day and nowhere else, as Kähler did, although they do see that this is where the turning point lies.

It was in form-criticism that Kähler's insights really bore fruit. The form critics showed that the *Sitz im Leben* of the gospel pericopes lies in the preaching of the Church. Their kerygmatic character rules out any interest in a chronological presentation of the life of Jesus. The real question is not whether it "really happened", but what the motives were which governed the growth of the tradition: "We may not therefore ask whether this thing or that could have happened or really did, but how, since when, for what purpose and with what meaning it has been handed down."[2] Of course, all this does is to postpone our prob-

[1] *Jesus von Nazareth, Mythus oder Geschichte*, 1910, p. 153.
[2] Dibelius, *Theologische Rundschau*, 1929, pp. 210f.

lem and raise it to a higher plane. Any *direct* connection between the kerygma and historically demonstrable occurrence is denied, though what connection there is between them is left unexplained.

This shift of concern can be clearly traced in the books on Jesus which emerged from this newer school of thought. In *Jesus and the Word*[1] Bultmann abandons any attempt to express a "viewpoint" about Jesus as a historical personality. Such attempts, he says, are often interesting, but they leave us in the position of neutral observers. For this reason "interest in the personality of Jesus is excluded" (p. 8). What Bultmann sets out to offer us is "an encounter with history" (p. 6). At first sight it looks as though even in limiting himself to the message and teaching of Jesus Bultmann is still pursuing the old quest, and is seeking to produce some historically objective material at least in regard to the teaching of Jesus. But he immediately scotches any such suspicion by insisting in unmistakable terms that it does not matter at all whether the material he uses goes back to the earliest stratum in the tradition, that is to Jesus himself. Bultmann is not seeking to reproduce the teaching of a "historical Jesus", but the teaching of a Jesus proclaimed by the Church. His message was essentially one of forgiveness offered in his word. Here Bultmann can even speak of the "facts of salvation", though with the important qualification that the death and resurrection of Jesus are not the kind of historical facts to which you can take up the attitude of an impartial observer, e.g. proving them and adding them to your stock of knowledge. If that were so, they would not be events which encounter me. In the final analysis, it is only the Word of Jesus which is an event of this kind (pp. 213ff., esp. p. 215). And the only proper assessment of Jesus' person is the recognition of him as the bearer of the Word. There is no external proof that this Word is true (p. 218). That kind of a solution to our problem does look somewhat arbitrary, it is true. Jesus' own proclamation of the Word of forgiveness and the acceptance of this proclamation by the earliest Church—this is what set the kerygma in motion, historically speaking. To be sure,

[1] 1926; E.T., 1934.

we ought not to make too much of Bultmann's denial that there is any "attestation of the truth of the Word". Before this he had already said: "The tradition of the Church has rightly held fast to the connection of forgiveness with an event, and speaks in this sense of the facts of salvation."[1] In other words, the kerygma is definitely rooted in an event distinct from the Word of Jesus himself. Only we must not suppose that this event is susceptible of proof. That would be quite wrong. Here, indeed, is yet another negative description of the relation between kerygma and history. The kerygma is not rooted in an occurrence which is susceptible of historical proof. The only positive thing one can say about it is that it is rooted in an event whose character is left undefined. Must we then rest content with this vague solution, or is there more to be said on the subject?

Schniewind, at any rate, would like to go further: "The careful historian, we would maintain, is bound to come up against the traces of this revelation, and where they are obscured it is a sign that there is something wrong with his historical methods."[2] Bultmann will have none of this: "All it (sc. historical research) can do is to confront us with the Jesus of history. Only the Church's proclamation can bring us face to face with Kyrios Christos" (op. cit., p. 118). This quotation from Schniewind is open to criticism, for Martin Kähler's contention that this is just what historical criticism cannot prove has been amply vindicated. Evidently, when Bultmann speaks of the historical Jesus he means something different from what it had meant in the old quest of the historical Jesus. What he means by it is "an abbreviation for the historical phenomenon with which we are concerned".[3] In other words, Jesus seen in the light of kerygma of the earliest Church. Hence the question is still open.

Schniewind refers in his "Reply to Bultmann" to Hoskyns and Dibelius. Hoskyns' *Riddle of the New Testament* (1931) offers the best résumé of New Testament scholarship in connection with our present subject of discussion. It has the limited purpose of demonstrating that our sources are shot through with the pro-

[1] P. 212: translation slightly revised by R.H.F.

[2] *Kerygma and Myth*, Vol. I, p. 84.

[3] *Jesus and the Word*, p. 14.

clamation of the Kyrios Christos, and that later developments, so far from being accretions to or perversions of the kerygma, are merely attempts to draw out its implications. Earlier than this, Dibelius' work on form-criticism had already pointed out the connection of the tradition with the early Christian preaching, which he regards as the controlling factor in the growth of that tradition. He also pointed out that this connection acted in two ways. On the one hand it resulted in a certain indifference towards the historicity of the stories narrated. On the other hand it tended to preserve the tradition and thus to insure the utmost reliability. Hence he can speak of the "relative trustworthiness" of the earliest tradition.[1] In his book on *Jesus* his aim is "to offer a portrait which will help the reader to make a genuine decision for or against him" (op. cit., pp. 13–14). He does not attempt the impossible by distilling a purely historical presentation out of the proclamation of the earliest Church. He is deliberately cautious about the Messianic consciousness of Jesus, confining himself to showing what "Christ" or "Messiah" would have meant when the gospels were written. In other words, he is interpreting the kerygma (pp. 90ff.). But he does broach our subject when he considers how the faith and proclamation of the earliest Church, which originated in the post-Easter faith in the Risen Lord, actually came into being. Even if we can postulate certain prior data for that faith, such as the Pharisaic belief in the resurrection of the dead (p. 140), this cannot account for the conviction that *Jesus* had risen from the dead: "But the New Testament narratives also show that, at least in the hour of crisis, the disciples had no such assurance. They fled (Mark 14. 50), and gave up Jesus' cause for lost (Luke 24. 19–21)." Something must have happened in between which in a short time not only produced a complete reversal of their attitude but also enabled them to engage in renewed activity and to found the primitive Christian community. This "something" is "the historical kernel of the Easter faith" (p. 141). This ought to satisfy Schniewind's desire that historical criticism ought to be able to uncover traces of the revelation. They are, be it noted, no more than traces. Dibelius

[1] *From Tradition to Gospel*, pp. 59ff., esp. p. 62.

cannot specify any event which is at once accessible to historical research and can account for the origin of the kerygma. When all is said and done, we are back at Kähler's point, which was that all we can establish is the effects of the revelation in history, and then make inferences from those effects to their cause. All we can prove historically is the kerygma of the earliest Church. We cannot prove that there was any direct connection between the proclamation and the disciples as they were during Jesus' earthly life. The very fact that we cannot necessitates the inference that there was some such event, though we meet it positively only in the Church's witness to the resurrection.

There is another work worth noticing which was particularly concerned with the results of form-criticism. We refer to H. J. Ebeling, *Das Messiasgeheimnis und die Botschaft des Markus-Evangeliums*.[1] Its author was killed on active service in 1939. He shows impressively how our problem was raised by implication with Wrede's recognition of the Messianic secret as a literary motif in the Markan gospel. He furnishes a detailed account of the course of the discussion since Wrede's original essay. Wrede was the first to replace "the psychologizing of the narrative by the psychologizing of the narrators" (p. 12). It was this that made him (Wrede) a pioneer in the enquiry into Mark's literary motives. He made only one mistake, and that was, he did not go far enough. He failed to see how impossible it was for the Church to impose a Messianic interpretation upon a life which, as Wrede maintains, and which the Church allegedly knew to be, un-Messianic. The form critics were the first to go the whole way and to drop the whole question of historicity. They sought to explain the gospels entirely as the expression of the Easter message. This development, however, rouses Ebeling's suspicions. It suggests that the gospels were actually anti-historical, and that the evangelists were completely indifferent to the life of Jesus. Here the form critics are one-sided, and fail to do justice to the literary evidence. For the earliest Church the life of Jesus, so far from becoming unimportant, acquired its real significance for the

[1] "The Messianic Secret and the Message of the Gospel of Mark". *Beiheft zur Zeitschrift für die neutestamentliche Wissenschaft*, Berlin, 1939.

first time as a result of the Easter message. The gospel evidence about the disciples' lack of understanding is an indication of their awareness that it was only after the resurrection that they came to perceive the true meaning of Jesus' signs. Unfortunately Ebeling's view obscures the real import of the Easter message itself. The comparisons he draws between the disciples' experience and those of Mohammed and Augustine leads him into the error of psychologizing the Easter faith, which is quite a different matter from psychologizing the actual witness. Ebeling should have paid more attention to Schniewind and his works, and he would then have had a clearer grasp of our problem. For although in his popular commentaries Schniewind treats the pericopes as straightforward historical narratives, his method here was only a kind of appendage—and a necessary one—to his professional work as a scholar. Unfortunately we have hardly any evidence of this except in notes taken at his lectures. Yet the contrast between his critical work and the ostensibly naïve treatment of the pericopes in his commentaries shows that when we have noted the evangelists' lack of concern with past history, this is not the whole of the story. Just because we recognize the kerygmatic character of the gospels we are able to pass on their testimony as it stands. The upshot of Schniewind's work, however, is to leave the impression that to distinguish between kerygma and history is not to solve the problem, but simply one way of stating it.

The Bultmann-Schniewind debate on demythologizing suggests that our problem, so far from being solved by demythologizing, has actually been accentuated. Since Bultmann's programme pushes the recognition of the kerygmatic character of the New Testament to its logical conclusion and stresses this character so remorselessly, it raises anew the same problem which Kähler was faced with by that same recognition—the relation between kerygma and history. All that Bultmann has done is to describe that relation in its negative aspect. Historical criticism, he says, cannot recover any traces of the revelation of God. The question is, can that revelation be described only in these negative terms? Can we say anything positive about it? Some solutions which have been offered in the course of the debate are one-sided, and are due to a less radical appreciation of the kerygmatic character of the New Testament witness. First, we should mention the contributions of Catholic theology and pietism. It is true that Catholic theologians agree that "the original form of the apostolic kerygma (is) the norm of our preaching and theology about Jesus Christ".[1] Geiselmann finds this original form in the speeches of Acts. They already have this invariable feature: "their nucleus consists of a summary of the history of Jesus of Nazareth" (ibid.). We might also agree when he says: "The apostolic preaching is in every respect concerned with the history of Jesus of Nazareth" (ibid.). But Geiselmann does not mean that the apostolic preaching is concerned with a figure of the immediate past. What he wishes to suggest is that the Messiahship of Jesus is susceptible of historical proof. That Jesus is Messiah is not just exclusively the assertion of the kerygma. The kerygma simply reproduces a fact which as Karl Thieme makes the same point with greater precision: "We are left with the resurrection of Jesus as a historical event. More than that, it is *the* historical event *par excellence*."[2] Lest faith should be reduced to the mere acceptance of a historical proposition, he adds elsewhere that the function of these events is to "prepare for the personal experience of salvation and to make it effective".[3] Yet he cannot avoid the consequence of making faith the confident acceptance of an extra-personal reality in space and time, the acceptance of the staggering event of "Christ's resurrection from the grave" (ibid.). Here is the parting of the ways, and there seems to be no point carrying on the discussion any further. It is the inevitable consequence of two different conceptions of faith, Catholic and Protestant.

This is, indeed, what Catholic theologians themselves think, as is shown above all in an article by Adam Fechter entitled

[1] Subtitle of an essay by J. R. Geiselmann, "*Jesus, der Christus*", *Katholisches Bibelwerk*, Stuttgart, 1951.

[2] *Frankfurter Hefte*, 1953, p. 113.

[3] *Theologische Quartalsschrift*, 1952, p. 401. Cf. in the same periodical Geiselmann, "*Der Glaube an Jesus Christus, Mythus oder Geschichte?*", 1949, pp. 257ff. and 418ff.

"*Entmythologisierung, Methode oder Manie?*"[1]. This "disease", as he calls it, set in at the Reformation, when the young Luther told philosophy to go to the devil—and note, it was the Church's philosophy!—and based his exegesis on his own feelings. As a result, "Luther's famous lectures on the psalms took a line somewhat similar to Bultmann. To start with, he followed the Church's traditional method of tropological exegesis, but interpreted the object of faith, Christ, in the light of the self-understanding of contemporary (sixteenth century) man. Sixteenth-century man was in despair about the visible Church, with its papacy and its legalism and its secularized conception of the sovereignty of God. Conscious of his total depravity and his fallen state, he flung himself upon faith in the grace of Jesus Christ as a 'mathematical point'." Fechter does a good job in tracing the connection between the existentialist interpretation—if we may use the term here, following the parallel drawn by Fechter—and the despair at the possibility of establishing the truth of the faith and the claims of the Church by secular proofs. This is the real reason behind the Catholic rejection of demythologizing. Once the view was abandoned that the Church's claims could be proven the same conclusion was bound to be drawn with regard to the kerygma. Here is yet another endorsement of Bultmann's appeal to Luther.

Among the pietists Bultmann's denial of the "historicity" of the resurrection has been the real stumbling block. This is due to their failure to see the difference between *historisch* (past historical) and *geschichtlich* (of permanent, historic significance), as Martin Kähler distinguished them. Otherwise Reinecker, who is shocked by demythologizing and flatly rejects it, would hardly have overlooked the fact that the passages he cites from Bultmann do not stand alone, but are balanced by positive statements about the Easter *faith*. It is indeed a tragedy that the pietists would have made up their minds solely on the basis of Bultmann's negative statements about the resurrection, thereby failing to appreciate the resources he offers for their own preaching of the

[1] "Demythologizing, method or madness?" in *Wort und Wahrheit*, 1953, pp. 898ff.

gospel message. Pietist preaching has always suffered from a failure to see where the shoe pinches over the relation of the kerygma to history, and as a result they have contented themselves with a one-sided solution. They regard the kerygma simply as the proclamation of events which have happened inthe history of the past, at least to the extent that past historical events need proclaiming at all. They should have noticed the indifferent attitude of the gospels towards past history. Surely that would have opened their eyes to the problem. Instead, they have confined themselves to trying to harmonize the gospels; which has proved an embarrassment in present-day evangelism, since the would-be convert is no longer confronted with a genuine challenge. They above all people should have seen this. It should have taught them that demythologizing is not the bogey they think it is, not an attempt to water down the gospel message, but an honest endeavour to do justice to what the pietists themselves are so concerned about, to challenge our contemporaries to a genuine decision. They will never see this until they realize that their rejection of demythologizing springs from a one-sided view of the whole programme. Not only does Bultmann emphasize that redemption is a real event: it stands at the very heart of his thought. They should show more confidence in the power of God's word to prevail over man's fallible interpretations and to use such endeavours as those of Bultmann to bring men to faith. That would make them more cautious in their judgement of him.

We find exactly the opposite criticism of Bultmann in the Berne school.[1] We might first mention Ulrich Neuenschwander's *Die protestantische Dogmatik der Gegenwart und das Problem der biblischen Mythologie*.[2] But the chief representative of this school is, of course, Fritz Buri. In his contribution to the second volume of *Kerygma und Mythos* he had already laid it down as a matter of fundamental principle that "There neither can be, nor is there any need for a kerygma, a proclamation of a divine act of salvation in Christ" (op. cit., p. 96). In other words, there is no connec-

[1] The Swiss liberals, see above p. 33 (R.H.F.).

[2] "Contemporary Protestant Dogmatics and the Problem of Biblical Mythology", Berne, 1948.

tion between kerygma and history. The kerygma belongs entirely to the sphere of myth. Its meaning and validity depend on the degree to which the particular understanding of existence it enshrines can be interpreted. In his contribution to the third volume of our series Buri has outlined a "theology of existence", which he further developed in an outline of dogmatics bearing the same title (Berne and Stuttgart, 1954). The latter work provides a more detailed account of Buri's views on the kerygma and history. All Christological statements, even the most rudimentary form of the kerygma, "Jesus is the Christ", have a symbolic character. This character must be laid bare "by seeing it as the mythological expression of an experience of 'redemption', which in turn must be interpreted in the light of an analogous experience of Self" (p. 87). He hopes to offer "an objective criterion for the adequacy of any given Christology". This is "the creative activity of God through which men partake of salvation in suffering and guilt" (p. 89). But despite this attempt to reassure us, there is nothing to stop him from interpreting this experience of Self without reference to its cause. It no longer points to an event which brings it into being.

The kerygma is thus unleashed completely from its historical moorings. It originates not in an event of history, but in the experience in which "existence comes to apprehend its relatedness to Transcendence, and thus becomes conscious of its freedom and its givenness" (p. 89). The only connection between the kerygma and history is that the kerygma emerges in history. You can hardly call this "revelation" as Buri does, at least not in the normal sense of the word. "It is the formative power in history which this faith possesses in Jesus and his disciples, and the truths of human existence which it disclosed that impart to this entity a special revelatory quality for us" (p. 90). The early Christian confession is divine "revelation" only because it is a legitimate mythological symbol. Buri's endeavour to do better than Schleiermacher and to find a higher starting point than liberalism had, is obvious. So is his agreement with the solution Bultmann offers to the task of hermeneutics. But he cannot escape from his liberal presuppositions, because for him the criterion of genuine understanding is the understanding subject himself. "Just as the mythological imagery may serve existence as a mode of expressing its self-understanding, so, conversely, traditional mythology can only be understood in the light of existence" (p. 85). Hence there can be no causal connection between history and the kerygma. The divergence of view exhibited here is still more evident in the Bultmann-Jaspers controversy (see below, pp. 133ff.).

In these two controversies, between orthodoxy (catholic and pietist) and Bultmann on the one hand, and between the Berne school and Bultmann on the other, we have the two most pregnant controversies in the whole of the debate. The rest of the discussion has proceeded within the area thus delineated. The main burden of criticism in official Lutheran orthodoxy, as we find it in the volume edited by Ernst Kinder[1] is its insistence on the objective factualness of the redemptive event. The chief danger of demythologizing is the elimination of certain elements from the kerygma. Ernst Kinder is indeed aware of the problem of kerygma and history. He too recalls Kähler's distinction between *historisch* and *geschichtlich*, but misconstrues it and gets bogged down in a barren controversy. Of course, when Kähler said "not susceptible of proof by the methods of historical criticism" he did not mean "it never happened". That would be a false dilemma, and one which never so much as crossed his mind. The opposite of "not susceptible to historical proof" is "with permanent historic effect". Kähler was just as insistent that the latter applied to the whole New Testament tradition as he was in denying the former. Kinder is asking of the tradition something which, if we follow Kähler, we cannot allow. We cannot claim that everything happened precisely as the New Testament relates it, nor can we claim the reverse. The gospels never raise the question, and it is wrong for us to do so. It is up to the orthodox Lutheran theologians to prove the objective reality of the events as best they can, since they agree that it cannot be done by the methods of historical criticism. Is there any other way of getting at what actually happened? Evidently Kinder thinks there is—through

[1] See above, pp. 17f.

faith. Hence we get such nonsensical statements as this: "If these supernatural realities are only disclosed to faith, they are still objective realities which really happened" (Kinder, op. cit., p. 52). Objective reality requires a percipient subject, an openness for perception. Faith becomes an occult science when treated as the only way of arriving at perception, and thus enters into competition with scientific perception. Of course it is legitimate to speak of perception through faith, but it is essential always to remember that it is perception through *faith*. It is impossible to speak in this connection of objective reality.

Walter Künneth puts his finger on the real difference between both parties when he criticizes Bultmann's views of the relation between revelation and history. "Revelation is not merely 'address' *in actu*: it is communication of a fact, the message of an event of salvation which has already happened, of something accomplished, something done" (ibid., p. 78). The kerygma is first and foremost a communication of facts. It is not clear whether Künneth realizes the consequences of what he is saying. It means that the kerygma is completely dependent on the results of historical research, an intolerable situation, which is just what Kähler was so anxious to avoid. And it is to be questioned whether such a view of revelation can find any support from the New Testament. It has long been established that the earliest Christian kerygma is primarily address *in actu*. This, however, does not mean that the relation of the kerygma to history is the opposite of what Künneth maintains, and the fact that this is so is just the problem. Künneth oversimplifies that problem when he asks Bultmann: "Why is the origin of the new self-understanding shrouded in such obscurity? You say it originates in Jesus of Nazareth. But we know so little about him. He could have been anyone else." The answer is that it pleased God that our salvation should have come from this name and from none other. And as a matter of fact he is not so obscure as all that. For the earliest Christians he was a figure of the immediate past, and was therefore open to exhaustive investigation. It was just this that made Christianity so different from the mystery religions, as Bultmann himself admits. Here then is one positive link between the kerygma and history. Of course this does not mean that we can prove from history that Jesus was the Christ. That was the point at issue between Bultmann and Schniewind, and is indeed the crux of the matter. The question is not whether there is any relation between the kerygma and history, but whether the truth of the kerygma can be proven from history. People ask Bultmann whether he is really trying to hold fast to the Christ event as a unique occurrence in Jesus of Nazareth as a figure of past history. But that is beside the point. There can be no doubt about that. But Künneth is unable to dissociate this question from the question of its susceptibility to proof. To confound the two questions in this way is inevitably to court error: they must be kept strictly apart.

We turn now to Friedrich Gogarten's *Demythologizing and History* (E.T., London, 1955). This essay is directed specifically against the criticisms of the official Lutheran theologians. Gogarten traces the source of their arguments back to the supersession of the metaphysical by the historical understanding of faith. The metaphysical understanding, which comprehended eternal and divine reality with the temporal and earthly life of man in a single whole, is no longer tenable. It has been dissolved by the historical understanding. Faith can only be understood historically (pp. 34f.). The Lutheran theologians realize this, and are trying to do justice to it by tying faith to the objective factualness of the revelation. By history they mean primarily past events. That is why they are concerned so exclusively with the "trans-subjective reality" of the redemptive event. Everything else must be subordinated to that. The alternative view outlined by Gogarten is that "actual history—and, one must add, the actual historical character (*Geschichtlichkeit*)—of the events recorded in the New Testament is not to be sought in the 'objective' and historically (*historisch*) ascertainable fact of their having taken place, but in the kerygma, the proclamation and witness that in the events of this history God turns with grace towards mankind and their world" (pp. 37f.). This describes the connection between the kerygma and history in both negative and positive terms. It is not that the kerygma includes allusions to certain historical occurrences. It lies in the kerygma itself, which testifies to God's gracious turning to mankind in these events. Gogarten has thus put into his own words what Bultmann has said about the relation between the cross and the resurrection. The kerygma proclaims an event of past history, the crucifixion of Jesus, but claims that this is the event of redemption, and this is something we encounter only in the kerygma. The proclamation of Easter is conceivable only as proclamation. It can never be ascertained as an event of the past.

The first reply to Gogarten came from Erwin Wilkens.[1] This was followed by a more detailed refutation from the pen of Ernst Kinder in an article in the same journal entitled *Die Verbindlichkeit des neuzeitlichen Geschichtsdenkens für die Theologie*.[2] He promises to elaborate his argument further in a work of the same title. The only quarrel Kinder can pick with Gogarten is his exclusive attachment to a particular terminology. Gogarten had pointed out that the orthodox Lutherans' insistence upon the objectivity of the redemptive event is rooted in the subject-object pattern of thinking, to which he prefers the historical pattern of thinking. But—and this is what Kinder fails to see—he did this only to rebut the charge that Bultmann was subordinating theology to philosophy by introducing the terminology of modern historical thinking. Gogarten agrees that this terminology has no exclusive claim to validity: "Needless to say, this truth does not have to be learnt from Heidegger. If one thinks one can learn it better from another source, all well and good. But, in one way or another, learnt it must be" (p. 52n.). Kinder has no convincing reply to Gogarten's gravamen against the Lutheran insistence on the subject-object terminology. Moreover, as Gogarten shows, these terms, "objective", "trans-subjective" and the like, are not the only ones the Lutheran theologians use. They bring in, quite inconsistently, statements about "the reality which cannot be proven historically". This inconsistency is the real problem about this Lutheran theology. Gogarten complains that they

[1] *Evangelische-Lutherische Kirchenzeitung*, 1953, pp. 297f.

[2] "Must theology be tied to modern historical thinking?", op. cit., pp. 381ff.

never iron out this inconsistency (p. 43), and Kinder cannot say anything in reply. All he says is that the terminology objected to is used only incidentally, in an auxiliary way; though he cannot make out any case for this argument (p. 382). He ought to have made this clear somewhere along the line, for that is not exactly the impression we get from the official Lutheran pronouncements. Rather, it seems to be for them a matter of life and death to maintain the objective factualness of the redemptive events. Perhaps this is because they want to keep a solid front against Bultmann, as Kinder suggests (p. 382). But all they can do is to keep harping on the point, and make that the centre of their attack. And if that is all they can do, they should show what direction this auxiliary function takes, if that is really the case. They should tell us *why* these terms are so important, instead of repeating them *ad nauseam*. Yet Kinder assures us that he finds much in Bultmann with which he can agree (ibid.), which makes it all the more necessary for him to explain what he means by auxiliary functions. Once again, the Gogarten-Kinder controversy points up the real problem—not the factual character of the redemptive events, but the place of history in the kerygma.

Wilhelm Kamlah[1] criticizes Gogarten from a somewhat different angle. Gogarten's essay, he tells us, fills him with both apprehension and gratitude. But has Gogarten really proved his case that the dogmatic formulae of the New Testament represent historical as opposed to metaphysical thinking? Even Gogarten is constrained to speak about a mystery which "takes place in eternity between God and Jesus", yet he contends that this is historical rather than metaphysical thinking! Now, Kamlah asks, can this be done in a strict, Heideggerian sense? To prove his point that this is really historical thinking, Gogarten introduces the idea of responsibility as the clue to Jesus' obedience to the Father. In this obedience is exhibited the structure of the revelatory act of God in Jesus. It is "the redemptive event which takes place in Jesus' delivery of His message of salvation" (p. 74).

1 "*Gibt es wirklich die Entscheidung zwischen geschichtlichem und metaphysischem Denken*" ("Can we really decide between historical and metaphysical thinking?"). *Evangelische Theologie*, 1954, pp. 171ff.

Kamlah doubts whether the concept of historicity, which Gogarten so stoutly maintains, is adequate to convey the Biblical affirmations. What he does not notice is that Gogarten is still faithful to Heidegger's conception of historicity. Has not Gogarten, he asks, fallen into the same trap as those who use the term "supra-historical", of which he is himself so critical? Kamlah, however, goes on to ask "whether historicity can be applied to the historical character of individual human existence without which, Gogarten contends (p. 38), there can be no such thing as history". This discussion is worth pursuing further. Kähler's distinction between "historical" and "historic" (*historisch* and *geschichtlich*) no longer covers all the problems involved. The official Lutheran theologians must be made to clarify their terminology, so must Gogarten himself.

We turn now to Karl Barth's critique of Bultmann. In the last analysis he shares the Lutheran theologians' anxiety lest history should be abandoned in favour of a general truth divorced from history. As Barth rightly sees, the issue becomes a burning one when we come to the historicity of the resurrection. Barth starts with a penetrating analysis of the Easter message, for the moment in complete conformity with Bultmann: "The event of Easter is, as it were, the prism through which the apostles and their communities saw the man Jesus in every respect of his relation to them—as One who 'was, and is, and is to come' (Rev. 4. 8)" (*Church Dogmatics*, III, 2, p. 442). He continues along the same lines as Martin Kähler: "For the New Testament this later history is not just an appendix or afterthought to the main theme, but essential and indispensable. And it is all this, not in a different sense, but exactly in the sense in which the New Testament takes it" (p. 443). He praises Bultmann for his correct and emphatic appraisal of the Resurrection (ibid.). Equally justified is his criticism of Werner Kümmel's *Promise and Fulfilment*[1] and of Oscar Cullmann's *Christ and Time*.[2] Both books fail to do justice to the centrality of the Easter message. Cullmann gives the impression that the Christian Church had its concept of time already to hand and simply read the Christ event into it. This at once

[1] E.T., 1957. [2] E.T., 1950.

invites the counter-question to Barth as to whether in his controversy with Bultmann he presents a necessary alternative. Is "the memory of the forty days" (ibid., p. 442) the necessary alternative to the contemplation of a "timeless and non-historical truth", as he calls it? Certainly, the Easter history is "the axiom which controls all their (sc. the Evangelists') thinking about this man in His time" (ibid., p. 443). But why should he go on to draw this antithesis: "It is not just a mere reflection of their memory of Jesus or of their present life in communion with Him or of the hopes they set upon His person"? By setting up these false alternatives, Barth lays himself open to the same criticism which Gogarten brought against the official Lutheran theology. He writes: "The real Easter event, which belongs to that eschatological occurrence, is the rise of the Easter faith of the first disciples. This was not based on any event in time, but only on the supra-historical, supra-temporal act of God" (ibid., p. 444). It is hard to see how this differs from the statement of Bultmann which he had already criticized, viz. that the Easter event is the rise of faith in the Risen One. The only difference is that Barth infers from this faith the "supra-historical and supra-temporal act of God", an inference which counts for very little, since supra-historical and supra-temporal are meaningless terms. "For, if language is still to have any meaning, whatever is 'supra-historical' or 'historically comprehensible reality' is quite certainly not history" (Gogarten, p. 41). For the moment, however, Barth sticks to formulations with which one cannot but agree: "For the Easter faith of the later Church and for our Easter faith, it *has the significance* of an act of God" (ibid., p. 444). If only he would confine himself to asserting all this of the Easter *faith*. But he at once goes on to mis-interpret Bultmann by describing the faith of the disciples as the movement in which "the disciples made up their minds about Him and about His death in particular" (ibid., p. 445). The inference he draws: "Nothing happened between Him and them" is hardly what Bultmann says. It is true, as Barth says, that it is impossible to get back behind the faith of the first disciples, and that our only access to Christ is through their proclamation. But this is not to say that faith is merely "making up their minds", merely a subjective experience. Bultmann never says that nothing happened between the Risen Christ and his disciples. All he says is that our only access to what did happen is through their proclamation. In his polemic Barth simplifies the issues and thus distorts the views of his opponent.

In the last resort, however, the crux of the problem lies in the terms "historicity" and "factualness". Barth is not satisfied with the idea that an event can only be acknowledged as having really happened when it is a "historical" fact, i.e. when it is open to verification by the methods of modern historical scholarship (p. 446). He objects to the argument that acceptance of the factualness of the resurrection in this sense involves blind acceptance, intellectual insincerity, a *sacrificium intellectus*, the degradation of faith to the level of a work. By contrast, he maintains, the New Testament regards the Easter message as something which it is a joy and privilege to believe. For the same reason he opposes those who claim the universal validity of the modern world view, and the impossibility of reconciling the gospel message with it. He points to the believer who, without being any the less a modern man, can accept the Easter message "freely and gladly" even to-day (p. 447). Here again is a confusion of two different things, and as a result, a false controversy to cloud the issues. The good news of the New Testament is at the heart, not the resuscitation of a corpse, but the possibility of the New Being disclosed with the Easter message. Similarly, the present-day Christian does not accept the Easter message because of a resurrection from the dead, but because he finds here the gesture of a gracious God. Hence acceptance remains an act of faith in response to the Word of God spoken to him. It cannot be identified with the acceptance of something that merely happened in the past. Faith is not a fiducial assent to a miracle-story. All we would insist on is that the early Christian's assent, like that of his present-day counterpart, is an assent of faith in response to God's word. It must not be surreptitiously distorted into an epistemological judgement, however articulated. This confusion of issues runs like a thread all through Barth's thought, and is the only reason why he lands himself into a false controversy with Bultmann.

Walter Klaas[1] is a disciple of Barth whose first contribution to the debate was very critical of the whole programme. More recently, however, he has offered an impressive corrective to Barth's error.[2] His essay is preceded by one from Günther Bornkamm, who accuses Barth of trying to carve out on *a priori* grounds room for the revelatory event. This is what Martin Kähler did when he spoke of a great, pre-eminent event which God has made immune from human fallibility. Bornkamm argues that the reality "of which the kerygma speaks . . . encounters us only in the Word, whose appropriate mode of apprehension is faith, and faith alone" (p. 20). Klaas then takes up the cudgels with a discussion of Barth's attempt to anchor the revelation in an occurrence which, though inaccessible to historical research, is nevertheless a real occurrence (though the way we come to apprehend it is still uncertain). He then proceeds to expound the relation of kerygma and history in Bultmann's thought: "Bultmann distinguishes *Historie* from *Geschichte*. The distinction is like that between thing and person. He is concerned with the genuine, significant-historic character of the figure and fate of Christ, and with the historicity of faith and the Church" (p. 46). Everything turns here upon the sense in which Bultmann uses the term historicity. As Ernest Fuchs has shown in his lengthy review of Bornkamm and Klaas,[3] the distinction is always a formal one. So is his use of the word "Church". It has the same eschatological dimensions as it has in Barth. "The Church itself is the revelation of God in space" (col. 17). Any discussion of kerygma and history must therefore take the Church into account. In the Church's proclamation the kerygma has a definite and direct relation to history. There is only one point where Fuchs, along with Bornkamm, feels he cannot go along with Bultmann. This is his retention of the word "reality". Yet he cannot accept Bornkamm's attempt to solve the problem with a refurbished definition of history.

[1] "*Der moderne Mensch in der Theologie Rudolf Bultmanns*" ("Modern man in the theology of Rudolf Bultmann"), *Theologische Studien*, No. 24.

[2] G. Bornkamm and W. Klaas, "*Mythos und Evangelium*", *Theologische Existenz heute*.

[3] *Theologische Literaturzeitung*, 1952, col. 11ff.

F

This is where F. K. Schumann comes in with his essay *Wort und Wirklichkeit*.[1] Schumann tries to show that this is inadequate for theological statements about the revelatory action of God. "If reality denotes this world of change and effect, reality is just what God is *not* insofar as Christianity is right in understanding him as Word, Logos" (p. 22). "Theological statements, even when formulated in strictly conceptual terms, must therefore of necessity be quite different from conceptual judgements in the realm of the real world" (p. 22). This is just the distinction that is missing in Karl Barth. Next, Schumann criticizes Künneth's arguments. Since the whole of creation is determined by the Word, it is wrong to think of it as a chain of cause and effect operating by itself. Hence the modern discoveries of uncaused incidents within the microcosmic structure of the atom have no decisive importance "for the Christian doctrine of God and creation" (p. 23, footnote 12).

Schumann then offers an interpretation of the kerygma in the light of his doctrine of creation as determined by the Word. This brings him to our problem. He does not like Bultmann's description of the kerygma as "that which gives meaning to an occurrence to whose historicity it testifies" (p. 48). Instead, he proposes as an alternative: "(The kerygma) testifies that while the occurrence in question (earthly life, crucifixion and resurrection of Jesus?—the allusion is not clear) takes place in the context of other historical occurrences, it has an additional character of its own. It is an event in a way that no other historical occurrence is. This is how I should distinguish between 'event' and 'occurrence'. 'Occurrence' means something which happens in the real world, and is therefore historical in the proper sense of the word. It can be demonstrated within the historical order, and can be proven by it. 'Event' is something which occurs within the historical order to the degree that it has entered into it, but it is not an intrinsic part of that order. It inserts itself into that order and assumes a place within it, but it is not derived from it" (p. 48). And here is Schumann's crucial point: "We cannot speak (of this event) as we do of historical occurrences: we can only

[1] "Word and Reality".

speak of it as a message which we proclaim" (p. 49). We must insist by analogy that our perception of such an event is quite different from our perception of an occurrence. "Only the disciples experienced the resurrection as an occurrence" (ibid.). There can be no doubt but that this takes us a step forward in the discussion. But where does it get us to? Does it mean that in the last resort we should resolutely abandon the search for historical proof of the kerygma? Is the search for a direct causal relation between kerygma and history—a search which Catholic theology, pietism and in the end even Karl Barth are so bent upon—really a problem at all? Would it not be best to drop it for good and all, recognizing that it is a problem which never so much as entered the heads of the evangelists? Should we not be satisfied that the only thing we can prove historically is the earliest preaching of the kerygma? That preaching is its only link with history—not some implied occurrence at the back of it. Of course there is still the question how the kerygma actually emerged—in that sense there is still a problem of its relation to history. This was the theme of Gloege in the main lecture delivered at the theological conference in Berlin in 1954.[1] Its title, *Offenbarung und Ueberlieferung* (Revelation and Tradition), indicates the real question which the kerygma poses: What, within the kerygma, is the relation between revelation and tradition, which is the form in which revelation confronts us in the kerygma? In the Old Testament revelation is historical in three senses. It is itself an event. It aims to produce decision. And it embodies historical occurrences. Revelation provides the foundation of *Geschichte* in the sense of a continuous chain of occurrences in past history (*Historie*) (col. 220). Gloege has reversed the question. It is not that the kerygma has a historical basis, but that history has its basis in the kerygma. But Gloege was obliged to deal with the first question. For the New Testament replaces a theophany by a Christophany. "True, the Christophany claims to be a theophany under a different guise. But it can only be seen as such through the Spirit in whom the Kyrios is present: only so can it be interpreted and expounded as a theophany. . . . In the New Testament

[1] *Theologische Literaturzeitung*, 1954, cols. 213–236.

it is only Jesus who reveals himself. . . . Of course it is not denied that God acts in a revelatory manner 'In Christ'. But the formula is not so much Christological as pneumatological'' (col. 224 and note 67). Gloege has thus made the kerygma self-authenticating. It is kerygma only because it is the medium of the Spirit's activity, and the Spirit or pneuma in the New Testament means the invisible presence of Christ. Now this means that he will not base the kerygma on an event or occurrence of any kind, but only on the testimony of the Spirit. Quite obviously this raises some fresh issues, and they certainly look more promising than much that has been discussed hitherto. There has been far too much discussion about the factual character of the occurrences or their immunity from proof.

But does Gloege succeed in getting beyond his own criticism of Bultmann? In his first contribution to the debate[1] he deals with Bultmann's rejection of the resurrection in any miraculous sense. Gloege criticizes this position with the support of an analytical treatment of the evidence. He argues that the Easter event is not presented as a miracle, but in a different light: ''In what sense is it an event if it is the eschatological word and deed of God for us?'' (p. 75). By taking the statement *Wunder ist Mirakel* merely as a synthetic judgement ''we do justice to the objective historicity of the resurrection, as an event which followed upon the historical event of the crucifixion'' (ibid.). But does the first proposition necessarily lead to the second, viz. that the resurrection is historical? Of course, Gloege is not trying to prove by the use of scientific historical methods that the resurrection actually occurred. That is why he cannot use the term historicity in the strict sense of the word. His coining of the term ''God's action-word'' (*Tatwort*) is a sign of this. Surely we ought then to be satisfied in finding this action-word of God in the kerygma. We can take that as the starting point of our considerations and abandon for good and all any attempt to get back behind the proclamation. Is there any sense in continuing to speak of historicity if we are using the word in quite a different sense from that which it normally bears?

[1] *Mythologie und Luthertum*, 1952.

The problem of kerygma and history has not assumed the same importance in the English-speaking world that it has had in Germany. Perhaps the reason for this is that English-speaking theologians have long been accustomed to using the word kerygma to imply a clearly defined entity, beyond which there is no need for us to go. Since it is the explication of the primitive Christian testimony, "Jesus is the Christ", the kerygma is regarded as a uniform entity. That this is in fact the English-speaking view is shown by such an early work as Sir Edwyn Hoskyns' *Riddle of the New Testament* (1931) and a little later in C. H. Dodd's *History and the Gospel* (1938). Along with this recognition of the kerygma there is, of course, as William Manson shows, more confidence in the reliability of the synoptic narratives, so much so that attempts are made to find the roots of the kerygma in the earthly history of Jesus. There is much talk of Jesus' self-manifestation as the Messiah. Thus the revelation is brought into direct connection with his earthly life. Ian Henderson's statement may be regarded as typical: "There must have been something about the actual Jesus at the time at which He was on earth, to make the New Testament witnesses summon men to decide for or against Him. Even Kierkegaard, with all his emphasis on the Divine Incognito, admits that. And if it is so, the historical facts about Jesus, and the mythological element in His life cannot have quite the subordinate rôle that Bultmann allots to them" (p. 49). As regards the kerygma's roots in history, English-speaking writers are content with what Dibelius says about the "x", the "something which must have happened". The factual character of this "something" has never had the importance it has unfortunately acquired in the German-speaking world.

Results

It will be sufficiently obvious that the debate thus far has not issued in anything like general agreement. We could hardly claim that there has been in all the various phases of the controversy even an agreement to disagree. Further, the whole debate has been marred by too many misunderstandings. There have been too many red herrings strewn along the path. All the same, it would be wrong to conclude that there has been no advance at all.

Perhaps the most important result has been the widespread recognition of the importance of hermeneutics and the many problems it involves. Bultmann's radical picture of the hermeneutic situation has at least brought these problems to the surface. It seems now to be generally recognized among Protestant theologians that we have an inescapable responsibility in this highly difficult matter, and the course of the debate has enhanced our awareness of it. We are nowhere near to general agreement on the extent of the task. And there are limits to what has been achieved, as for instance is shown by the obstinate defence in some quarters of the "objectivity" of the facts of salvation. An assessment of the objective element in the gospel narratives is neither necessary, nor, in the strict sense, possible. If that is the real intention of the gospel narratives—to communicate objective facts—then there can be no real hermeneutic problem. If, however, we do agree that there is such a problem, the implication is that we recognize the situation as Bultmann depicts it.

Closely connected with the hermeneutic problem is the homiletic aspect, the importance of which has been stressed particularly by the English-speaking contributions. It is from this quarter that we have been warned of the danger of being so out of touch with our people that our sermons offer them no genuine possibility of decision. That warning should be taken to heart. There is therefore no need to have any qualms about using terms borrowed from contemporary philosophy. Gogarten observed that Bultmann's critics use philosophical terms just as much, and that it is indeed impossible to avoid their use should it damp the ardour of those who harbour the illusion that there is a sacred theological language which is *ipso facto* legitimate. The relation of kerygma and history is still the burning topic in the debate. One side insists at all costs on the historical foundation of the kerygma, with the result that they reject demythologizing even when they admit that there is a real problem of communication. On the other side we have Bultmann's view, that the sole connection between kerygma and history lies in the earliest preaching, thus ruling out any attempt to get back behind the kerygma. This view has never been refuted. To some extent we have begun to clarify such terms as "reality" and "historicity", or at least to examine the way in which they are used. That must be carried further. Only then will we be able to see how far we can do justice to the concern of Bultmann's critics, a concern which thus far has taken the form merely of repeated insistence on the objectivity of the facts of salvation. The suspicion voiced by Thielicke in the early stages of the debate, that the crucial event is located in the human consciousness, has either been dropped altogether, or, as time went on, has been refuted by invoking the "intentional" character of self-understanding and the nature of the kerygma itself as event. It would be pertinent to ask whether the upholders of the objectivity of the salvation event would be satisfied with the assertion that this event occurred *extra nos* but also *pro nobis*.

When we have recognized that the kerygma is the sole object of our theological concern, and that it is impossible to get back behind it, we have by no means solved the problem of its relation to history. To begin with, it leads to the further problem pinpointed by Gloege, viz. that of revelation and tradition. And there is still the question of the separate pericopes and their significance for the proclamation. Only at one point can we register anything like a consensus of opinion: this is that the pericopes are used in the service of the kerygma. Otherwise exegesis must judge each pericope on its own merits.

The more we pursue the course of the debate, with the resultant impression that the controversy over the significance of history is being worked to death, the more convinced we are that this is the real issue, as we suspected all along. Undoubtedly, Martin Kähler thought that the only solution was to appeal to the "basic fact" of the resurrection. Yet it is equally certain that this is a *cul de sac*. And it is equally obvious that to reject the whole problem out of hand is merely to carry Kähler's solution to its logical conclusion. We have the kerygma, and it is the kerygma we have to preach and the kerygma we must get people to believe. Surely, if we stopped there we should escape from the dilemma which Iwand finds in the two words of God. And at the same time we should be rid of the dilemma which Gloege detects in demythologizing. Then, and only then, would we truly appreciate the formal character myth and at the same time Barth's fear of any kind of prior understanding would cease to worry us. Ought not this to offer the solution to most of our controversies? And should not reflection on the kerygma and its exclusive significance restore to the whole debate its character as a common search in a responsibility which is that of the Church herself? That this question should have been forced on to the centre of the stage is to my mind the most important result of the debate up to now. And the line taken by the Catholic theologians merely serves to underline this. For them demythologizing touches the very nerve of their controversy with Protestantism. Bultmann's claim that he is simply carrying to a logical conclusion the doctrine of justification by faith in the sphere of epistemology has been confirmed by both Gloege and the Catholic theologians. Just because of this it would seem to be a crying need for the (Lutheran) Church to exploit to the full this extension of the inner logic of Lutheranism.

There are two further questions which, to my mind, too little attention has been paid thus far. On the one hand, no attempt has been made to answer the numerous pronouncements of the Catholic theologians. They have pointed out to us in somewhat superior tones that all our difficulties spring from the Reformation understanding of the Church and the Word of God. What they are asking us, is whether the pillars of Luther's doctrine of justification have crumbled. This doctrine of justification, they keep telling us, was the base from which Bultmann launched his programme. He is fighting with his back against this pillar.[1] Here they are taking up the words of Bultmann, which have been quoted so much in the discussion, and to which so much objection has been taken, about the parallel between demythologizing and Luther's doctrine of justification. Bultmann's contention has never been refuted, nor has it been taken with the seriousness it deserves. The Catholic theologians are asking us whether we are

[1] Adam Fechter, *Wort und Wahrheit*, 1953, p. 904.

still prepared to stand by this *articulus stantis et cadentis ecclesiae*, even if it deprives us of our ultimate security in the sphere of epistemology and of doctrine, where we thought we still had it.

But there is still another way in which the debate leads to the question of our very existence as an evangelical Church. Many have looked for a decisive pronouncement from the authorities of the Church. Fortunately, the pronouncement of the bishops' conference was not taken as such. Our Catholic brethren have called attention in this connection to the first heresy trial in Wurtemberg—though the victim was not one of Bultmann's disciples, but a pastor with Romanizing tendencies. People have talked derisively of the "Swabish pope". How, our Catholic brethren ask, does this square with the Lutheran doctrine of the Church, which leaves the last word to the congregations instead of to Canon Law? All the way through, they say, we have been hampered in the debate because we have no authoritative magisterium. It would be a good thing if it were laid down in black and white that the policy of the authorities is to give advice, but never to anticipate the personal decision of the individual.

Yet another question has been touched upon in the debate. This is the bearing of demythologizing upon the Church's preaching. Here, in my opinion, the situation is the exact opposite to what is generally supposed. This is what Jaspers thinks about it: "Theologians sometimes dodge the existential claim by speaking about it, by acquiring an intellectual knowledge of faith, and by working for the preservation of the Church."[1] In both Kierkegaard and Bultmann "a doctrine intended to counteract a false rationalism unwittingly provides the unbeliever with a means to persevere in his faith with a good conscience, at the price of violence to his reason".[2] The trouble is, Jaspers fails to see that demythologizing arises from a concern for the Church's preaching. Such an evasion on the part of the sceptic is actually made impossible by demythologizing. As a preacher I am confronted by the witness of the New Testament. This is all I have to trust in. I can only preach when I have taken my stand upon this witness and have accepted it myself. It is Bultmann's critics, in my view, who are

[1] See below, p. 159. [2] P. 162.

guilty of this evasion by their insistence on the objectivity of historical facts, if by facts they mean not the testimony of faith. For faith no longer needs the props of objectivity. If theological language is exposed to the danger which Jaspers and many of Bultmann's theological critics see, the danger, I would contend, is a real one only so long as we disregard the whole purpose of demythologizing, which is to communicate the Church's message. If, however, that is its real purpose, the danger is really on the other side, although that is something which has not yet come out in the discussion. Jaspers is unconsciously putting his finger on this danger when he speaks of "working for the preservation of the Church" (p. 159). As for Bultmann's critics, we must ask them whether the unavowed motivation of their criticism does not lie in a rearguard action of this kind. But this point has not as yet come out in the discussion. Yet it would seem to me that this—as well as the challenge of the Catholic theologians—is the next point to be taken up in the theological enterprise.

KARL BARTH

RUDOLF BULTMANN—AN ATTEMPT TO UNDERSTAND HIM

THE name of Rudolf Bultmann is inseparably linked with the idea of "understanding". The connection will be obvious to anyone in the future who undertakes to write the history of theology in our day, and it is equally obvious to all who have kept abreast of theological trends during recent decades. Bultmann has impressed this idea, or rather the problems it brings to light, upon our consciences with extraordinary force. And he has offered many answers, and quite logical ones, to the problems it raises. Nor has he left us in doubt as to what he means by "understanding", particularly as regards the New Testament and its practical bearing. Many of us too have joined the fray "for and against" him.[1] I have myself joined in from time to time. It has often disturbed me that as a writer Bultmann is not at all easy to understand, a fact which has endangered the basis of the whole discussion. In this he is like the authors of the New Testament, perhaps even worse! What is really at the back of his mind? It is so easy to find ourselves at sea as we read him in one passage because we have overlooked some hidden dimension, and in another passage because we suspect such a dimension where none exists. Sometimes we are too sure, at other times we are not sure enough. Sometimes we fail to do him justice, at other times we give him more than his due. Sometimes we draw what seem to be obvious inferences, sometimes we neglect to draw them.

I must confess I know of no contemporary theologian who has

[1] An allusion to the Tübingen Memorandum (see above, pp. 39f.), entitled *Für und Wider die Theologie Bultmanns* (R.H.F.).

so much to say about understanding, or one which has so much cause to complain of being misunderstood. More than a few of his disciples and his critics upset me by the cocksureness with which they seem to have understood him. Yet when it comes to agreeing or disagreeing with him over a particular piece of exegesis (or even to thinking we can take him in at a glance, as the authors of the Tübingen Memorandum seem to), we must, it seems to me, reach agreement about something else first. Before we can express our agreement or disagreement with him over the method or results of his exegesis of the New Testament, we must first of all agree about what kind of exegesis is appropriate to it and the texts it contains.

What follows is simply an account rendered of the way I feel I have been able to understand him so far. I shall then try to come to some sort of provisional attitude towards him and his thesis. For good or ill one cannot avoid doing that. My present purpose is, then, not to speak for him, nor even, strictly speaking, against him, but, if I may put it thus, alongside of or around him. In saying this I would like to emphasize that I am concerned with my own attempt to understand him so far. And I must hasten to add that at best that attempt has proved unsatisfactory, not to say fruitless. I have the impression that many, if not the majority, know the answers no better than I do, but only behave as though they did. If anyone is clearer about Bultmann, he is of course, at liberty to help me—and any others who feel about him as I do—by sharing with him his better understanding. But to claim that he is easy to understand is not enough, whether it is his friends or critics who make the claim. Am I not right in thinking that somehow or other the whole discussion about Bultmann has got into a rut? Is it not therefore high time to reconsider his starting point?

I

First, I hope I am not wrong when I say that Bultmann's primary aim is to present the New Testament as the document of a message (kerygma, proclamation, preaching). It is that and that alone. This means that the usual lines of demarcation between exegesis and systematic theology are entirely abolished. It also means that we understand the message as something meant for ourselves and that in expounding it we become vehicles of the message. We neither understand nor expound the New Testament if our object is to extract general or theoretical propositions about God, the world or man, or even neutral historical data about events which happened long ago, or the record of religious, mystical devotional or even ethical experiences which happened once and can happen again to-day. If the New Testament contains such things they are only by-products, neither essential nor proper to it. Any such approach to the New Testament would be wrong. It would be wrong to hear it, think of it, and speak about it in any of these ways. None of them represents what the New Testament writers meant to say, what they intended, or what in fact they did say. Everything they say is conditioned by the message they delivered. They can only be understood by sharing the life of their message. To understand them means to believe them, and to expound them is to preach their message. Do I understand him rightly, thus far at least?

I will now try and follow him a step further. We can share in the life of the New Testament message, and we are required to do so, because of the message itself, not because of the theories, records of fact or religious experiences it incidentally records. The essential content of the New Testament is a unique event, a truly singular occurrence, with a significance far beyond anything the New Testament writers themselves or their contemporaries ever dreamed of, a significance for men of every age. Further, by the constant repetition of that message all men of every age can become contemporary with it and are meant to do so. The quintessence of the message, its very foundation and power, lies in the word which proceeded once (once for every Now) from God and was spoken in this act which happened once (once for every Now). This act takes place once for every Now of every man. God's word is spoken once for every Now of each one of us. Such is the message of the New Testament. Thus it brings us face to face with God, and challenges us to the decision which faith demands, to the choice between offence and obedience. In the obedience of faith which the message aims at producing we come to share its life, a sharing which challenges and enables us to understand ourselves by understanding the message. Quite apart from the historical and philological attention it demands, the understanding of the New Testament becomes an "existential" act, whereby its true understanding becomes an event. Am I still following Bultmann?

Not quite, perhaps. I can see that we can only interpret the New Testament aright if we share in the life of its message and in the obedience which responds to it. I can see, too, that this sharing takes the form of interpreting the message and my own faith as one who hears or reads it. But I cannot see why this should involve an act of *self*-understanding on my part. That hardly seems the right way of putting it. The message may bring me face to face with God and with myself as the one who hears it. It may lead to the obedience of faith. But how astonishing then and how incomprehensible I would find *myself*! How little should I be able to say about myself! Indeed, there is nothing I could say. How can I understand and explain my faith, of all things, unless I turn away from myself and look to where the message I believe in calls me to look? How can the understanding of the New Testament be an "existential" act, except in the sense that I am compelled to renounce any understanding and explanation of myself, thus finding it contradicted everything I thought I knew about myself, and finding myself called to account for that with which (or him with whom) I have been brought face to face? How can this come about when in actual fact I am engaged in turning away from myself and looking to where the message calls me to look? Is that what Bultmann really means to say? I should like to know, for it is just this that I cannot be certain about.

Perhaps I have begun to raise questions too soon. Therefore, while we are still concerned primarily with Bultmann's general orientation, let me go on listening. The New Testament records its unique message in a specific historical form. It is equally true that this message bears witness that the Word was made flesh. The message is brought to me at all times through the medium of the New Testament, but it is cradled in the language, terminology, thought-forms and ideological presuppositions of the particular period in which these documents came into being. It is this cradle which is the real problem in any attempt to come to grips with the message. But if it is to become contemporary with men of other ages, the message of these documents must first be understood in its original historical form. Only then can it be translated into other forms, into the language, terminology, etc. of later ages. In particular it must be translated into terms which are intelligible to those who in any particular age are trying to understand and expound it. Only so can it be a relevant message for to-day, for modern man and his contemporaries. Only so can it bring them face to face with God and challenge them to the decision of faith. Only so can it be heard with true faith, or at least as an authentic scandalon: only with contemporary ears. The substance of the message may be the same, but its form must be different to-day from that of yesterday. Its form must be understood and expounded anew to-day. Am I doing justice to Bultmann's intention?

If so, I could agree with all this. In every age all forms of theology—exegesis, dogmatics and preaching—must certainly undertake this kind of translation. It is an important task, and one which must be done rightly to-day as always. I wish, however, I knew how to introduce within the framework of Bultmann's concern, something else which seems to me to be even more important. Who is it, or what is it, in the New Testament which before all else calls for constant new understanding and exposition? Is it the "cradle" of the language, the thought-forms, etc., in which the message is enshrined? Or is it not before all else the message itself? Ought our primary concern in understanding and expounding the New Testament to be how we can convey it to our children, or to myself as a modern man, or to my contemporaries? Or should that be our exclusive concern? Does not what the New Testament says in its particular historical form, or rather, does not he who meets me as I read it, stand out in almost every verse, in gigantic proportions? Does not it—or he—continually cry out for a new enquiry about himself? And is it not true that in our understanding and expounding of these writings, our first endeavour must be to stop and listen to what the New Testament actually says? Must we not try to come to grips with him who confronts us there, and try to do it just a little better than we have before? Then, indeed, as we seek to grasp the message of the New Testament, we must grapple with the task of translation and somewhere confront contemporary man. The task of translation is a secondary concern, and it can only be done well if both reader and exegete take in hand the primary task first. No doubt I am not understanding Bultmann correctly here. Yet I am quite sure he would agree with me about what I have called the primary task. But there he is, still hammering away with unparalleled persistence, at the various historical forms in which the gospel is enshrined. Apparently he already knows *what* is in the New Testament. Apparently that is why he wants himself and he wants us to concentrate entirely on translating it from one language and one set of terms into others. For we already know what it is we are trying to translate. He seems to imagine that this secondary problem (which is certainly important) can be tackled and solved as it were *in vacuo*. Here Bultmann and his followers seem to agree with several of his critics, like Walter Künneth, to mention only one. They are strangely at ease just where in my opinion we ought, all of us, to be uneasy. For as far as the message itself is concerned we are in fact anything but *beati possidentes*. Some of my readers, no doubt, are itching to interrupt me here and show me just how my incomprehension might give way to understanding. To such let me say at once that I shall not be satisfied if they simply reassure that Bultmann and I are really after the same thing.

II

Permit me now to devote a little space to the historical background of Bultmann's position. No doubt we are right in finding its centre in the kerygma, which is founded and motivated by the act and deed of God. Here Bultmann's theology would seem to combine two important tendencies in the developments of recent decades. According to the Tübingen Memorandum, one of these tendencies is the return to the Reformation and its theology, the other the liberalism of the eighteenth and nineteenth centuries. There are vestiges of the latter even in Bultmann.

For the moment I will not contest what the Tübingen scholars say about Bultmann's liberalism. Historically, of course, it came first. Perhaps, however, since we are concerned with the idea of kerygma, it would be more illuminating and indeed more concrete if for liberalism we substituted form-criticism. Form-criticism began about thirty years ago to replace the history of religions school, which, with all that went before it, was then supreme in the field of New Testament studies. Form-criticism made use of principles in which some of us at any rate thought we could detect something more than a mere continuation of liberal exegesis. It looked like the beginning of a new appreciation for the objective character of the New Testament documents.

In that extraordinary springtime in the early nineteen twenties, it was not Bultmann's allegiance to Wrede, Bousset, Jülicher or Harnack, still less to their liberal predecessors, nor was it, as the Tübingen theologians assert, his training as a historian or philologist, but rather his status as one of the pioneers of form-criticism, that led him for the time being to throw in his lot with us—although most of us came from quite different intellectual and spiritual backgrounds—in the venture called *Zwischen den Zeiten*. All of us found in the kerygma (which, as Bultmann has himself so frequently emphasized since, is directed against the history of religions school) a common terminology for our enterprise. We thought we understood him and we believed he understood us. We were all trying to hear and reproduce better the real message of the New Testament. Even at that early date Bultmann was already talking about understanding. Did that mean he was already stressing the need to translate the message from one language into another? None of us, with the possible exception of Gogarten, were interested in that during those early days. If Bultmann was stressing it then, we never noticed it. It did not seem necessary to follow from the lead we had been given by the form critics—and it was as a form critic that we understood Bultmann. After all, there were other form critics, like Martin

Dibelius and Karl Ludwig Schmidt, who showed nothing of that particular "understanding". I still cannot see how it was a form critic that Bultmann came to set such store by translation as his primary concern, as he has done since. As for the other side of Bultmann's heritage, the return to the Reformation and its theology, I find this even more difficult. I suppose what the Tübingen scholars are referring to is the return to Luther and his doctrine of justification, etc. They mentioned not only Karl Holl (was he of particular importance to Bultmann?) but my own name too. I may therefore remark in passing that this new interest in the Reformation was not the original source, but a further consequence of my work. At that time I was only remotely interested in Luther himself. But it may have been quite different with Bultmann, and we should not forget how close he stood to Gogarten in this connection. Perhaps we should call him in all essentials a Lutheran, though, of course, a Lutheran *sui generis*, and on a higher plane! But that is a matter to which I shall return. As a form critic he was able, and as a thinker stimulated by the Reformation and particularly by Luther (though no doubt indirectly, rather than directly) he was bound, to give his support to the "theology of the Word" as it was called in those days, and to put the kerygma at the centre of his theology.

I can follow him thus far. But in the light of *this* heritage I find it even more difficult to see how he came to give "understanding" and "expounding" the predominant sense of "translating". On p. 5 of the Tübingen Memorandum we find an indication of the context in which Bultmann is to be viewed:

> For more than two centuries theology has been preoccupied with the Enlightenment, the new understanding of man and the world based on reason and revelation which had penetrated the whole of Western civilization.

This was in fact the situation. The great and, in fact, the sole theme of theology, the message of the Bible, was relegated to the background or completely neglected during those centuries. Theology was engaged in a discussion with a court of appeal which was quite foreign to that message. Its authority rested in the fact that it seemed to be establishing or to have established itself in the eyes of that court. But was this not obviously a departure from the Reformation and its theology? The Reformation never discussed matters with that kind of authority. In what way then is Bultmann returning to the Reformation, if his work represents part of the well-known reaction against its theology? Or, to put it another way, if Bultmann believes he is rooted in the Reformation and especially in Luther, how can he regard the problem of translation as the great theme? For that was the theme of the anti-Reformation, or at least the un-Reformation, during those two hundred years. I would like to know where Bultmann stands, but this problem baffles me, I am afraid.

III

Let me now try to describe what seems to me to be the outcome of Bultmann's understanding of the New Testament thus far. There is no doubt that he wishes to pass on the New Testament kerygma as he has heard it. What does that kerygma contain?

Basically, it is concerned with two factors which govern all human existence. First, it exposes the "old" determination of that existence. Secondly, it exhibits a new determination, and summons man to accept it. These two factors, and the transition from the one determination to the other which takes place when faith occurs, must be united by yet another factor. This is the saving act of God as experienced and known to faith and completed in the transition just mentioned. This succession, not in time but in fact, is a constant theme of Bultmann's, and is integral to our understanding of him. First, as hearers of the message, we experience ourselves as we were and are, and as we ought to be and shall be. Next, through faith in the message, we experience ourselves in transition from the one state to the other. Finally, we experience ourselves in the process of this transition as objects of God's saving act, or concretely in our being in Christ.

Here, however, I am already at a standstill. I cannot say I recognize in this translation the basic pattern of the New Testament message. It reminds one, of course, of the young Melanchthon's formula in 1521 (was it the same as the young Luther's?): *Hoc est Christum cognoscere, beneficia eius cognoscere.* Many people have been fond of quoting that slogan, first Spalding, then Bretschneider, then Ritschl and all his followers, and now Bultmann. All right, we're listening! There is nothing to be said against it. It is sometimes a very useful slogan, for instance against abstract objectivism. But we must not fall into the opposite danger of abstract subjectivism by elevating it into a kind of systematic principle. I suspect this is just what Bultmann has done and, I must say, it surprises me. For I cannot see how this sequence of events corresponds to the message of the New Testament. It may be we often think nowadays in that sequence. But does the New Testament begin with man's subjective experiences, with man as the recipient of its message? Are the New Testament's affirmations about God's saving act and about man's being in Christ primarily statements about man's subjective experience? Is not this reversing the New Testament? If so, the consequences will be far reaching. It may sometimes be justified to turn things the other way round, but only on occasion, and never as a fundamental principle of hermeneutics. The contours of New Testament thought are often different from and even the reverse of what modern man is used to. That is a hard fact, but if we are to translate the New Testament we ought not to conceal it from him.

But first let us hear what Bultmann has to say about these two determining factors of human existence. First, how does the New Testament address man? The answer is, as a sinner, as one who belongs to this world, who lives in the flesh. Man lives from his immediate environment, from the sphere of visible, tangible, measurable reality. He puts all of this in God's place, God, who is the sum of invisible, intangible, immeasurable reality, beyond man's control. By thus asserting his own autonomy, man incurs the judgement which falls upon this world. He is condemned to inauthentic existence and becomes a prey to fear and anxiety, at loggerheads with his fellows and subject to death (i.e. the past). He knows already, if only in outline—and existentialism can fill in the blanks—that there is such a thing as inauthentic, fallen being. The New Testament, however, focuses, corrects and radicalizes this knowledge of man before faith. It tells him not only that he is inauthentic and fallen, but that he is powerless to extricate himself from his plight. Every attempt to lift himself by his own strength merely involves him more deeply in his inauthentic state.

There is certainly much we can recognize here. There is something here of the Reformation doctrine of sin, something of Paul and John, something of the Synoptics. But do these contrasts between visible and invisible, tangible and intangible reality play the part Bultmann assigns to them in the message of the Bible? Does the Bible identify God with invisible, intangible reality? Does disobedience to God, i.e. sin, consist in preferring the sphere opposed to him? Surely, from the standpoint of the Biblical God, both spheres are very much in this world and, therefore, very much in the flesh? When the gospel speaks of pride, faintheartedness, falsehood, is that no more than a radicalizing of what man before faith, oscillating as he does between the two spheres, is able to know about himself and is capable of experiencing? Or are the statements of God's Word to man about himself as the "old man", about his sin, about his *servum arbitrium*, about the judgement he stands in something entirely new compared with man's self-accusations and laments?

Of course, the sequence Bultmann has chosen cannot tell us that. I can quite understand it. But I do not understand why Bultmann should have chosen that sequence and thus made it impossible for himself to show that sin is a wrong human decision, so that he is driven into a description of its consequences which are remarkably reminiscent of Platonism. I grant my difficulty with Bultmann here is the same as I feel with traditional orthodoxy as a whole. For in describing sin abstractly, apart from what God has done to remove it, he is, by and large, following the line of orthodoxy. He also follows it in using terms derived solely from natural law. And I quite see it would be asking too much of him to break with orthodoxy over this rather than anything else.

And what is it that the New Testament challenges man to accept? Faith, confidence in the unseen, unknown intangible reality. The surrender of all worldly or personal security. A life of having as if we had not (I Cor. 7. 29f.). To turn aside from our present to God's future, from fear and anxiety to freedom, to freedom for others, to love of God and our neighbour. In a word, he is called to accept the eschatological existence of the new creature, the authentic and truly natural form of human existence. Of course, man has always been aware of this, though only in a provisional and sketchy fashion. All the message does is to bring it to light and promise it to man as his proper destiny, and hold it before him as the end of his existence.

No one would want to deny that much of this is well said and accurate enough. In Calvin's language, we can catch the echoes of the *vita christiana* in the *vivificatio* which follows the *mortificatio* in the *meditatio vitae futurae*. And there are echoes of Paul too. Of course, the same problems that vexed us before are still here, and indeed more acutely. And there is something oppressively formal, legalistic and cold in this part of his translation. Can we really subsume under the rubric of "detachment from the world" all that the New Testament has to say about life in faith as the life of the new man? Can we for the purposes of translation ignore the fact that life in faith, eschatological existence, as presented in the New Testament, is a life of gratitude and response to the grace of God? There is something seriously lacking here. Can we ignore the fact that the New Testament always connects this new existence with a Lord who stands over against us, who is there before we are, warning and comforting us? I can understand why Bultmann wants to leave all this out. He obviously wants to describe the *beneficia Christi*, Christian existence considered in itself. Only then will he tell us how it has come into being. Only then will he tell us that it is founded in Christ, in God's saving act.

But that is just the point. How can we expound the New Testament if we relegate God's saving act which is the foundation of Christian existence to a secondary position? How can we do it if we understand God's saving act only as a reflection in the mirror of Christian existence? I cannot see why such a translation is necessary, or where it gets us. It seems to be purchased at too great a price, by narrowing down to the New Testament message and failing to do it justice. I know I should understand why he attaches so much value to his chosen sequence, but I am afraid I cannot.

This is, in fact, the crucial point about Bultmann's translation of the New Testament, which shows us more than anything else how he understands and expounds it. The kerygma is historical in the rarefied sense in which Bultmann uses that word, for it demands and evokes hearing and obedience. It proclaims the history of man's transition from the old life to the new, from himself to himself, from inauthentic to authentic existence, from his past to his future. It proclaims the Christ event, the event in which that transition occurs. The *Christ* event? The Christ *event*? Where does Bultmann think we should place the emphasis? Or is it wrong to ask that question at all? Yet when can one hardly refrain from asking it when the New Testament attaches such importance to it.

Bultmann tells us that the transition is the *Christ* event. Clearly that is where he would put the emphasis, not perhaps absolutely or exclusively, but certainly to a considerable extent. Nor does he do so merely because of the historical accident that the kerygma which proclaims that transition comes from the New Testament, which unmistakably connects that transition with the name of Jesus of Nazareth and his appearing, with his life and death as testified by the first bearers of the kerygma. This point is important to Bultmann because that transition claims to be history, with a beginning and ending in time, a history distinguished from other histories by a particular historical name, distinguished from them as something that happened once and for all. The New Testament kerygma makes this claim because it proclaims Jesus Christ and the saving act of God which he announced, the act of God which originated in this man and was done for us to whom the proclamation is addressed. Are there any other reasons why Bultmann insists that this transition is the Christ event, any other reason than that it has about it certain indispensable marks of genuine historicity? I look about me, but for the moment I see no other reason.

Should we then stress that it is the Christ *event*? While it began in the life and death of the man Jesus and derives its name and title from him, is it actually located not in him, but only in the kerygma about him and in those who accept this kerygma and obey it through faith? Or is the kerygma linked rather with history? Is that what gives it such historicity as it possesses? Or is the content of the kerygma not the man Jesus, but the transition, and the obedience of faith which that transition demands?

Kerygma of the Christ event? That I could understand. But it is hardly what Bultmann means. Christ event in and through the kerygma? That is what he seems to mean. And I cannot understand that as a reproduction or translation of the New Testament kerygma. That *Christ* is the kerygma is what the New Testament appears to say, not that Christ is the *kerygma*. Bultmann seems to be trying to reverse the New Testament. Or perhaps I have overlooked something, or suppressed or distorted something, and maybe that is why I feel so much at a loss in trying to understand this part of his argument. Yet perhaps there may be something in my way of putting it after all.

In traditional terms we might say that Bultmann is obviously insisting on the unity of Christology and soteriology, and the kerygma as the proclamation of this unity. Thus far I have no difficulty in following him. But as I see it, that unity is an articulated one in which Christology is prior to soteriology without being separated from it, and in which soteriology, while it is part and parcel of Christology, is nevertheless secondary to it and derivative from it.

The kerygma contains one story, the *Christ* event and the Christ *event*. Its locus, the locus of the saving transition from the old life to the new, is the life and death of the man Jesus of Nazareth. It is in him that we find the content, the substance, the backbone, the *locus communis*, in a word, the principle of the Christian message. Is this a sound reproduction of the New Testament message? Is it a good translation when Jesus Christ is thus relegated to the margin? Is it right to leave the cause of the transition so obscure and mysterious as Bultmann does? Can a fair and square translation of the New Testament dethrone Christology and merge it into soteriology? When this happens, Christology ends up by being the name and title of soteriology, its only importance being to ensure the "historical" character of the soteriology.

There is something else that puzzles me, something which seems to be connected with what we have just said. The whole doctrine of the Christ event must surely be intended to show how the transition, which is beyond man's capacity, has become a possibility and a reality. That being so, what is the position if this doctrine is not so much a doctrine of Christ but a doctrine of the happening of the transition, which only had its beginning in Christ, which only derives its name and title from him? What if Christology has no function of its own, but is absorbed into soteriology? What I mean is, supposing Jesus Christ becomes an obscure, marginal figure, without any independent significance of his own, what then? What if he becomes "significant" only as he enters into the kerygma and finds obedience among its hearers? What if the point of kerygma is the summons of faith it addresses to its hearers and the demand that summons imposes upon them?

Is the kerygma, thus conceived, a *gospel*—a kerygma in which nothing is said of that in which or of him in whom its recipients are to believe? What is it but a new *law*? I must press these questions because this is where I particularly fail to understand Bultmann. How far does this kerygma really speak, as the kerygma is intended to speak, of an act of God? How far does it speak rather of an act of man (strictly speaking), of the transition which man achieves by his own obedience—though he is supposed not to be capable of it? What meaning must we attach to the statement that the Christ event took place "for us", *pro nobis*? What I want to know is, whether Bultmann means any more by this than that the content of the kerygma concerns us, that it is significant for us, that we should accept it as the law of our decision and realize it in our act of faith, in the *imitatio Christi*? Is that all it is? That is what I am asking.

Let us try and follow Bultmann in detail at this crucial point. There are, he maintains, two elements in the Christ event, which have to be differentiated, yet held together. One is the cross, the historical event of Jesus' crucifixion, so described because of the beginning, name and title of the event. But, he hastens to add, the cross must be understood in its significance "for us". It is the word of the cross, in which man's transition from inauthentic to authentic existence takes place. For the death of Jesus Christ means that it sets man on the way to a radical, mortal judgement on his inauthentic being. It calls him to tread this way as the path to grace and salvation. We may also add that the kerygma has this import because the death of Jesus Christ, understood not only as a historical event but as the act of God, has been taken up into the kerygma so as to participate in its meaning. As the recipient of the kerygma responds with the obedience of faith it demands, the death of Jesus Christ acquires particular significance for him. This significance becomes concrete as the believer appropriates the cross of Christ and undergoes crucifixion with Jesus Christ. Thus he sets out on the road that leads to mortal judgement, to grace and life. This event is an act of God, *the* act of God. For the origin and purpose of both—the crucifixion of Jesus Christ as a historical event and man's faith in its significance—occur in the sphere of the invisible and intangible and are, therefore, identical with God. This event is God's act of salvation because it puts man on the road and opens the gateway to grace and life, i.e. to salvation. It is the eschatological event of redemption which takes place in man's eschatological existence and shapes and determines that existence.

I understand, but once again there is only one thing I understand. I can see that the New Testament message presents the cross of Jesus Christ not only as a historical event but also as an event which in its uniqueness and concreteness in time is significant in every age. Bultmann likes to speak of its "cosmic" significance, and rightly so. But I do not see why it only acquires this significance by being taken up into the kerygma and evoking the obedience of faith. On the contrary, it seems to me that the New Testament describes the cross of Christ as an event with an inherent significance of its own. It is just because it has this inherent significance that it can become significant in the kerygma and for the faith of its recipients. I am disturbed by the way Bultmann reverses the sequence of events. I can see further that the New Testament message speaks of the passion and death of Jesus as being completed in the life of the believers, e.g. in the injunction to take up the cross and follow him, or in Bultmann's favourite text, Col. 1. 24. But I do not see that faith, in the New Testament sense, faith in which the believer comes to realize the significance of the cross of Christ for himself, is exhausted in this completion. Rather, it seems to me, the New Testament regards this completion as the result of faith. For the New Testament asserts that in faith the believer attaches himself to something which is wholly and entirely outside himself, something without him and in spite of him, something which took place for him on God's initiative in the death of Jesus Christ. I am also disturbed by the way in which Bultmann's doctrine of the cross looks suspiciously like Catholic passion mysticism. Finally, I can see, of course, that the New Testament proclaims the death of Jesus Christ in such a way as to include faith in its significance as God's incomprehensible—and we might even say paradoxical—act of salvation. But I fail to see how Bultmann can suppress the fact that the New Testament describes the death of Jesus Christ as something which, for all its incomprehensibility, is still comprehensible, and which for all its hazardous character is meaningful. I think I can see light falling from both sides here: it was not just anybody who was crucified, it was God the Lord who humbled himself and became a servant and man; he was the servant exalted by God to be the Lord, vindicated as the witness and prophet of the kingdom of God.

So I think I can see in the New Testament message of Christ crucified the subject who has already suffered the judgement of death which brings salvation to all men, who has already effected their transition from the old existence to the new, their translation into eschatological existence; who has not only inaugurated, but completed this process. Although much of this remains obscure and is not susceptible to proof, I can, I think, see certain contours and colours. I can see a person and his work. I can, I think hear a word which is self-explanatory, where all Bultmann can see is darkness and silence, where all he can see is that the cross is God's saving act. Bultmann's doctrine of the cross comes perilously near the devil's temptation of Jesus to throw himself down from the pinnacle of the temple to prove his divine Sonship and demonstrate the supreme paradox of his faith, and it disturbs me. Bultmann once wrote: "The saving efficacy of the cross is not derived from the fact that it is the cross of Christ: it is the cross of Christ because it has this saving efficacy."[1] I should like to hear an authentic interpretation of this notorious passage from Bultmann himself. I should find it difficult to expound it in any sense consistent with the New Testament message. It may well be that my questions about Bultmann's doctrine of the cross (and indeed about his doctrine of the Christ event as a whole) are due to my failure to understand this passage.

According to Bultmann, the second element in the kerygma and, therefore, in the Christ event, is the resurrection. But by this he means the revelation of the saving significance of the cross. It is called the resurrection because of its beginning and its name. What took place in this resurrection? Bultmann says it was the emergence of the faith which realizes, understands and affirms the significance of Jesus Christ "for us"—the beginning of the "Easter faith" which consists in the believer's participation in the cross of Christ in a struggling freedom from sin, anxiety and human discord. Further, it is this decision, the decision of Easter faith, which produces the kerygma itself, with the cross of Christ as God's saving act forming its central affirmation. It is the Easter faith also which is the origin of the Church and the sacraments(!).

It is obvious that for Bultmann the crucifixion, while a unique event in the past, occurs and is intended to occur with the same uniqueness in every way now. The whole process is part of what he calls the eschatological event of redemption. The process as such depends on the resurrection of Jesus into the Easter faith and the kerygma. Bultmann's contention is that our understanding of the Christ event as the act of God must include this further aspect—dare we call it the noetic aspect? Yet apparently even here, nothing can be said about its being an act of God on its own right quite apart from its happening in the kerygma and in faith.

[1] *Kerygma and Myth*, Vol. I, p. 41.

Nothing can be said about it as the foundation and content both of faith and of the kerygma. And, therefore, nothing can be said about the risen Christ as such. He is not allowed any life of his own after he rose from the dead. Nothing can be said about Jesus' own interpretation of his earthly life and death, nothing about his intercourse with his disciples before they came to believe in him or were charged with the kerygma and gathered to form the Church.

Bultmann does, indeed, insist that the resurrection of Jesus Christ is the act of God. But apparently this does not mean that men beheld the glory of God in the Word made flesh and put to death in the flesh, or that they beheld him raised from the dead in space and time as the outcome of his previous earthly life. They apparently beheld his glory only in the kerygma, only when he was preached and believed in. It was not Jesus himself who taught them to see the meaning of his crucifixion, nor had the crucifixion any intrinsic significance of its own arising from the person and work of him who was crucified. That "on the third day he rose again" does not appear to be the basic fact of Christianity, but only an explanation of the kerygma and of faith, and one which could be dispensed with if necessary. The real life of Jesus Christ is confined to the kerygma and to faith. This is what I cannot understand, and I must confess it astonishes me. I can only hear distant echoes of the New Testament. I can find no justification for such a translation of its message. Or am I wrong? Does everything indeed depend on the priority of the personal resurrection of Jesus Christ over every other resurrection there may be in the kerygma, in faith, in the Church or in the sacraments? Can we give the same priority to our own resurrection in him? Or is it all due to my own failure to understand Bultmann? He seems to think that in the kerygma Jesus Christ is on his way to rising in us. And that is just why I cannot understand him.

Here then it would seem is the act of God which is presupposed in the dialectic of human existence, or rather in man's transition from the old existence to the new. In its ontic aspect it is crucifixion; noetically it is the Easter event. This is the Christology contained in Bultmann's soteriology and deducible from it. True, he emphasizes that this act is history, and indeed the history of Christ, and this is something which neither his critics nor his disciples should overlook. Undoubtedly, his intention is to give adequate expression not only to Pauline doctrine, but to the New Testament as a whole. Yet people like Jaspers and that Jasperian theologian, Fritz Buri, think that for this very reason he is just as bad as the rest of us.

This being Bultmann's intention, we can hardly write him off as a liberal, whether of the older or the newer kind. If only he carried out his intention so clearly that it was beyond all doubt! If only he spoke of the cross and resurrection of Jesus in terms compatible with his emphasis on their inter-relation and on the Christ event as a whole! Bultmann has been widely criticized for not doing so, and, it would seem, with a good deal of justice. I am sorry to have to say this.

IV

I thought it best to concentrate to begin with on the positive aspect of Bultmann's work, his presentation of the New Testament message. I have not yet mentioned the word by which his work has become so widely known and discussed, not only among German theologians, but all over the world. I refer, of course, to the demythologizing of the New Testament. This is, of course, no nickname given to it by a third party. It was invented by Bultmann himself; and not only is it a barbarism, but it is unnecessarily provoking. And it was Bultmann who bandied the term about so much, e.g. in his primary essay, "The New Testament and Mythology",[1] which is of crucial importance for the whole subject. If the wicked (Christian) world fails to understand him, much of the blame is due to his invention of this word, so uninspiring and negative. But we must not be put off by the word itself, for that would not do him justice. It is not itself the real clue, or at any rate not the only clue to his position. I, for one, would regard the demythologizing of the New Testament of secondary importance compared with the positive results of his

[1] *Kerygma and Myth*, Vol. I, pp. 1–44.

exegesis, and the positive principles by which he reaches them. It is, in fact, the positive side which disturbs me even more if anything, than the negative side, or demythologizing proper. But since Bultmann himself has introduced the term and evidently sets such store by it, I shall have to give it due attention and follow him along this path too.

Once again I shall begin with his positive account of the New Testament message, at first in purely general terms, and simply point out Bultmann's omission of certain elements which are characteristic of it in its original form. He has no use for those elements at all, and he tells us so quite plainly. He suggests—and in his original essay with almost frantic insistence—that the primary task of exegesis and translation as he sees it is to circumvent these elements and eliminate them. Let me hasten, however, to correct this impression. He expressly contrasts himself with the older liberals on this point. His aim is not, except in a few border-line cases, to suppress or circumvent these elements. Rather, they must be translated out of the language, imagery and terminology of the New Testament into our own, into those of contemporary man. For, says Bultmann, it is just these elements which require translation. We can hardly complain that he actually omits them except in a few marginal instances. They are certainly there, though in a new guise. What has been allowed to disappear, what is missing, he claims, is the forms in which the New Testament expresses those elements, not their essential meaning. This, then, is the crucial question about Bultmann's work, taken as a whole. Is the essential meaning of these elements and the function they fulfil still recognizable in spite of the different form in which they are expressed? And if so, to what extent? Or, to put it in Bultmann's own terms, does the removal of the New Testament forms of expression enable us to recognize more clearly the intention of the elements in question? More than this, is it the case that their intention can only be recognized when they have been transformed and the New Testament forms of expression replaced by another? Can I, therefore, claim that the questions I raised under section III were posed correctly, at least in a formal sense, from Bultmann's point of view? In that section I was in fact concerned with the problem of recognizing in Bultmann's presentation the New Testament message itself. Since this presentation was at least partly—and Bultmann sometimes gives the impression that it is absolutely—determined by his transformation of them, it is reasonable to suppose that it is just the transformation of them which makes it difficult, if not impossible for me at least to recognize the original message. That is what I was trying to explain there.

What kind of elements does Bultmann find room for in his restatement? He divides them into two groups, though how he does so I find difficult to understand. First, we have those elements in the language of the New Testament which directly or indirectly reflect the distinctive world view of late Judaism and Hellenistic gnosticism. There is the three-storied universe, the intervention of supernatural powers, and their influence in human existence. There is Satan and the demons, sin and death on the one hand, and God, angels and miracles on the other. There is imminent end of all things in a cosmic catastrophe, the resurrection of the dead, and divine sentence of salvation or damnation directly pronounced upon them. Secondly, there is everything that corresponds to that world view in the New Testament portrayal of salvation. This includes the idea that the end is ushered in with the mission of the pre-existent Son of God, his birth of a virgin, his bodily resurrection from the dead as the first stage in the dethronement of Satan, sin, death, and the demons; his exaltation as king and Lord and his reign in heaven; his visible return to consummate his saving work—an event which Paul himself expected to experience; the Church, baptism and the Lord's Supper as means of uniting believers to their Lord, the indwelling spirit as the pledge of their final status as sons of God.

Does this mean that a viable translation of the New Testament depends on the proper treatment of these respective elements? That in some cases they should be eliminated, and in others transformed? Here I must pause for a moment to ask Bultmann why he has raised these elements to central importance in his exegesis. As we can see from what he has written elsewhere, and particularly in what his disciples have written, there is a tendency to describe these elements a little crudely, a little ironically, even to caricature them. Does he do it in the interest of the spirit, content and scope of what the New Testament says? If so, he should pay more attention to the context in which these elements occur, and the value attached to them in their context. That would give him elbow room to consider them, more patience and inclination for doing so. He would look at them with less irritation (pardon me for saying so), less detachment, less temptation to lump them all together as a series of curiosities. He would be less inclined to exalt them into a problem for their own sake, still less to make them the main problem of his exegesis.

Why this procedure? Where does he find his common denominator? Is it the core of the New Testament message as he conceives it? Or is it some kind of historical analysis which makes him feel free, or rather compelled to turn such a detached interest to the structural idiosyncrasies of the New Testament statements? For it is clearly historical analysis which provides him with the clue to the common features in these various elements. What is not clear to me is what kind of transformation this is if Bultmann, as he seems to have done, had taken just one of the possible results of historical analysis and elevated it into the problem of all problems for New Testament exegesis, and made it into the sole criterion for its solution. Hence, even if we were merely concerned with Bultmann's *modus operandi*, I feel I can hardly go along with him thus far with a good conscience.

Assuming that he is right first in lumping all these elements together and then treating them separately, what does he actually do to them? Let me repeat that he does not deny, eliminate or expunge them from the kerygma, except those elements which are untranslatable, such as the three-storied universe, Satan and the demons, the angels, the virgin birth, the empty tomb and the ascension. He *interprets* them. Let us examine the way he presents them. Some of the important elements are certainly there. There is sin, death; God, his revelation in Christ and in Christ alone;

the Holy Spirit, the divine sonship of the believers, the Church and even the sacraments and the eschatological hope, the last being the dominant principle. All these are there, each in its proper place and each duly translated and "interpreted". He does it with an earnestness which puts many a more orthodox expositor to shame. No wonder many liberals think Bultmann is too orthodox to be one of themselves. He has on more than one occasion disowned the name of liberal; he is not eliminating these indigestible elements but interpreting them! This may not be quite fair to some of the earlier liberals like Biedermann. And did not Schleiermacher, who was also suspected of being too orthodox, aim chiefly to interpret and to confine himself to that? But who reads Schleiermacher nowadays, let alone Biedermann? It is good to remind ourselves that there is nothing new under the sun—only the names have changed, that's all. But enough of that!

V

But why do these particular elements in the New Testament need interpretation? That is the first and foremost question here. And supposing they do, how far should we go? Bultmann's answer is that they need it—and here is his cardinal principle of criticism—because they are couched in the thought and language of the world of those days. They are mythological expressions of the truths they seek to convey. Myth and mythological language, according to Bultmann, are to be found wherever the divine is described in terms of this world, the other side in terms of this side, the non-objective as objective. In this form myth speaks of the power or powers which man allegedly experiences as the ground and limit of his world and of his own activity and sufferings. In this form myth is an expression of man's self-understanding. Thus the New Testament message, Bultmann thinks, in the historical forms in which it is enshrined in the texts, is a mythological expression of a distinctive human self-understanding. That is why the New Testament demands interpretation and its records require translation. This implies, on the negative side, that they must be demythologized, i.e. removed from their present form and placed in another. Such a procedure is possible since the mythological form was at best only a temporary necessity. There is nothing specifically Christian about it, and it can easily be detached from the message itself, which is the specifically Christian self-understanding. This operation is necessary since the mythological form obscures the real meaning of the New Testament message. Why? Because the mythological view of the world and of man is as obsolete as the age which produced it. Another view of the world and man, the modern one, is irresistibly forcing itself upon us, and we cannot avoid presupposing it in our thinking. It would be senseless and impossible for the Christian preacher to expect modern man to swallow the ancient world view, or to accept those features in the New Testament's presentation of the redemptive event which conform to that world view and which he can only regard as obsolete. Such a *sacrificium intellectus* would be as impossible as it would be downright dishonest. It would reduce faith to a human achievement, which, as Wilhelm Herrmann pointed out, would be immoral. It would in no way confront man with the real stumbling-block, or challenge him to a genuine decision between faith and belief. We must, therefore, stop expecting it of him. The task of exegesis, shared as it is by the dogmatic theologian and the preacher, is thus in the first place a negative one. It is to show from the texts themselves that the New Testament message is couched in imagery derived from late Judaism and Gnosticism. This imagery must then be removed on the ground that it is irrelevant for the understanding of the message, so as to make room for an exposition of the message itself. The demythologizing of the texts is the *sine qua non* for their understanding. This process, thinks Bultmann, is all the more justified since there are in the New Testament not only obvious contradictions between the various images, but also a process of interpretation which itself tends towards demythologizing. We can see that as we compare Paul, and especially John, with the Synoptic gospels. Bultmann claims that this is just what he has provided by his presentation in its positive aspect: he has met the need which the New Testament itself requires.

As I listen I am amazed; I should like to follow but I cannot. Is it possible to understand any text, be it ancient or modern, if we approach it with preconceived notions about the extent and the limit to which it can be understood? Is it not preferable to come to it with an open mind, and patiently follow what it has to say? Can we understand it if we think we have some criterion to enable us to know in advance what parts of the text are intelligible, and thus differentiate the outward imagery from the actual substance? Are we to suppose that the text can only be made intelligible and gain a hearing if it is first translated? Surely, if we want to understand any given text, the provisional clue to its understanding must be sought from the text itself, and moreover from its spirit, content and aim. Surely we should be condemning our text to silence in advance if we approached it with such a criterion, alien alike to its spirit, content and aim. How can we decide even before we have read the text what it actually says, and what is only temporary imagery? And what happens if we use this alien criterion as an infallible instrument rather than as a provisional clue? Is not Bultmann's very concept of myth, the infallible criterion which dominates his hermeneutics, quite alien to the New Testament? Whether or not it is the contemporary fashion, as Bultmann claims it is, the question is how can it be used to decide what belongs to the substance of the New Testament and what is merely outward imagery?

Bultmann says the exegete must be honest and sincere. To whom does he owe this obligation primarily? To what is he responsible, the presuppositions of his own thought and of the contemporary world, and to a principle of understanding determined by that thought, or to the actual text he is trying to understand, and to the criterion to be derived from its spirit, content and aim? I do not mean to suggest that this canon should be applied rigidly; it is only a flexible rule for further research.

From another point of view it may be asked whether it is right to stigmatize everything mythological as though it were *ipso facto* absolutely useless for modern man. Why should not the divine be described in terms of human life, the other-worldly in terms of this world, the non-objective as objective? And is not this too formal a definition of myth to cover all the different kinds we know in history, the Indian, Babylonian, Egyptian and Teutonic mythologies? Or the myths of the modern world, the myth of the twentieth century, the Marxist myth, the myth of the Christian west, etc.? Has myth always been the representation of some general relationship and correspondence within the realm of nature or history, decked out as a superhuman tale of the gods? The controversy over the meaning of myth is not without its importance. For if Bultmann used a definition which covered the content rather than the form, he could still find plenty of mythological imagery and terminology incidentally accepted and used in the New Testament. As for the actual content of the New Testament message, however, he could hardly describe it as mythological in form, proceed to dismantle it from top to bottom and replace it by some other form, supposedly more intelligible and relevant to modern man. However much the New Testament writers borrowed their imagery and language from the surrounding world, it could hardly have occurred to them to produce their message as the proclamation of general cosmic truths disguised as a tale about the gods and their doings. After all, that was just the kind of thing they were attacking. Perhaps demythologizing the New Testament would have made more sense if Bultmann had not chosen this curiously formal definition of myth and made it the criterion with which to distinguish between the form and substance of the New Testament. I wonder what voice from heaven it was that led him to choose this crude definition of myth to describe the dubious elements of the New Testament. He would have done better to reserve his fire for the supernaturalism of the Bible, as it used to be called, if indeed he had to attack anything at all.

Since, however, he has chosen that definition all I can do is to put to him the real theological question on which everything devolves. Is the demythologized kerygma allowed to say anything about God's having condescended to become this-worldly, objective and—horror of horrors!—datable? Apparently it is not allowed to say that the New Testament God is the kind of God who is capable of such condescension. Nor can it admit that it originated in the concrete fact that the disciples saw with their own eyes, heard with their ears, touched with their hands, in space and time, not only the dereliction of the Word made flesh hanging on the cross, but also the glory of the same Word made flesh risen from the dead. Nor apparently can it say that the disciples' faith was born, not by a kind of parthenogenesis, but through a revelation, the revelation of one who had been crucified on Golgotha, a revelation occurring not in some invisible, supra-historical, celestial sphere, but in their own visible, historical, earthly sphere, a revelation as human, worldly, this-worldly and objective as the cross itself? Apparently the demythologized kerygma must remain silent about what causes faith. It has a cause, it is not just a paradox, but it is not "susceptible of proof". Apparently the kerygma must suppress or even deny the fact that the cross and resurrection of Jesus Christ, the total Christ event, is the event of our redemption, that it possessed an intrinsic significance of its own, and that only because it has that primary significance has it a derived significance here and now. Yet this event is the ground of our faith and of the kerygma, and faith and kerygma are only secondary to it and derivative from it. Apparently the kerygma must suppress or even deny the fact that the Christ event has founded a community which throughout its history has had a Lord distinct from itself, a Lord whom it follows in discipleship. All this would, it seems, have to go by the board if we demythologized the New Testament à la Bultmann. What is the purpose of the alleged mythological elements if not to demonstrate that we are not left alone in this human, worldly, this-worldly, objective existence of ours, that our faith does not depend on some unknown distant deity, some supra-cosmic transcendent, non-objective reality? On the contrary, are they not meant to show that he who was crucified and rose again at a particular time and place is our divine Lord and human brother whom we are privileged to know as one who is both near and far, as one who lives and reigns over us even before we come to believe in him and even in our unbelief, as the one in whom God *first* loved us. How else can all this be expressed except in the way Bultmann calls mythological? It is just this truth—or am I mistaken?—that Bultmann has left out in his demythologizing. What service is it to modern man, ourselves included, to suppress the cardinal truth of the kerygma like this? I am most embarrassed: much as I am loath to charge Bultmann with heresy, I cannot deny that his demythologized New Testament looks suspiciously like docetism. Perhaps this has something to do with his inability to make anything of the Old Testament. It is too historical, too down to earth for him! Schleiermacher had just the same difficulty with it. And perhaps it also has something to do with his difficulties over the synoptic Jesus, with his ministry of word and deed and his course from Jordan to Gethsemane. I cannot as yet see how this all fits together, but I must confess that if interpreting the New Testament means demythologizing it, and if demythologizing means what Bultmann with his definition of myth means by it, it seems to have singularly little to do with the gospel of the New Testament.

VI

Now for our second question on the positive side of Bultmann's hermeneutics, a more interesting question than the first. Granted that these problematic elements in the New Testament do exist, how far are they capable of being interpreted? How can they be transformed and what will they look like when they have been? Bultmann's answer is that the only honest exegesis, dogmatics and preaching is the *existentialist* interpretation. By this he means one which exposes the specifically Christian self-understanding enshrined in the mythological form. Existentialist interpretation understands and explains the New Testament affirmations as existential statements.[1] Why this interpretation in particular? For two reasons says Bultmann, two reasons which come pretty much to the same thing. Both the New Testament message itself and the mythological imagery in which it is conveyed are attempts on man's part to understand himself. The message, let us

[1] Anyone who engages in a discussion with Bultmann or his pupils should beware of confusing "existentialist" and "existential". Failure to do so is the unforgivable sin—other misunderstandings may be forgiven, this one never!

recall, deals with the transition from fallenness to authenticity, from unbelief to faith, and man's self-understanding in that transition. But the same is true of myth, for myth deals with man's experience of the powers which determine the world he lives in, his own actions, and his consequent self-understanding.

I do not know if I am correct in combining these two things together. There is a structural affinity between the New Testament on the one hand and myth on the other. Both are attempts on man's part to give an account of his own existence. It is, therefore, only natural for Christians living in a mythical age to use the mythical imagery and terminology of their contemporaries. The conclusion is inescapable: both myth and the message itself cry out for anthropological, or more precisely existential interpretation. The imagery and terminology must be interpreted in an existentialist sense, i.e. as man's attempt to explain his own existence.

This has two great advantages. First, the real meaning and intention of the New Testament are at last brought to light. Secondly, this is done in such a way that modern man, whose thought is no longer mythological but anthropological, can understand it. Christian proclamation, whether in exegesis, dogmatics or preaching, then offers no inauthentic stumbling-block. There is no need for any *sacrificium intellectus*, no need to pretend to believe anything which we cannot honestly accept. We are at once confronted with a genuine choice between faith and unbelief.

All this is so illuminating and so dazzling that we can well appreciate its appeal to so many present-day theologians. It is almost like the light which, according to the "mythological" account in Acts, illuminated and temporarily blinded Saul on the road to Damascus.

What a coincidence of academic and practical interests! What an anwer to the questions of young theological students thoroughly disillusioned by National Socialism, the débacle of 1945, the prisoner-of-war camps and other bitter experiences, disillusioned by all conventional language, particularly that of Christianity. These young people want something to believe and to preach, but it must be honest, sincere and straightforward. Demythologizing makes theology so simple. It allows it to concentrate on essentials. It enables us to get rid of some of the awkward elements in the New Testament canon, e.g. in the Book of Acts. That was something that badly needed doing, and it opens up the way to a deeper appreciation of the other parts of the New Testament, especially the Pauline Epistles and the Johannine literature. It brings us much closer to Luther's original intentions. At last theologians can be true to their faith, and in a new and exciting way: yet they can still keep both feet firmly in the real world of to-day. What an exciting prospect!

Unless you can appreciate how attractive this all is, and feel it in your very bones, unless you can see how everything tips the scales in favour of Bultmann and his existentialism, you are not qualified to dispute with him. Rhetorical denunciations of his negative tendencies, his elimination of this or that article in the Bible or creed will get you nowhere. Bultmann's positive appeal is too strong for that. The sullen looks with which Bultmann and his entourage meet such denunciations, insisting like Shylock on their pound of flesh, are proof enough. In any case, they make me think.

Yet their sullen looks make me uncomfortable. For it is just the positive side of Bultmann's hermeneutics which to my mind rest upon a questionable assumption. Take a look at the history of theological development. Have such admirable solutions or coincidences ever been discovered or has there ever been a time when everything was so simple, and theologians were able to concentrate on their job, when everyone has been so sure of being on the winning side and so entitled to glower at others?

As far as I can see, this has really happened when their initial assumption has been that they have received a new revelation of the spirit, content and scope of the New Testament. But it has often happened when they have discovered some new *philosophical* key and put it to use. Then, and generally only then, have they come up with such theological illuminations.

It is no secret that something of this kind has happened in Bultmann's case. His particular philosophy is the existentialism of

Martin Heidegger in his earlier days. Whether he uses it as a handmaid or as a queen is a nice question, as it always is in such cases. Heidegger provides him with a certain prior understanding with which to approach the New Testament texts (and not them alone). Prior understanding—that is what he calls it. In the first place this denotes a particular interpretation of the general concept of understanding. All understanding is concerned, in one way or another, with man's understanding of himself, his self-understanding. Secondly, it is a particular way of understanding man's self-understanding, a self-understanding caught in the polarity between inauthenticity and authenticity, between a situation he can control and one he cannot, between past and future. Thus the primary concern of the New Testament is with anthropology, an anthropology structured in this particular way. This is the prior understanding required of the exegete, and with this he must approach the New Testament. It is obvious how this works out in Bultmann's understanding of man's old, sinful existence and his new eschatological existence in faith. It is equally obvious how it controls his doctrine of the Christ event. For the essence of that event, as we have seen, is the transition from one state of human existence to the other. It can take no form outside of this restricted anthropological sense. There is one thing, and only one thing which he does not get from Heidegger, and that is his description of the transition as an act of God. This is the point where he is speaking independently as a theologian. With this single exception, the whole of his positive presentation of the New Testament message is encased in the strait jacket of this prior understanding. Of course, this means that we can only discuss things with Bultmann if we share his prior understanding, i.e. Heidegger's existentialism, and are prepared to learn its unusual and somewhat difficult language. If we don't understand it we shall always be met with Bultmann's cool and distant reply. "I do not understand."

This is just what *I* do not understand. I do not see why I have to don this particular strait jacket in order to understand the New Testament. All honour to Heidegger, even to the younger Heidegger in his anthropological strait jacket! But neither Heidegger to-day nor Bultmann thinks that the Heidegger of 1927 has *the* philosophy, or that it dropped from heaven, as people used to think Aristotelianism had, or as Hegel used to boast of his own system. There is, therefore, only one reason why Heidegger's philosophy should be canonized like this, and this is because it is the philosophy *par excellence* of our day and age. This is what Bultmann seems to mean. And who would deny that it is certainly a highly important expression of the spirit prevailing in the first half of our century? We all speak or think existentially to a greater or lesser degree nowadays. But this is not the only expression of the spirit of our age; there are others, and quite different ones at that. In his later writings Heidegger himself seems to have passed beyond the phase—the anthropological strait jacket, which has had such a strong influence on Bultmann. In the U.S.A. they have not for the most part got as far as existentialism, while in Russia they think they have outgrown it long ago—it is so thoroughly bourgeois! I wonder, seriously, whether there are so many "modern men" in the rest of the world, even among the educated classes, who feel that existentialism is just the very thing, particularly Heidegger's version of it. If so, is there any reason why theology should be particularly beholden to it? Does this philosophy rest on such broad and firm foundations, both materially and historically, that we are obliged to adopt it, if only because it is fashionable, for the sake of the modern man? Must we become existentialists on principle, and existentialists of this particular brand? Is it the indispensable prerequisite for the understanding of the New Testament, of all things? After all, it may always have to be modified in the light of the latest research. It is the force of this claim that I cannot understand.

The first reason for this is that I cannot even admit that myth can be interpreted entirely and exclusively, in a totalitarian fashion, so to speak, as the expression of particular self-understanding of man. No one would deny that it is in part such a self-understanding. But there have always been an immense variety of myths, not only in the past, but even in our own day, so that we can hardly believe that myth is only an expression of man's self-understanding, and nothing more. Was not Christian Wolf of Halle nearer the mark long ago when he propounded for the benefit of all "lovers of the truth" what we might call the myth of the eighteenth century, the rational beliefs about God, the world and the soul of man, and all things in general? What kind of myth is it that recognizes the existence only of the human subject, and so requires an exclusively existentialist and anthropological interpretation?

But the theological question is even more serious. What will happen to the New Testament message if we clamp it thoroughly, exclusively and in a totalitarian fashion in this vice, asking only about man's self-understanding which it enshrines and with a certain preconceived understanding of it at that? After all, it is the message of Jesus Christ; it asserts an event between God and man, and it is just as certainly couched in the form of a *human* testimony. Are we not, therefore, bound to distort it if we confine it to an existentialist interpretation—especially since we have already demythologized it—and deprive it of its most important and obvious element? Is not this bound to happen if we allow this element to stand merely as a memorial to the name of Jesus Christ and of the act of God which took place in him? Whereas, of course, it is the *Christ* event which is determinative of all else, controlling and dominating it. Will we not distort and diminish the message if we remove the Christ event, interpret and transform it into something which is at best only a secondary element in the message, something which is true and important only in its relation to the Christ event? We can love Bultmann and give him full credit for breaking away from existentialism at this one place—much to the annoyance of Fritz Buri! Yet even Bultmann himself is not sure whether the retention of an act of God is compatible with demythologizing, and I do not think he has answered his question satisfactorily. In spite of this notable inconsistency, he has certainly made it difficult, if not impossible, for us to recognize the New Testament message in this new existentialist garb. We can recognize it in the hymns and meditations of Gerhard Teerstegen, or in Biedermann's dogmatics. We might even, with a modicum of goodwill, recognize it in the

Roman Mass. I don't know how many of our contemporaries have been helped by Bultmann and his disciples to know the real joy of believing. I shall not ask, but just hope for the best. Speaking for myself, I must say I find it hard to imagine how Bultmann could inspire me to study theology, to preach, or even to believe. And I think this has something to do with the extreme arbitrariness of this interpretation. That is where, judged by the text it professes to explain, it falls short.

VII

And now, before I proceed to sum it all up, I would like to step back for a moment and see what I can make of the phenomenon of Rudolf Bultmann as a whole. What am I to think of him? During the past ten years I have often been uncertain just where he belongs in the history of theological development. That even I, an old neighbour of his, should find it so difficult, is a clear indication of the stature of the man and his work. And it would certainly have been good for others who have found it so easy to pigeonhole him, if they had been aware of this difficulty. Where does Bultmann really stand? Let me tell you of some of the attempts I have made to answer this question over the years.

1. To a great extent, Bultmann has only himself to blame if he gives the impression of being concerned mainly to do battle for a more modern world view against the ancient or mythological view, particularly against its survival in the Church, its theology and preaching. He looks like a rationalist with the austere Marburg passion for sincerity! A new David Friedrich Strauss! A bedfellow of the Berne School, with its enthusiasm for the one truth necessary to salvation, the delay in the parousia! Away with superstition! We are children of the enlightenment. We use electric light and the radio. How can we believe in the New Testament world of spirits and miracles? These things simply aren't compatible!—such is the somewhat chilly note which Bultmann often strikes. Buri has taken great pleasure in interpreting Bultmann in this light, objecting only to his failure to carry his cleansing of the temple to its logical conclusion. But, of

course, the other side has interpreted him in the same way too, and with some excuse considering the first part of his famous lecture. The reader should take another look at what he says there in the name of modern man. There is so much that he cannot "understand", so much that he must dismiss as obsolete. Bultmann can hardly be surprised that many people were so shocked that they refused to read any further. And why did he coin the word demythologizing, which, as we have seen, only covers the negative side of his enterprise?

Yet there is certainly a misunderstanding here. Demythologizing in the narrower sense of the word has a great significance for Bultmann, but only a subsidiary one. It is only intended to make room for his existentialist interpretation, which he has so much at heart. He takes the modern world view and modern thought as his criterion—as a good Marburg man Bultmann is more interested in methods than results—just because it is modern, because it is our own, and, therefore, an indispensable ingredient in our self-understanding. The older rationalists, following Strauss, *believed* in a modern world view. I suppose the Berne school does too. Bultmann does not. He knows it is only relative. It has only a *de facto*, not a *de jure* authority. At any rate, that is how I think we should understand him. Of course, I wish we had said so in so many words. Then we should have known where we stood.

2. Or should we treat Bultmann as an apologist—of Schleiermacher's stature, of course, though with an individuality of his own? Is he simply concerned with the authenticity of the Christian proclamation in our day and age? Is it his sole aim—Schleiermacher wanted nothing more—to make Biblical exegesis, theology in general, and preaching in particular, relevant and interesting for its cultured despisers?[1] It has been observed in more than one quarter that Bultmann's original lecture shows an unmistakable pastoral concern for modern man with his electricity and atomic physics. For, of course, he cannot understand the gospel unless it is demythologized and given an existentialist interpretation, let alone recognize it as a viable faith, or

[1] An allusion to the subtitle of Schleiermacher's addresses *On Religion* (Trans. by John Oman, 1893). (R.H.F.)

even genuinely reject it. Remove or sublimate the myth, speak to him in Heideggerian terms, and all will be well. Bultmann and his disciples are annoyed if we call him an apologist. But there must be some truth in that description, otherwise he would not be so bent on communicating the gospel to modern man. And I really do not see why "apologist" should be a term of abuse. Surely theologians have always been apologists in some sense; they could hardly help it. It is clear, however, that this is only one side of his work, and hardly the most important side for him. At best it is a by-product, though a notable by-product, to be sure.

3. Or is he simply a historian, a unique historian in his own way, but one who stands in the great tradition of the nineteenth century? Is he a scholar divesting himself of all his prejudices and presuppositions and studying the New Testament as part of the civilization, culture and religion of late antiquity, concluding that the synoptic version of the kerygma is only one version of it, and that the genuine form is to be found in the Pauline Epistles interpreted in a Johannine sense? Has he simply, as an unprejudiced exegete, discovered that the New Testament is the proclamation of a particular human self-understanding, and that a demythologized, existentialist interpretation of it is relevant even from a purely historical and scientific point of view? His *Geschichte der synoptischen Tradition*[1] and his recent book on *Primitive Christianity*[2] suggest that we should be right in interpreting him simply as an academic scholar. Indeed, these works, together with his commentary on John and his *Theology of the New Testament*[3] include so much research and so much material important and interesting in their own right that we can largely ignore his existentialism (which not every historian can swallow) and if need be, the particular purpose of his demythologizing? I think it is at least possible. So, too, unfortunately, is something

[1] Third ed., 1957. Eng. Trans. in preparation (R.H.F.).

[2] *Primitive Christianity in its Contemporary Setting*. Thames and Hudson, 1956. Trans. by R. H. Fuller (R.H.F.).

[3] *Das Johannesevangelium*, 1941 (Eng. Trans. in preparation); *Theology of the New Testament*, Vol. I, 1952, Vol. II, 1955. Trans. by Kendrik Grobel, S.C.M. Press.

else. It is easy to be put off by his lofty arrogance as a historian. (Much of this he has inherited from his great predecessors from 1890 to 1910.)

We should have to shut our eyes to a great deal if we were to stop short here. There is a good deal of intellectual, if not spiritual pathos in his writings, the onesidedness of which has rather a sectarian attraction, and is certainly strongly religious. And this has nothing to do with pure history. It does not simply ask "what actually happened". His idea of the kerygma, the very fact that he can identify the tasks of exegesis, systematic theology and preaching, should be enough to warn us here. I should like to see a pure historian say this as emphatically as Bultmann says it. In his historical and philological criticism of the Gospel of John, Bultmann comes near to the conclusion that the authentic text, with its alien accretions peeled off, tends to demythologize an earlier tradition. Hence the only rightful exegesis is to carry on the good work. Indeed, the Gospel of John is a powerful vindication of Bultmann's own hermeneutics and theology. We can but admire this, whether it be some accidental, pre-established harmony, or the skill of a very determined *systematic* historian. And, in any case, it is most illuminating. Thus even the interpretation of Bultmann as an academic scholar, though it comes nearer the mark, is only a partial solution, and not permanently satisfying.

4. Or, to take exactly the opposite position, does the secret of theology lie in the discovery of a new philosophy and his enthusiasm over the discovery? As we have already suggested, such a discovery is always a great moment in the history of theological development. Is this the greatness of Bultmann's hour? If so, the day of his conversion was when he first met Heidegger. Tired of positivism, idealism and romanticism, all that our fathers stood for, he must have found in existentialism the key, at any rate for our time, to every kind of ontology, anthropology, cosmology, soteriology and eschatology, even those of the New Testament itself. So he proceeds to translate it into the language of this philosophy, demythologizing being only a by-product. However this may be, it would mean that Bult-

mann's work would be only a new form, just one form of something which is always going on in theology, *semper, ubique, et ab omnibus*, with varying degrees of verve and emphasis. If this is how many people have understood Bultmann, the fault is largely his own. Must we confine ourselves to the strait jacket of a terminology and a language which is far from universally accepted or recognized? Must we, as it were, learn Chinese before Bultmann can help us to get to the real Paul and the real John? Such an impression is not altogether unjustified. This need not, of course, condemn him out of hand for this. Augustine used the language of Neoplatonism, Thomas Aquinas that of Aristotelianism, F. C. Baur and Biedermann were Hegelians, just as Bultmann is now a disciple of Heidegger. The impetus and energy with which he propounds his philosophy are undoubtedly reminiscent of those great exemplars. There is an element of philosophy in all theological language. But Bultmann attaches such an exclusive importance to his use of existentialism, and indeed it is the very hall-mark of his theology which is what makes it such a problem. On the other hand in all fairness we should not overlook his protest that he uses existentialism only as a tool, and only because it seems the most viable philosophy for our age. But can philosophy be used merely as a tool? Does it not become much more? A tool which turns out to be the key to open all, or nearly all, the locks is a very remarkable one indeed.

Nevertheless, it would be quite wrong to say that Bultmann is a philosopher and not—in his own way—a theologian. It was Buri, not Bultmann, who said that one particular type of existentialism was the only true theology.

5. Let me boldly suggest that the nearest solution will be that Bultmann is simply a Lutheran—*sui generis*, of course! I feel we have been given a right to press this suggestion by the group of Bavarian theologians who published *Ein Wort Lutherischer Theologie*.[1] My friend Georg Merz, in particular, exhibits Bultmann's affinities with Luther, in spite of his own reservation towards his work.

Now, of course, the heritage of Lutheranism is a highly com-

[1] See above, p. 9.

plex one. I have already pointed out the parallel between Bultmann and the original version of Melanchthon's *Loci communes*. In the first meeting of a seminar I held on Melanchthon this was spontaneously discovered by the students, who could hardly suppress their glee. The earliest work of Protestant dogmatics is apparently already moving consciously and exclusively within the anthropological triangle of law, sin and grace, law being interpreted as natural law. The Pauline epistles are already being treated as the canon within the canon. While such mysteries as the Trinity and the Incarnation may be subjects for prayer and adoration they are not included in the *loci communes*, for they are not capable of further theological explication. The *historia* of the New Testament is apparently only *historia*. All this looks like a cold demythologizing of the New Testament. And the young Melanchthon was a faithful disciple of the young Luther. I have long been waiting for a treatise on the distinctive place and function of Christology in the young Luther. How did he relate Christology to the soteriology with which he was so preoccupied? I know that both Luther and Melanchthon came to see the question in quite a different light in their later years in the course of their controversy with the *Schwärmer* over the Real Presence. Still, Luther's main preoccupation continued to be the application of salvation to man (law and gospel, etc.), and justification by faith. There are places in the final version of his commentary on Galatians where Christology almost merges into soteriology, passages which Bultmann might well cite in support of his own existentialist methods. He could easily appeal for support in his strong distinction between "flesh" and "glory" to Luther's theology of the cross. His ethics, with their strong individualism, would fit in quite easily with the Lutheran doctrine of the two realms. It is not surprising, for instance, that he is not too far from the Lutheran bishops on political issues, especially on the practical decisions which Germany faces to-day. What kind of doctrine of Church and state would Bultmann offer? I ask all this not to cast aspersions on him. I have too high a regard for Luther and Lutheranism for that. All I want is to understand Bultmann as best I can. After all, he learnt his theology from

Wilhelm Herrmann, and he is fond of quoting him. In justice to Bultmann, we must remember all he could have learnt and probably did learn from Herrmann long before he ever heard of Heidegger. I am referring to his constant simplification of the Christian message, his emphasis on its ethical and anthropological aspects. I am also thinking of his reverence and respect for the autonomy of the secular world and its science, his abhorrence of conservatism, which goes on clinging to outworn shibboleths and is really a quest for righteousness by works. And it was surely Herrmann who maintained the genuine Lutheran tradition, albeit a narrow one. It is just these elements in his theology which have influenced Bultmann so much. And, as everyone knows, there were two other theologians who stood behind Herrmann, Tholuck, the theologian of the heart, and Ritschl, dry-as-dust. Were not they also good Lutherans? Then, of course, there is Kierkegaard the Danish philosopher and father of existentialism. He, too, was a Lutheran. Bultmann's work is inconceivable apart from his Lutheran background. Of course, this is not the whole story. But those who throw stones at Bultmann should be careful lest they accidentally hit Luther, who is also hovering somewhere in the background.

VIII

To return to the subject, my attempts to understand Bultmann converge on one point: What do we mean specifically when we talk of understanding the New Testament? And what do we mean by understanding? I am deliberately placing these questions in that order. Both are pressed upon us by Bultmann.

First, with regard to the New Testament, can there be any genuine understanding of its text if we presuppose as our norm a fixed canon of possibility, truth and importance—the prior understanding, as Bultmann calls it? Surely, to understand the New Testament kerygma means to understand in faith the Word of God to which it bears witness. And this Word of God can only confront and illuminate man as truth and reality if it is seen to run counter to his whole natural capacity to understand; yet it enables him for this very reason to make it his own. If I do not believe, how shall I be able to understand by my own reason and strength? What do we mean by capacity for understanding if it depends on the illumination of the Holy Spirit? Of course, this understanding which is subservient to revelation will turn out to be a very limited affair, often inadequate and often baffled. But we have no right to provide our own answers for what lies beyond its scope. We have no right to try and barricade ourselves behind the limits of our understanding in order to protect ourselves from the Word of God. Of course, everyone approaches the New Testament with some kind of preconceptions, as he does any other document. We all have our prior notions of possibility, truth and importance. We all know what we think is our capacity to understand. And, of course, as we seek to understand the New Testament, our first reaction is bound to be one of self-defence against its strangeness. We shall want to cling to our prior understandings and preconceptions. More than that, we shall always be trying to confine this strangeness within the strait jacket of our prior understandings and preconceptions. We shall always be trying to incorporate and domesticate its strange elements. But have we any right to elevate all this into a methodological principle? To defy that strangeness with a "thus far and no further"? What business has the modern world view here, however tenaciously we cling to it and imagine we are morally obliged to uphold it? And what business has existentialism and anthropological interpretation here, however much we ourselves may be convinced by them and accept them as binding for ourselves? What is the relevance here of idealism or positivism, to which our fathers were so attached? Or—as may occur and has in fact occurred to some—Marxism or some kind of nationalism? Do these elements of the world make us competent to quibble with the Spirit and the Word of God? How can we listen to the New Testament if we are always thrusting some *conditio sine qua non* between ourselves and the text? To do so is to invite all kinds of wrong exegesis, if nothing worse. Surely it would be better to cultivate as flexible and open-minded approach as we can, instead of donning the existentialist strait jacket? Better by far to wait and see if we can understand it first. Let the New

Testament serve as the catalyst of our capacity to understand. Do not make our capacity to understand the catalyst of the New Testament! Accept the New Testament's understanding of ourselves before we take our own self-understanding too seriously and try to force it on the text. If we adopted this procedure, we should find our understanding of the text enhanced. Of course, it would mean we should have to swallow a good deal of what Bultmann would call mythology!

Any attempt to understand the New Testament is fraught with two dangers. Either we shall omit and distort the text, or, in Bultmann's sense of the word, we shall mythologize it. Of the two, surely the former danger is the greater, and must be avoided at all costs. It was the young Melanchthon who gave positive expression to all these questions:

> Unus est ut simplicissimus, ita certissimus doctor: Divinus Spiritus qui sese et proxime et simplicissime in sacris literis expressit, in quas ubi animus tuus veluti transformatus fuerit, tum demum absolute, simpliciter, exacte . . . comprehendes.[1]

And it was Luther who said in his *Table Talk*:[2]

> Sacrae literae volunt habere humilem lectorem qui reverenter habet et tremit sermones Dei, (lectorem) qui semper dicit: Doce me, doce me, doce me! Superbis resistit spiritus!

There can be no more effective way of communicating the New Testament message to modern man (ourselves included) than to point towards this possibility of understanding. Would this be expecting too much? Would it be putting on pressure? Would it produce insincerity? I think not. Rather it would be leading men to the truth.

This brings us to the concept of understanding as such. Biblical hermeneutics is not so much a specific application of a general hermeneutics, but the pattern and measure of all others. It is impossible to understand another person or a text, e.g. a mythological one, if we do not allow it to question us with the

[1] *Loci communes*, ed. Kolde, 1921, p. 105.
[2] As quoted by Ellwein from the *Bavarian Anthology*, p. 32.

utmost frankness. It would, perhaps, be going too far to speak of being unreservedly open to the text, for that is rarely possible, either with the Word of God or with the word of man. But if our aim is to understand it, we must surely try to approach it as open-mindedly as possible. That is a matter of principle. It is impossible to understand any other person unless we are ready to let him tell us something we did not know before, something we could not find out for ourselves, something we have hitherto been prejudiced against, perhaps with much justification. We shall never understand him if we are sure we know beforehand the limits of our understanding. We shall never understand him if we lay down these limits before we have given him a chance to speak for himself. These limitations, it is true, are found in all personal relationships. They are signs of real narrow-mindedness. Thus it is certain that even if we manage to be completely open-minded, it will take us a long time to reach a perfect understanding. No doubt from time to time we shall be jolted out of our narrow-mindedness and widen our sights for a moment. But it is quite another thing to regard as our sacred duty and an iron law to confine ourselves within our narrow-mindedness and refuse to budge an inch. I do not see how I can understand another man or a text unless I am ready to show a certain amount of flexibility. Otherwise my understanding will not only be incomplete, but not even genuine and I shall, therefore, not be able to understand at all. If I close my mind to the text on principle and refuse to make the effort necessary to understand it, no one else will understand me either. I shall only get annoyed and perplexed, concluding that I am speaking Chinese, while the other man wants to talk Japanese, and is angry because I won't. To understand another I shall have to overcome this unsympathetic attitude, and cease to maintain it as a matter of principle. Such sympathy, or its absence, can never be taken for granted, whether towards others or towards a text. It can never be guaranteed or contrived artificially by our own reason or strength, any more than we can contrive it in our relation to God. For genuine understanding between man and man, however incomplete, the discipline of the Holy Spirit will undoubtedly be necessary. For it is only through the Holy

Spirit that the Old and New Testaments can be appreciated as a testimony to the Word of God. Not even myths or persons like Goethe for instance can be understood without this initial sympathy, that is, without something of the discipline of the Holy Spirit. The erection of this doctrine of the prior understanding as the norm, which lies at the root of Bultmann's hermeneutics, would seem to be the death of all right and genuine understanding. For it appears to compete with the Holy Spirit and unduly to restrict his operation. We are surely justified in approaching this doctrine with scepticism—and the use to which Bultmann puts it. For it rules out all genuine communication.

Thirty years ago, when we launched the new movement in theology, our aim—or at least mine—was to reverse the current understanding of the New (and the Old) Testament; and understanding in general, man's knowledge, as we saw it, depended on his being known by the object of his knowledge. We were concerned with the Word, God's gift and message to man. We felt that the Word of God also throws light on the words men address one another. Our aim was to emancipate understanding, both of the Bible and of things in general, from the Egyptian bondage in which one philosophy after another had tried to take control and teach us what the Holy Spirit was allowed to say as the Word of God and of man in order to be open to understanding. Although we did not know the Word, we were seeking to demythologize the belief that man was the measure of his own understanding and of all other understanding. It turned out a long and arduous path. We stumbled upon many obstacles, sometimes alone, sometimes in company with our colleagues. There were many bypaths and false turnings, and we had to be constantly recalling ourselves and our colleagues to the main road. I am far from thinking we have reached the end of the road. But we were quite sure this was the right road. Now, as I see it, Bultmann has forsaken our road and gone back to the old one again. He has gone back to the old idea of understanding which we had abandoned. Here is the main reason why I don't want to pursue my attempt to understand him any farther, at any rate for the time being. Unlike most of those who cannot follow him, I am perplexed not so much by his resolute opposition to anything smacking of the supernatural, or the denials and eliminations in his restatement of the kerygma, as by—shall I call it—the "pre-Copernican attitude" which lies behind them.

Nobody knows whether his work will prove to mark the turning point in theology for the second half of our century. It could be, if only because the younger generations have never known the Egyptian bondage first hand, the era of Ritschl, Harnack, Troeltsch, and their predecessors and are, therefore, unable to appreciate why we were so eager to escape from it. Already some of them seem to think that it was they who discovered America! What I mean is that they have just found out that there is nothing better than radical criticism, whereas *we* had found out that there was something even more important. Maybe, of course, they are more in debt to the general return to ecclesiasticism than they are aware of. Of course, I would not wish to measure everything by what we did in the twenties. Nevertheless, at the final meeting of my seminar on *Kerygma and Myth* during the Winter Semester of 1951–2 I could not help reminding my students how the people once lusted after the flesh pots of the Egypt they had left behind, and how soon they got tired of the manna and the quails. I ended with a pious hope which I should like to repeat here. If theology in the second half of our century becomes a theology of demythologizing and of existentialist interpretation, with a prior understanding as its *sine qua non* and its own framework of imagery, let us at least hope that Israel will not be punished with too many quails!

But perhaps heaven (mythologically speaking) has not yet decided that this will be the theology of the future!

Appendix

I had just finished the manuscript of this article when the recently published second volume of *Kerygma und Mythos* came into my hands.[1] It is dedicated, curiously enough, to the World Council of Churches at Geneva.

[1] Ed. by H.-W. Bartsch, Hamburg-Volksdorf, 1952.

To my mind this second instalment bears out my belief that the Bultmann discussion has reached an impasse. This need not have happened. The new symposium contains several essays which might have led to some advance.

Let me hasten to add that, of course, I cannot include in this judgement the attempt of those two forceful and able young men, Otto Hartlich and W. Sachs, to put me in my place, humble as I am and ready to learn, and much as I admire their erudition. Forty years as a theologian have taught me to take it, and so I bear them no malice. But there is a remarkable thing about Bultmann and his disciples. That is, if we cannot follow their exegesis they tell us brusquely to study its underlying principles. And when we tell them it is just these that we have difficulties with, they get angry and ask us why we are not prepared to engage in exegesis with Bultmann (p. 125). In my case this means learning that the New Testament and the Christian faith are not concerned with an event in space and time or with an assessment of that event. Indeed, to engage in exegesis with Bultmann is to enter upon a critical examination of Bultmann's exegesis and its hermeneutic principles. The dog is chasing its own tail! I bow to their judgement, but I am astonished that the master himself regards their essay as the best contribution to the debate (p. 179).

I would mention first Prenter's essay "*Mythus und Evangelium*" as representing a real advance in the discussion (pp. 69f.). Here the relation between the negative and positive elements, demythologizing and existentialist interpretation, is given a thorough spring-cleaning. We must admit, whatever our own attitude may be, that that is something which needs doing, and which is not clearly evident in Bultmann himself. There is also an essay by W. G. Kummel entitled "*Mythische Rede und Heilsgeschehen im Neuen Testament*" (pp. 153f.) in which the writer attempts to distinguish between myth in the New Testament which is adequate to kerygma and myth which is not, between myths which can and myths which cannot be demythologized. We may argue about this, but it is certainly a point worth discussing. Kummel, incidentally, is one of those historians who show little interest in the existentialist side of Bultmann's hermeneutics. Finally, there is Fritz Buri's ultra-radicalization of Bultmann's radicalism, entitled "*Entmythologisierung oder Entkerygmatizierung der Theologie*" (Demythologizing or dekerygmatizing of Theology). Note this further enrichment of our German language! "The kerygma is a last vestige of mythology to which we still illogically cling" (p. 96). It requires very little understanding of Bultmann to see that this is an attack on the very foundation of his theology. Yet it is based on Bultmann's own presuppositions, and makes out a good case for itself.

I am, therefore, all the more astonished that in his "Reply to his Critics" which forms the climax of the whole symposium (p. 180f.; E.T. (part only), *Kerygma and Myth*, I, pp. 191–211) hardly takes any note of Kümmel except to say that his suggestion on page 85 is absurd. Nor does he or any of his pupils answer Prenter or Buri. Or perhaps we must take it that Buri's essay is disposed of in the editor's remark (p. 6) that "no German theologian would agree with it". Why not? I for one would be most eager to know what the master and his pupils had in mind to counter Buri's arguments. And the scholasticism so patently manifested in their replies (which are only a rehash of what they had said already) seems to me a poor substitute for their curious silence over Buri, Prenter, and Kümmel.

The only new thing I came across in Bultmann's Reply (and it was a point which had already been singled out by the advance publicity was the parallel to the Pauline and Lutheran doctrine of justification. Demythologizing, we are told, is that doctrine pushed to its logical conclusion in the field of epistemology. I am surprised that this is Bultmann's own "self-understanding", but I am not sorry that I myself said just as much, and indeed thought it the best place to put him in in the history of theological development (cf. p. 121 above).

No, there is little new in the second volume of *Kerygma und Mythos*. How could there be with things as they are? Another publication I received after completing my manuscript was Hellmut Traub's *Anmerkungen und Fragen zur neutestamentlichen Hermeneutik und zum Problem der Entmythologisierung*, Neukirchen, 1952. It contains important material, particularly for developing the suggestions in section VIII of my essay. It would be better if there were a little more give and take on both sides. Bultmann can hardly be serious when he complains we do not want to understand him, or that we have not paid enough attention to the questions he has asked. He can hardly complain, either, that we have neglected his suggestions in the realm of exegesis, or the principles which underly it. Have we not all stood round him for the past ten years, racking our brains, and wondering how we can possibly meet his challenge? And does he realize that other people have their own questions and desires, with a different slant and emphasis from his? Surely, he hardly expects us to submit to cross-examination from him to see whether we are prepared to take his line and go as far as he does both in what we affirm and what we deny. Can he understand anyone but himself and his own programme? Does it surprise him that there are others who cannot identify themselves with him, cannot understand him, and cannot help misunderstanding him? Can Bultmann or his pupils contemplate any discussion except one in which they do all the talking and everyone else agrees? Whenever anyone raises an objection, it only shows he has failed to understand him! There is apparently little likelihood of there being anything in the reservations which other people have expressed about him, nor could he profit from a discussion with them. After all, he has never yielded an inch—admirable doggedness in its own way, but such as to preclude any real meeting of minds. One wonders where the New Testament comes into all this, especially when one thinks of the contributions to this second volume of *Kerygma und Mythos*. And, finally, what is the debate really all about? The holy evangelists and apostles? Or that apparently immutable and majestic hypostasis, the demythologizing of the New Testament? Must demythologizing become a subject of discussion for its own sake? Must everyone be concerned with it, and with nothing else? Surely, something has gone wrong here. It is all too dogmatic for words. And as I look back over this essay of mine, I wonder what desert I have landed myself into too. No doubt Bultmann will put me in my place. There seems little point in going on with the game any further. Much better to mind our own business. I had to throw all these questions into an appendix, because the second volume of essays gives the impression that the whole debate is in danger of getting bogged down in sterility and boredom, and if it is continued at all, there is little prospect of any improvement.

KARL JASPERS

MYTH AND RELIGION

Background of the Discussion

NO philosophy can comprehend religion either as a historical phenomenon or as a living faith. Philosophic thinking confronts religion as an ever-perplexing ultimate, a weight it cannot lift, or a resistance it cannot surmount. When, occasionally, it seems to us that the resistance has been surmounted, we do not experience the gratification produced by the discovery of a truth; rather, we feel something like terror, as before a sudden void.

That is why I begin my lecture with some hesitation. I am to speak of a world in which I am not at home, of which I have no right to speak by virtue of practice or office. Beside the theologian's, my learning is inadequate. Nor am I sufficiently informed about contemporary religious movements. Here I am like a traveller in a foreign country, looking at things from the outside. My only hope is that here, too, an outsider may notice things which the native misses, but which are nonetheless important.

And yet, a sense of inadequacy remains. I venture to speak to you, since you have asked me, but the fact remains that the philosopher should not interfere in the affairs of the minister or the theologian. What happened to Hegel and to Schelling is a sufficient warning.

However, to-day we are faced with a peculiar situation. Bultmann's views on demythologizing, which have aroused widespread and lively discussions, have assumed the proportions of an event touching the very essence of religion. This alone is enough to shake the philosopher out of his aloofness, even though the question is outside his field. But there is more. Bultmann's ideas evolve within the sphere of philosophy (up to a point that will be named later), and hence are subject to philosophical criticism. For both these reasons philosophical discussion is indicated. Since I run the risk of trespassing on others' territories, I hope you will permit me to make assertions which in view of the restricted scale of this lecture, will not be supported fully. However, the issues under discussion do most seriously concern my philosophizing.

1. *Two Weak Premises*

Bultmann's demand for the demythologizing of religion is based on two premises. The first is his conception of modern science and of the modern view of the world, which leads him to negate many articles of the Christian faith. The second is his conception of philosophy, which enables him to give an existentialist interpretation to certain contents of faith, that, in his opinion, are still true. He thinks that such an interpretation derives from scientific philosophy. These premises are the main pillars upon which his argument is built. These pillars seem to me not strong enough to bear its weight.

Modern Science and the Modern View of the World

Bultmann speaks of a modern view of the world which asserts a self-contained causality and tolerating no miraculous intervention. He speaks also of the modern view of man, which asserts mankind's unity against the alleged intrusions of gods and demons from outside. Finally, he speaks of the principles of scientific method, characterized by testing and verification. What does he mean by this?

Has Bultmann in mind a certain mode of thinking that is overwhelmingly current to-day and that is the distinguishing characteristic of modern man? It scarcely seems possible. The Resurrection, for instance, was just as implausible to the contemporaries of Jesus as it is to modern man. To exaggerate the spiritual differences between one age and another leads to overlooking the identical elements that characterize man as such. Thus, materialism and a naturalistic realism have always been with us; similarly, man's disposition to believe in the absurd is as unchanged as ever, no less strong to-day than it was then. It is only the contents of this faith in the absurd that are partly new: for example, belief in the advent of a definitive happiness for all in a classless society magically brought to birth through violence. This modern belief is analogous to the early missionary faith that the Kingdom of God will be realized simultaneously with the end of the world at the moment when the Gospel shall have been preached to all mankind (as the Bible prophesies). The absurd faiths of the modern era, ranging from astrology to theosophy, and from National Socialism to Bolshevism, suggest that superstition has no less power over the human mind to-day than it had formerly. Such permanent elements of human nature are universal, and have nothing to do with modern science, no more than with similarly permanent elements of rationality. Absurd modern faiths may very well make occasional use of scientific results, without grasping their origin or meaning.

Or does Bultmann have in mind modern science proper, which is actually something new in history, having begun in the late Middle Ages, although its realization dates only from the eighteenth century? This science, however, whose name is invoked by everyone, is known to surprisingly few: indeed, there are many scholars, and Bultmann, a serious historian, is apparently one of them, who are unfamiliar with its principles. A crucial feature of modern science is that it does not provide a total world-view, because it recognizes that this is impossible. It was science that liberated us from total views of the world, and for the first time in history. All previous epochs (and even our own at the level of the average man) have clung to general conceptions of this kind. Because it takes seriously the principles of cogent, universal, and systematic knowledge, science is always aware of its limitations, understands the particularity of its insights, and knows that it nowhere explores Being, but only objects in the world. It studies these methodically, aware of its boundaries at any given moment, and of its inability to provide guidance in life. Modern science has developed the new knowledge, which the ancient Greeks foreshadowed in their mathematics, medicine, geography, astronomy, mechanics, and political thought, failing to attain a general and basic scientific approach for lack of patient and systematic co-operation. In consequence of this development, the insights achieved by scientific method are available to, and are accepted as valid by all men everywhere who can grasp them. No earlier rationalistic system, no philosophy, was ever as successful in this respect as modern science has been, with its methodology and specialization. But where questions of faith are concerned, the impact of modern science is no more disintegrating than that of the universal rationalisms of earlier times. Only a basic misunderstanding of modern science, such as is very common to-day even among specialized researchers, leads to such a conclusion. Down to the present, this science has been accessible to the masses only in the form of final results referring to the totality of things, a form that absolutizes and distorts the actual results of science, giving rise to spuriously scientific total views. These reflect modern scientific superstition rather than real knowledge or insight into the meaning, content, and boundaries of science.

When Bultmann speaks of modern science, he uses various traditional expressions in a fairly summary way. For instance, he refers to mythical and scientific thinking as mere contraries, and he says that scientific thinking is prefigured in operational thinking. In each instance he has hit on a partial truth. But he completely misses the meaning of modern science when he asserts that scientific thinking arose out of the Greek search for the ἀρχή, or the principle that introduces unity into the manifold. This question was and remains a philosophical question; science cannot ask it methodologically, nor can it answer it. Only systematic theories are scientific: they are built on assumptions which are always hypothetical, and are guided by unifying ideas which can never bear upon the whole of Being. Questions are scientific only when they indicate starting points for genuine methodological investigations. Bultmann's statement, "The unity of the world in scientific thinking is matched by the unity of scientific thinking itself" is completely false. The opposite is true.

The Notion of a Scientific Philosophy

According to Bultmann's premise, which reflects no more than the average rationalistic spirit of any epoch, science has destroyed a large number of Biblical beliefs. But Bultmann's purpose is not to destroy religion: he wants to rescue it. And he effects this rescue by means of what he calls "existentialist interpretation". For this he needs a philosophy, which he calls "scientific philosophy". In his opinion this scientific philosophy achieves a natural understanding of human existence, this empirical existence which is concerned about itself, which is orientated towards death in Fear and Care, which is finite and rootless, flung into the world without origin or destination, inherently precarious, and so on. About this philosophy professed by Bultmann, the following must be said:

(*a*) Bultmann bases himself explicitly and, in effect, exclusively, on Heidegger's book *Sein und Zeit*. Whether he understood this book in Heidegger's sense is a matter for the philosopher to decide. To me, it seems that we are confronted with a peculiar situation. Heidegger's book is a complicated affair. In the form of an objective phenomenological analysis, he draws up a list of existentialist concepts, the so-called *Existentialia*, an analogy from the [Kantian] categories, and presents us with a doctrine as well knit and coherent as a steel structure. The whole is not motivated by the mere will to know reality as it is, but by *a* fundamental experience of human existence, not by *the* fundamental experience of human existence, in the sense of universally valid experience. Heidegger renounces all faith, taking up an attitude which in its openness to Nothingness appeals to "modern" men, and approaches Being with foreboding. This endows his construction with life and gravity.

This philosophy seems to me grounded in ambiguities. It operates with existential terms; in fact, it derives from Kierkegaard, Luther, and St Augustine. But at the same time it operates scientifically, phenomenologically, objectively. The appeal to selfhood, to authenticity, and to actual being—a sinking into the original, historical facticity (*Sosein*), in order to be appropriated—

the appeal to earnest questioning in a hopeless situation, is present as it is in the great philosophical tradition, though the ideas of that tradition tend to acquire a hollow sound. At the same time, Heidegger's thought is presented in objective terms, as a doctrine, and as a result it commits us no more than the traditional systems. What we have, then, is a noncommittal, phenomenological knowledge, and by the same token, a learnable, usable knowledge that is a perversion of philosophy. This is why psychiatrists were able to employ *Existentialia* to describe certain states of mental illness, both chronic and acute, often not without success. And this is also why Bultmann can employ the *Existentialia* as an alleged discovery of scientific philosophy, useful for the exegesis and appropriation of Biblical texts. Such a use of the *Existentialia* was made easier by the fact that they themselves originate in a thinking rooted in the Bible.

(*b*) Because Bultmann confines philosophy to one book by Heidegger, and, as I suspect, misunderstands that book when he emphasizes its "scientific", objective, scholastic aspect, he in effect cuts himself off from all philosophy. His writings reveal this in other ways as well. Whenever Bultmann refers to the history of philosophy in his studies, he is concerned with statements that can be quoted with the superficial correctness of historical data; he is not concerned with philosophy itself. He appears to be untouched by the least breath of Kantian or Platonic thinking. His conception of philosophy, which I believe foreign to Heidegger himself, is that of nineteenth-century academicians or Hellenistic doxographers. Heidegger himself would surely be surprised at any theology based upon it.

(*c*) If the various attempts at philosophizing which are to-day lumped together as Existentialism have anything in common despite their differences of tendency, form, and content, it is, negatively, the rejection of so-called scientific philosophy, and, positively, the affirmation of a moral earnestness foreign to mere knowing. Now, this state of affairs is veiled by a distinction which once again gives an opening to philosophical inauthenticity, namely, the distinction between existentialist analysis and existential thinking. I don't know whether Heidegger himself has drawn such a distinction—it would be in keeping with the ambiguities of his thought referred to above—or whether it was introduced by Bultmann. The consequences of this distinction are: Existentialist analysis seeks to formulate with scientific objectivity that which can have meaning only in terms of existential thinking; what was meant by the *Existentialia* only as a sign, an indication, is turned into a thing; what has meaning only as a summons to awaken, or a stimulus to unrest, is treated as universally valid cognition. What can be achieved only through inward commitment becomes a matter of noncommittal knowledge; responsibility for things said is confined to scientifically rational responsibility, instead of extending to inner meaning and consequences; thinkers take the liberty of speaking in the name of "abstract consciousness" where they are entitled to speak seriously only for themselves; an illusion of knowledge is created in matters where everything depends on the ground that is never known and that, since Kierkegaard, has been called *Existenz*; conceptual definitions congeal what only a transcending thinking can achieve step by step, each meaningful only to the degree that it evokes an inner resonance and becomes real in the actual life of the thinker.

Furthermore, this turning of signs into objective *Existentialia*, this concern for scientific philosophy, implies a new dogmatism, which is expressed less in concepts than in the general attitude: a modern mode of despair thus achieves self-understanding without transcendence. Resolution (*Entschlossenheit*) as such, without content, suffices unto itself. An alleged knowledge of what we are or can be or want to be or allegedly cannot help being, begets a new intellectual intolerance, presenting as universal truth that which is valid only for the thinker's own life, on the grounds that it is modern, of the age. The tendency of many rebels to absolutize their own rootlessness in nothingness originates in that false idea, not in any scientific advance by a scientific philosophy.

Bultmann, although he keeps aloof from the tendency we have just described, believes in such a "scientific philosophy". That is why he isolates the philosophic ideas contained in Heidegger's book *Sein und Zeit* and interprets them as a scientific, universally valid insight into human existence. This interpretation may describe one incidental, though scarcely unequivocal, aspect of the book. Detached from its context and made noncommittal, this thinking becomes an instrument for the intellectual assimilation of existential propositions in the Bible by means of existentialist exegesis. It is a deceptive instrument. At all events, it makes one blind to philosophy. As for what it does to the Bible, I have my doubts. Why do things that have resonance in Heidegger sound so hollow in Bultmann? It seems to me the reason for this is Bultmann's scientific prejudice with regard to the possibilities of philosophy, his superstitious belief in a "scientific philosophy".

Existentialist analysis can never give scientific insight or replace moral earnestness. Existentialist analysis, when it is philosophical, is never neutral in the manner of science, is never universally valid, but is at the same time existential: it speaks out of moral earnestness with a view to commitment, out of deep emotion to arouse emotion. It speaks with a sense of responsibility, not for scientific correctness, which must not be sought and which cannot be found here, but for the truth of that which I will do and am, and in appeal to others to respond. Philosophical language is responsible for the goal of its thoughts, for that into which they transform me inwardly, and for the consequences that follow in external action, in concrete decisions, and in everyday life. I escape from commitment by the linguistic distinction between existentialist and existential. It is not a critical, clarifying distinction, but one that seduces into noncommitment. It paralyses instead of awakening. It leads to endless talk, which does not advance. It gives a hollow tone to what is said.

2. *Bultmann's View of Transcendental Philosophy*

In thus venturing to characterize Bultmann's position as alien to both science and philosophy, have I not been guilty of exaggeration, to say the least? Has not philosophy still another task, which I have overlooked in my discussion so far, namely the clarification and critical delimitation of all our modes of knowledge and belief? Actually, it is in this area that Bultmann tries to establish the possibility of faith with the help of his conception of myth and of the relation between knowledge and faith. This philosophical task bears upon the form, not the content, of the ideas involved. Demythologizing, we are told, by exposing a historically obsolete form of thinking, which has become false, will liberate religion from that form. We are here entering the domain of philosophical investigation which was first explored by Plato, which since Kant has been called "transcendental", and which is to-day carried on in various ways, among others, by elucidating the modes of the Encompassing. Such transcendental reflection, as distinct from philosophical speculation proper, which discloses meaning, cannot be regarded as scientific in the full sense of the term, although it comes close to scientific cognition in so far as it claims universal validity.

Once again I shall confine myself to a few theses:

Immediate Experience and the Modes of the Encompassing

Everything that is real for us and that we really are, is present in immediate experience. But this immediate experience cannot be grasped in its moments of plenitude or impoverishment, in its vital concentration or dispersal—it cannot be grasped as a state at all. It remains the site of all actualization (*Verwirklichung*), yet it remains unknowable as a whole and as an object. But with regard to everything that is asserted, we raise the question whether and how its content is actual for us, a question which is answered not in terms of reason, but in terms of the given reality in this immediate experience. Without such an answer there is only empty talk.

In immediate experience a conscious mind is directed at objects which it sets before itself. All clarity, all thought and language, is in this split between the thinker and the thing he has in mind, between subject and object. This split is the luminous crest of a wave surging above unfathomable depths; it may also be compared to a flame that is nourished by the flow of the inexhaustible Encompassing. If the flow stops, if awareness of the deep ground is absent, if there is only the split between a conscious mind and the objects it intends, then we have no more than a rustle of withered leaves, the random swirling of dead husks of words, producing a semblance of external order and meaning in endless, arbitrary variation.

By various methods, philosophy seeks to comprehend the mind and its deep ground in the whole range of its potentialities. It sets up levels of cognition, from sensory knowledge to the supersensory intuition of the godhead (antiquity and the Middle Ages), or it analyses the faculties of the human soul, namely the faculty of thinking as apprehension of objects, the faculty of the will as capacity for execution, and the faculty of feeling as awareness of psychic states (Kant), or it elucidates the modes of the Encompassing, within which the split between subject and object takes place. Such modes are empirical existence in an environment, abstract consciousness with its world of objects, the spirit with its world of forms, and *Existenz* with its transcendence. When philosophy, following any one of these paths, covers the whole range of immediate experience, the unity of the distinct modes of the Encompassing becomes clear in their interplay and counterplay, in their inseparability, and in their meeting in abstract consciousness. As a totality, this unity is called man, or reason; or, when we give a name to that which we may encounter in immediate experience, it is called Being, God, or the All-Encompassing.

One feature all these philosophical explorations have in common: they try to give a scientific form to something that cannot be an object of science. They speak of something that is the ground of all objectivity, but that is not itself an object. Therefore, Kant called them "transcendental". They do not transcend in a forward direction, so to speak, away from all objects towards something that lies beyond, but in a backward direction, away from all consciousness of objects, towards the ground of possibility of this diverse objectiveness. This accounts for the inadequacy of all propositions advanced in such explorations, although such propositions remain meaningful.

We cannot think unless something becomes an object for us. To be conscious means to live in that clarity which is made possible by the split between the I and the object. But it also means to live within the walls constituted by the split between the I and something known to be an object. We attempt to break out of this prison by becoming conscious of this split in our reflection; and then we realize that wherever men live in serious commitment, the wall has been breached. Objectivity is a mode in which the Encompassing that is lost in the mere object becomes clear. The fact that the Encompassing has also a non-objective aspect becomes apparent in the objectifications of the Encompassing; in each of its modes, objectivity has meaning only in relation to the pertinent subjectivity. This objectivity is the tangible presence of the object in the mode of empirical existence, and logical objectivity in the mode of abstract consciousness. In the mode of *Existenz*, the objective aspect of the Encompassing assumes the form of the tangible presence of transcendence in the myth. If we forget that myth is also a code language, a cipher, it loses all reference to transcendence, it becomes mere tangible presence.

Since nothing becomes clear until it has been made an object, it is not objectification that merits reproach, but only false objectification. Thus, when transcendence is the object of thought in speculation about Being, this object is present in such a way that only its disintegration through the movement of thought shows what was meant. In that way what has been conceived as object is transformed into a sign of possible *Existenz*; when treated as objective *Existentialia* such signs lose their authentic meaning. The question is always how we grasp the indispensable objectivity of things without losing sight of the fact that objectivity alone is insufficient, and how we distinguish it from false objectification.

Now, these are laborious philosophical investigations, worthy of extensive elaboration. It is as someone whose philosophizing has been clarified by such investigations that I shall venture the following remarks on Bultmann's theses.

Myth and Science

Bultmann, in keeping with a tradition that goes back to Aristotle, distinguishes between myth and science. He regards mythological thinking as obsolete, as something scientific thinking has left behind. However, in so far as the myth conceals a content that was expressed in a language suitable only to the age in which it was created, it must be translated. The myth, says Bultmann, is to be interpreted, divested of its mythological garb, and transposed into a truth valid to-day.

I deny this. Mythical thinking is not a thing of the past, but characterizes man in any epoch. It is true that the term "myth" is by no means unequivocal. It contains the following elements:

(*a*) The myth tells a story and expresses intuitive insights, rather than universal concepts. The myth is historical, both in the form of its thinking and in its content. It is not a cloak or disguise put over a general idea, which can be better and more directly grasped intellectually. It explains in terms of historical origin rather than in terms of a necessity conceived as universal law.

(*b*) The myth deals with sacred stories and visions, with stories about gods rather than with empirical realities.

(*c*) The myth is a carrier of meanings which can be expressed only in the language of myth. The mythical figures are symbols which, by their very nature, are untranslatable into other language. They are accessible only in the mythical element, they are irreplaceable, unique. They cannot be interpreted rationally; they are interpreted only by new myths, by being transformed. Myths interpret each other.

How wretched, how lacking in expressiveness our life would be, if the language of myth were no longer valid! To fill mythical forms with banal content is to commit an unpardonable error. The splendour and wonder of the mythical vision is to be purified, but must not be abolished. To speak of "demythologizing" is almost blasphemous. Such a depreciation of myth is not enlightenment, but sham enlightenment. Does the splendour of the sunrise cease to be a tangible, ever new and inspiring reality, a mythical presence, just because we know that the earth is revolving around the sun, so that properly speaking there is no sunrise? Does the appearance of the deity on Mount Sinai or in the burning bush cease to be a poignant reality even when we know that in terms of space and time the phenomena in question were human experiences? To demythologize would be to do away with an essential faculty of our reason. Nevertheless, the impulse to demythologize contains a half-truth derived from genuine enlightenment:

The Degradation of the Myth. The truth of mythical thinking has been perverted in all periods, including our own: the myth is interpreted not as a code, but literally, and material reality is ascribed to its symbols. Contact with true reality by way of its unique language slips into materialism of tangibility and usability. Therefore, thinkers of all ages, and Bultmann, too, are right in denying assertions which give myth the tangible reality of things in the world, a reality that is accessible to our quite different real knowledge, a knowledge that modern science has developed and clearly delimited. A corpse cannot come to life and rise from the grave. Stories based on the reports of contradictory witnesses and containing scanty data cannot be regarded as historical facts. Because materialism is a common way of thinking, the cipher language of myth will always be degraded into a language of the tangible, which is guaranteed and provides guarantees; this took place among the earliest Christians, and has taken place everywhere in the world. Every epoch has the critical task of correcting such perversions. Bultmann hits on something true in so far as he means by "demythologizing" the fulfilment of this task—that of denouncing reification, or conceiving the myth as an alleged reality, opaque and tangible.

Recovery of the Myth. But the demand for demythologizing is justified only if at the same time it insists on restoring the reality of the mythical language. We should seek not to destroy, but to restore the language of myth. For it is the language of a reality that is not empirical, but existential, whereas our mere empirical existence tends continually to be lost in the empirical, as though the latter were all of reality. Only he has the right to demythologize, who resolutely retains the reality contained in the cipher language of the myth.

The real task, therefore, is not demythologize, but to recover mythical thought in its original purity, and to appropriate, in this form of thinking, the marvellous mythical contents that deepen us morally, enlarge us as human beings, and indirectly bring us closer to the lofty, imageless transcendence, the idea of God which no myth can fully express for it surpasses them all.

Mythical thinking can achieve a unique and legitimate effectiveness in our lives provided that two critical ideas are not lost sight of.

First: Whereas mythical language is historical, and hence its truth can lay no claim to the universal validity of knowledge, it is precisely by virtue of this quality that it can lend the historical *Existenz* something of the unconditional. The unconditional thus brought to light remains conditioned in expression, historically relative, and objectively uncertain. It is one of the basic insights of philosophical reflection that universally valid truth is valid only relatively, from the standpoint of abstract consciousness, while it is existentially neutral; and that existential truth, on the contrary, which becomes identified with the thinker so that he lives and dies in it, precisely for that reason must be historical, and cannot achieve universally valid expression. Only he has a right to live in the mythical who does not confuse the unconditionality of historical *Existenz*, which becomes clear to itself in myth, with the universal validity of an assertion, which, being an assertion concerning an empirical reality, is valid for all. Indeed, the reality that has come down to us in the myth would be lost if it were dissolved into general philosophical ideas.

However, it is impossible to foresee where mythical language achieves validity in the moment of unconditional decision. To learn this language, to appropriate the vision it expresses, makes decision possible and prepares us for it. But even that takes place historically. By entrusting ourselves to our own historical origins we are brought closer to the Bible and to antiquity, despite the partly oriental contents of the former.

Second: All mythical images are ambiguous. This idea is inherent in the Biblical commandment: Thou shalt not make to thyself any graven image. Everything mythical is a language that grows faint before the transcendence of the one godhead. While we see, hear, and think in the language of myth conceived as code, while we cannot become concretely aware of transcendence without a code language, we must at the same time keep in mind that there are no demons, that there is no magic causality, no such thing as sorcery. There, nevertheless, remains a deeply moving series of images—the three angels visiting Abraham, Moses receiving the tablets of the law, Isaiah seeing in his vision not God himself but only his manifestation, God addressing one man in thunder and another in a gentle breeze, Balaam's she-ass possessed of better vision than her rider, the Risen One saying, Touch me not, his Ascension, the Descent of the Holy Ghost, and so on to infinity.

Now, the three distinctions—between the tangible presence and the language of cipher, between mythical contents and the transcendent God, and finally between unconditional historicity and relative universal validity—are proper only to the philosophical consciousness. What we thus distinguish may have been one originally, and it becomes one again where it is alive. For the philosophically naïve, tangible presence and cipher language are not distinct. Some pious people conceive of this tangible presence as an empirical reality. True piety, as a matter of course, eliminates the materialistic, magical, and utilitarian misuse of literal interpretation. There is also an impious, materialistic conception of the myth as tangible reality, which no longer regards the myth as a cipher, and which leads to superstition.

Struggle for Existential Possibilities of Faith. However, the great and most essential task for anyone who enters the field of mythical thinking is to struggle for the true faith within that thinking. One myth confronts another, not in rational discussion, and not necessarily with the aim of destroying it, but in spiritual struggle. This struggle is fought dishonestly if the outward form of the myth is attacked, if its opponent denounces it as a mode of thinking, denying that such a mode of thinking is necessary to his own faith. Such a struggle is fought fairly and illuminates when it goes back to the original meanings, to the deeper sources. Depending on the consequences a given myth has for a given individual, he will accept or reject it, realizing how it affects his actions and conduct. But no man can deny in the name of all what he rejects for himself. He must concede that a myth which he cannot accept may be valid for others. What is in question is existential truth, which is spiritually efficacious only in mythical thinking, but which without the myth would remain beyond our horizon.

We acquire strength when we read the Bible not in a spirit of slavish literalness, but participating in the inner meanings, rejecting or appropriating them. The mythical contents put the reader in certain states, which he experiences as possibilities; he sees their meanings in the various and variously important images that appear to him, and that all point beyond themselves to something no image can express. It is not rational knowledge, but existential clarification in the sphere of the contradictory, mutually exclusive or complementary possibilities of the Bible that gives us the daily strength to go forward or to resist. For us, the Bible is the favourite arena of spiritual contest; another one is provided by the Greek epic poems and tragedies, and still another by the sacred books of Asia.

Translation, explication, and interpretation in terms of universal concepts—methods which have been practised since antiquity—may help us to appropriate the contents of the Bible in a limited sense; but the clarifying struggle in which the rejected elements are not destroyed, but retained as discarded possibilities, requires that we come to grips with the living contents of the myth.

Now, it seems to me that in this struggle for the truth of certain Biblical contents against other Biblical contents, Bultmann reaches conclusions which I cannot accept. Here lies the crucial point of the debate. Bultmann, who has made important contributions to our historical knowledge of the New Testament, is interested in all of the Bible as a historian; but as a theologian, he appears in an entirely different light, namely, as a man whose interest in the Bible is singularly restricted. He is almost indifferent to the Old Testament. Study of the Synoptic Gospels proves to him that we have little historical knowledge of Jesus, and that many views contained in those books were a common possession of the non-Christian world at the time. But he attaches the highest value to St Paul and to the Gospel according to St John. For him the revelation is found not in a historically knowable Jesus, but in a redemptive history which can be discovered in these later texts. The redemptive history conceived by Christ's disciples and apostles is the very meaning of these texts. Here the emphasis lies on the mythical idea of justification by faith alone—an idea which is most alien to our philosophizing. As a believing reader of the New Testament, Bultmann is attracted by the theology expressed in it, but less so, if at all, by the actual teachings of Jesus. The spiritualized Christ of the Gospel according to St John, though noble and captivating as a fairy tale hero, seems to us far less significant than the living figure of Jesus in the Synoptics. But Bultmann is not concerned with this. He is scarcely troubled by the absurdity of the Gnostic myth in the Gospel of St John—although he was the first to recognize it clearly as a myth—and he interprets this Gospel as a surmounting of the myth. His interpretation goes into detail, yet he is scarcely troubled by the fact that this Gospel mythically justifies the earliest Christian anti-Semitism, absent from both St Paul and the Synoptics and indicative of the sort of faith animating the author of this gospel of love. Selection, emphasis, evaluation, and acceptance or rejection of given contents of the Bible can be clarified only if these are discussed in terms of mythical thinking itself, and we can do this (and do it) to-day as always.

Faith and Comprehension

Bultmann presented his ideas under the title of "Faith and Comprehension". Comprehension is the theme of almost all of his discussions: exegesis is his special field, and "existentialist" interpretation is his method of comprehension. Faith is presupposed, and its essential character is brought out through the process of comprehension, namely, as faith in the redemptive history, not as faith in the Resurrection of the Body. Bultmann justifies his comprehension of faith by texts, ascribing to St John's and St Paul's writings a higher meaning than to the Synoptic Gospels—and he achieves comprehension of the texts by means of his faith. All comprehension is based on such an inevitable hermeneutic circle, but here the process has a special form because of the absolute character of the faith. Now, the concept of "comprehension" is taken for granted by Bultmann; yet he seems to overlook some of its crucial aspects.

Immediate reality combines elements at which we arrive through critical reflection, and elements present as an inseparable whole in a fulfilled life: significant encounters and meaningless happenings; the personal interventions, demands, and assistance given by the Thou, and the impersonal resistance of things which we conquer or which conquer us; dark powers and clear causes; that which is directly perceived, and that which is logically inferred; passing moods and iron necessity. What is implied by such distinctions within immediate reality, we shall discuss here in greater detail with reference to the meaning of comprehension.

Explanation and Comprehension. We grasp reality either by explaining it or by comprehending it. What we perceive from the outside as the Other pure and simple, we call nature, and we explain it as a process governed by laws. What we perceive from the inside as the other, but a related Other, we call the soul or the spirit or the person, and we comprehend it as a meaningful whole. In actual fact, in so far as empirical investigation is possible, we explain nature, the cosmos, matter, the unconscious life; we comprehend man and the contents of his spiritual history.

Primary and Secondary Comprehension. In a broader sense, we call "comprehension" every mode of conceiving reality. Whether we think nature, man, the powers, the gods, God, we speak of "comprehension". In this sense, everything is "comprehended" —nature, the self, God, and so on—and comprehension is the mode of awareness of the Being that we are. Being is the actuality and the effective range of this comprehension.

But here another distinction arises. Anything comprehended by anyone anywhere can be comprehended by us a second time, even though we did not actually participate in or witness the thing in question. We can comprehend Caesar without ourselves being Caesar (Simmel), we can comprehend works of art without creating them ourselves, and scientific discoveries without making them ourselves. In this sense, we not only comprehend, but we comprehend what was comprehended (Böckh: The knowing of the known). This latter type of comprehension is practised in the grand style by philosophy and the historical sciences that philosophy makes possible—the history of myths, of religion, of art, of language, of literature, of politics, of law, and of philosophy.

What in the sciences we call comprehension as opposed to explanation is a secondary comprehension, not the other, the primary comprehension. Primary comprehension is the reality of comprehension itself; it is in possession of itself and of the thing comprehended; with regard to that reality, secondary comprehension is removed into its own weaker reality. Primary comprehension distinguishes between good and bad, true and false, beautiful and ugly; secondary comprehension, or comprehension of the comprehended, confronts its object from a distance without commitment, and distinguishes only between the correct and the incorrect in determining the actual meaning once intended. Primary comprehension passes judgements of value at every moment; secondary comprehension suspends judgements of value to the extent that it is correct (Weber).

Unity and Tension of Both Types of Comprehension. This seemingly clear distinction, however, is not actually a clear-cut distinction between two spheres, but the expression of a tension, in which the maximal will to clarity in secondary comprehension provisionally attempts a suspension of value judgements, although the source of all insight and comprehension is actually primary comprehension with its value judgements.

We shall try to make clear this difficulty in the case of the history of ideas, conceived as an empirical science. This history depends upon documents, testimonies, works, and languages in space and time, on things that are present to our senses now, and things that we perceive in the past or over a geographical distance; second, it depends on our ability to comprehend. Just as sensory perception in natural science presupposes sensory organs, so comprehension in the historical sciences presupposes, in addition, a certain intuitive ability. At this point, what we have just asserted as fact, namely, that we can comprehend Caesar without ourselves being Caesar, becomes, instead, a question: How is it possible? What is the relation between comprehension of the comprehended, this reality-less comprehension, to the primary, real comprehension? What is the relation between secondary comprehension and appropriation of the comprehended in one's own reality? The fact that the same term is used for both types of comprehension, the primary and the secondary, shows that there is a connection between the two.

Once again we must make a fundamental distinction, in terms of goals.

The seemingly clear distinction between primary and secondary comprehension is transcended in the primary comprehension itself, which always arises out of something previously comprehended. It is of the essence of the spirit to be born out of its own past. Its primary comprehension feeds on what has been comprehended: spirit itself is history, is spirit by virtue of its own tradition. Spirit, when it is primary, is already past its origins. It always presupposes a previous comprehension (Hegel). This primary comprehension, arising out of a secondary comprehension, transforms and appropriates but does not possess a yardstick for comprehending correctly what was meant in prior comprehension. Or, it sets out to comprehend the author better than he comprehended himself (the phrase is Kant's, but he himself expects his readers to do just that).

Opposed to this is the other mode of comprehension, the will to comprehend only what has been comprehended, to know and correctly determine what was actually meant in past thoughts, beliefs, works of art, and poetry. It does not let itself be diverted from the goal of correct knowledge of past spiritual creations by the idea, dangerous to the historian but meaningful for the theologian, that one should comprehendingly bring out what was implicit in such creations. Rather, it aims at demonstrating empirically, and as far as possible cogently, what was actually meant, and nothing more.

Now, in that which is primarily comprehended, there is truth and falsity, good and evil, beauty and ugliness. In so far as the late-comer sees these things more clearly in his own primary comprehension, he can have a more complete general view of what was once actually meant, and then demonstrate the errors empirically contained in past spiritual realities. But this applies unequivocally and clearly only to scientific knowledge. Elsewhere there is no general view based on greater knowledge and susceptible of producing better judgement. Rather, the uniqueness of the primary comprehension, which speaks to us out of the past, is, by its very nature, inexhaustible. Wherever this is not the case, the past spiritual content presents no real interest, no more than past scientific views whose falsity has been demonstrated. The subsequent, secondary comprehension, where it is confronted with an irreducible primary content, must come to grips with the past, without having an absolute yardstick at its disposal. This coming to grips is only suspended, by no means dispensed with, when the historical reality is studied for the purposes of an empirical comprehension.

In other words, this pure, self-effacing secondary comprehension is not a process of passive reproduction. It rests upon one's own latent primary comprehension, now merely suspended. Hence, capacity to comprehend in the historical sciences is individually limited, and cannot be uniformly presupposed in all, as we presuppose the presence of sensory organs in all normal persons. For this reason, the achievements of the historical sciences are less cogent, seem less universally valid than those of natural science, and are to a far greater degree stamped with personal character.

The capacity for secondary comprehension implies the possibility of being that which is comprehended; it is itself set in motion by this possibility, and is thus participation in some measure. This is true of political insight in the man who has been prevented from political activity; it is true of artistic insight in the man who can grasp but not create it, who has the capacity for vision but not that for creating aesthetic ideas; it is true of the religious insight of a man who may long for faith but cannot achieve faith, or is prevented from doing so by the self-assertion of his reason.

This tension between primary and secondary comprehension has important consequences. There is a wide gap between the man who is himself originally in the act of comprehension, and the man who merely comprehends what the other comprehended. The comprehending observer may range farther, may gain greater insight than the active participant. But breadth of insight is his at the price of bloodlessness and, moreover, a fundamental limitation: in every case, important elements must elude the mere observer's insight, for the very reason that he is not himself what he comprehends. And our emotional absorption in the experience of secondary comprehension easily leads us into the error of mistaking that comprehension for our own reality. Habituated to such behaviour, we fall victim to an illusion: we imagine that comprehension of other people's possibilities can replace our own authentic *Existenz*. For example, we may mistake an uncommitted, aesthetic way of life for our own reality.

Contact with the Incomprehensible. Primary comprehension comes always into contact with the incomprehensible, which assumes two forms: the incomprehensible which is the obscure pure and simple, and is a natural process capable of explanation; and the incomprehensible which is real in every life, which is also obscure, but which is capable of endless comprehending clarification.

These two types of the incomprehensible correspond to the two methods we have mentioned above: the external, scientific method of explaining the origin of reality in the absolute, unclarifiable obscurity of the Other pure and simple; and that of comprehension, which unfolds meanings and thereby gains insight into historical uniqueness.

The two paths are endless: that of explanation leads to knowledge of the laws governing the processes of nature, which never discloses its inwardness, and which has no inwardness for this type of knowledge; that of comprehension leads to knowledge of meaningful wholes, which always point to deeper meanings. As knowledge advances, we realize ever more unmistakably that in the former case we are coming to grips with an absolute obscurity, with contingent facticity (*Sosein*); in the latter case, with a potential clarity, with something that is fundamentally striving for complete openness.

Each of these cognitive methods leads to a radically different result, but in the transcending thinking of metaphysics the two may coincide. This is suggested by the fact that human *Existenz* at the profoundest level of awareness seems to unify that which is naturally given and universally explorable with that which is historically comprehensible *ad infinitum* in its uniqueness. For *Existenz* shares in the ambivalence of the incomprehensible itself, which is revealed to the deepest comprehension both as obscurity and as potential clarity.

Comprehension at its best always comes to grips with both aspects of the incomprehensible. In contact with the incomprehensible, secondary comprehension becomes primary comprehension: it comes to grips with reality, as a factor of our own historical realization.

Criticism of Bultmann. Seen in the light of the foregoing distinctions, Bultmann's discussion of comprehension would seem to justify the following conclusions. Because Bultmann, while undoubtedly aware of the difference between primary and secondary comprehension, does not take it into account, the great tension between the two is absent from his writings. He alternates between empirical, philological exegesis and a theological appropriation of religion. The two great opposing goals, which are the historical investigation of religion and the primary comprehension of faith, do not add up to a convincing statement, but rather collapse for lack of tension and clarity. Instead of producing a work that moves us by its inner struggle, Bultmann attempts to be true both to history and to theology, thus keeping his argument at an inferior level. We begin to feel this when we recall our situation with regard to the incomprehensible.

When we have run headlong into the wall of the incomprehensible, are we still within the range of comprehension? Is clarification still possible at this point? Only in one sense was the incomprehensible a fundamental limit: the more our knowledge of nature advances, the greater and the more unsurmountable the obscurity of the ultimate incomprehensible. We encounter this limit even in the realm of the spirit in so far as it is tied to nature, for instance, when we are deaf to argument, inaccessible to rational persuasion, when comprehension breaks off, or when the incomprehensible asserts itself concealed within the superficially comprehensible. But in the other sense, the incomprehensible confronts us with the possibility of an infinite progression in comprehension, with the striving of rational *Existenz* to disclose itself.

When the will to comprehend (which does not content itself with external cognition) runs headlong into the incomprehensible, the latter either shows itself in mythical figures and speculative concepts, as though it were striving to disclose itself, but still concealed in magnificently ambiguous language—or the incomprehensible becomes accessible to endless existential communication between men.

Faith sees the two aspects of the incomprehensible as one, by a primary comprehension, first in mythical, then in conceptual terms, without really comprehending it. Faith runs headlong into the incomprehensible and makes us aware of it in those terms. This faith can be communicated to others, and thereby lays claim to being comprehended. Only what can be comprehended can be communicated.

Therefore, when Bultmann combines faith with comprehension, he goes to the heart of the matter. A question, however, remains: how is comprehension effected when it comes up against the incomprehensible? "Existentialist" interpretation scarcely provides scientific insight; its objectifications are false. Even when this objectification is consciously rejected, its effects linger, though they may be unnoticed. The result is a false knowledge, and a faith inauthentic in its modes of communication. On the other hand, it is true that comprehension of faith, when it has weight, is "existential" interpretation in terms of communication. Such comprehension has nothing to do with scientific method; it is a voice from the source. We cannot achieve such comprehension in the noncommittal spirit of scientific cognition, for there is no scientific cognition here. We can achieve it only in the spirit of responsible commitment and acceptance. In these matters, to comprehend is to circle around, to describe, to discuss, to transform. To speak from faith is itself faith, preparation for the existential moment, recall to the eternal ground in the language of mythical images—or, in philosophy, in the language of speculative concepts.

All of us live in images, even if we go beyond them in philosophical speculation. We might think of them as constituting an unavoidable myth—a myth that may be shallow or profound, that may inspire a madness concealing boredom, that may gratify, for one destructive moment, a craving for the monstrous, or that may lead to the most extraordinary self-sacrifice in failure. Philosophically speaking, the myth is the rational *a priori* form in which we become aware of transcendence. Psychologically speaking, it is the mode of experiencing the real. But neither rational *a priori* form nor psychological experiential form is a guarantee of truth. Either of these forms may serve as vehicle for the hysteria of every sort of magician or Pied Piper, every sort of opportunist who believes and yet does not believe, who lies and is taken in by his own lies, who dazzles and spellbinds his victims, whether in the guise of the aesthetic snob or that of the nihilistic politician. All of them are destructive, whether of self-knowledge and possible authenticity, or of life itself.

The truth of the myth is not inherent in the *a priori* form or in the psychological disposition. Only moral earnestness can arouse moral earnestness. The man who speaks in mythical language has assumed a real risk. He has taken upon his conscience to identify himself with his works, not just for the moment, but for ever.

Bultmann speaks neither as the nihilistic spellbinder nor as the authentic man of faith. He speaks as a scientist, and his intentions are of the best. But because he advances theological propositions in the name of "abstract scientific consciousness", steeped as he is in false notions of modern science and misled by his belief in an allegedly scientific philosophy, his words lack palpable conviction. Theological propositions, just like philosophical ones, lose all meaning when they hide behind science, i.e. when the pneuma does not inform them. It is for just this reason that theology grounds its comprehension in the Holy Ghost. No one can, of course, be sure whether the Spirit bloweth or bloweth not at a given time and place; but he to whom the Spirit speaks, however faintly, must say when he was moved by it, and when he was not. He should also be able to describe the silence of the Spirit. When the mythical contents are genuinely appropriated, the speaker communicates his conviction out of the faith in whose name he speaks; he is not then troubled by the inherent implausibility of the myth in its literal aspect. Now, Bultmann, we feel, assumes scientific responsibility for his statements, a responsibility which is fully adequate in historical investigation, but which is insufficient when theological questions are at stake. The true man of faith speaks out of the Encompassing, in which the objectivity of what is said and the subjectivity of the speaker are not separated. But when the subjective aspect is neglected in favour of the mere objectivity of the content of faith or of the objectified subjectivity of existentialist thinking, the genuine theological or philosophical commitment—a commitment which is impossible in science—is lost; serious commitment is also lost when the objective aspect is sacrificed in favour of an arbitrary or fanatic subjectivity. Bultmann seems to mistake exegesis for comprehension of faith. It is as though he had thrown overboard the broad range of possibilities, the tensions and decisions, which are inseparable from genuine comprehension.

3. *The Forces Behind the Discussion: Transformation and Appropriation of Biblical Religion*

To sum up: The transcendental analyses that branch out into the methodology of comprehension and exegesis are ambivalent in character. On the one hand, they open up and divide the areas of our knowledge, of our consciousness of reality, of our self-understanding. They are critical, i.e. they guard against confusion. By going back to the original sources, they enable us to preserve meaningful contents that have falsely been declared invalid. They strive to be critically neutral, not to prejudge anything regarding the contents of myth. They clarify the ground on which meanings expressible in words can confront each other. They keep open the possibilities for awareness of the real.

On the other hand, such discussions always serve as a curtain behind which something else takes place, something that really matters: in our case, the issue is the appropriation of the Biblical faith and its transformation into a faith effective to-day. When we step behind the curtain, the questions at once take on another complexion. What so far has been touched upon casually, now becomes the theme.

A genuine transformation of living religion cannot be effected by deliberate planning. Such a transformation must be actually under way before one can speak in its name. The critique of theology will then raise the crucial question—a question that cannot be expressed in scientific terms—namely, whether this transformation has any meaning for contemporary believers, and what this meaning may be.

Theologians sometimes dodge the existential claim by speaking about it, by acquiring an intellectual knowledge of faith, and by working for the preservation of the Church: of course, the tendency to self-perpetuation is inherent in every human institution. Theology may also serve an entirely different purpose—that of ingeniously remoulding a religion which is no longer believed, but is still desired, into a form acceptable to "the cultured despisers", while passing over in silence the vital issues. Such a theology may be motivated by social considerations and by whatever still remains of the traditional beliefs.

How do we relate Bultmann to such ideas? Once again, we must first define the horizon within which an answer is possible. We shall discuss three points. First, the minister in his congregation; second, the struggle between liberalism and orthodoxy at the level of faith; third, the unification of theology and philosophy, both as aspiration and as threat.

The Ministry

Biblical faith is not acquired by study, but by the practice of religion. The language of faith is not acquired by translating the myths into supposedly non-mythological terms, but by transforming the content of the myth itself, by giving it meanings cogent in our own time.

Bultmann seems to solve this problem by criticism and the elimination of the scientifically untenable, as though the mere negative effect of such a purge sufficed to bring about a rebirth, as though mythical language should be discarded as such. Because Bultmann fails to recognize that the mythical language conveys an untranslatable truth, his thinking does not strike us as inspiring. In my opinion, it is poor, and even stultifying. The element of truth in the myth, which persists throughout its transformations, cannot be separated from its historical garb, once the latter has been stripped away. Exegesis, let alone existentialist interpretation, cannot supply anyone with a "knowledge" of the Biblical faith.

Generally speaking, the task of acquiring faith is only secondarily a question of theological scholarship; primarily it is a matter of the minister's own theology in his daily practice, as he comes to grip with specific human situations and proves his worth. Nor is it a task for philosophy, even though philosophy may formally illuminate the approaches to the transcendent, may clarify the transcendent at the existential level, and may help to decipher the cipher language of the transcendent.

The practical minister (and to-day the cure of souls is widely practised—in a highly questionable manner—outside the churches, in the fields of psychotherapy, anthroposophy, Christian Science, etc.) is confronted with an extraordinary task. He boldly sets out to understand the language of transcendence (which he conceives as the language of God) and to speak it himself in his congregation, commenting on men and events, human aspirations and failures. Only a man who is himself permeated with such language has the right to use it. It is authentic when spoken by a man who actually participates; it is inauthentic in a man who merely thinks it, or, worse yet, merely uses the words. Where it is authentic, and hence efficacious—as at the deathbed, at weddings, burials, in times of adversity—it serves its purpose. At such times it gives us a sense of our own finiteness, helps us to arrive at certainty. The minister who thus proves himself can do things unattainable by philosophizing: he can perform the communal rites and administer the sacraments, and celebrate the holy feasts in holiness.

The priest who performs the sacred rites, the pastor who preaches the revelation, the theologian who knows the secrets of divinity, together constitute a primal human phenomenon, which, under a variety of names, is always manifesting itself anew. When we realize the tremendous responsibilities implied in such a calling, we are filled with admiration and concern. This is indeed a bold venture, to seek salvation through one's own life and in one's own commitment, not merely for the self, but for all. The minister's action is not confined to sympathy and aid; it also commands belief through his personality. Even when he struggles unremittingly, even though he has no direct knowledge of salvation, he stands already in the truth. In him the mythical language acquires efficacy. He makes the mythical world his own, and gives it present meaning, not with the help of the theories of philosophers and theologians, but by the genuineness and the depth of his own experience of faith.

The implications of all this will perhaps be clearer if we recall what may bar the way to the religious vocation. This calling is impossible for all who are susceptible of disappointment in the majority, of disillusionment with the human community, its lack of understanding or honesty. A man for whom faith has become absolute inwardness, to whom all that is temporal has become unimportant, who regards all material objects of worship as external and hence to be repudiated—such a man cannot be a priest or a pastor. The religious calling is incompatible with a view that radically negates the world as total evil, with the belief that the world is at an end, is lost, that there remains only contemplation in despair. Men like Sebastian Franck or Kierkegaard, who possessed such characteristics, attempted in vain to be or to become ministers.

There is perhaps a certain analogy between the callings of the minister and the physician. In both cases, the practical aspect of the work takes precedence over theoretical knowledge, which is only an auxiliary. The future of the physician's art is not determined in the laboratories devoted to medical research, nor is the future of the Biblical faith decided by academic theology.

Intellectual refinements have little bearing on practical achievements in these fields. Kierkegaard's conception of the Christian faith as absurd is admirably consistent and seductive. If this conception were true, it would, as it seems to me, spell the end of the Biblical religion. Without comparing it to Bultmann's more anodyne conception, we may observe that Bultmann's radical purge of religion in favour of a redemptive process implies belief in another absurdity, which, however, avoids Kierkegaard's consequences. In each case, a doctrine intended to counteract a false rationalism unwittingly provides the unbeliever with a means to persevere in his faith with good conscience, at the price of violence to his reason.

To-day the crucial practical elements of the physician's art and of Biblical religion are passed over in silence, while medical research and theological speculations are loudly publicized. Thus, a kind of acoustic illusion is produced, which misleads as to the true state of affairs.

The analogy between modern man's attitude to the pastor and to the physician may be illustrated by Bultmann's statement that "it is impossible . . . to avail ourselves of modern medical and surgical discoveries, and at the same time believe in the New Testament world of miracles and spirits". The fact is, we can do this very well. There is worse: modern superstitious belief in medicine is frequently just as absurd as the literal belief in spirits and miracles. And physicians infected by the psychoanalytic religion or by similar contemporary movements descend into demonology, although they express themselves in a somewhat different language.

Bultmann wastes his critical energies on denouncing relatively insignificant dangers. But against the real dangers that threaten us to-day, against the deceptive hopes and expectations derived from fear and conceived in helplessness and confusion, against the facile expedients resorted to by medicine, politics, and theology with uniformly ruinous effects, Bultmann provides no remedy. He does not take part in the struggle against them. He confines himself to theoretical discussion, which combines shallow enlightenment with religious orthodoxy, a discussion which, for all its differences, is essentially carried on in the spirit of the rationalistic theology that Lessing once repudiated in favour of either genuine orthodoxy or genuine liberality. We shall discuss this point at greater length.

Orthodoxy and Liberality

What is actually hidden in the debate on demythologizing is the struggle of orthodoxy against liberalism. Where does Bultmann stand in this struggle? Before answering this question, we must agree on the meanings of the terms "orthodoxy" and "liberality".

The Liberal Faith. Liberality is not based on abstract, intellectual understanding or on unhistorical criticism. The liberal thinker knows that philosophical justifications of religion, as well as theological speculations, serve no purpose if the main thing is lacking, namely, faith. And what matters is not the verbal expression of religious ideas, not creeds, but men living in a community of faith. This community is rooted in a historical tradition whose authority is respected, but is nevertheless subject to change.

In other words: Liberality recognizes the validity of both the objective and the subjective aspect of faith, and regards the two aspects as inseparable. Liberal faith is characterized by its conception of the objective aspect. The features of physical presence and knowledge are pushed into the background without being completely eliminated. The language of liberalism is less positive than that of orthodoxy. Liberality furthers faith, not by credos, but in the actual conduct of life. It gives up all superstition, i.e. all absolutization of the object. It preserves, within knowledge, an area of non-knowledge, which comprises the symbols of transcendence. It recognizes the physical aspects of faith as such symbols, not as actual presences of transcendence in the world.

The liberal faith is self-sustained, drawing its strength directly from transcendence, seeking no guarantee in the sensory world or in tradition, though the tradition awakens it and makes it capable of testing the traditional truths. The liberal faith needs no external props, not even a redemptive history conceived as an objective absolute event, the prerequisite of all faith.

In liberality everything is centred on the responsibility of man thrown back upon himself. It is through freedom, and only through freedom, that he experiences how he is given to himself by transcendence in freedom—not by freedom.

Orthodox and Liberal Attitudes Towards the Incomprehensible. We have previously referred to the limits of comprehension. Everywhere we run headlong into the incomprehensible. We encounter it as a wall, as silent nature which does not answer our questions, either when we master it or when it resists our efforts or even destroys us. We also encounter the incomprehensible in men who cannot be moved, who speak but do not answer, and in our own selves, where it often makes us act against our will, and pretends to be ourselves.

Our comprehension is a movement in an area that is surrounded by the incomprehensible on all sides—a movement which on the one hand confronts the incomprehensible pure and simple and recognizes it ever more clearly as the dark ground of the natural process governed by laws. On the other hand, this movement experiences the incomprehensible as something that can be clarified endlessly, as something that is not fundamentally and absolutely incomprehensible, but rather striving to be comprehended.

Orthodoxy and liberality are characterized by their attitude towards this movement of progressing comprehension. Where the progress is arrested, we have orthodoxy; where it goes on, we have liberality. Everything ready-made, every kind of self-sufficient dogmatic knowledge is illiberality. Illiberality can be discovered in every man at the point where he no longer listens or gives answers, or where he answers inadequately; we discover this temptation in ourselves. To know this, to try to detect illiberality in ourselves, to recognize that our opponents help us in this self-testing and to welcome them for that reason, are fundamental traits of the liberal attitude.

Liberality and Enlightenment. Liberality is in alliance with enlightenment, but the genuine kind of enlightenment—the irresistible, responsible movement of reason, which is never completed. Sham enlightenment, on the other hand, is rational knowledge taken as complete.

The sham kind of enlightenment exists in all historical periods. It is, in effect, a form of unfaith which superstitiously believes itself to be firmly grounded in rationality. It is seduced by cogent insights, which are in contradiction to falsely understood, or even perverted, statements of religious faith. It has a certain power in so far as it is based on such insights.

This is why theologians attempt repeatedly to defend faith against enlightenment by accepting the unavoidable insights with which enlightenment threatens to destroy faith. They hope to defeat the adversary by seizing his own weapons. In this battle, Bultmann applies a familiar strategy: he appropriates a maximum of enlightenment, only in order to assert faith all the more resolutely. But it seems to me that he appropriates an enlightenment that is not genuine, and a scientific philosophy that is not scientific—in the end to assert an absurd dogma and cling to it at all costs, with a determination that smacks of violence. As a result, we are once again confronted with the defects that characterize all such enterprises: they fail to satisfy the unbeliever, and implant doubts in the believer. From the liberal point of view, Bultmann offers a deceptive solution, in order to bolster orthodoxy with the help of the method of existentialist interpretation.

Liberality, which is inspired by genuine enlightenment, by the unending movement of reason, emancipates itself from all scientific superstition, from all allegedly scientific philosophy, as well as from orthodoxy. It does not try to defend religion. Lessing, the prototype of the liberal, and one of liberality's greatest manifestations, turned against the violent kind of orthodoxy, against the enlightened rationalistic theology that wanted to defend or conserve religion by reinterpreting its teachings, as well as against the destructive ideas of Reimarus, so complacent in his rationalism. Lessing stood aloof from such as these, never imagining that he saw the whole truth. With his endless critical energy he remained open to the contents of the Bible. He condemned half-truths, obscurity, self-delusion. Therefore, without being an orthodox believer himself, he favoured straightforward, devout orthodoxy in its naïve form (without, however, approving the dishonest intolerance of a Pastor Götze). He respected Reimarus' arguments as important for getting at the truth, but he recognized their limits and where he went beyond them. Least of all did he favour the rationalism of the theologians, who, inconsistent and irresolute, wanted to conserve religion, but, for all their good intentions, became untruthful. In Bultmann I find nothing of a Lessing, a Kant, a Goethe, none of the liberal spirit, but something of their opponents. Occasionally he seems to be giving a new form to the old theological rationalism; at other times, to be re-founding orthodoxy.

Ambiguity of the Terms, Enlightenment, Liberality, Conservatism. Enlightenment, liberality, conservatism are ambiguous terms. They are confusing unless one distinguishes between enlightenment as progressive emancipation from one's self-caused immaturity (Kant), and enlightenment as know-it-allness (sham enlightenment); between liberality as limitless openness to reason—i.e. communication for the purpose of furthering all genuine insights, however opposed to each other—and liberalism as the intolerant absolutizing of an allegedly definitive intellectual knowledge of the freedom and equality of all men, which would in effect justify all arbitrary impulses; and between conservatism as reverence for tradition and resistance to wanton destruction of the past, and conservatism as hostility to progress, as an attempt to freeze human institutions and ideas.

Genuine enlightenment, liberality, and conservatism form a harmonious whole, and are opposed to the powers of sham rationalism, false liberalism, and reaction, which, though often in conflict with one another, are related in spirit.

The Idea of Revelation. Liberal faith is distinguished from orthodoxy by its attitude towards the idea of revelation. The belief that God manifests himself at a given place and time, that he has revealed himself directly at one place and time and only there and then, makes God appear as a fixed thing, an object in the world. This objective entity is supposed not only to be revered on the basis of tradition, but also to possess the absoluteness of godhead. In the canonical writings, in the creed and in the system of dogmas, in the sacrament of Holy Orders, in the Church as *corpus mysticum Christi*, and in other forms, the revelation and the grace it bestows are conceived as physically present.

Liberal faith rejects this conception of revelation. It recognizes that the revelation of truth is a mystery, a series of sudden illuminations in the history of the mind; it recognizes that we are ignorant of how men arrived at this revelation, and that some of its elements have not yet been comprehended. The fact that we use the same term, "revelation", to denote both an absolute and unique divine intervention and this process of the gradual revelation of truth, must not cause us to overlook the radical difference between the two.

The liberal faith is criticized by orthodoxy on the ground that it makes man the master, who by his own thought determines what God can and should do, and what God can say. On this basis liberality is identified with disbelief, and it is argued that instead of doing all the talking, man should let God speak to him. According to the Bible, man is capable of knowledge only in so far as he is known by God. Hence, the great alternative is ultimately formulated in these terms: Is man with his reason master and judge of everything that is, can be, and should be, or must he listen to God? (Fries, in *Tübinger Theologische Quartalsschrift*, 1952, p. 287.) Orthodoxy demands profession of faith in revelation—for instance in "the gospel of Crucifixion and Resurrection"—and asserts that what is at stake in our attitude towards this gospel is "the decision between faith and unfaith, and in this decision, the issue is between eternal life and eternal death" (*Denkschrift der Tübinger Fakultät*, p. 34). The reply to this, from the standpoint of liberal faith is:

(*a*) How do we recognize revelation? What criterion of truth is given for the direct revelation of God? The point at issue here is that, according to orthodoxy, the revelation is its own criterion. But in actual fact, whatever is said and done in the name of revelation, is said and done in worldly form, in worldly language, in human acts and human perceptions.

Those who believe in a revealed faith argue that its divine

origin guarantees the revelation. Revelation, they maintain, is distinguished from all myth by the exclusiveness, uniqueness, and absoluteness of its demand for faith. This assertion, however, does not change the fact that revelation has all the features of myth. Liberal faith does not deny that God can act as absolute transcendence, but it insists that all it can perceive is the actions, the sayings, and the experiences of human beings.

(*b*) What is crucial is that God is hidden. Whatever is posited as an absolute in the world, as God's word or God's act, is in each case a human act or human word that demands that we recognize it as God's. However, the idea of the hidden God can be interpreted mythically in rational terms, as Kant did. According to Kant, God manifests his eternal wisdom by remaining hidden. For if God himself in all his majesty appeared before us or spoke to us, he says, we would be reduced to the status of marionettes, unable to move save when our strings were pulled. But God willed that we should find our way to him by means of our freedom; and this way leads to him, because our self-responsible reason in the world perceives his ambiguous hints, and arrives at him through the reality of our moral life.

Liberal faith refuses to arrest its movement in time by a revelation frozen in its definitiveness. It strives to keep itself open, ready to recognize the language of the godhead in everything that is real. It perceives the hidden God's demand upon us, a demand inherent in the fact that he is hidden. This faith, therefore, forbids absolute obedience to the words of a sacred text or to the authority of an ecclesiastical official, because (according to it) every man can be in direct relation to the godhead in his freedom and reason, which constitute a higher authority. And this higher authority may require that every revered transition be tested anew and transformed.

Speaking in mythical terms, we may say: liberal faith opposes the assertion of a direct revelation, not out of a will to empty freedom, but out of its idea of God as actualized in mankind's relations with the hidden, all-guiding transcendence.

(*c*) The orthodox objection against liberality—that it fails to recognize the objective character of God's actions and that it invests the human subject with supreme authority—is misleading.

The attempt to play objectivity against the subject, like the inverse attempt to play subjectivity against objectivity, is based on failure to recognize the fundamental structure of our empirical existence and consciousness. There can be no object without a subject, and no subject without an object; the Encompassing in which we exist and which we are, is clarified through the interaction between the two; it eludes us if we confine ourselves either to subject without object, or to object without subject. Empirical existence implies an environment, abstract consciousness implies objectivity, and *Existenz* implies transcendence.

Transcendence, God, the All-Encompassing never become clear to us as they are apart from our subjectivity. The reality of transcendence is present for us objectively only in the language of the code or cipher, not as it is in itself. Transcendence is reality only for *Existenz*. Both transcendence and *Existenz* manifest themselves in empirical existence and in consciousness, but only as languages. God's countenance, God's action, God's word—all these are only code symbols by means of which a subject with potential *Existenz* conceives, perceives, and questions that which is manifested to it as a reality.

It is not true that the liberal believer presumes to decide what is and what is not possible for God. But as a philosopher he is aware that objective knowledge is subject to conditions rooted in the structure of Being as it is given to us.

As we have said, the Encompassing is clarified within the split between subject and object. This does not mean, however, that we determine that which our thinking discloses as the Other. We are moved by the Other, and we conceive it as independent of us, as something that is even without us. At the same time, we become aware of the subjective conditions governing our awareness of everything objective. Reality is disclosed to us only in so far as we are empirically existent, as knowable only in so far as we are abstract consciousness; and as transcendence only in so far as we are potential *Existenz*. The unfolding of subjectivity implies the coming into view of a pertinent objectivity. The one does not produce the other, but the object appears only to the subject, and the subject can realize itself only through the object.

From the standpoint of liberal philosophy, the thesis that the revelation of God is an event taking place in the world is based on a confusion. For it is a fallacy to say that transcendence is the object of *Existenz* conceived as subject, and that the one is related to the other as the known is related to knowledge in the world. The transcendence that does not speak ambiguously in the language of code but is there unambiguously in the revelation, is, after all, merely the Bible, the Church, merely an assertion by men who claim to have seen God, to have heard his voice, to have witnessed his acts. They demand belief in their assertions, and call this belief faith. Thus, a wordly authority, which in every instance has a human and historical foundation, lays claim to have its source in God.

Now, we may ask: Does the revelation as an objective reality come first, and does faith follow from the perception of its reality? Or is faith in the revelation at one with, and inseparable from, the revelation itself, which produces the faith? As in all our awareness, here the subject is bound to the object, and the object to the subject. Is revelation that which always takes place when there is faith, when God is believed in? Have such revelations occurred whenever they have been asserted in history, not only in the West (Judaism, the various Christian denominations, Islam), but also in Asia?

Or do we go counter to the meaning of revelation when we assert that it is a general phenomenon, of which the revelations of Jesus Christ or of Moses are only special cases? Are the other cases—of the eternal Vedas to the Rishis, or of the canonical books to the Chinese—not cases of revelation? Can the claim of a revelation to uniqueness be justified, or is it inherently unjustified?

Or, are we to conceive of revelation so broadly that every man in his freedom has the possibility of experiencing himself as being given and guided by transcendence, despite the ambiguity of all the worldly signs?

Such questions can be answered when we keep in mind that

the subject and the object are inseparable in the Encompassing, which is clarified by their division. Hence, the answers logically take the form of a circle. We say either that revelation is the process of becoming revealed to the subject, which conceives revelation in itself as something objective; or, that reason in the movement of reason subjects its revelation to the test of rationality. We have here the circle of subject and object which, in various ways, condition, justify, and support each other. Inescapably, the circle is the fundamental form of all our awareness. The discovery that an idea implies a circle does not necessarily prove the falsity of this idea. What matters, rather, is to ascertain the depth or shallowness, the adequacy or inadequacy of a given circle, the consequences of thinking or living in a given circle. We do not emerge from such circles, even when we surmount each separate circle. Nor can we, from a purely logical point of view, prefer one of the circles to another. For instance, materialism, too, implies a circular reasoning: the world is a product of our brain; the brain is a product of the world; and through the brain the world perceives itself in this product. The circle of reason in liberal faith, and the circle of the revealed faith in orthodoxy, are in conflict not because either has a right to reject the other on the ground that it involves a circular reasoning, but only on the basis of the content and consequences of each.

(*d*) Liberality recognizes the historical sources of our spiritual life, whatever they may be. For instance, we Westerners recognize the importance of the Bible. But liberality repudiates the idea of an exclusive truth formulated in a credo. It recognizes that the way to God is possible also without Christ, and that Asians can find it without the Bible.

Liberality understands the importance of history and its language for faith. The main thing for liberality is to see to it that faith is not weakened by the denial that historical objectification is absolutely and universally valid, i.e. by the denial that faith can find objective guarantees in the world. Philosophical reflection (e.g. Kant's transcendental philosophy and its successors) is a necessity for liberal faith, and can be helpful, not because it can provide us with contents of faith, but because it opens our minds to faith by clearing the ground and enabling us to become aware of the truth inherent in faith, as contrasted with unfaith and with orthodoxy.

Every tradition is valid as a possible language, and becomes a true language not abstractly, but in given historical situations for *Existenz*, which discovers itself in them. The historical struggle at the existential level takes place in the medium of the mythical. Rational and mythical modes of awareness are only the foreground of a never-ending process of existential clarification and comprehension.

(*e*) While liberality repudiates an objective redemptive history conceived as an absolute event and as a prerequisite of salvation for all men, it accepts this history as a myth. As in the case of other myths, the validity of this one must be tested existentially, and judged on the basis of the strength that emanates from its language, the truth that arises from it in the reality of life. Liberality recognizes faith in revelation, including belief in the truth of the redemptive history as a possible truth valid for him who believes it—in so far as the believer does not, by his deeds or his words, draw consequences destructive to the freedom of men who find themselves directly before God, nor attempt to coerce others by violent means.

Considering the kind of theology that is still current to-day, Buri displayed great courage in drawing the ultimate consequences from Bultmann's demythologizing. Buri admits candidly that the redemptive history is no more than a myth. But he does not want to demythologize in order to destroy. While recognizing that the language of religion is mythical through and through, Buri asserts its validity as a language, and tries with its help to gain awareness of our beliefs, moral duties, hopes, and goals. Now it is no longer the creed that guides us, but moral earnestness and serious commitment undertaken in uncertainty, without outside guarantees. Clarification of transcendence is based upon the concrete situation.

(*f*) The conflict between the claims of orthodoxy and the liberal reaction they provoked was extraordinarily passionate because of the importance of the issue—the decision concerning our eternal salvation. We can still feel faint echoes of this passion to-day.

For almost two thousand years orthodoxy has threatened us with eternal death, condemning our self-deification, our pride, our presumption in setting man, i.e. ourselves, above God. These judgements fill us with amazement, as do the uncritical, curious assertions that condemn the non-believer to eternal torments and promise the believer eternal bliss.

Is God absent from our lives? Is our trust that God comes to our aid in a manner that is for us incomprehensible, unpredictable, and incalculable—that when we act with goodwill he can be with us in the terrors of destruction and death—a mad delusion? Bultmann says that the idea of God without Christ is to be described as madness "from the point of view of the Christian faith".

Are we not justified in thinking that God would not damn us for our honest efforts even if orthodoxy were right, and even though these efforts continually fail and deceive us? Did not God side with Job against the orthodox theologians?

He who lives by human reason must not, in struggling against others, justify himself by God, but only by worldly arguments. For God is my adversary's God as well as my own. But what if orthodox fanatics deny us the right to serve God, to strive to live in obedience to God, denouncing our idea of God as a delusion? Against intolerance only intolerance is effective, but fortunately this is no longer a matter of life and death. Heretics are no longer burned at the stake in the name of the revelation (although we should never forget that the extermination of heretics is consistent with such beliefs); to-day they are destroyed in the name of authorities other than God. Fortunately, since the anathemas the orthodox theologians still pass are inconsequential, we may refrain from answering them on this point.

Is Bultmann Liberal or Orthodox? In the light of the foregoing observations, we may attempt to answer the question, Where does Bultmann stand?

However reliable and many-sided Bultmann may be as a historian, as a theologian he leads us astray. He seems to be saying something but in the end does not; he seems to be saving the faith, but he does not save it. When—and this is crucial—he asserts a frozen orthodoxy of redemption, he undermines it at the same time by the high-handedness of his assertion. His rehashing of the old problems of enlightenment, ostensibly intended to salvage an essential minimum of faith, must delight secret unbelievers among the theologians, because he dispenses them from believing a great number of things; at the same time, he must displease the orthodox believers, because he deprives them of so many of their best arguments.

He has not discovered a new form for the language of faith, although he thinks that his existentialist interpretation provides a new method for the true acquisition of faith. This idea is not only untenable philosophically, in my opinion, but I should also imagine it to be of little practical value to the pastor.

The philosopher cannot help being taken aback when he sees what this salvaged minimum of faith turns out to be—the residue of faith which, according to Bultmann, is not mythical, and is the essential element of religion: namely, justification by faith alone, faith in the redemptive history. For a philosopher this is the most alienating, the most outlandish of beliefs—this Lutheran dogma with its terrible consequences scarcely seems any longer even denotative existentially. Bultmann himself sums up and discloses the meaning of his enterprise in the statement that "Radical demythologizing is a parallel to the Pauline-Lutheran doctrine of justification by faith alone apart from the works of law." It seems to me that Bultmann's position is in effect altogether orthodox and illiberal, despite his liberality as a man and a historian.

Bultmann's illiberality may be characterized as follows:

A philosophy that conceives empirical existence as hopeless (and Heidegger's *Sein und Zeit* can be interpreted as such a philosophy) finds it natural complement in a doctrine that promises salvation through faith in the redemptive history. The sinner, who realizes the full extent of his sinfulness only through grace, sees this grace as an objective event which can save him if he believes in it.

But such an analysis of empirical existence is not universally valid. It does not reflect a general human truth, though some, perhaps many, but certainly not all, men recognize themselves in it. The reality of man is not a radical sinfulness which is overcome only by an alleged divine intervention that took place in a foreign country a long time ago.

We find in the Biblical faith itself an entirely different conception of man—namely the conception of man's God-created inborn nobility, *nobilitas ingenita*, as the Pelagians called it. Man, always in danger, is humble in the knowledge that he is not self-created, and that in fulfilling the task assigned to him he must be given to himself in order not to lose himself. According to this conception, man is determined by God, the source of everything man can be, but only in the direct relation of his own freedom to the godhead, and without the help of an external agency. Thus man is confident that he can fulfil the will of the hidden God by an effort entirely subjected to his own responsibility, and that he will be helped by God in an incomprehensible and unpredictable way. This God-given *nobilitas ingenita* is called in Biblical thinking "the Christ in me", and is not a possession, is not ours once and for all, but must be continually conquered, and can be lost. This conception of man, of his freedom, and of his task, is that of liberality.

The Unification of Theology and Philosophy

The natural tendency of liberality—a tendency for which it is criticized, regarded with concern, or viewed with satisfaction—seems to be in the direction of a meeting of philosophy and theology; these might ultimately be united, as they were in Plato, in the Stoics, in Origen, in St Augustine, and in Nicholas of Cusa. Should this come to pass, we must keep in mind an important distinction: theology and philosophy may become one, but not religion and philosophy. In religion there flows a stream of communal life that lies beyond the reach of philosophy—a living relationship to shrines, to sacred actions, objects, and books, to rites and prayers, to the office of the priest, in short to the physical presence of symbols. Here philosophy ends and is confronted with something that is not philosophy.

Philosophy and all great philosophers stand outside this sacred world. A philosophy that could cross this gulf would not arrive at one particular religion, but at a religion embracing all religions (thus Proclus called himself the hierophant of the whole world): from the religious point of view, a contradiction in terms. It would be the abolition of the historicity of religion, of its historical earnestness. What has been called "philosophical religion" would be a religion without any of the features of a living religion, it would be what was left after all the rituals, the prayers, the religious communities, and the Scriptures had been subtracted. Schelling's philosophy of mythology and the revelation, which aims at such a philosophical religion, ends, it is true, in Christ, and even seems the narrower thereby. But Schelling's positive philosophy of the historicity of the real implies elimination of the Christian idea.

Philosophy should not offer its services to those who seek to formulate a philosophical alternative to religion; rather it should warn against itself.

When theology becomes philosophical to such a point that it loses touch with the specific elements of religion, the philosopher may very well be alarmed. It is as though his indispensable adversary, in struggling against whom he clarifies and rekindles his own impulses, were no longer there. He wonders what form the old adversary, now hidden, has assumed. It is as though he could not do without his adversary, whom he had actually never wanted to destroy, but only to induce to speak with the utmost frankness.

The philosopher is alarmed about the fate of the majority because he is aware of the impotence of philosophizing. A theology that has become identical with philosophy might bog down in the same impotence. Now, the philosopher's right to address himself to individuals is denied to theology, which must address itself to every member of the Church. The question is whether the very thing in which philosophy must fail is not indispensable to the majority of us—namely, religion as worship, as community, as tangible and authoritative physical presence. The philosopher may fear lest the things that philosophy cannot do, and that it legitimately expects religion to do—in as much as not everyone remains content with philosophical insight—may now not be done at all.

Furthermore a unification of theology and philosophy may adversely affect the fate of the Biblical teachings. The Biblical impulses which for us are irreplaceable may be watered down, as a prelude to their complete disappearance, instead of being remoulded and renewed.

Finally, the philosopher to-day knows that men who have become helpless through their reliance upon mere understanding, and have not attained to philosophy, fall prey to a tyranny which is all the more terrible because it recognizes no transcendence. Then they once again obey unconditionally, but without the Biblical faith; to us Westerners such a life is completely meaningless.

However, we must keep in mind that the unification of philosophy and theology does not necessarily involve religion. Even if theologians and philosophers were in agreement as to the method of clarifying the Encompassing, there would be no uniformity in religious practice. And it is in the realm of practical religion, in the performance of the rites, in preaching, in interpreting the mythical language, that the minister puts his calling to the test.

Bultmann's Spiritual Personality

Anyone, whether theologian or philosopher, who makes claims which in effect go beyond science, even if they falsely assume a scientific form, must put up with being scrutinized personally. For here issues and personalities are inseparable, casting light on each other.

The discussion about demythologizing was touched off by Bultmann, perhaps to his own surprise. His original paper on the subject, "New Testament and Mythology," is the second essay in the book *Revelation and Redemptive History*, published in 1941. It is by no means presented there as being of special importance. Possibly something had been smouldering in the world of theology, and Bultmann's essay merely fanned the flames. Nevertheless the ensuing debate has been stamped by Bultmann's personality to such an extent that we cannot help becoming interested in him.

Bultmann is a historian whose investigations provide us with uncommonly reliable information. He has the rare honesty of acknowledging uncomfortable or awkward facts, as when he wrote the sentence: "Jesus was mistaken." I confess that as a layman I have learned more from him and from Dibelius than from any other contemporary theologian. Bultmann presents his historical studies in a wonderfully clear style, and he holds his reader's interest.

But when Bultmann passes to "existentialist interpretation", as he repeatedly does, he becomes boring as a historian, there is no more to learn from him. At the same time he seems to fail in his objective, or he achieves it only rudimentarily. I don't know whether his views can stir a pastor. At all events they do not stir a man who does not share them out of his own faith. In his existentialist interpretation Bultmann remains learned and argumentative in a scientific fashion. He shrouds the splendours of the Bible with an enveloping layer of dry, objective language. His style is neither ponderous nor light, but conveys an atmosphere of sullen rigidity.

But to note a certain discrepancy between the historian and the theologian is not to play one against the other. Because he is a great scholar we must not expect him to be a good theologian. If—perhaps—he is a bad theologian, one who makes promises that he does not keep, this does not put in question his scientific historical work.

Yet, I suspect that if Bultmann were praised for his honesty, he would take such praise for granted as a natural tribute; he would not be taken aback, he would not reply, for instance: "No man can really succeed in being honest. Though honesty is a human requirement, it is a tremendous one; I am afraid I do not come up to it." Now, there is no doubt that Bultmann is always guided by his honesty when he works scientifically, but it seems to me that his honesty, without his realizing it, is severely strained when he speaks of religion not as a historian but as a theologian. Yet who can be sure in such a matter! Here everyone confronts the mystery of the other, whom he never sees wholly. One can only voice the aspect that was disclosed to one, and not in judgement, but only as a question.

What does Bultmann represent? He is not a liberal and not an orthodox authoritarian. It is quite possible that a naïve piety rooted in childhood memories would not be shaken by his views, for all that they are disintegrating—in my opinion, they are a betrayal of both theology and philosophy. He is influenced by a modern, supposedly enlightened world-view; he speaks as though he could have scientific knowledge of the matters he discusses. so that we are not aware of an appeal to faith and commitment. If this jumble of science and theology represents anything, it is, in the last analysis, orthodoxy. It seems to me a most peculiar mixture of false enlightenment and high-handed orthodoxy.

Combined with his self-assurance regarding scientific method, this no doubt accounts for his unshakable dignity. This would also account for the ease with which he broke off communication with an orthodox adversary, whose views he did not care to discuss at length: "I think that I can settle my dispute with him peacefully, provided each of us makes one concession to the other: I will concede that I do not understand a thing about *Realtheologie*, and he, that he does not understand a thing about demythologizing." It is doubtless physically impossible to answer everyone who expresses himself privately or publicly in such a large debate. It is also a fact that dialogue often seems pointless. But the will to communicate, which has its roots in Biblical thinking, must not break down so readily. Granted, this will must keep silent all too often; but when such silence is combined with a coldness that denounces a radical inability to comprehend in a tone of biting irony, it seems to me indicative of a shut-in obstinacy. We often hear remarks, uttered in the most casual tone, like: "I cannot understand this" or "We shall never understand each other." This casualness is also Bultmann's. To me it seems the hallmark of every orthodoxy, and not only the Christian one.

It would seem that in venturing afield, the great scholar has disappointed both the philosopher whom he leaves without a philosophy, and the minister to whom he actually shows no path at all. For the views Bultmann advances can scarcely be comprehensible to the pastor and his flock. Do they help those who candidly seek self-clarification in a spiritual experience capable of bearing the whole burden of life?

RUDOLF BULTMANN

THE CASE FOR DEMYTHOLOGIZING: A REPLY

I WAS at first pleased, indeed, I felt honoured when Karl Jaspers expressed himself on the issue of demythologizing. But after reading and re-reading his remarks,[1] I found it difficult to reply to them. I feel ever more strongly that they have little in common with the spirit of genuine communication. Their style is not that of a Socratic-Platonic dialogue, but rather of an *ex cathedra* pronouncement.

Jaspers has made it impossible for me to make any answer to a number of things. For were I to defend myself against the criticisms that I am "untouched by the least breath of Kantian or Platonic thinking", that my conception of philosophy is "that of nineteenth-century academicians or Hellenistic doxographers", or that I confuse "genuine enlightenment" with "sham enlightenment", I should seem a ridiculous figure. Nor can I reply to his doubts about how useful my theological work may be to the pastor. As for his characterization of my personality, no one can expect me to comment on that. You don't argue about your obituary.

I shall, moreover, refrain from dealing with Jaspers' criticism of my "assumptions", on which, he says, my theses rest "as upon two pillars". It may become clear indirectly, on the basis of what follows, that I neither hold that modern science provides us with a "world view" in Jaspers' meaning of this term, nor do I base my thinking on a philosophical doctrine. Regarding the latter question, I may gratefully refer to the analysis by Kurt Reide-

[1] First published in *Schweizerische Theologische Rundschau*, 1953, No. 3–4, pp. 74–106, and later in *Merkur*.

meister,[1] who has shown that demythologizing involves a hermeneutic problem arising from a concrete situation, and that in this situation, which is not defined by any special method of philosophizing, the distinction between "existential" and "existentialist" is unavoidable. Further, I can refer to Friedrich Gogarten's work *Demythologizing and History*,[2] which makes it clear that we do not necessarily subscribe to Heidegger's philosophical theories when we learn something from his existentialist analysis. The fact is that Heidegger attacks a problem with which theologians have grappled since Ernst Troeltsch, namely, the problem of history, which has become more acute for theology with every advance in historical understanding of the Bible. Trying to clarify the dependence of human existence on history, and by the same token, on historical comprehension, and going beyond the traditional "subject-object schema", theology is willing to learn from Heidegger. "Needless to say, we may learn from others besides Heidegger. If we can learn those things better elsewhere, it is all to the good. But they have to be learned." And it is true, more generally, that "he who reflects critically on the concepts he uses, whether theological or physical, by the same token comes close to philosophy and utilizes its conclusions" [Gogarten]. Whether theology is advanced or not by its recourse to modern philosophy depends not on arbitrary choice or individual preference, but on the historical situation: for both theology and philosophy have begun to realize how questionable is the thinking that has prevailed in science down to the present time.

Would not a genuine discussion of demythologizing have to begin by clearly formulating the problem involved? Does Jaspers see this problem? He takes it for granted that I want to salvage faith in so far as it can be salvaged in the face of scientific insights that cannot be ignored; that I want to give the unbeliever "a means to persevere in his faith with a good conscience". Now, this is most certainly not my intention. The purpose of demythologizing is not to make religion more

[1] Published in *Sammlung*, VIII, 1953, pp. 528–534.

[2] E.T. S.C.M. Press, 1955.

acceptable to modern man by trimming the traditional Biblical texts, but to make clearer to modern man what the Christian faith is. He must be confronted with the issue of decision, be provoked to decision by the fact that the stumbling-block to faith, the *skàndalon*, is peculiarly disturbing to man in general, not only to modern man (modern man being only one species of man). Therefore my attempt to demythologize begins, true enough, by clearing away the false stumbling-blocks created for modern man by the fact that his world-view is determined by science.

Such an attempt does not aim at reassuring modern man by saying to him: "You no longer have to believe this and that." To be sure, it says this among other things, and may thereby relieve his pangs of conscience; but if it does so, it does so not by showing him that the number of things to be believed is smaller than he had thought, but because it shows him that to believe at all is qualitatively different from accepting a certain number of propositions. It is by striving to clarify the meaning of faith that demythologizing leads man to the issue of decision, not by "an intellectual assimilation of existential propositions in the Bible by means of existentialist exegesis", nor by "a new method for the true acquisition of faith" through existentialist interpretation.

It is this—to disclose what the Christian faith is, to disclose the issue of decision—that seems to me the only, the crucial thing that the theologian must accomplish in the face of "the real dangers that threaten us to-day . . . the deceptive hopes and expectations derived from fear and conceived in helplessness and confusion . . . the facile expedients resorted to by medicine, politics, theology, with uniformly ruinous effects". He must clarify the question that God poses to man, such a stumbling-block for the "natural" man, because it entails the sacrifice of all security attainable by his own unaided efforts.

That Jaspers has no clear conception of this stumbling-block is shown, on the one hand, by his obvious belief that it consists in Christian revelation's claim to absoluteness (to which we shall return later), and, on the other hand, by his reduction of Biblical faith to trivial "consciousness of the God-created nobility of man"—he even equates this consciousness of the God-given *nobilitas ingenita* with the Biblical (incidentally, Pauline) "Christ in me"—by his failure to understand the Pauline doctrine of justification by faith alone without the works of law, and by his opinion that the Gospel according to St John: "mythically justifies the earliest Christian anti-Semitism".

The real problem, in other words, is the hermeneutic one, i.e. the problem of interpreting the Bible and the teachings of the Church in such a way that they may become understandable as a summons to man. But Jaspers, it seems to me, despite his lengthy disquisition on comprehension, has not really grasped the hermeneutic problem. Of course, we cannot reproach him for not having personally experienced the responsibility involved in interpreting a Biblical text. But had we not the right to expect that he would make an attempt to understand this task and the responsibility it involves?

He is as convinced as I am that a corpse cannot come back to life or rise from the grave, that there are no demons and no magic causality. But how am I, in my capacity as a pastor, to explain in my sermons and classes texts dealing with the Resurrection of Jesus in the flesh, with demons, or with magic causality? And how am I, in my capacity as a theological scholar, to guide the pastor in his task by my interpretations? How would Jaspers interpret, say, Rom. 5. 12–21 or 6. 1–11, if he had to? When he says that the redemptive history, which actually is related in the New Testament in the form of a myth (for instance, Phil. 2. 6–11), must "be tested existentially and judged on the basis of the strength that emanates from its language, and the truth that arises from it in the reality of life", I can only reply to such a vague statement by the question, "Well, how is this done?"

The magic word with which he dismisses the hermeneutic problem is "the cipher" (occasionally also "symbol"). The mythological statements in the texts, according to him, are "ciphers", and the mythological language is "a cipher language". What is in cipher? Is it "transcendence", is it the transcendent

God? "Myth is the language of reality that is not empirical, but existential."[1]

To define the myth as a cipher of transcendence merely describes the problem of interpretation; it scarcely solves it. All mythologies have this in common (if we set aside the purely etiological myths), that they refer to a reality situated beyond empirical reality, independent of man. But is that reality—and hence human existence—understood in the same way by all mythologies? In Indian, in Greek, and in Biblical mythology? Naturally, Jaspers cannot ignore the richness and diversity of the "ciphers". But is this diversity a matter of indifference, in as much as all myths are merely ciphers of transcendence? When Jaspers says that the revelation of truth is "a series of sudden illuminations in the history of the mind", he seems to look upon the diversity of myths as a purely accidental fact, determined by historical concretion.

Or do I misunderstand him? After all, he also says that myths are opposed to myths, and that it is possible to struggle for what we believe to be the true faith within the terms of mythical thinking. Since Jaspers gives no examples, confining himself to the general remark that for us the Bible is the favourite arena for such spiritual struggle, and that another arena is provided by the Greek epic poems and tragedies, and still another by the sacred books of Asia, I cannot imagine how, in his opinion, this spiritual struggle should be fought. Must we not interpret the various myths with regard to the existential understanding expressed in

[1] Disregarding the question of whether this reality can be expressed only in mythological language, as Jaspers maintains, I should like to ask whether his conception of the myth, in so far as he defines it as a statement in cipher, is so different from my own. When I say that the myth expresses man's knowledge of the ground and limits of his being, is this so different from what Jaspers implies? At all events, I agree with him that the myth is misunderstood when the reality it denotes is conceived of as empirical, and its language as that of "a guaranteed and guaranteeing physical presence". In my opinion such misunderstanding is not accidental; rather it is a characteristic of original myth that in it empirical reality and existential reality are not distinguished. Mythical thinking is just as objectifying as scientific thinking, for instance, when the former represents the transcendence of God in terms of remoteness in space, or when it personifies the power of evil as Satan. This is precisely what makes demythologizing necessary.

them? Is it only in philosophy that there are existential differences, between Jaspers and Heidegger, for instance, not in mythology, too?

In short, Jaspers does not seem to have grasped the hermeneutic problem or to have taken it seriously. His assertion that assimilation of the mythical language of faith must be effected by transforming the content of the myth itself, by giving it meanings cogent in our own time, tell us nothing at all about what such a transformation may actually be, or what is transformed by it; nor does he tell us what is the element of truth that persists throughout the transformations of the myth.

Jaspers also eludes the hermeneutic problem by denying that the task of interpreting the Bible objectively is the scholar's: he assigns it to the minister who "boldly sets out to understand the language of transcendence (which he conceives of as the language of God) and to speak it himself in his congregation". Must not the minister, in order to understand the language of the Bible as the language of transcendence and thereby as the language of God, also understand the Hebrew and Greek languages? And if he does not know these languages, must he not rely on scholars who do know them? Does translation into contemporary German amount to no more than transposing foreign words into German ones? Does not the minister need for this purpose a deeper understanding of the language, of its conceptual pattern, of the thinking that guides it? In other words, is not translation always interpretation as well?

Furthermore, must not scholarly translation be "correct" (in so far as this is attainable)? Can the exegete, who strives to comprehend that which was "primarily comprehended" (to use Jaspers' term) understand the primarily comprehended with its "valuations" of good and evil, true and false, beautiful and ugly before he has correctly understood the text? "Biblical faith is not acquired by study", says Jaspers. It certainly is not—but when have I maintained that it was? Comprehension of religion (surely this must mean believing comprehension), Jaspers also says, has nothing to do with scientific method. It certainly has not—yet religious-comprehending appropriation of the Biblical word is possible only when the Biblical texts are translated into a language understandable to-day. Is such a translation possible without methodical study?

Now, it is true that such methodical study (aiming at "secondary comprehension") is impossible unless a potentiality for primary comprehension is present in the student, i.e. unless he has a primarily comprehending, existential rapport with the subject treated in the text he is to interpret.[1] Therefore, when he wants to show what the text regards as good or evil, true or false, etc., he can do this only if he himself experiences good or evil, true or false, as existential possibilities. This does not prevent him from suspending, i.e. from keeping under question, his own "valuations". Objective interpretation of what is "correct" leads the hearer or reader *indirectly* into the situation of decision. But interpretation itself can only discover and strive to show what is "correct". In so far as it discloses possibilities of existential understanding through indirect appeal to the hearer or reader, it does not deprive him of decision. Naturally, it cannot prevent the hearer or reader from misunderstanding what has been said, when he has failed to perceive the appeal.

What is true of every interpretation applies also to interpretation of the Bible. Here, too, what is "correct" can only be discovered and demonstrated when the interpreter stands in definite relation to the matter in question. But this does not imply the impossible requirement that the interpreter should assume that he has faith; what it does imply is that he must be vitally concerned with the existential question, to which faith is a possible answer, though not an answer that can be demonstrated by the interpretation.

Jaspers' failure to understand the predicament of the interpreter seems to me linked with his denial of the possibility of existentialist analysis. Why the latter should be impossible, I cannot see. Certainly, what Jaspers calls "existential clarification" differs from Heidegger's phenomenological analysis of

[1] Cf. my paper "Concerning the Hermeneutic Problem", in *Glauben und Verstehen*, II, 1953, pp. 211–235. E.T. in *Essays Theological and Philosophical*, Tr. by J. C. G. Greig, S.C.M. Press, 1955.

empirical existence in this, that existential clarification is effected only in the act of existing, and is inseparable from "existential communication". But Jaspers cannot help explaining what he calls "existential clarification" in such a way that it becomes universally understandable, i.e. he is obliged to objectify it as a doctrine. And if Jaspers were to claim that the objectification is transcended in genuine (existential) comprehension, much the same could be said of Heidegger's analysis. Heidegger's phenomenological analysis of empirical existence as self-contained and self-resolved in Being towards death does not debar anyone, not even those who are convinced by this analysis as a doctrine, from the existential venture. Rather, it shows that the existential venture is always personal, and it clearly emphasizes the appeal, which Jaspers regards as basic, "to selfhood, to authenticity, to actual being, to a sinking into the original, historical facticity (*Sosein*), in order to be appropriated—the appeal to earnest questioning in a hopeless situation".

Whether such propositions of Jaspers as this one: "Everything is comprehended. . . . Comprehension is the mode of presence of the Being that we are" are or are not to be termed "existentialist analysis", seems to be a purely verbal question. The same goes for his statement about "the responsibility of man thrown back upon himself. It is only through freedom that he experiences how he is given to himself by transcendence—in freedom not by freedom". Or his remark that "every man in his freedom has the possibility of experiencing himself as being given and guided by transcendence". Were a reader to accept such sentences as a clarification of his Being, would he be accepting a scientific philosophy of the kind evolved by "nineteenth-century academicians"? Jaspers, too, it would seem, can be misinterpreted. But to misunderstand or abuse existentialist analysis is surely not to demonstrate its impossibility.

In my opinion, Jaspers comes closest to the hermeneutic problem when he reflects on the relation between subject and object. But if he were interested in a genuine dialogue, i.e. in a joint search for the truth by means of reciprocal critical questioning, he could not fail to see that the problem of the relation between subject and object also motivates my hermeneutic efforts: for my purpose is to arrive at a genuine comprehension of past existential insights, a comprehension that would go beyond the horizons of objectified thinking. I feel that Jaspers misses the point when he suggests that I am not subjectively committed to my objective conclusions, that in my case "the objectivity of what is said and the subjectivity of the speaker" do not coincide.

For my part, however, I would not agree with Jaspers' view that such a coincidence, when it does take place, is attributable to "the Encompassing"; rather, it occurs when the subject perceives the object as a summons to him in the genuine encounter. To account for it by "the Encompassing" is, in my opinion, not only to engage in superfluous speculation, but also to miss the earnestness of the summons, of the encounter. In Jaspers' thinking the Encounter and the Summons play no part whatever; and as I see it, this means that he has failed to grasp the full importance of the historicity of human existence. In so far as I can judge from his analyses, he understands by historicity merely the fact that man is always situated at a certain point in time, that he lives under accidental historical conditions and is influenced by historical traditions.

For the same reason Jaspers' concept of transcendence seems to me questionable. Transcendence obviously has at first for him the negative sense of the non-objective; then, the insight that *Existenz* does not belong to the world of objects leads him to hypostatize the non-objective as the All-Encompassing, indeed, as God. This enables him to speak in the language of myth, which, according to him, is indispensable. Thus he says that man has the possibility of experiencing himself as given to himself and guided by transcendence, and that the liberal faith does not regard it impossible for God, conceived of as absolute transcendence, to effect anything. This All-Encompassing reminds us of the "universum" of Schleiermacher, to whom Jaspers occasionally refers rather maliciously. Other statements remind us of Kant. According to Jaspers, direct relation with the godhead is possible for every man in his own responsible freedom of reason. "In the direct relation of his own freedom to God", man knows that he is determined by God. In the last analysis, what is this transcendence but that which was formerly called "the spirit"?—the spirit which, to be sure, is transcendent in relation to "physical presence", but is immanent in human reason! Is such transcendence the transcendence of God? And since, according to Jaspers, "the mystery of the revelation of the truth" is disclosed in sudden illuminations within the history of the spirit, his transcendence seems also to be immanent in history.

Jaspers' concept of transcendence now leads him to his interpretation of the revealed faith. He says that the belief that "God manifests himself at a given place and time, that he has revealed himself at one place and time and only there and then, makes God appear as a fixed thing, an object in the world". Very true! It is also true that the Christian churches often interpreted and still interpret the revealed faith in that way. But does not Jaspers see that such a conception of the revealed faith has been fought against repeatedly? Does he not know that what I am fighting against is just this fixation of God as an objective entity, against misconceiving the revelation as an act accomplished once and for all? Does he not grasp that the purpose of my demythologizing is to interpret the mythological eschatology of the New Testament in such a way that the process of revelation is given its genuine meaning of an "eschatological" process? He may regard my conception as false, but can a genuine dialogue take place if one of its participants ignores the intention of the other?

Now, I have the impression that Jaspers thinks it impossible to have a genuine dialogue with me, on account of what he calls my orthodoxy, or because as a Christian theologian I assert the absoluteness of the Christian revelation. Does Jaspers realize that wherever a revealed faith speaks, it asserts, and must assert, the absoluteness of its revelation, because it regards itself as the true fulfilment of the commandment: "I am the Lord thy God. . . . Thou shalt have no other gods before me." Everyone is free to regard such a revealed faith as absurd. But a man who does, should not talk about revelation. At all events, it is absurd to look for various instances of revelation in the history of religion or the spirit. As a historian I can only discover various instances of faith in revelation, never of the revelation itself. For the revelation is revelation only *in actu* and only *pro me*; it is understood and recognized as such only in personal decision.

It follows that it is also absurd to ask: "How do we recognize revelation? What criterion of truth is given for the direct revelation of God?"—for such questions presuppose that we can ascertain the truth of the revelation before recognizing it as revelation. When we speak of revelation in the true sense of the word, such questions cannot arise, and the impossibility of applying criteria is part of the stumbling-block inherent in the revelation. As though God had to justify himself to man! As though every demand for justification (including the one concealed in the demand for criteria) did not have to be dropped as soon as the face of God appears! As though man's justification were not a gift to the man who has fallen to his knees before God! After all, that is the meaning of the doctrine (which Jaspers regards as mythological) of justification by grace alone without the works of law. For "the works" denote here the actions of a man who strives to justify himself before God by his own strength, who boasts and asserts his claims before God.

If this doctrine of justification by faith alone without the works of law is the content of the revelation, then it is true that the Christian faith must assert a revelation "frozen in its definitiveness". Otherwise it could not speak seriously of revelation. It is, however, clear—and I think that Jaspers should have seen this—that this content of the revelation can never be accepted as a doctrine in the sense of an orthodoxy, without at once losing its truth. If this were to come to pass, Jaspers' liberal faith would be perfectly right in refusing "to arrest its movement in time by a revelation frozen in its definitiveness". But, after all, revelation is truth only in the event.

Does Jaspers imagine that I fail to realize that "whatever is said and done in the name of revelation" is "said and done in worldly form, in worldly language, in human acts and human perceptions"? After all, the Christian doctrine of incarnation explicitly says this very thing (in mythological language!). What matters is that the incarnation should not be conceived of as a miracle that happened about 1950 years ago, but as an eschatological happening, which, beginning with Jesus, is always present in the words of men proclaiming it to be a human experience.

If the redemptive history were an objective event in a remote past, if it were "an objective redemptive history" in *that* sense, liberal faith would be perfectly right in repudiating it, "as an absolute event and as a prerequisite of salvation for all men". But in the Christian conception, faith is not "weakened" by the denial that historical objectification is absolutely and universally valid, i.e. by the denial that "faith can find objective guarantees in the world". On the contrary, it is only when there is no such objective guarantee that faith acquires meaning and strength, for only then is it authentic decision.

When the revelation is truly understood as God's revelation, it is no longer a communication of teachings, nor of ethical or historical and philosophical truths, but God speaking directly to me, assigning me each time to the place that is allotted me before God, i.e. summoning me in my humanity, which is null without God, and which is open to God only in the recognization of its nullity. Hence there can be only one "criterion" for the truth of revelation, namely, this, that the word which claims to be the revelation must place each man before a decision—the decision as to how he wants to understand himself: as one who wins his life and authenticity by his own resources, reason, and actions, or by the grace of God. The faith that recognizes the claim of the revelation is not a blind faith, accepting something incomprehensible on the authority of something external. For man can understand what the world of the revelation says, since it offers him the two possibilities of his self-understanding.

But we must also say that faith accepts the incredible on authority! For the possibility of living by the grace of God can, by its very nature, be given only to me; it is not a possibility open to all for the taking. If it were, the very meaning of the revelation—the grace given to man who is nothing before God—would be lost. Man does not live by the *idea* of God's grace, but by the grace *actually granted him*.

Thus the revelation has to be an event, which occurs whenever and wherever the word of grace is spoken to a man. The "demythologized" sense of the Christian doctrine of incarnation, of the word that "was made flesh" is precisely this, that God manifests himself not merely as the idea of God—however true this idea may be—but as "my" God, who speaks to me here and now, through a human mouth. And the Christian message is bound to a historical tradition and looks back to a historical figure and its history only to the extent that it regards this figure and its history as evidence of the Word of God. The "demythologized" sense of the assertion that Jesus Christ is the eschatological phenomenon that brings the world to its end is precisely this, that Christ is not merely a past phenomenon, but the ever-present Word of God, expressing not a general truth, but a concrete message, that Word that destroys and in destruction gives life. The paradox of the Christian faith is precisely this, that the eschatological process which sets an end to the world became an event in the history of the world, and becomes an event in every true sermon, and in every Christian utterance. And the paradox of theology is precisely this, that it must speak of faith in objective terms, like any science, while fully realizing that its speaking becomes meaningful only if it goes beyond the "objective" formulation.

For Jaspers, the Christian faith's stumbling-block is its claim to absoluteness. Perhaps I should be quite satisfied with the effect my attempt at demythologizing has had on him. After all, the purpose of demythologizing is to make the stumbling-block real. However, I doubt whether I have been successful in this with Jaspers; for I doubt that he has correctly understood the stumbling-block. Viewed as an assertion of the absoluteness of the Christian *religion*, it is not correctly understood. As such, it would be meaningless. The Christian religion is a historical phenomenon, as other religions, and like the latter it can be considered with regard to its spiritual content and its existential understanding of man. Certainly, the religions of this earth can be classified from the point of view of their spiritual content and the depth of their existential insight. But even if, in attempting such a classification, we were to give the Christian religion the highest rank, if, for instance, we were to assert its irreplaceable value for human culture, this would mean something fundamentally different from the claim of the Christian faith to absoluteness. This claim can—but also must—be raised by the believer only, not on the basis of a comparison with other modes of faith, but solely as answer to the word that is concretely addressed to me. And this answer is: "Lord to whom shall we go? thou hast the words of eternal life" (John 6. 68).

HANS-WERNER BARTSCH

BULTMANN AND JASPERS

THIS critique of Karl Jaspers is written from a very different attitude towards Bultmann and his theology from that of Jaspers himself. Let us first examine this difference and give reasons for it.

Bultmann embarked upon his programme of demythologizing as a servant of the Church and her proclamation. His concern springs from the constant endeavour of the preacher to make the New Testament message intelligible to his hearers. Whether or not this is how Bultmann himself regards it, this is in fact the place it occupies in the development of New Testament studies. The enterprise we have come to call demythologizing is simply a continuation of form-criticism. The essential result of that earlier movement was its insight that the *Sitz im Leben* of the gospel pericopes was the preaching of the earliest Christian community. The sole purpose of the gospels is a kerygmatic one. This is what links Bultmann with the theology of Martin Kähler and his disciple, Julius Schniewind. Of course, Schniewind had reservations about this connection,[1] but that there is such a link is unquestionable. To ignore it would be to divorce demythologizing from its setting in history. And it would make it impossible to explain the influence Bultmann has exerted over the *younger* clergy from the days of the Church struggle, and still enjoys to-day. This influence is primarily on their teaching, and only in the second place on their theology.

Bultmann has made use of terms and ideas which he found in Heidegger. There he found an understanding of human existence which up to a certain point agrees with the New Testament. In confronting man with its message the New Testament takes for

[1] See *Kerygma and Myth*, Vol. I, pp. 45ff. and 102ff.

granted this understanding of his existence. So it is clear that even in his use of Heidegger Bultmann has a pastoral and evangelistic concern.

Now we must examine Jaspers' criticisms of Bultmann and try to determine how far they are the result of misunderstandings. These misunderstandings would seem to spring from Jaspers' failure to notice this kerygmatic concern. How far are they due to the difference between the respective tasks of the philosopher and the theologian?

I

As Jaspers sees it, demythologizing rests upon two premises, on Bultmann's views about modern science and the modern view of the world and man, and upon his ideas on philosophy. These two pillars, Jaspers contends, are too weak to bear the weight that Bultmann imposes upon them.

Actually, however, these things are not the premises of demythologizing. Rather, the mainspring of Bultmann's concern is the incompatibility between the modern world view, determined as it is by the growth of modern science, and that of the New Testament. The terms he adopts from existentialism are linguistic tools which he exploits for the interpretation of the New Testament message. But Bultmann does have a premise, and this is that the New Testament message is, in fact, open to interpretation. Whether he is right in this assumption is something theologians have been discussing ever since the debate started. One party rejects it, while the other welcomes it with open arms. It looks as though they will both continue to do so.

This is not to deny the force of Jaspers' criticisms. Even if his arguments leave the premises of demythologizing unaffected, his questioning of Bultmann's views on modern science and his use of existentialist terminology would, if justified, throw doubt on Bultmann's success in making the gospel intelligible to modern man. Jaspers raises quite different issues from Bultmann's theological critics. The latter are concerned about the legitimacy of the enterprise. Jaspers asks whether there is any need for it at all, and whether Bultmann's particular methods offer any prospect of success. If Jaspers is right, demythologizing, even if legitimate, is in the last analysis futile, for it leaves the gospel just as unintelligible to modern man as the New Testament does itself. If, as Jaspers claims, man's realism and materialism are, like his "disposition to believe in the absurd", as unchanged as ever, it is hard to see what need there can be to restate the New Testament message.

But it is a real question whether Jaspers and Bultmann are talking about the same thing when they speak of modern man. Bultmann is thinking of the potential convert to the New Testament message. The would-be believer is conditioned against the New Testament by his world view. That message no longer speaks to his condition, and seems irrelevant to his existential concerns. It is no longer *kerygma*. Is Jaspers thinking of the same person when he speaks of man's chronic disposition to believe in the absurd? We wonder even more when he speaks of modern science as having emancipated itself entirely from any world view.

Jaspers is just as guilty of overestimating this chronic condition as he thinks Bultmann is of underestimating it. For him (Jaspers) faith, in the New Testament, is essentially belief in the absurd. It is on a par with modern superstitions, such as National Socialism and Bolshevism, and the popular cult of astrology.

In thus arguing, Jaspers unintentionally corroborates the need for demythologizing, no matter whether Bultmann himself is successful at it or not. For it is not man's incapacity for faith in the New Testament sense which makes restatement necessary, but the very fact that Jaspers attests, namely that the New Testament faith is dismissed as equivalent to belief in the absurd. Jaspers shows by the self-same token that he is blind to the real import of the miracle stories—whether we believe that they happened literally or not. He cannot see that they have any other import than that they did actually happen. This is the very reason why the New Testament requires interpretation. The New Testament faith refuses to be written off as belief in the absurd, as so many people write it off to-day.

The differences can well be illustrated by the examples Jaspers himself chooses. Modern superstition, as manifested in National Socialism and Bolshevism, in astrology and theosophy, is not comparable to the earlier missionary faith in an imminent second coming, as Jaspers supposes. National Socialist and Bolshevist man believes in Utopia, in final and perfect bliss magically "brought to birth through violence". But it is this use of force, it is his own power and might which he trusts in to bring about this secularized version of the kingdom of God. Modern man's superstition lies in his exclusive trust in his own powers. The earlier missionary faith in the coming of the Kingdom of God was a very different affair. It looked forward to an event which was the burden of their testimony—the eschatological action of God. Now there can be no doubt it is modern science which has led to the growth of modern superstition, for it has increased man's confidence in his own powers. But even such a superstition as astrology is part of the same picture: the shape it takes nowadays is inconceivable apart from this self-confidence of modern man. It has thrown a vivid light on the miraculous character of all marvellous occurrences, and induces man to use all kinds of magical practices to gain control of everything that otherwise eludes his power. By contrast, the miracles of the New Testament bear witness to the action of God which surpasses all human power and control. This is the real purport of the miracle stories. But, as Jaspers himself shows, they have ceased to have meaning for modern man. It is modern science which led man to take the miracle stories as literal reports (whether they believe in them or not).

Bultmann, himself, is partly to blame for Jaspers' failure to grasp the real intention of the miracle stories in the Gospels. Jaspers is right when he questions Bultmann's statement that "it is impossible . . . to avail ourselves of modern medical and surgical discoveries, and at the same time believe in the New Testament world of miracles and spirits."[1] But Bultmann has put his finger on the real issue over the question of faith and superstition: "When belief in spirits and miracles has degenerated into superstition, it has become something entirely different from what it was when it was genuine faith",[2] a point which

[1] *Kerygma and Myth*, Vol. I, p. 5, quoted by Jaspers, p. 162.
[2] Op. cit., p. 5, note 1.

comes clearly to the fore in the distinction between "thaumaturgy" and miracle—a distinction to which Jaspers has paid too little attention.

Of no less consequence is Jaspers' claim that "a crucial feature of modern science is that it does not provide a total world-view, because it recognizes that this is impossible" (p. 135). We cannot but agree. But it would be pertinent to ask whether even science can get along without a world view. The preacher of the biblical message, however, is confronted not by science as such, but by the modern layman, who cannot get along without a world view, even though he may be aware that modern science does not provide him with one ready made. Certainly he may be aware that his world view is only provisional, for that seems to be widely realized to-day. And this certainly means that the Church's apologetic task is not quite as acute as it was. Yet this change should not be exaggerated. Nor does it make any fundamental difference, since the preacher still has to face men who are caught in the toils of a particular world view, a view determined by the current position of scientific research, whatever that may be. Jaspers, himself, is aware of this when he says that even our epoch "at the level of the average man" (p. 135) clings to a world view. It is *this* man, the man who has a ready ear for science, whom the preacher has to face. For as Jaspers says, "this modern science has been accessible only to the masses in the form of final results referring to the totality of things" (p. 136). It is he whom he has in mind when he says that "the unity of the world in scientific thinking is matched by the unity of scientific thinking itself" (p. 136).

II

There is a reason for Jaspers' criticism of Bultmann at this point. As a philosopher he does not see that Bultmann is concerned as a preacher of the biblical message to demythologize it. Bultmann is not concerned to do this as an academic theologian and a scholar. That is why he does not realize what man it is whom Bultmann seeks to serve by his restatement, and whom he portrays in the introductory part of his original essay, in order to show why a restatement is needed. It also explains his criticism of Bultmann's distinction between "existentialist" and "existential": "What can be achieved only through inward commitment becomes a matter of noncommittal knowledge . . . conceptual definitions congeal what only a transcending thinking can achieve step by step, each meaningful only to the degree that it evokes an inner resonance and becomes real in the actual life of the thinker" (p. 139). These remarks are all the more weighty since they coincide with much that the theologians have had to say. The apparent detachment of the existentialist interpretation seems to obscure its intention of evoking an existential decision. It is intended to force a man either to accept or reject what is stated in those terms. The fact is, it is a mistake to think that existentialist interpretation can impart a neutral knowledge of the Christian faith without challenging a man to decide and to do something about it. In Christian theology there can never be knowledge without commitment. Though we can agree with the point Jaspers is making, his criticism of Bultmann arises from a misunderstanding, and one which is all the more explicable since so many theologians have fallen into the same trap. What we have to ask is how to avoid such a misunderstanding. Does transcendental thinking offer the possibility of relevant restatement in such a way as to make its intention clear? Can we communicate the necessity of an inner response? Is not the very thing that Jaspers misses in Bultmann the task of the preacher? And is not Bultmann trying to stop him from running away from that task? Is he not trying to give him the tools for the job? The preacher is bound to understand Bultmann's intention to be just what Jaspers expects it to be.

A further consideration should make this clear. At first sight Bultmann creates the impression that all he finds in the biblical witnesses is their subjective experiences, and that the sole aim of exegesis is to interpret those experiences. But this is only an impression. In the shift of self-understanding from unbelief to faith, a shift which Bultmann's existentialist interpretation makes clear, we can discern the creative force behind the shift, which is the eschatological action of God. Not that we can discern it directly, in an objective kind of way: it is only manifested indirectly through the shift itself. Bultmann helps us to see that it is to this action of God that the witnesses are really testifying. They do this by speaking of it in objective language, making it visible by means of miracles, etc. All that is openly visible is the shift of self-understanding, which points to the action of God. But that action cannot be perceived or known: it can only be accepted or rejected in decision. By translating the New Testament into existentialist terms Bultmann is achieving the same goal as the original witnesses did, though perhaps in a way which is not immediately obvious.

III

Jaspers cannot see that the real aim of demythologizing is the proclamation of the Word, a word which confronts us with the claim to be the very Word of God. Maybe the reason why he cannot see it in this light is that it can only become clear to one who experiences the Word as personal address. This is the only conclusive argument against Jaspers' position, and all we can do is to repeat that this is Bultmann's aim; we cannot prove it. This same blind spot recurs constantly in the course of Jaspers' paper. It goes to show how the theologian as the servant of the Word and the philosopher are bound to be at loggerheads. This comes out particularly in Jaspers' criticism of demythologizing as an existentialist interpretation of myth.

"To speak of demythologizing is almost blasphemous. Such a depreciation of myth is not enlightenment, but sham enlightenment" (p. 144). How can Jaspers say such a thing? Because the only thing he can see in myth is a "poignant reality" (ibid.), even although he realizes that "in terms of space and time the phenomena in question were human experiences". He is against demythologizing because it would result in an impoverishment of human life. Yet Bultmann's attempt contains a "half truth". By means of a critical operation he is trying to prevent "the cipher language of myth" from being "degraded into a language of the tangible, which is guaranteed and provides guarantees". This is something that needs to be done over and over again, in every successive age. Bultmann, of course, would hardly agree that this is the purpose behind demythologizing. Myth for him has not the same intrinsic value it has for Jaspers. The theologian sets store by it only as a vehicle of the New Testament proclamation. For the same reason it is no business of his to distil the "poignant reality" which the philosopher discovers in myth, or to preserve it, mythological language and all, as the cipher appropriate to that proclamation. *His* responsibility is to keep open a hearing for the concrete claim enshrined in the biblical mythology. For in New Testament times the mythology itself was able to win a hearing for the claim. It challenged men to a life and death decision. Jaspers is, himself, evidence that it has lost that power to-day: at least it has not the immediate and universal appeal it had then. The claim of the word and its challenge to decision are no longer audible. The myths are merely ciphers for a "poignant reality".

In spite of all this, Jaspers finds much in Bultmann with which he can in practice agree. But with him the upshot is very different, and it is no good ignoring it. He expected something very different to come out of demythologizing from what Bultmann intended. For instance, he "insists on restoring the reality of the mythical language" (p. 145), a requirement which, incidentally, demythologizing often does fulfil in practice. This was never brought out in Bultmann's original essay, nor has it been in the ensuing theological discussion. But it is bound to come to the fore when the preacher tries to put into practice the principle of demythologizing. For the preacher does not abandon the mythological language. He still goes on talking about the miracle of the resurrection, because he knows no other way of speaking illuminatingly of the eschatological action of God. But all the time he knows what he is doing. He is bearing witness to the eschatological action of God, not to the "objective truth" of a miraculous event or the "poignant reality of the myth itself".

The preacher's need for mythological language is simply a pragmatic one. There is no other way of speaking directly or objectively of the eschatological action of God. All he can do is to bear witness to the effects of that action. In this way, the myth is made to point beyond itself. For Jaspers, however, myth has an intrinsic value of its own, a value which must be preserved at all costs, and which must emerge more clearly through what he is prepared to sanction as a surrogate for demythologizing. All that matters is that we should remember that myth is only a cipher or a code. We must never lapse into "an impious, materialistic conception of the myth as tangible reality, which no longer regards the myth as a cipher, and which leads to superstition". Thus, for Jaspers, the need for mythical language is axiomatic. It is not just a pragmatic necessity arising from the inadequacy of all human language.

Here we have the inevitable and fundamental difference between the theologian and the philosopher. It hinges upon what Bultmann calls the redemptive event, but it is the same thing as what we have called the eschatological event. Any such notion is meaningless to the philosopher; at least he cannot talk about it like that. Their disagreement is, therefore, inevitable, and Jaspers cannot possibly accept the "degradation" which results from demythologizing. Here, as Jaspers recognizes, is the parting of the ways.

IV

Now as Jaspers sees it, "in this struggle for the truth of certain Biblical contents against other Biblical contents, Bultmann reaches certain conclusions" which he cannot accept (p. 148). Bultmann, he complains, seems to concentrate on Paul and John to the exclusion of the Old Testament and the Synoptics. His characterization of Bultmann's theological position is accurate enough: "For him the revelation is found not in a historically knowable Jesus, but in a redemptive event, which is disclosed in these later texts (viz. Paul and John). The redemptive event, conceived by Christ's disciples and apostles, is the very meaning of these texts" (ibid.). It is the second of these two sentences which is misleading. Bultmann's argument (which Jaspers is trying to reproduce in this sentence) is that the redemptive event is not something thought up by the first eye-witnesses: it is nothing more nor less than the eschatological action of God. All the disciples and apostles are doing is to bear witness to that event, just as the later theology of the Church draws out its implications. Once again, Jaspers betrays the limitations of his understanding. He cannot see any difference between the two viewpoints because he has no use for a redemptive event which is inaccessible to direct observation. The redemptive event is identified with the myth (which has actually no independent value apart from the event) and by the same necessity it is identified with the testimony of the disciples and apostles. There is a grain of truth here. For, as Bultmann puts it, we know nothing of the redemptive event except through the testimony of the disciples, and then only in mythological statements which are the vehicles of that testimony. This is the same point which has led Bultmann's theological critics to accuse him of eliminating the redemptive event and of reducing the kerygma to a subjective religious experience. For, they allege, Bultmann has eliminated the Easter event and reduced it to the Easter faith of the disciples. But this is a hasty conclusion which assumes an ontic identity where all we have is a necessary vehicle for testimony and apprehension.

Instead, Jaspers would get back to "the actual teachings of Jesus" (p. 149). There is much more in the "living reality of the figure of Jesus in the synoptics than in the spiritualized Christ of the Gospel according to St John" (ibid.). The Johannine Christ is nothing more than a "noble and captivating . . . fairy-tale hero". In view of his remarks about the reality of myths, we can easily imagine what he means by the reality of Jesus. He agrees that that reality is not dependent on the historicity of this or that story about Jesus. It is a reality which cannot be translated. It can only be expressed in myths, as it is in the gospels. But it is not a word with a claim and a challenge.

Jaspers' contrast between the Pauline (and Johannine) Christ and the synoptic Jesus shows a pitiful ignorance (though perhaps a philosopher may be pardoned for it) with recent New Testament scholarship—with form criticism and the study of the traditions behind the written documents, and with the History of Religions. Apparently he knew nothing about these things until he read Bultmann's essay on demythologizing, and then it came as rather a shock. If Jaspers and his colleagues had read an account of form criticism, etc., like that of Sir Edwyn Hoskyns in his *Riddle of the New Testament*, he could never have drawn that particular contrast. It is impossible to draw a contrast between the "actual teachings of Jesus" and the proclamation of the redemptive event. Jaspers might then have realized that the proclamation of this redemptive event lies behind those very teachings of Jesus which he talks about, and that the New Testament from cover to cover is simply the unfolding of that proclamation. There may be different versions of the proclamation in various parts of the New Testament, but it is always at bottom the same proclamation, even (to take a well-worn example) in the Epistle of James compared with those of Paul. Jaspers' attempt to interpret Bultmann's essay as exhibiting a preference for some parts of the New Testament over against others will not do. Bultmann is looking for the very kernel of the New Testament, for the key to its total understanding. And this is the proclamation of the Christ. To have discovered that was the achievement of form criticism, a movement in which Bultmann played a notable part.

V

One question is therefore settled. The redemptive event, which is the starting point for demythologizing, and to which it seeks to bear witness, is for Jaspers just one element among others in the Bible, an element which he feels at liberty to contrast with other elements, and to prefer in the search for truth. In other words Jaspers rejects the testimony to the redemptive event. Here we have the heart of the matter. This accounts for everything he has to say, especially when he complains of the lamentable effects of demythologizing. For that interpretation exposes the redemptive event as the very heart of the New Testament. Those other features by which Jaspers sets so much store simply go by the board. No wonder Jaspers does not like it. But this does not mean that he has no use for demythologizing at all. For he goes on to put it to the test in order to see whether it has enabled Bultmann to make faith in the redemptive event intelligible. He starts out with an important distinction in the definition of understanding.

Authentic, primary understanding is "every mode of conceiving reality" (p. 150). It is "the mode of awareness of the Being that we are" (ibid.). Then he draws a distinction between primary and secondary understanding (understanding of the understood). It would seem more in keeping with Jaspers' own definition, as well as more relevant to demythologizing, to speak of the understanding of someone else's previous understanding. This is not quite the same thing as the understanding of the understood. Our proposed alternative would also fit in better with Jaspers' remark that the distinction is not meant to imply a complete divorce between the two modes of understanding, but simply to register the tension between them.

The two modes of understanding cannot be completely divorced from one another. This is because we can never really suspend our own judgement or participation; indeed, such judgement is the source of all the insights which lead to understanding. The understanding of the understood always leaves the door open to an authentic, primary understanding.

But there is just as much danger of evading the tension as there is of confounding the two modes of understanding. That is exactly what happens when we objectify what we understand, pretending that it represents our own personal experience. Jaspers expected to find in Bultmann authentic, primary understanding. All he found was the secondary kind, which pretended to be the real thing, but was unable to produce genuine participation: "Even when this objectification is consciously rejected, its effects linger, though they may be unnoticed" (p. 156). One could hardly find a more acute and perceptive condemnation of Bultmann's procedure. But what is Jaspers after? "Theological propositions," he observes (p. 157), "just like philosophical ones, lose all meaning when they hide behind science, i.e. when the pneuma does not inform them. It is for just this reason that theology grounds its understanding in the Holy Ghost. No one can, of course, be sure whether the Spirit bloweth or bloweth not at a given time and place; but he to whom the Spirit speaks, however faintly, must say when he was moved by it, and when he was not. He should also be able to describe the silence of the Spirit. When the mythical contents are genuinely appropriated the speaker communicates his conviction out of the faith in whose name he speaks; he is not then troubled by the inherent implausibility of the myth in its literal aspect. Now, Bultmann, we feel, speaks from a sense of scientific responsibility." An "only" should be inserted here, and it should be added that the Encompassing Reality which strikes a chord in the listener and turns the spoken word into a personal message and challenge to faith is not something that can be felt by the senses.

It is impossible to answer this criticism, or even to mitigate it. Jaspers is listening for the Embracing Reality, which is the source of all theology. He wants to feel the breath of the Holy Ghost. It is, however, pertinent to ask whether Jaspers is not beating his head against the barrier of all scientific theology as contrasted with proclamation. If so, his criticism may not be damaging after all. In any case it cannot be expressed in scientific terms, as Jaspers tries to do when he says: "Primarily it is a matter of the minister's own theology in his daily practice, as he comes to grip with specific human situations and proves his worth" (p. 160). But is there any answer to the question at all? Can there be any scientific proof? All we can do is to testify that this is what theology is driving at, and that is for the believer a living truth. In the same way the preacher can testify how much Bultmann has helped him in his preaching. It is in the pulpit that the real and living faith Jaspers is looking for will be found. But it is just as easy to give the opposite testimony, to say that the whole thing is meaningless, and to send the enquirer away empty-handed. Both these possibilities exist. And if we are looking for an objective proof, we need only substitute "spirit" for "Holy Ghost" and credulity for faith. Once more, Jaspers is beating his head against the barriers of intelligibility: beyond them all is mystery. The Spirit bloweth indeed where it listeth and faith grows where God wills. All we can say is: *ubi et quando visum est deo.*

Yet Jaspers' question has a relevance not only for Bultmann, but for all theology. It is a perpetual warning to the theologian of the danger he stands in, as he pursues the ends of scholarship. It may be true that "theologians sometimes dodge the existential claim by speaking about it, by acquiring an intellectual knowledge of faith, and by working for the preservation of the Church" (p. 159). This is just as great a danger for conservative theologians, though no doubt they can shelter behind their orthodoxy and remain blissfully unconscious of it. On the other hand there is no proof that they succeed in avoiding the danger. In the last resort, Jaspers knows he is asking from Bultmann something he cannot give, because it can only come by proclamation and the response of faith. He sees that "primarily it is a matter of the minister's own theology in his daily practice, as he comes to grip with specific human situations and proves his worth" (p. 160). Jaspers holds that it is the task of the theologian to provide a remedy "against the real dangers that threaten us to-day, against the deceptive hopes and expectations derived from fear and conceived in helplessness and confusion, against the facile expedients resorted to by medicine, politics, and theology with uniformly ruinous effects" and complains that Bultmann does not provide it. But the only way to do it is by offering that very hope and expectation which the early missionaries proclaimed. In other words, it is the theologian's task to lead men to an understanding of the understood, with all the tensions that that entails.

Jaspers complains that Bultmann is over-academic in his approach: he tries to combine a shallow enlightenment with orthodoxy. This is a serious charge, and is rooted in the tension between the two kinds of understanding described in the previous paragraph. For Jaspers is afraid that Bultmann runs away from this tension. Such an accusation is, however, inevitable. Any theology which tries to understand and interpret a faith experienced in the past is bound to incur it.

VI

Jaspers then complains that Bultmann does not offer him what he is looking for. What he wants is genuine "liberality". He, therefore, continues by distinguishing this desideratum from pure orthodoxy and the position of Bultmann.

> The liberal faith is self-sustained, drawing its strength directly from transcendence, seeking no guarantee in the sensory world or in tradition, though the tradition awakens it and makes it capable of testing the traditional truths. The liberal faith needs no external props, not even a redemptive history conceived as an objective absolute event, the prerequisite of all faith (pp. 163f.).

Liberality, as Jaspers conceives it, is opposed to rationalism and liberalism, to that form of unfaith "which superstitiously believes itself to be firmly grounded in rationality" (p. 166). Liberalism is "the intolerant absolutizing of an allegedly definitive intellectual knowledge of freedom and equality of all men" (ibid.), whereas liberality is "limitless openness to reason, i.e. communication for the purpose of furthering all genuine insights" (ibid.). This kind of liberality is also opposed to all orthodoxy, in which this openness, the permanent movement which liberality signifies, ceases, and knowledge takes its place.

As a matter of fact, this is where Jaspers comes closest to Bultmann, and it ought not to be difficult to reconcile their positions. "Does the revelation as an objectivity reality", Jaspers asks, "come first, and does faith follow from the perception of this reality?" (p. 170). Bultmann's answer is, No. The conservatives, who set such store by the objectivity of the redemptive event, would say, Yes. (By objectivity they mean that the redemptive event is independent of and prior to faith.) For Bultmann the redemptive event is at once the object and ground of faith and therefore not something objective, which can be apprehended apart from faith. Faith alone can apprehend it. Jaspers asks a second question: "Or is faith in the revelation at one with, and inseparable from, the revelation itself, which produces faith?" Bultmann's answer here would be, Yes.

Thus they agree on the essential point, apparently. Their differences would seem to be peripheral. Some of them, of course, are due to misunderstandings. But the real difference lies deeper, as is shown by Jasper's next question:

> Is revelation that which always takes place when there is faith, when God is believed in? Have such revelations occurred whenever they have been asserted in history, not only in the West (Judaism, the various Christian denominations, Islam), but also in Asia?

Revelation thus takes various forms: every instance offers the possibility of revelation, provided it is accepted in faith. But it is always accepted as a possibility, never as an absolute. This brand of liberality "repudiates the idea of an exclusive truth formulated in a creed. It recognizes that the Asians can find it without the Bible" (p. 171). Here Jaspers is consciously following Lessing, whom he regards as the type of liberality *par excellence*.

We would agree that orthodoxy is wrong in claiming the priority and exclusiveness of revelation. Up to a point there is a great deal to be said in favour of this kind of liberality, when it says there can be no revelation apart from faith. As Jaspers says, revelation cannot claim to be an objective datum; it can only be testified by faith. But this is not to say that revelation assumes various forms and is always relative. *Christian* faith at any rate cannot admit it. For Christian faith is tied to an historical person. That has always been its distinctive feature. It was based on a figure of the immediate past, not on a mythical figure of pre-historic times. Christian faith has never wavered over this point. One mythical figure can always be replaced by another. The same philosophy of life can be expressed in ever-changing forms. The only historical element in them is the form they assume in any given religion at any particular time. Hence they are always the product of the believer's faith, even when "the importance of history and language for its faith is understood" (ibid.). This importance, however, depends exclusively on the validity of the given faith. It does not imply belief in a definite person, like Christian faith.

Yet faith and revelation are inseparable. The person of Jesus Christ is not apprehended as revelation independently of faith, nor is it recognizable as such. Only faith can say of it that it can be apprehended. This is never true prior to faith or apart from it. Revelation is perceived only in faith. Therefore, for the non-believer Christ is just as relative as any other figure of faith. He is just one of the various instances of revelation. Faith, however, cannot admit that there are such varieties. It may distinguish between faith and revelation: the one is the ground of the other. But this distinction is made *a posteriori* in the self-reflection of faith. It is compelled to make this distinction since the ground of faith is a historical person and not a mythical figure who could easily be replaced by another.

Consequently demythologizing is the necessary reflection of faith on the historical foundation enshrined within the mythological imagery it uses. Buri and Jaspers, of course, maintain that the foundation itself is just as mythological, but that is because they have departed from Bultmann's definition of myth. For Bultmann does not regard the eschatological action of God as a mythological notion. It is only the forms in which it is testified that are mythological. This is substantiated by the way God's eschatological action does not seek to prove itself capable of apprehension. It merely testifies to its own occurrence and leaves the hearer to decide whether to accept it or not. It, therefore, does not resort to objectification like mythological language. Revelation does not demand "that we recognize it as God's" (p. 168). The witness merely declares the gift of faith he has received, knowing that this gift can become available to others when and as it pleases God. For God is at work, in a hidden way, in the acceptance or rejection of the testimony. Jaspers desires that the hiddenness of God should be respected all the way through. He has, therefore, what he wants. It is never infringed, only God breaks through it in his freedom where he wills, where he discloses himself to the believer in faith. But his breaking through is never susceptible of proof.

It is, therefore, inevitable that Jaspers and Bultmann should disagree, and we can see why. The witness to the divine revelation cannot speak, as Jaspers does, of "serious commitment undertaken in uncertainty, but without outside guarantees" (p. 172). It is not the believer storming the gates of heaven. He is overwhelmed, seized upon by God, and this seizure cannot be reduced to the same level as any other. Hence Christian faith can never regard itself as one possible language among many others. For a believer it is always the language of truth, even in the context of other faiths. But it proves its claim only in the concrete historical situation.

Hence faith never claims to possess the key to universal salvation. This is something that rests in the power of God. Faith simply owes its existence to that power and bears witness to it. It cannot perceive that action of God anywhere else. God may be at work everywhere, but his work is never open to perception anywhere else. For faith it is idle even to raise such a possibility, since it knows where it does perceive God's work. It has one task, and one task alone, and that is to bear witness of the encounter. But this is not intolerance. It does not pass judgement on any other faiths. But it does exclude the indifferentism which regards all faith as a search for the truth and "accepts this history as a myth among other myths" (p. 172).

The tolerance Jaspers looks for springs from the knowledge that a believer can never force the sceptic to believe. For the believer has no knowledge of his own at his disposal: he can only apprehend the revelation in faith. He never possesses the truth or the revelation, as Jaspers seems to think. All he can do is to say with Paul: "Not that I have already obtained this or am already perfect; but I press on to make it my own, because Christ Jesus has made me his own" (Phil. 3. 12). That kind of faith is never stationary, it is always on the move. Thus it is just what Jaspers wants, and what he contrasts so unfavourably with orthodoxy. But faith is equally aware of the "radical sinfulness of man", which Jaspers is at such pains to deny. Faith will have no truck with the *nobilitas ingenita* which Jaspers is so anxious to assert. Jaspers' interpretation of "Christ in me" as it is conceived in the Bible is entirely mistaken, for it is always a gift, and never an innate quality. It only emerges into the clear light of day through death and resurrection. By it Paul means the "not I" of the new existence, which the believer acquires through being apprehended by Christ.

Jaspers goes on to say: "God would not damn us for our honest efforts even if orthodoxy were right" (p. 173). This is completely misleading. For our apprehension by Christ is not the result of honest effort, any more than we can be blamed for not being apprehended by him. It is just that kind of notion which, as Bultmann has shown, has been demythologized in the Gospel of John. To be rejected, to stand under judgement is something that happens now as we are confronted by the eschatological action of God. The proclamation can only bear witness to the fact: "Now is the judgement of this world" (John 12. 31). It is superfluous to repeat that this is not a verdict on the work of the philosopher.

VII

In the last part of his paper Jaspers discusses the relation of philosophy, theology and religion. Once again his purpose is to show up Bultmann's shortcomings.

> The philosopher cannot help being taken aback when he sees what this salvaged minimum of faith turns out to be—the residue of faith which, according to Bultmann, is not mythical, and is the essential element of religion: namely, justification by faith alone, faith in the redemptive event. For a philosopher this is the most alienating, the most outlandish of beliefs—this Lutheran dogma with its terrible consequences scarcely seems any longer even denotive existentially (p. 174).

This is where Bultmann comes out in his true colours. He is "illiberal", wedded to orthodoxy. He fails to achieve the ideal of liberality, in which philosophy and theology are united.

Of course, this ideal is a limited one, and in Jaspers' view cannot include religion.

> In religion there flows a stream of communal life that lies beyond the reach of philosophy—a living relationship to shrines, to sacred actions, objects, and books, to rites and prayers, to the office of the priest, in short, to the physical presence of symbols (p. 175).

Here, again, Jaspers' interest in myth is evident. Myth offers the physical presence of ciphers.

It could, of course, be questioned whether Jaspers' observations on religion in general apply to the Christian faith and proclamation. Be that as it may, we are bound to ask whether Bultmann has not, by speaking of the redemptive event, demonstrated "this source of reality which philosophy can neither reach nor explain". The question is answered in the affirmative when Bultmann speaks of the "vestiges of mythology" which remain after demythologizing. Jaspers prefers to speak of the practice of historical religion, of which the gift of "mythological language" is the appropriate expression. Their difference here corresponds with that which exists between religion in general and the Christian proclamation. Only thus can we speak of the vestiges of mythology as Bultmann does, though from his point of view Jaspers would add that we do so inauthentically. Religion is extricably bound up with mythological language. It uses that language as a vehicle to convey what is ultimately mysterious and ineffable. The ciphers remain a barrier behind which everything is shrouded in obscurity. They can only attempt to describe and name it, but can never cast any real light upon it. For the Christian proclamation mythological language is also a cipher for something which cannot be expressed in everyday terms, and is, therefore, bound to look like a vestige of mythology. But it testifies that this is God's eschatological action, something far removed from all myth. In such a connection it is inauthentic to speak of "mythological language".

Religion is inexorably bound to myth. Demythologizing makes sense only by putting myth in its proper perspective. In practice it can never dispense with that kind of language because it is its very life-blood. Only so can it present the enigma of human existence in such a way as to throw light upon it. But self-conscious reflection will always remind it that its descriptions are no more than ciphers. It may throw light, but only to point up the obscurity which lies behind it. It cannot do without the language of myth. The Christian proclamation avails itself of this language in the same way as a cipher. But it does so to express its faith and to bear witness to the eschatological action of God which has brought the ground of human existence out of obscurity. In Christian usage, therefore, mythological language is a cipher which, so far from being inexplicable, is actually open to explanation. Demythologizing is faith reflecting on the language it uses, despite the fact that it goes on using that language and can never dispense with it.

Theology is the pursuit of this kind of reflection, based on the redemptive event, the eschatological action of God. It thus escapes the danger of becoming "philosophical to such a point that it loses touch with the specific elements of religion" (p. 176). Bultmann has recalled Christian preaching to the centre of faith. He has opened the eyes even of the philosopher to where this centre lies, as Jaspers himself admits, even if he feels uncomfortable about it. He has thus rendered a signal service for the dialogue between philosophy and theology. He has laid bare the frontier between the two disciplines. Each has its own particular perspective. Theology speaks in the light of a redemptive event. It bears witness to that event, and it is always in practice, though never in principle, obliged to use mythological language. Philosophy on the other hand speaks from a spirit of liberality. It can only regard faith as a possible choice. Thus it is bound to regard a redemptive event as even more intolerable than mythological language itself.

GUSTAV BRØNDSTED

TWO WORLD CONCEPTS—TWO LANGUAGES

THE occasion for this essay is the recent philosophical and theological attempt at rescuing the Christian proclamation from its entanglement in the form of a remote age, at liberating the "essential" gospel in order that it might be heard and accepted by men of our own age.

To that extent its subject is the gospel and theology. Where a proclamation is made, a theology is bound to arise. It cannot be otherwise. However much the proclamation appeals to the emotions or is directed at the will, it must always contain a "what" and a "that". The attempt to clarify the content of the "what" and the "that", whether for oneself as one listens to the proclamation, or for others to whom the proclamation is addressed, is itself already theology. This theology will create dogmas, as well as a world view and a philosophy of life. Dogmas are the form which the proclamation assumes wherever the Church seeks to hold on to it as its property, its treasure. The world view and the philosophy of life will be shaped and reshaped by the clash between the proclamation and the varying views of life of successive ages and their understanding of themselves. It is an illusion to imagine that the proclamation may be kept free from theology. It is an illusion to imagine that the Church should be able to keep its teaching free from contemporary currents of thought; it has never been able to do so, and if it were able, the proclamation would die for lack of a language.

It has always been the case, that wherever the gospel has been proclaimed, not as mere "teaching", but as gospel, it has been made contemporary, proclaimed in time, against time. "Time" is the place in which we necessarily stand, and in which alone we can hear. The time is the place for the gospel, but it is also the place of our self-assertion and self-sufficiency, of our opposition to the Gospel, and its forms of culture and thinking may emphasize this. Therefore the language of the proclamation is the eternal problem of the proclamation, and creates all that theology, which from of old has been called dogmatics and apologetics, and which in our own age meets us as "existentialism" and "demythologizing".

What I shall here attempt to provide is neither apologetics nor dogmatics, nor any solution for the problem of the gospel and our own times, whether in accordance with the existentialist attempt at a philosophy of life of a Christian character, or the attempt of "demythologizing" to attain an "essential" interpretation of the apostolic gospel. On the other hand, the aim of this pamphlet is not a refutation of existentialism and demythologizing, even though to a considerable extent it is concerned with those movements and takes a position with regard to them. The aim of Bultmann's demythologizing must be understood from that situation in the Church and in theology which has "facts" for its slogan, and in which the pattern is that of subjective *v.* objective, those trusty assistants of rigid orthodoxy and the heresy hunt, and, therefore, also of defection from the Church. This pattern, so handy a weapon for controversy, has had better conditions in Germany than in this country, where Grundtvig's proclamation of "the word" long since has achieved something similar to that reaction of Bultmann, that it is in *the word* alone that we encounter the saving act of God—an assertion which he proceeds to rationalize philosophically and theologically.

I will, however, attempt to point out a principal reason why the question of the gospel and our age is one, which is insoluble *qua* problem, why no theology opens a way for the gospel. Theology is not proclamation, but reflection and formulation. Theology is thinking. The core of the matter is hidden in the question of the competency of thinking, not abstractly and philosophically, but in a practical and compelling manner. On this depends the fulfilment of the hopes for a renewal of the language of the gospel. Here, too, conflicts arise with old theology, which seeks to maintain the gospel, and new theology, which seeks to rescue it.

Old questions present themselves in a new form for every new generation. In the following pages it is not solutions, but reflections, which I seek to present. They are reflections and specimen explanations before science and theology, rather than a presentation of the whole subject, which the topic does not demand. Yet, after it has been read, it ought not to be ambiguous what I have intended and what I have stated. The problem itself is the old one, but I have sought to state it more broadly and more simply than is customary in these discussions, which have taken place mainly in Germany. It concerns us all, not only the great contemporary philosophers and theologians with their difficult language and easily misunderstood categories. I have attempted to make the essential nature of the problem plainer by confining it to the fundamentals of each of the two world views which find their expression in the proclamation of the apostolic age and in contemporary civilization, and which speak through the primitive and mythical language of the Bible and the analytic and naturalistic language of our own times.

The two world views and the two languages are expressions, not only of past and present, but, wherever the gospel is preached, of a tension in which we live day by day. It is as men of the present that we are confronted with the traditional proclamation of the gospel and stand within it. The questions press upon us and show us the duality of the world in which we as Christians live, the duality of the position in which we as theologians find ourselves, as those who proclaim the apostolic gospel and participate in the contemporary culture pattern.

Two world views, two languages. Is there any bridge between them? Is it possible to speak of the one in the language of the other? Is it possible to proclaim the gospel in a language which is proper to the world of research? And if not, why not? And what then?

No person lives in one single age. Even though, on the whole, our consciousness bears the stamp of that which passes for the contemporary mode of thought, yet a vast area of our world of concepts is a survival of other ages, even perhaps remote ones. Some of this comes to the fore forcibly, at times even decisively, in our whole response to our environment, while some appears but vaguely and obscurely, as dim shadows or as nuances and overtones of emotion, in different ways and to different degrees. Here the artist differs from the technician, the historian from the archaeologist (and historians are rare, while archaeologists are as numerous as the sands of the sea, statistically, culturally, theologically). The intellectual life of any given society has no definite date, no absolute age. These "thoughts of the age" which cleave their way into the future like a cutting edge or a front are but part of an age, and not always, by any means, its most essential part.

Similarly, in the various races and peoples of the world, widely divergent ages live on side by side. It will, therefore, always be something of an abstraction to speak of "the contemporary mode of thought" and "the contemporary world view" and to attempt to systematize them and describe their characteristics in contrast with a similarly abstract "primitive world view". Yet such an attempt may have its uses, since it is always useful to seek to clarify one's own world of thought. To do so gives a sense of perspective and assists in an evaluation of reality; it is a condition for mature hearing, seeing, and reading.

For a theologian it is useful, and indeed necessary. In the tradition and proclamation of the Church he is confronted with a world which reaches far back into a "primitive" age, yet simultaneously extends into our own age, which itself must recede into the past. For this last reason a description of the outlook of each of these two ages and a comparison between them would in itself be no more than archaeology, were it not that the voices which reach us from distant ages, and which, before reaching us, have resounded through the most diverse periods, themselves speak *to* us and speak *about* us—and that with more authority than all other voices. Otherwise it would not be a proclamation, indeed *the* proclamation, which resounds. It is on the one hand as close to us as our fellow-man whom we encounter on this very day, on the other hand as remote from us as if it were uttered from another planet.

It is the theologian's task to acquaint himself with this strange world, this strange language, to hear its speech, and to help others to hear it. It is a craftsman's task, and as a good craftsman he must know his tools and use them with due regard to their limitations. Since he is dealing with material he must use his knife—and thought *is* a knife—and because it is speech he must be a living, hearing, and complete man.

It is not, of course, my intention here to attempt to draw a comprehensive picture of the thinking of the time of the New Testament, and another of the civilization and mode of thought of our own time. Both have been done many times. I will, however, attempt to make a very brief excursion into each of these two ages and, in a few glimpses, to survey things which are already well known to you.

First of all I must state that it is *not* a question of an ancient Graeco-Roman world picture contrasted with a modern one. The difference here is considerable, yet secondary. Thucydides is easily read and correctly understood by a modern reader; and the difference between the natural science of the Greeks and that of the present is mainly one of degree of wealth of material and of accuracy, and is thus due to a shift in technique. The religious and animistic vestiges which remain in classical antiquity have no essential influence on its method. Thus the objections of Graeco-Roman intellectualism against Christianity and its attacks upon it, such as those of Celsus about 180 A.D., are in the main the same as those of the age of the Enlightenment and of the present day.

The boundary separates the age of the New Testament on the one hand from classical antiquity and our own time on the other. The two latter have the same 'language', the apostolic age another.

Furthermore, in relation to the men of the New Testament, to them even more than to those of the Old Testament, we may be overcome by a feeling of hopeless remoteness. We do not understand them. It is not so much the two millennia and the language, which separate us. As has been stated, there are other points in the cultural history of Europe where the cultural distance in those respects is not felt. It is less their remote ideas and opinions than the persons themselves. Worse still, they do not understand *us*. They would speak to us, but they do not share our mentality. They have enough of profound seriousness and biting sarcasm, but they do not know the light jest, the blessed sense of humour, that irony about oneself which is at one time both gay and serious, the trusty helper of truth. Nor do they know the joy of knowledge, the craving for inquiry, the food of art which gladdens soul and body. Our very selves are incomprehensible to them, and they to us. From a humanistic point of view the world of the New Testament is narrow and petty, strait-laced and short-ranged. Its skies are low, its soil is barren, the air in its dwellings stuffy as that of the conventicle.

Yet it may happen that a word from that world of small men gives life to our own world, so rich, yet so poverty-stricken. At the very least, it has shaped two millennia of history. Is it then strange that some persons stake their all on building a bridge between the two worlds, for instance, by attempting to translate the thoughts of the New Testament into contemporary thoughts, to find and express that which is essential in the gospel for us too? Yet, apparently, without success. Like continental land masses the two worlds inevitably drift apart. Every bridge breaks.

These are old problems which repeatedly press upon us, problems which we must formulate day by day, and which we, day by day, must overcome rather than solve, in order that we may live.

And so I shall begin entirely from the outside.

Wave and wave the many-coloured mountains arch themselves towards the distant horizon. They are naked and barren, but the valleys sprout with abundant verdure. The winter rains have been copious, and with a life-giving latter rain the Lord God has blessed the orchards and the fields. From the stores of heaven he has bestowed his bounties upon the earth. The springs flow with life, the brooks gladden the stony gorges, they give thanks with flowers and verdure, and the birds sing their joyful song. But the naked mountains and the fertile valleys proclaim that the Lord God apportions life and death according to his own will. He touches the mountains, so that they smoke and melt like wax. But even to the mountains he gives life, if it be his will, the great forest-clad mountains afar off, those upon which the treasures of the snow have been poured, where the cool streams flow down and give life and growth to herbs and bushes and the great tree-trunks of the primaeval forest. There swarm all manner of creatures, there creeps the serpent, there the bird flies, there the wild beast lies in wait for its prey, there hart and hind leap, there all creatures, clean and unclean, dwell together, for so the Lord God has willed it. And behind mountains, ravines, and valleys, the plain, and the Great Sea itself, is the realm of Leviathan—Leviathan, with his mighty teeth and his heavy armour, whom the Lord created for himself to play with him—the realm of Leviathan, bestowed upon him by God as his fief. No foot of man has trodden its depths, no eye has seen its terrors, but on its back it carries the sons of Adam to distant coastlands. There they serve strange gods, and demons bear rule over them, yet the eye of the Lord God watches over them and their works, and his angels record them in the heavenly books which are to be opened on the day of reckoning, the day of judgement. The children of Abraham, too, travel across the Great Sea to dwell on strange coasts and islands as strangers among strangers. The eye of God follows them, seeing whether they are faithful to his laws, and the recording angels write down whatever injustice and violence is done to them, whether in foreign parts or at home in the Holy Land which the Lord God has given to the children of Abraham as their heritage. Their lot and law is to be clean amid the unclean, to be the people of God among the nations, the proclaimers of the Lord, until he separates the righteous from the unrighteous and establishes his kingdom for all those of Adam's race who do his will and obey his holy Law.

He is the Lord. All the heavens belong to him, he is the Father of the heavenly lights. All the powers of the air obey his command, the storm and the rain, the gentle winds, and the cooling dew of the night. All the kingdoms of the earth are his; all the treasures of the deep, the silver and gold, are the Lord's. His are all that the children of men have built and wrought. All that lives by the dwellings of men, on plains and in forests, are his. His will is inscrutable, and all destiny is in his hand, the joy of life and the horror of death. All the powers of light obey him with awe, and the spirits of darkness tremble before his avenging word. To him every creature shall bend its knee, in the heavens, on the earth, and in the underworld.

He is the Creator, by whose word all has come into being. He sustains all things by the word of his power. And at his word sea and earth will eventually perish, be dissolved like smoke, the heavens be rolled up like a carpet, the stars fall like dust, sun and moon fade and vanish. All will be annealed by the fire of the Lord, all the powers of darkness and all their minions suffer the eternal penalty, while the righteous shall shine as suns in the kingdom of their Father.

But until that day the tares will grow among the wheat on the field of the earth. No one but God himself and he whom he sends is able to separate the good from the evil. No one to whom he has given life is dead; their souls are preserved in hidden habitations. The pious know this, those to whom God has revealed it, those who "meditate in his law both day and night". Adam knew it, and so did Eve; they knew Paradise, the Garden of God, the land as God had created it. They knew the bliss of obedience and the horror of disobedience; they tasted death, but their children recorded their utterances, and the devout continued to read books about the life of Adam and Eve. Enoch knew the ways of God, the structure of the world, the spheres of the Powers, the task and the place of the Virtues, for Michael had revealed all of it to him; he had led him through heavens above the heavens, shown him the angelic powers which are set over the courses of the sun and the moon and the stars, and taught him exactly the laws that have been given to them. He revealed to him the deeds of the rebellious angels and their punishment and the places of punishment, carried him to the uttermost bounds of the world, to the dwellings of the winds in the north and in the south, in the west and in the east, and taught him the tasks of their angels. He carried him over deserts and immense mountains to Paradise in the east, and showed him wondrous creatures on the way in the distant regions. He carried him over all the lands in the west and in the north, over the outermost sea, and set him on the brink of the vast abysses where the souls of the dead are hidden, where chasms separate the evil from the good, until the day of judgement. And the guiding Angel showed him the wondrous ways of God with his people down through the ages, his will for the future, his hidden counsel, conceived before the foundation of the world was laid, eternally living before the face of God and revealed, made visible on the earth as the compass of the world and its course. He showed him in the midst of the worlds and times the chosen People and their city Jerusalem, where everything is, as it were, recapitulated and gathered together, the throne and temple of God, and at its foot Gehenna, the Valley of the Dead. Here, too, the fulfilment is to take place, the judgement is to be pronounced. Here the throne of glory is to be raised, the heavenly, eternal Jerusalem is to descend and be built upon earth, from hence the eternal kingdom of God is to begin.

And still his revelations live among the devout in Israel. Among the first Christians, too, and in the following generations his words[1] are read as a holy revelation and a true picture of that world which God has created and which he sustains until "that day".

As the world is described in the great Book of Enoch (and I have here merely touched a few features), as well as in many other apocalyptic and "wisdom" writings, both Jewish and Christian, so it was conceived in broad outline already in the days of the Prophets. Through the influence of the Old and New Testaments

[1] The book of Enoch, which, among others, even Tertullian (c. 200 A.D.) decidedly includes among the canonical books, belongs to the second century B.C. In the generations around the time of Jesus it is cited and utilized by Jewish writings such as the Book of Jubilees, the Testaments of the XII Patriarchs, II (IV) Esdras, and the Apocalypse of Baruch, and by Christian writings such as the Epistle of Jude, the Epistle of Barnabas, and the Apocalypse of Peter. Paul, too, read and used the Book of Enoch.

it lives down through the history of the Church, in its preaching and hymnody, in its catechetical instruction[1] and popular speech.

Out of this world view, rooted and ground in these thoughts, the gospel was proclaimed since the days of the apostles. It was the joyful message that now the hour had arrived, so longingly awaited by the devout. God had intervened, his work would unfold itself speedily, visibly and openly. God's world, corrupted by Satan and all evil powers, would be dissolved, purged, and renewed within and without; all evil would vanish, the will of God prevail, there would be a new earth, a new heaven, the eternal abode of the righteous. For the man Jesus of Nazareth was the Voice of God; his crucifixion was the plan of God's salvation, his resurrection the seal of God. He was the Christ, the divinely chosen King of Israel and of the world, the Son of God. He was "the Son of Man", the heavenly One, prepared from eternity for this hour of God. He was the Word, through whom and in whose intent and measure the world had been made. Born of a Virgin, he enters into this world of sin; holy and blameless in body and soul he ascends into heaven, from whence he is now to come again, very soon and unexpectedly, clothed with all the authority of God, as Judge of the world and Lord of all.

"The Lord delayed." The gospel traversed lands and ages. Still it was proclaimed as though time were standing still; thoughts did not change. And when Gnosis and neo-Platonism in antiquity, Renaissance, humanism, and, more recently, rationalism would modernize the gospel, only the new trappings remained.

Precisely where the gospel has spoken most strongly to contemporary man, the connection between the proclamation and the biblical world picture has been most intimate and most conspicuous. Who of us has not smiled at the very thought of the monstrous conservatism of a Luther or a Grundtvig as regards their world picture? Who of us has not felt profound indignation at the Church's attitude to Galileo? And who of us has not noticed with amazement and at the same time a certain feeling of

[1] Cf. the mediaeval work *Lucidarius*, originally written in Germany for the laity at the instigation of Henry the Lion.

insecurity that among these men, who paid most attention to the need for a renewed world picture, the gospel sounded feebly and faintly, or else like something alien and redundant, however much that renewal was carried out "for the sake of the gospel"?

Why? Is the gospel then really bound to an obsolete world picture, or rather, is the gospel itself but a part of a vanished past? Is it impossible for it to be spoken and heard in a new language?

In its essentials the world picture which which we work and with which we live is clear to us all. It is a further development of our heritage from the Greeks. It is learned in school, it extends through all our understanding and knowledge; it is unfolded astronomically and physically in one direction, biologically and sociologically in the other. Between these the historical subjects live, or else crumble into dust. The fact that Galileo's astronomy has been relativized by Einstein, that physics is being rearranged by the atomic and quantum theories, and that the goal of biology becomes psychology—all this is no more than a shift in technique and emphasis, not a change in principle.

The vault of the heavens is broken. The starry canopy has vanished. Principalities and powers on high are no more. There is no up and down beyond that which is locally expressed by the law of gravitation and attraction on each spot of the globe and in the universe. All connection is relative, all opposition likewise. All that we see is formed by our senses, and our senses in turn are formed by the forces of the universe, borne by light and electricity, indifferent to organic and inorganic, yet acting and existing. The fact that the law of causation and the fixity of identity at first prevail in our age, and then are subjected to doubt because matter and energy no longer appear to be separable and are superseded by electro-magnetic fields, all this is merely a battle of words, since at the same time the attempt is made to fix temporal and fractional relationships for the transition from the one to the other. Both in analysis and description it is impossible to work with any other instrument and standard than that of logic, which by use becomes more rigid than ever, however much the material, astronomical, physical, chemical, and biological seems elastic and evasive in the grip of thinking and shifts under our very observation. Analysis and logical summary are the natural methods of work and measurement. Complementarism, the subject of so much debate and hope, is but the expression of a certain hesitation and testing in the progress of the work, determined more by its materials than by thought. As an outlook on life it is sheer nonsense. There has been some talk of "the limitation of causality which atomic physics has taught us", of "non-causal quantum leaps". I would strongly deprecate making such considerations the basis for religious or moral hopes. Here is a case of verbal confusion. The world picture of physics has not been destroyed by atomic research, but merely refined. If research into matter and energy, carried out on "matter-and-energy" by means of thinking biologically derived from "matter-and-energy", can logically prove non-causality to me, and even degrees of and places for this non-causality, then I will immediately and spontaneously cease to think, and calmly contemplate logic proving itself to be illogical.

Astronomy and physics seek to form for themselves a picture of inorganic matter and its "behaviour patterns", whether in the old-fashioned way one speaks of finite *or* infinite (which is mastered merely as a border-line concept), or of matter *and* energy, or of electro-magnetic fields. Biology, in its widest sense, seeks to form for itself a picture of that which is organic and of its behaviour-patterns, whether the division is made between living and dead and the "living" is spoken of in other senses than of that which is molecularly "mobile", or, with greater consistency, is understood as a continuation of particularly complex chemical molecular combinations.

In biology evolutionary physiology seeks to clarify "the whole history of living matter". The separate individuals are merely parts of "the continuous stream of living matter", and "the structure and dynamics of living matter are the expression of finely balanced molecular processes" contingent upon "the capacity of carbon for building up complicated structures". If there is to be any sense in the evolutionary theory, we must assume that life has arisen from that which is "lifeless". "The secret of life, then, is . . . that molecules of complicated structure *must* behave as they do by virtue of the universally recognized laws of physics and chemistry." This living matter has two thousand million years behind it and boundless time before it. "The term 'species' covers a chemical peculiarity which is deeply anchored in the sexual cells of the individuals" which carry on the stream of life. Somewhere in this stream is man, whose behaviour pattern and "character" are similarly determined by molecular processes. "It is the great goal of biology to help men by means of the methods of natural science to understand our genetic type and to adjust our environment in the most appropriate manner for our genetic type . . . to give us a greater understanding of our own actions and of the behaviour of our fellow-men, to find still more rational means and ways of achieving our ethical endeavours, to make life easier for us all."[1]

Indeed, every field of research has its own infinitude. Analysis binds the investigator to his own quality of truth, even where he as a human being seeks to make truth useful for living.

But surely research is more than mere analysis? It is. All pioneering in research demands more than analysis of details and stringent thinking. There is need of intuition, of artistic imagination, if something significant is to be produced. But in this connection it is irrelevant. It does not touch the problem of proof, of verification, of how a scientific truth is validated and operates with compelling force. There is thus no bridge of thought from our world into the primitive world, in which proof is not objective and by means of details, but by means of authority, wholeness, imagination, and by the forcefulness of the presentation itself.

It is quite irrelevant that some natural scientists, despite their recognition of the flux of existence in terms of physico-chemical laws, concede to individual human beings person consciousness of liberty and responsibility. It is either meaningless, since this consciousness is itself an expression of an undoubted cerebral process, or else it means that man, besides being a rational being who wants to understand "life", is a fool who wants to live it.

[1] Quoted from articles of H. V. Brøndsted.

One can hardly object to this conclusion.

In order, then, that we may "render to Caesar the things which are Caesar's, and unto God the things that are God's", we resort to the expedient of halting somewhere on the road between the Bible and chemistry, on the road of secularization.

But to what avail? What does it avail to yield one step, to Galileo and all his consequences? Or two steps, to Darwin and all his consequences? Or three steps, to contemporary biology and biochemistry and all their consequences? It is the road itself which in principle is closed to the gospel, it is the "secularized language" of analysis and demonstration, of which the motif and object, as well as the standard, are incommensurable with those of the gospel.

It is also entirely irrelevant whether the modern world picture is incontrovertibly a closed one, or whether or not there are enough lacunae in modern knowledge to enable us, as has been attempted from the earliest times, to insert a few contradictions of nature, such as Creation, the Deluge, Jonah in the whale, Elijah in the chariot of fire, the Virgin Birth, miracles of healing, and the Resurrection. Faith cannot live on such lacunae or hide itself in those "unsolved problems", even though these are equally welcome to many psychologists and natural scientists, yet "breathing holes" as irrational as was "the missing link" in the descent of man for churchman during the last century. *Faith* cannot live on gaps in our knowledge nor on "historical possibilities". The denial on the part of science arises from its methodology, that of rational demonstration, and not from its more or less incomplete material; otherwise it would have no right to deny the possibility of centaurs and such like, but it makes the denial and *must* make it. "God" as a principle of cosmic coherence it will not deny, but both from the standpoint of science and of Christianity this is irrelevant. It is the biblical God who *acts*, as well as spirits and souls; and it is life, responsibility, sin, and salvation in their *Christian* sense that science is compelled to deny.

It is true, indeed, that there are natural scientists who "believe in God". But that is because they, as human beings, possibly only at a certain point, escape from, abandon the world in which they have been imprisoned by their methods and their theories, abandon it with the reservation "and yet". Possibly the gospel has become too strong for them; possibly they feel compelled to do so in order to save their own humanity; possibly also it is merely because the oppressiveness of their world picture invites them to seek escape.

Every person needs an escape. Astronomers do, for astronomy is reputed to be a very exacting subject, rigidly bound by formula, and so astronomers sometimes escape into spiritism. Natural scientists often escape into the humanities. Such escapes may well have their repercussions on the subject itself. In our own day, when most subjects, even "cultural" ones, are dominated by the natural sciences, congresses make solemn pronouncements that everyone agrees that basically existence is exceedingly mysterious. The result will probably be that natural scientists will take over the cure of souls. At present it is in the hands of the doctors; in times past it was in the hands of priests, in a more remote past in the hands of medicine men with their magical skills.

But, *as scientists* to make room for irrational matters such as guilt and responsibility and thus for freedom of the will, because these things are of such great social value—that is inadmissible. *It would mean ascribing the same value to the consciousness of a thing as to the thing itself*, on account of the effect of that consciousness. It ought to be clear that it is right to speak of them only as psychological concomitants determined by molecular reactions, unless we are willing to be thrown back into the "myth" of the God who acts and demands.

Two world pictures and two world views, mutually exclusive —that is the situation in which the proclamation of the gospel finds itself in our generation.

First, then, it is our imperative duty to take pains that the question is raised in a radical way and is honestly insisted upon. It is *our* duty, and thus not merely that of the proclamation of the gospel, but also of scientific research, since the "we" includes both those who proclaim and those who are engaged in research. Whether we are theologians, physicists, and biologists, or engaged in practical activity, we are living on the fruits of scientific research and think in its terms. Whether our life-work is the one or the other, we live together in mutual dependence as human beings who are born, are happy, suffer, and die.

Therefore, in all our dialogue concerning these present matters, we must think synthetically and inclusively, without deceiving one another or ourselves by making concessions in details, however important, or by abandoning the dialogue when it approaches certain areas which are embarrassing for one party or the other, intellectually or emotionally. Every person has the right to refuse discussion and mind his own business; we have no right to force tasks or plans of living upon each other. But discussion with reservations is not honest discussion, and no one is helped thereby.

It is not the case that a series, whether long or short, of problems concerning details adds up to the whole. Nothing has been gained in clarity if one party at the demand of natural science sacrifices, e.g. the biblical record of creation and receives in return the concession, e.g. of the geological verisimilitude of the narratives of Sodom and Gomorrah; nor if one party sacrifices the patriarchal stories to historical research and in turn receives the concession of the Israelite monarchy, or else writes off the Pastoral Epistles in return for the authenticity of the Epistle to the Romans, etc. Nor is there any gain in surrendering demons and possession by spirits to biology in return for the right to feel the freedom of the will for the sake of morality, or by surrendering miracles to natural science in return for the assurance that even a world bound by law may belong to God. And if, after great agonies of soul, he sacrifices the messianic concept, the Virgin Birth, and the Resurrection, in order that psychology may concede an idea of God, and biology an inclusive concept of life, it avails him nothing, it compensates for nothing. It is not *that* God which the gospel proclaimed, nor *that* life with which the proclamation is concerned. Discussion of individual problems, whether great or small, may assist in clarifying one's own stand as well as that of the other party. But however many individual problems the biblical writings contain and which at various times become prominent in the tradition of the Church, their mere addition does not constitute that totality with which it might be possible to make a final reckoning. The totality is not the sum of its parts, but lies behind it.

The same, however, is no less true of the other party. However many separate notions of history, physics, or biology the contemporary scientific world picture contains, notions which may be separately listed and drawn up in contrast with corresponding details in the biblical world picture, as has been done with increasing frequency during the past few centuries, it is not by the mere addition of those details that the totality is produced, with which a complete reckoning might be expected or hoped for. Here, too, the totality is not in the sum of its parts, but lies behind it.

It is the whole, more than the details, the goal even more than the whole, which matters—that whole which is not the sum of the details, but their essence.

A world picture. If it really were possible, as is constantly being attempted, to see the two world pictures, the biblical and the contemporary, under one heading, even if it were merely in terms of category, and thus lift oneself above them both!

It is not absolutely impossible to compose a picture of the world or of existence as it was conceived in the mind of a normal Jew approximately at the time of Jesus. Not one, but many Jews of that period have spoken with awe and to the glory of God concerning the structure of the universe and the process of existence. Of course, they did not so speak with complete consistency or harmony. But would this be any more the case with a modern picture of the world, whether astronomical or biological, even though it is entirely possible—as has actually been done in our own times—to describe the structure of the universe and the process of existence? Such expositions display an internal unity which could not reasonably be denied.

To that extent it would seem to be in order. The two world pictures ought to be able to be viewed together, confronted with each other and compared with a view to testing them and rejecting that which is found wanting. The earth is flat, therefore science is wrong; the earth is round, therefore the Bible is wrong. To that extent the two world pictures ought to be capable of being viewed under one heading, since they belong to the same category. They are both world pictures. This, however, is the case with them only in a very secondary sense, and with qualifications.

Even the common standard which we apply to the two world pictures to test the validity of the one by the other, is not applicable to them both. It is one derived from our modern point of view, but since it seems so abstract and neutral we do not readily perceive its real nature. The notion that a world picture as such aims at physical and conceptual coherence is one that centres on ourselves as observers. It is arrived at by observation and verified by repeated observation.

When we speak of two world pictures—and for the purpose of discussion bring them together under the one category of "world picture"—we have at once accepted for this purpose a "common standard" which is not applicable at all. It has validity, at any rate, only to the extent that the Jew of that period, as well as Christians of subsequent ages, consciously or unconsciously objectified their world pictures and thus allowed themselves to be drawn into a valuation of a world picture derived from their cultural environments, Greek, Roman, Renaissance, etc. As has been previously pointed out, such cultural environments were far closer in their world picture to our own times than to the apostolic age, even at the time of the gospel itself, and that not only in the subject matter of their knowledge, but, which is more important, in their goal, their essence.

Wherever a common category was postulated or conceded, it was only reasonable that the consequences of the dialogue between the parties down through the centuries should be criticism, mockery, re-interpretation, hair-splitting, legalistic quibbling, arbitrary use of authority, denunciation, evasion, and, under the best of circumstances, the mutual exchange of irrelevancies, depending on the varying prestige and strength of the parties involved, from antiquity to our own times.

Even when, as occasionally happened, the diversity of categories was recognized and the consequences were drawn, dialogues and encounters continued, in the main, on the same plane as that on which they had begun, and thus had a tendency to remain academic and abstract like the encounters between faith and knowledge in times past.

Meanwhile the new world view is at work. This is apparent in all departments, in culture by the reorganization of the behaviour pattern of society which is socially, morally, and religiously conditioned by technology. Technology involves a fundamental readjustment of the conditions of life, of the structure of the family and all the values based on it. The content of the significant words of the language is semantically altered, the content of concepts such as right, community and purpose is changed and thus becomes useless as a basis for the translation of the gospel. And without being translated, the gospel remains a relic of the past, an anachronism, indeed it is bound to do so.

It will, perhaps, be said it is but self-evident that the natural science of the West and the world picture based on it, have, from the days of the Greeks to our own, given occasion for the Church's revision of concepts connected with a popular *oriental* world picture, which has been capable of surviving in the West only by virtue of its continued intimate association with the whole of Western culture by means of the Bible. It is hardly surprising that our thought forms are in conflict with those of the apostolic age—but what is the whole question worth?

It is easy to come with a pronouncement that the question is without interest, mere "academic" theology, a hackneyed problem from the days of scholasticism, the Renaissance, the Enlightenment, that although it is more acute in our times, it is still the same problem, and no more than that.

But what avails the attempt to shake off the question, merely because for some people its elucidation is no more than an antiquarian curiosity and for others no more than a theological thinking game? The question is still with us because it is *not* "just a problem", an intellectual matter. It is with us because *the world picture of the gospel is not a mere world picture* which, by being placed beside the contemporary world picture can raise questions concerning such matters as the Ascension of Christ (what and where is "heaven"?), visions of angels and expulsions of demons (what are "powers" and what is sickness?), man's origin (what is Creation, what is the soul, what is life?), biblical history and the history of humanity (what is religion and what are the religions?), matters which together indicate the difference between the world pictures. Over several generations up to our own times the attempt has been made, under violent conflict, quantitatively and point by point, to solve the question by replacing one form of expression with the other, wherever the world picture of the gospel was in contradiction with that of Copernicus and Galileo, which has entered into the very blood stream of our generation as truth. The question is with us because the world picture of the gospel is in reality *not merely a world picture, but a world view, an attitude towards existence* which, in the guise of a world picture, speaks of man in a way which is incapable of being translated in terms of the way in which *our* world view speaks of him. Our world picture, too, is something else besides a world picture. It, too, is a world view, an attitude towards existence, qualitatively different from that of the gospel. Each has its basic character and *speaks its own language. It is impossible to translate* from one of these languages into the other. They are incapable of contributing material to each other.

A wall has been erected all of a sudden, and on either side of it are two parties who were about to begin a dialogue. A curtain falls and I stand on either side of it, divided by it. A word of the gospel has been spoken to me. It has been proffered me as judgement and as a gift, and there I stand. To old-fashioned, straightforward temptation has been added something novel and meagre, doubt. Temptation is dissolved, overcome, but by doubt, not by faith. The gift that was proffered and which we perhaps seek to recover is, according to this new world view, obtained only in the form of salvation of oneself or of mental hygiene—a philosophy, a mere shadow of what was alive behind the words "temptation" and "faith".

Every time the gospel is heard, read, or sung the question is raised afresh. We seek to work ourselves free from it, or else we attempt to work ourselves through it. We attempt to make it powerless by minimizing it, or else we give it weight by equating it with "the scandal of the gospel", a *crux intellectus* which God lays on the shoulders of believers. Or else we attempt to divide it by consigning one area to preservation and another to destruction, thus adopting the sham solution of demythologizing.

Are then all our attempts at solving the question mere make-believe? Is the question itself but make-believe in order to preserve a piece of the past beyond its natural span of life?

In terms of *theology* it is so. As an attempt at reaching a solution by means of a formula it is but make-believe. As theologians who seek to explain we are spectators of the thoughts of the past as well as those of the present, and a common formula, however subtle, cannot be found. *Nothing* can be safely rescued across the abyss. *Biblicism* seeks to preserve all of the gospel, including its words, but succeeds merely in rescuing words. *Existentialism* seeks to preserve ideas, but not even they are preserved, since they are torn out from their embodiment. As theology all our attempts are empty make-believe.

But *must* the gospel be silent for us, for us who cannot escape from our own world?

We live in two worlds and in two languages, even apart from the gospel. The one "language" works with *definition* and aims at *control*; it is, *inter alia*, the contemporary speech of natural science, which has gradually merged with the science of our age. The other "language" works with the *symbol* and aims at being *a bridge between the minds of men*. Definition cuts out and arranges, while the symbol hints and suggests.

Both tendencies have always existed side by side in all human speech. This lies in the nature and necessity of life. Definition cannot work without the contribution of the symbol, and the symbol cannot speak and communicate without the contribution of definition. By this I mean that each of the two "languages" has its fundamentally different character. They are languages for fundamentally different "worlds"—and we are in both.

In our perception and communication in speech and writing we move simultaneously on the primitive and the analytic planes of language. Sometimes the emphasis is on one, sometimes on the other, depending on the demands of subject, atmosphere, and popular attitude. We need but think of our perception and description of nature; how different, even contradictory, are the elements which they contain in even a relatively brief sequence of thought! Or consider our perception and description of each other and of each other's opinions, actions, and characters, not only when we speak practically, but also historically and socially. The primitive predominates in poetry, the analytical in science. But in both poetry and science we work on mixed elements, capable of separation only by renewed contemplation from without, by observation. The subject matter and the aim determine which of the two "languages" will predominate, and we thus speak of scientific or poetic attitudes and representation.[1]

[1] My attention has been called to Povl Diderichsen's statement concerning science and poetry, "To these complementary trends in understanding there are two corresponding opposite tendencies in language" (*Videnskab og Livssyn*, 1952, pp. 35ff., in a review of *Leviathan*, by Martin Hansen.

Povl Diderichsen propounds fundamental difference between the language of specialized sciences and that of poetry. Science aims at technical control and must therefore work with sharply defined expressions, fixed in concept according to the need of each subject. Poetry makes sovereign use of language in order to create new and living psychic experiences by means of "unexpected connections". Diderichsen draws examples from Povl la Cour, such as

grøn Vind grønne Grene
grønne Solskyers Strime.
("Green wind, green boughs,
Green streaks of sunny clouds").

or, programmatically, from Archibald Macleish,

"A poem should not mean
But be".

He praises this use of language in strong phraseology, since it keeps the inner side of our mental life mobile and fresh, expressing "the flowing change of emotional life". Science and poetry are "opposite in understanding. For this very reason they can never come into conflict. Neither of them believes in any absolute truth about man or nature. . . ." "Even life and death flow together in glittering, streaming light."

I hope that it is apparent that Povl Diderichsen and I speak of totally different things. What for him is the great intermediate mass of everyday speech, vaguely

And the two languages are in conflict. Each tacitly concedes certain areas to the other; but not only are there always border areas, and consequently mutual accusations of aggression. In the acute phases of the struggle the very existence of the opposite party is regarded as an act of aggression. Naturally there are times and persons among whom everything primitive, including poetry, becomes rationalized; but generally it is the case that either party is confident in its own truth and final rightness. Thus "science" concedes to its opponent no more than the right of being something which gives "colour" to existence, as well as relaxation. Its opponent concedes to "science" merely the right of supplying technical assistance in the practical tasks of living. Each of them has its faith, and to understand the other's faith is beyond them. Neither of them wishes to lose itself.

The two languages are concerned with two basic relationships, two functions in our human situation, one that *receives* and one that *takes*, to gives them a provisional description. *Each of these basic relationships creates language, each in its own way.*

The one pertains to that world in which, without being able to change anything, we are placed in a relationship of dependence on nature and one another, and in which, willingly or unwillingly, we must live in this relationship from the cradle to the grave. This world is *primitive*, however complex it may appear under certain conditions. Here everything is placed in a relationship to those with whom we share our fate. Everything in nature and in history—and history means the interaction between nature and

---

defined, is for me that which is essential, living by virtue of containing the speech of many ages, comprising also that which *I* call poetic language, alive by virtue of its origin and goal, that of *being a bridge* between men.

And I cannot quite understand why he has not realized that the science and the poetry, whose languages he distinguishes, basically express, not different aspects, but the same aspect of the world, and that what he calls poetic language is an extreme, constructed, artificial product, which aims at achieving psychological results by repeated "redefinitions", ever new emotional associations. Poetry thus becomes the *art* of poetry, and the art of poetry in turn an aestheticizing form of science, science mirrored in aesthetics.

In this Povl Diderichsen is right, the two can never come into conflict. "Neither of them believes in any absolute truth about man or nature." Exactly—observation and aesthetics belong together.

man—concerns us *in our relationship with our fellow-men.* Here in this world the sun rises over our joy and our strife and sets upon our wrath. The starry hosts see us; the mountains in their might, the abyss in its horror, speak to us. Here the bird sings, the forest becomes green, the field flowers, the fruit ripens, and we *receive* in fellowship with our neighbour. Here the day is light, and the night darkness, *for us*; here is good and evil, responsibility and guilt, *with us.* Here there is struggle, victory, suffering, here we are bound one to the other. Here poetry grows out of our outward and inward experiences, and we share with one another from generation to generation. Here language is not measured according to its exactitude or adequacy, but according to its ability to build a bridge, to convey experience from mind to mind. *To receive* is the key word of this language.

The other belongs to the world in which, whether as *observers or takers*, we aim at making everything our own. Here it is not the relationship of dependence, which is decisive, but that of *conquest.* It varies in accordance with times and places; it may be complex in the manner in which it appears, yet in its essence it is simple, yet it is never primitive, but *always up to date*, for the sake of conquest. Because it views all in terms of utility it draws all under its domination, whether in nature or history (in its widest sense). Its essence is *reason*, its means analysis, its test of truth logical consistency. Here in this world the sun and the stars are objects, and likewise men and man himself. Here the object is compelled to yield its external form, its properties, its effects, whether physical, biological, or psychological, by means of thought. Here a world picture is constructed out of the mass of experience, in which everything, under intellectual stresses and strains, bears the stamp of the means and method of the work. The means and method correspond to the aim of comprehending, of possessing, of ordering. Here language is measured and valued according to exactitude and adequacy; whether it is according to Greek philosophy or Einstein is merely a question of the progress of time and variety of usage; whether its character is academic or technical, its methods and goals are mechanical or biochemical and sociological, it is the same; whether it is for one's personal intellectual development or for the ordering and construction of society, it is the same. *To take* is the key word of that language.

In imagination take a stroll in our professional libraries between the miles of book shelves of literature on physics, astronomy, chemistry, biology, sociology, technology, etc., which is continually expanding and subdividing into new fields of specialization—what a sum of knowledge! Or think of our laboratories, physical, biochemical, etc., our research institutes and factories in the Old World and in the New. What a sum of competence, of strength, and of power! And all of it with the same goal, the same drive, summarized in one word—*to take!*

There is a great gulf fixed between this and that world of which the key word is, *to receive*. It is not that the key word of our civilization, *to take*, is bandied about in all its brutality. On the contrary, every moment that it functions it is de-brutalized, since our *taking* is only for the purpose of *giving*, to culture, to progress, to humanity. Yet this does not to the slightest degree change the nature of this taking. This is apparent not only from the progress and consequences of this same taking, such as competition in production, and wars, but it belongs to the very nature of the matter. Since there is no one who *gives* us all this, it follows that those who "obtain" become identical with those who "take". They "obtain" that only to which they, as economic supporters of the common endeavour or else as the wreckage of the machinery of society, have a "right" or "claim". If we are identical with nature, then our law is to take. This law may be refined, or rather, camouflaged, but it cannot be changed. But to *receive* presupposes a *giver*, and consequently a fundamentally different attitude to everything.

It is, therefore, impossible to "translate" from one language into the other in terms of adaptation, or at least only in an improper sense. The language in which we meet our *neighbour*, accept our *responsibility*, encounter our *guilt*, are judged in our *sinfulness*, accept life as a gift of *grace* by faith—such primitive language cannot be "sharpened" or adapted for verification. Nor can it be clarified by analysis, as two millennia of dogmatic theology have sufficiently demonstrated; it cannot be deepened by psychology. Like all living things it is plastic and flexible. It may, it is true, absorb foreign matter without harm to itself and eliminate it in turn without loss, but it cannot be reorganized and acquire a new fundamental character which is not primitive.

The language of receiving is irrational to the language of taking. This is true in daily living, and it is true in the case of the gospel. "Give us this day our daily bread" is irrational speech, because we *take* our daily bread, as far as we are able, and distribute it according to the law of necessity and compulsion. "Thy kingdom come" is irrational speech, since no other kingdom comes than that which is the result of our wills and actions. "Forgive us our debts"—that, too, is irrational speech. We are not indebted to anybody, except to those on whose welfare our own depends, whether emotionally or socially. Everywhere the gospel is fundamentally irrational speech.

With the language of taking, a language borne by analysis, men may conquer one another, but not live with one another and for one another. That language produces no words capable of building bridges between men, but destroys the primitive words which it absorbs. We know this very well from daily life. There is so much that vanishes by analysis, there are so many words which lose their content by rationalization. *Faithfulness*, once it is analysed, is no longer faithfulness. *Love*, logically rationalized, ceases to be love. *Grace*, if it is logically rationalized, is no longer grace. The desire to keep the words primitive and non-logical for the sake of human life may, of course, be labelled a desertion of the clear way of thinking, a conscious escape into a fog of myth. Yet to rationalize them by logic is to prevent them from serving as a bridge between persons.

The primitive language exists for all people. It aims at building a bridge immediately and completely. It is full of images and what science would label false analogies. It has one aim, that of reaching a person in a single matter with a simple, straightforward word. It cannot wait till it has found a clearly defined formula, and if it waits it loses its power of speech. Science, if need be, can wait for centuries, and is proud of it; but this language cannot wait, it must reach short-lived men and give them food here and now.

We live, however, in both these worlds and speak both languages. The aim and attitude to life are decisive, the "language" is merely the expression and the means.

The greater power for conquest the technological world view has displayed, the more dominant its "language" has become. Since, in practice, it appears that we *are* able to live by bread alone, we have given this other language the right of encroachment on the other, of correcting it, destroying it, and making it superfluous. This has happened to such an extent that even in poetry the words of the former language appear self-consciously or with an attached commentary or footnote, though not always an obvious one, supplied by the latter language, which is recognized as being "proper" because it is rational.

We have no other way of dominating our environment than thought. But we have another way to our fellow-man.

If, indeed, our fellow-man is no more than part of our environment, the object of knowledge, understanding, adaptation, something to "help", or dominate by force, interest, or by that helpfulness which professes to know better and thus obliterates him by assuming his responsibility and leading him along our ways, then we have no other way than that of thought, of conquest; then that way will really lead to its goal, then it *is* "truth" in its principle, its analysis, and its physical psychology. In that case it moulds, by its very conclusiveness, all that we feel and do, and the spread of civilization and progress shines with the self-satisfaction of him who knows better. Here is committed that placid rape which in international relations is the modern successor of the more massive violence of past ages towards "lower classes" and of cruelty towards "savages", which at least had the advantage of being understood for what it was and avenged as far as it was possible.

If, however, we and our fellow-men together are bound to a world which is *not* our property nor our spoil, but in which we *receive* everything, then all our ways, indeed our whole way to our fellow-man, are determined by this relationship of dependence, and thought is but a small element in the formation of symbols by which the language spoken on that way is constructed. In that case *primitiveness is not a manifestation of deficiency, but a necessity* for the building of bridges from one mind to the other, in order that the individual may give and receive through his neighbour and speak of giving and joy, of responsibility and gratitude.

The language which has been corrected by analysis is incapable of absorbing and transmitting that which presupposes primitiveness. It is not their primitiveness that makes ideas, such as those of the New Testament writings, to be "true" in themselves. There have been, and still are, numerous primitive notions about the world among the nations of this earth. But the very primitiveness builds a bridge from one living being to another, while analysis treats that which is living as if it were dead. And it is compelled to do so, otherwise it cannot retain it, take it, and dominate it.

There is thus no help in a psychology and philosophy created by analysis for a renewal of the language of the gospel, and its proclamation. In "translation" the very content becomes different. While the "original" deals with sin and salvation, the subject of the "translation" will be states of soul and their changes for the sake of the welfare of the ego.

True, both the two worlds and their respective languages are in a state of flux. But then all language is in a state of flux, from exactitude to symbolism. The very words of myth itself were once "exact", in so far as, speaking cosmologically, they contained an "objective" picture of the world, and were to that extent no more suitable for faith than any modern "objective" language. Furthermore, "objective" words of more recent date may themselves, through a process of attrition, cease to be exact, so that they are no longer useful for the conquering intellect, yet have thereby gained in usefulness for human life. They become well-worn words, suitable for tasks in relation to our fellow-man in that life, which is being lived, not merely observed. They become words that build bridges, that contain a common heritage, words left behind when specialization, technology, and speculation were no longer able to use them in their present worn condition as sharp tools of conquest.

All language, I suppose, is in a state of flux from analytical to naïve, and always the urge of conquest will sharpen its linguistic tools afresh. What matters is not what the language and its elements are *historically*, but what they are in the *given situation*.

One might well say that the Judaeo-Christian world of thought is basically an animism common to mankind and a primaeval mythological pattern of thought, and that it contains within itself the urge to control existence. But it was not for this reason that it was used in the New Testament proclamation.

There is more than a primitive understanding of the world and primitive science in mythical thinking. There is the *consciousness of dependence* and the *consciousness of being spoken to*, and it is this consciousness which makes the mythical form of thinking a fruitful language for the proclamation. The gospel has made address to the person the essential element in mythical language.

In reading Jewish and early Christian writings it is essential to understand that the world picture encountered there is not merely "primitive" in the sense of being naïve, and thus only to a slight extent the object of reflection and verification, but that it is also *mythical*. It is such not merely in the sense that it is ancient cosmology and the like, but in a far more essential sense, as something which in its continuity addresses man, as powers of good and evil, as the order and will of God, as struggle and victory. Thus "*objective*" *observation is meaningless here*. For this reason the language of this world picture can become the language of the gospel in a way no objectifying language, whether modern or ancient, has ever been able.[1]

The two world pictures, and consequently their respective languages, are first and foremost *different in essence*. Their relationship is that of religious to intellectual. The fact that, considered

[1] Even notions about nature, such as *popular* Greek ones in New Testament times, with their blend of ancient remnants of myth and "modern" fragments of natural science and astronomy, are objectifying. As an understanding of existence they are just as barren as "cultured" Greek mockery of them in its turn is coarse. One may think of examples such as Lucian's "Menippus' Voyage to Heaven" (Icaro-Menippus), a collection of grotesque jests and situations. Lucian, incidentally, concludes it with a tilt to the side, in that Menippus in his enthusiasm over his experiences in heaven finally announces, "Now I am going over to those philosophers who stroll in the 'Many-coloured Colonnade', to tell them the same joyful news".

as knowledge of nature, they differ in degree, that there is a process of change from the one to the other by a shift in the *elements* of their content, is, essentially, altogether secondary. Yet it is usually this which preoccupies both scientists and theologians, the contrast between the "three-storey" world of the Bible and the one-storey world of Einstein.

The apostles proclaim *good news* to their contemporaries in the hope and firm conviction that God will guide the course of his word, so that in every nation where it is proclaimed it will reach all those whom he has predestined from eternity and now is calling to salvation.[1] And the apostles proclaim this good news in their own language, "language" in the fullest significance, which is an inheritance from the Fathers created while Israel was becoming a people, saturated with power by the judgements of the prophets and their hopes, shaped in the days of the Exile and of later Judaism, when the thoughts of foreign peoples mingle with the thoughts of the prophets. It was strengthened in the tribulations and victories of the Maccabaean age, made flexible in the time of Roman domination, confirmed and renewed through the experiences in Jesus, in the days of the Son of Man.

True, language is outward garb and form, but language cannot be wholly detached from its conceptual content even when reduced to vocables, symbols of elements of thought. The New Testament may be translated, scantily and approximately, into languages such as those of Western Europe. Our languages have a common genealogy with the Hellenistic tongue in which it was written. Through the Church we share a common history with the New Testament in expressions, concepts and images. We have

[1] This is the meaning of the New Testament word *ἐκκλησία*, which we translate "congregation" or "Church" (*κυριακή*, the house or the assembly which belongs to the Lord). The word *ἐκκλησία* originally means the assembly of citizens duly summoned by the writ of the civic authorities. In ordinary daily speech it often meant no more than "assembly". But with Paul in particular it has received a deeper meaning, so that, linguistically, it has become a Christian eschatological deflection of the secular political word. The authority which summons it, calls it out, is now God, instead of the civil magistrate, and the body of citizens is the eternal people of God. The Church and its members are "citizens of heaven".

no lack of linguistic means for reproducing the words of the New Testament and causing them to live on even in indirect speech, in preaching and in hymnody. Naturally, much had been re-interpreted down the centuries or has received a different slant, yet it is possible, on the whole, through honest historical and philological labour to reach back to the original meaning, even, in a measure, to the original tone. Thus by translation and explanation we can transpose the writings of the New Testament into our time, speaking haltingly in our languages. But it is not *that* of which I speak.

Language is outward garb and form, yet not in such a way that it may be separated as the husk from the kernel or content, and so be clothed with a new husk, the form of another age. Yet we often think of something of this nature when the question arises of "translating" or transposing the gospel of the apostolic age to our own times, whether we regard language from an entirely superficial angle and make a "faithful" rendering from Greek into, e.g. Danish, or we dig somewhat deeper and regard much of the "content" as pertaining to the linguistic dress and, therefore, in need of explanation and transposition, such as customs, ways of perceiving events and contexts, etc. We still have a notion of something quantitative, the notion of a husk enclosing a kernel, of something movable, the wholeness of content, and of something dispensable, the form or the husk.

The "language" which is here in question is something more and something different, and the problem has a far wider scope. Were one to use an illustration, it would have to be that of an onion rather than a nut, since form and content, shell and kernel cannot be quantitatively separated. If one approaches *from without*, all is husk—on the outside the Greek language, then oriental custom and tradition, the Hellenistic dress of ideas, the late Jewish world of concepts and eschatology, the prophetic hope, the traditional morality, the God of the Fathers. It all acts as form, husk upon husk, till all has been peeled away. But if one approaches *from within*, it is all entirely different. Were one to meet a person in that distant age, were we to meet in the place where the message to him in *his* situation became a message to us in *our* situation, through him, all would be changed. His words, then, would break through all walls, whether of times, aesthetics, or world views. Then the "onion" would not be conjoining of wrappings or husks, but would itself be something with life. Then he would speak in *his* world and accompany us on our way through his world and into our own. We should not ask questions about content and husk, because that which was seen from without as a husk belongs to his words, bears his speech, constitutes his speech to us here and now. Then we should not ask about the appropriateness of the words, but about their ability to communicate as a bridge between man and man.

The way of the gospel goes from within. The way of theological inquiry goes from without and must do so, because it too, in its field, is explication and logic.

But the contemporary world, if it wishes to be true to its own nature and yet seek to include the "essence" of the gospel, must attempt to appropriate it from the outside.

The world picture into which the gospel has to be transplanted is capable of receiving something new only by absorbing it and assimilating it to its own nature, and the language which it speaks is one of conquest. It seeks to include: "nothing human is alien to it". The gospel, too, it seeks to include, in human fashion, and reproduce it in the same terms. Being analytic it would "clarify" it, and being humanistic it would "preserve values".

When the modern world picture with its language is confronted with the gospel it is confronted with an alien whole, as well as a number of separate concepts and words. Both the whole and its details suggest "values", which, however, it must test, sort out, and transpose.

The Church's gospel, so it is felt, is hopelessly doomed in the contemporary world and in the future; yet if the essence of the gospel is not preserved, then civilization itself is doomed. Contemporary humanism and contemporary existentialism are examples of the attempt to preserve the "totality" or the tone of the gospel for "contemporary man".

But in this attempt at saving the gospel the gospel itself ceases to exist. The language of the age into which it has to be transposed, leaves no room for it. Of this we could speak in many ways; I shall attempt to outline the matter by means of some examples of what happens to gospel words when they are "translated".

The New Testament word *sin* is connected with so many antiquated concepts. But from purely human presuppositions it is possible to retain it as a psychological concept, which does not break out of the humanistic cycle of thought. Sin, then, is man's moral deficiency, or, to put more strongly, his moral depravity. But in the gospel itself the word "sin" first receives its content in the form "a sinner" and "a debtor". At once the myth stands in the way of any attempt at appropriation. Here contemporary language, secularized language, is helpless, because sin now acquires a presupposition of an entirely different order, *God*, and the sense of this presupposition leaves no room for it in a modern psychological view. The gospel resists and says that sin is not moral depravity, sin is the attitude of our life towards God and man.

Forgiveness may become a humanistic word, but in the gospel the word first receives content in the context of *grace*, *the Cross*, *and salvation*. At once the myth exerts its pressure and secularized language is helpless. The words cannot be "translated" by means of the phenomena by which we attempt to render them in biological and psychological terms. *Forgiveness* is *not* man's "release to run a straight course". The words "grace", "cross", and "salvation" are mythical words which proclaim man's relationship with God, irrespective of the weight one would give the separate concepts each of them represents through their historical genesis. Grace, cross, salvation—no one would deny that the history of these words passes through concepts derived from experience of oriental despotism, sacrificial cultus, and the like. It is not, however, the archaeology of these words which is in question, but the words in the gospel context.

The word *faith* is psychologized and relativized. The known quantity "we" is substituted for the unknown and irrational one of "God", but the gospel word faith is unintelligible on the basis of this "we". Faith may become a moral concept, a concept of reverence, a concept of probability or possibility. But as a word of the *gospel* it cannot be "translated". It lies outside the self-consciousness of modern man, both when it is a question of faith in *God* in the biblical, that is, non-cosmic meaning, and when it is a question of faith in *the Cross*, in the Crucified, or, to use a contemporary term, the One who has been abandoned. Faith in, and confession of, him who has been abandoned is truth in the language of the gospel, in which the presupposition is man's responsibility before God and his submission to his judgement. It is untrue in secularized language, since that which had been abandoned cannot save. That which has been abandoned is, as such, deprived of all vitality, psychological as well as evolutionary.

None of the New Testament words is untouched by the goal which belongs to each of these two languages.

Christ is the truth, the proclamation in one language; it means that he is the only truth, the full truth about ourselves. *That* is the truth of the gospel, the absolute claim of Christianity. But if the truth of Christianity becomes a concept for *comparison*, we stand on the ground of the history of religions. We may then discuss the pros and cons of its absolute claims, we are in the world of relativities, the door has been opened for a concept of truth which has to do with observation and reflection, and it becomes irrelevant whether we think in speculative, religio-philosophical terms, or practical, rationalistic terms, scientifically or religiously. In that case truth is but a matter of comprehension. For ancient Gnosticism as for Neo-Platonism truth, in the final instance, is the common content of all concrete religions and of all religiosity. In the same way, for the rationalism of our centuries truth is the common core in the concrete great religions (cf. the ring and the rings in Lessing's "Nathan the Wise"), while for contemporary science truth is, and must be, a marginal concept, just as the mathematical concept of infinity is one. Truth becomes a question of degree of an intellectual nature, for us a relative and incomplete *insight*. So truth is never *among* us or addressed *to* us, but is pushed out ahead of us, into the future, into an infinitely remote future. Then truth is an idea without authority for the present in which we live, imposing no obligation upon us here and now. Then truth does not address us, but is merely a term connoting *our* manner of speaking about reality. *Into that language it is impossible to translate the gospel.*

The New Testament word *world*, the opposition to the kingdom of God, must needs be weakened and hollowed out, since for us "the world" involves no opposition, but embraces all that we know and all that we are, all the qualities of existence—all strength of emotion, all might of will, all power of knowledge, all grace and beauty, all fervour and depth of devotion, all constructive and destructive forces. It all depends on tensions and contrasts, inevitably so. If the world as we use the term encounters the world as the early Church used it, it encounters a vast constriction of meaning. It must then either itself become emasculated and as such lose its reality and vanish in monkishness and pietism, so that the gospel itself becomes saccharine and unreal, or else the world as the Church uses the word becomes a hollow and empty cliché by being measured by a standard which to us contains every possible meaning. The gospel, therefore, cannot be read and heard on the basis of this word of ours, except when the irrational idea of God the Creator stands behind this very word and divides it into categories of good and evil, *his* will and *our* will. We are thus beyond that realm of language; no psychology or philosophy are able here to create the means of translation.

The gospel cannot be humanized and survive. Secularized language, however humanistic its forms, cannot convey the message of the gospel. It is incapable, since it is itself a thing, not a form. That thing, which is identical with our will to conquest, our self-will, says "No" to the gospel. It has no room for the basic words of the gospel, neighbour, responsibility, guilt, sin, grace, faith, salvation, God. If these are to be admitted into it they must, as I have said previously, not merely be translated, but be *re-interpreted*, *dissolved*; they must slide into a world in which they are incinerated as thoroughly as a dead organism. Man, according to Epictetus, is dissolved into fire and water and air and ether; contemporary knowledge dissolves everything into elements, atoms, tensional proportions, relationships, mathematical formulae. No longer do even the basic words of the gospel speak from their own presuppositions, but from those imposed upon them by analytic thinking.

It is a question of the *taking* man and his nature, and consequently of the nature of analysis, of thinking. We touch upon the question of the competence of thinking as a means of technical orientation, as a criterion of truth, and as a light for life, but I shall not in this connection deal with it in detail. It is probably apparent what my opinion is on this matter, on the nature of thinking and of its language, which is the image of analysis and its servant. If we ascribe to it the quality of truth, which is the line from classical antiquity to Einstein, we must follow its way to the bitter end. It is not truth part of the way, so that it may be abandoned at one point or the other, where it is felt that it does violence to the gospel, or to religion, to morality, or to humanity itself.

Yet this is what is happening. In one way or the other help is being sought in the gospel to counter the effects of destructive thinking. This might be done in days gone by through a radical rationalism; in our own day it is being done particularly in conjunction with existentialist philosophy.

An emergency situation has arisen. We have been squeezed into a closed world, of which the determined course has been explained empirically, in which our minds make use of concepts and logic as its tools, yet our mind is merely a matter of chemistry. Then we rebel with the insistence that, in spite of all, we are something else. To be sure, existentialism is willing, in thought, to go the whole way, but it refuses to construct its understanding of life on that basis. It refuses to become fossilized in objectivity, in the mechanization of the analytic way, since it too has seen, indeed has insisted, that for him who exists man is more than a piece of complex biochemistry. It thus introduces, in the form of a mystique, a new kind of metaphysics. Although it is bound in a world enclosed by laws it seeks help for its need from the gospel, and finds self-knowledge in responsibility, self-determination in the world of death and meaninglessness.

Now *existence* is a concept with many meanings. With Kierkegaard, from whom the word was borrowed, often with a certain recklessness, there can be no question about existence and authenticity until man is confronted with the living God in an open world. For others the word connotes man's authenticity in a closed world. On the one hand, then, it is man in his authenticity in the presence of a God who judges, acts, and saves; on the other hand it is man in his authenticity as one who knows himself and achieves self-determination in a world that is closed, bound by logical coherence yet without meaning. With the word God myth has received its recognition, but with the word self-determination the door has been opened to mysticism. Both these concepts can be religious, the latter as well as the former, but they cannot both convey the gospel.

Of course every philosophy which is not content simply to recapitulate the specialized sciences of the day has the right of positing a basic axiom and building upon it, and thus becoming a philosophy of life. The axiom of existentialism, that man has power only as he knows, but is powerless as merely existing and subject to the alien authority of the other, and therefore subject to demands and responsibility in the midst of meaninglessness, is a borrowing from the gospel for the sake of rescuing humanity. It is idle to ask whether by borrowing in this way it has not become disguised theology. It has, however, borrowed this basic axiom without either the word or the concept, God. As a message it came into the world through the gospel, as a concept it has been appropriated by a philosophy. The question is thus merely, whether this basic axiom actually can endure in and by speculation, or whether it can only be maintained as faith, faith that man is subject to the *demand* of life through his fellow-man. This is proclamation. But who is the authority who proclaims this? Before what court is man summoned for judgement? Existentialism walks on a razor's edge between faith and speculation.

Wherever the determinate nature of the world acknowledged by contemporary thought is taken seriously, yet in some kind of intellectual mysticism, on the basis of human consciousness, authenticity and inauthenticity are being proclaimed, the struggle is being carried on in defence of humanity against the demand of speculation to dominate life. Yet no way has been opened to the gospel any more than a way has been opened for the gospel to clothe itself in the garb of existentialism. This would mean the dissolution, not only of all the forms in which the gospel is expressed, but of the very gospel itself. Existence in the mystico-philosophical sense, and life in the gospel sense, have nothing to do with each other. Self-abandonment, self-determination, are matters of ethics, possibly even of religion, but not of the gospel. All apparent contact with the gospel is an illusion.

The reality of subjectivity, *our* reality, must overcome the world of intellect, of concept. Yet, since the world is closed, it is the concept which overcomes.

There is a difference between guilt as a reality and guilt as a concept. There is also a difference between guilt and the *consciousness* of guilt. A philosopher may possibly explain for us how the consciousness of guilt may be dissolved and vanish, but not how the reality of guilt may be removed by forgiveness. The former is a psychological event belonging to man, the latter is God's act and belongs to the gospel.

Existentialism as man's understanding of himself cannot become a language for the gospel.

Just as existentialism, particularly in the case of Heidegger (for there are many kinds of existentialism), has in desperation borrowed from the gospel and used its borrowing in an alien manner, so others in turn have borrowed from Heidegger and sought to use their borrowings for the gospel. I am here referring, of course, to the movement known as "demythologizing".

It is this *use* of existentialism, rather than the actual attempt at translating the myths of the New Testament, which is decisive. By this use of existentialism the gospel in its translation receives a stamp which, despite all enthusiasm in the opposite direction, threatens to deprive it of its prophetic and historical character and transpose it into a timeless mysticism.

It is first and foremost Bultmann who has created this theology of demythologizing and existentialism. His goal is a theology capable of shaping a proclamation, one which is a true exposition of the apostolic preaching, but in terms of our own presuppositions and our own means.

Thus the question of the gospel and its language becomes more acute than ever.

In outlining my position in the following pages with regard to Bultmann's views and methods I must of necessity begin with a few introductory remarks about the issue as a whole. Bultmann's goal is the gospel, the means by which he seeks to reach it is a certain theology. There is a conflict between his goal and his means. It is almost impossible to attack any feature of his work with justice and not, at the same time, accuse him unjustly. From the basis of his argument, which is our modern understanding of the world and existentialism, he works in such a manner that the gospel is in danger of entirely disappearing in his re-writing of it, simply because he refuses to say more than his method justifies. Where, however, his essential aim shines through clearly, one realizes that the word existence in his argument and in his intention belongs to two different worlds. No one can read his final paragraph in *Kerygma and Myth*, I (p. 100) without perceiving how he aims at that which is central in the gospel. Some, however, myself included, are unable to read his explanations without agreeing to a very large extent with those who have misunderstood him.

Bultmann has never sought to secure the gospel by cutting its cloth in accordance with the world picture of objective science,[1] but he seeks "a language in which the proclamation as well as faith may speak unambiguously".[2] But the language which he accepts as valid, that of comprehensibility and logic, inevitably holds on to the gospel in a closed world, whether a mystical or a rational one.

Without doubt Bultmann has said, or at least has intended to say, that "it is indeed part of the *skandalon* that, as the Christian Church has always asserted, our salvation is One who is involved in all the relativity of history".[3] Yet the language which he recognizes as valid refuses him the possibility of actually saying so.

[1] *Kerygma und Mythos*, II, p. 187. [2] Ibid., p. 188.

[3] *Kerygma and Myth*, I, p. 111.

Furthermore, Bultmann's explanations, when compared, e.g. with his final paragraph, are a notable instance of how a language borne by definitions is incapable of expressing spiritual things, as compared with a language which, in the best sense of the term, is naïve, and which, following the example of Luther, proclaims the paradox and the simplicity of the gospel.

The New Testament proclamation of salvation is entirely rooted in myth. To this belongs not only everything which is the immediate corollary of the primitive world picture, such as the assumption that the world is governed by wills, demons, spirits, and God intervening in its course; death viewed as a penalty; this world separated from the world to come by the Day of Judgement; but also the very basic concepts of the gospel concerning Jesus Christ, his pre-existence, his atoning Cross, his Resurrection, his life in the Church and with God in eternity.

As thoughts and concepts these are all language altogether remote from contemporary man. It is not merely that it is meaningless for us, even though it was full of meaning for its contemporaries. Miracles, for instance, had their importance for that time because of the very content of the events; for us, however, they are meaningless because they break the order of nature. At that time, however, there was no conception of nature and the laws of nature; but there was a vivid awareness of men in action, of spirits in action, of God himself in action every moment, controlling the course of all things. Therefore, for the hearers of that age miracles were an eloquent language, since power over demons, the sign of God, evoked faith when the Word of God had opened the ear of the hearer. But for contemporary men, who think in terms of natural laws, it is silent; it raises questions about explanations and therefore begets doubt. But, more than that, the whole series of myths about heaven, Christ, eternal life, is for us not merely remote and foreign speech, but a barrier, speech that offends, not our ego, but our thinking. It is not the true and real offence of the gospel, which belongs to our standing naked before God, but an unreal, external, and false offence which may bar the way for that speech of God which both offends and saves.

It is all myth, but behind it the gospel lies hidden.

For many people the situation is, that the gospel must be set free by demythologizing in order that it may speak to contemporary man. A radical division and translation of the gospel is its only hope for survival in a future which must yield to realities, to our modern recognition of the true nature of earth and heaven, the nature of man as limited by time.

So two entirely unconnected factors enter into collaboration, the gospel message that God is speaking here and now, and the message of science. The attempt is made to hold on simultaneously to the God of the gospel and to naturalistic man. Here existentialism comes to aid. Bultmann wishes to translate mythical thinking into the language of existentialism in order to save the gospel for the present age.

"Not by myth, but by *the Cross* does the Church stand or fall."[1] The truth of the gospel is lost where we hold on to the myth. The truth of the gospel must be made valid anew and comprehensible to us, and its truth is *the Cross*, the abandonment and self-sacrifice of a man for his neighbour even unto death; hence it is the Cross both as judgement upon us and as victory over the tyranny of death, and thus as the renewal of life, as "resurrection" through self-sacrifice even unto death. As a person Jesus is dead, like all that has ever lived. As the Crucified he is the Resurrection and the Life. By faith in the Cross as the Word of God about man, man is liberated from his fallen plight and is saved, within this closed world of ours, for reality as man, for existence, for his authentic being, for new life, for obedience, for living for his fellow-man. That gospel, says Bultmann, is actually both *the true intention of the apostles* and also capable of being heard by contemporary man and accessible to him. It removes the false stumbling-block which originates in that which is merely a cross for thinking, while retaining the true stumbling-block which is expressed in man's refusal to hear *God* speaking and to receive God's salvation through the life of an individual man bound in the relativity of all history.

The theology of Bultmann has been under sharp debate for well

[1] Harbsmeier in *Kerygma und Mythos*, I², p. 67.

over a decade, not only in Germany,[1] but elsewhere as well. Many have taken his side, and many have violently attacked him. Both parties have, however, this in common, that they think that *theological* work can clarify the question, possibly even decide it. Theology is thus assigned a task which no theology can fulfil, because it, too, being borne by concepts and logic, is bound to a language which cannot contain that which is primitive.

Barth's argument against Bultmann[2] does not clarify matters. His theology is in essence the old supernaturalism which is nothing else than naturalism repeated on a celestial plane. Barth cannot justly reproach Bultmann both as a systematic theologian and as an exegete for "his silent presupposition of modern science", when Barth himself presupposes and employs his earthly logic on a higher plane or, to take a specific instance, argues for the possibility of the Resurrection as event in time and space beyond verification on our part. In that case revelation becomes no more than a series of sporadic penetrations from the higher plane to one below "perpendicularly from above", and to their mutual disturbance. Truth thus becomes akin to probability and faith becomes an assertion of the category of knowledge. It is really of no avail that Barth can give reasons.

To take another example, Thielicke[3] makes a great effort to discover a fixed boundary between the mythical element which belongs to the historical dress of the New Testament and which for us can thus be no more than a pictorial expression of reality, and another mythical element which is a direct expression of supernatural, yet historical, realities. This is a hopeless task, for where is the criterion for such a distinction? The boundary may be drawn with equal justification anywhere. Thielicke himself, to take an instance, draws a line between the Virgin Birth, which lies on the side of imagery, and the Incarnation of the Son of God which, like the Resurrection, lies on the side of reality. A generation ago, in the very same circles within the Church, the

[1] See the various contributions in *Kerygma and Myth*, I.

[2] See above, pp. 83ff. and the replies of Hartlich and Sachs (*Kerygma und Mythos*, II, pp. 113–149), commended by Bultmann (ibid., p. 179).

[3] See *Kerygma and Myth*, I, pp. 138–174.

Virgin Birth itself would have been on the side of reality. Such a drawing of lines will never be anything else than the expression of an arbitrary halt somewhere on an ever-receding line and aims in reality at nothing else than the establishment of a minimum standard of faith.

The presupposition is still that exegesis and reasoning, that is, theology, must be capable of establishing and rescuing that which is essential. This is nothing else than failure to recognize the destructive nature of analysis.

Is not this, however, equally true of Bultmann's theology, or rather, of his method? Is it an accident that Bultmann's construction is demolished on existentialist grounds by his disciple Kamlah? When Bultmann wishes to replace the myth with a new language to convey the gospel, a language based on comprehension, logic, and method, does he not by this very act capitulate, in the first instance to that existentialism which was his starting point, and in the final instance to naturalism?

Modern science by its understanding of nature, and modern man by his self-consciousness, exclude the speech of the New Testament myth to its very last vestiges. While Bultmann shares this understanding of nature and this self-consciousness as his presuppositions, and desires to "interpret the New Testament in the categories of Heidegger's philosophy of existence",[1] yet he wishes to use this philosophy as a "prior understanding", rather than remain in it. Unlike all philosophy since the time of Socrates he refuses to permit man's recognition of his own fallenness to become identical with his liberation therefrom or to become the means whereby it is achieved. He wants to hear the words of the gospel to the effect that this very thing, like "justification through the works of the law", is itself man's fallen plight, man's pride, man's sin, his rebellion against God. He wants to hear the words of the gospel, that it is not by man's choice, but through the *act of God* that man is saved for freedom and obedience, that he is saved from himself as he is, that God regards him as that which is *not*, that "the arbitrary one . . . is freed from himself. It is that very thing which the New Testament preaching proclaims. This

[1] *Kerygma und Mythos*, I[2], p. 33.

is the meaning of the Christ-event. It states, that where man is unable to act, God acts, and has acted for him."[1] This is a forceful summary of Luther's interpretation of Paul. The connection with the New Testament consists not in thoughts about the Incarnation, not the Resurrection, but the Cross. Everything else is demythologized to the vanishing point.

That is what the Cross comes to mean, when existentialism is the starting point of understanding, or its "prior understanding" —if this understanding really opens the door to the "intention" of the apostles themselves.

It is true, indeed, that every true understanding demands a prior understanding, prior presuppositions. This is true of all human things, of art, of history, of our fellow-man himself. The ear must be attuned to that which it hears, otherwise it hears wrongly or not at all. Hence there is so much historical science and so much understanding of the gospel which is beside the point.

The gospel *has* its "prior understanding", its presupposition for being heard. This presupposition, apart from all externals such as language, civilization, ability of perception, etc., consists in *being* human, not in a philosophy about human existence. If a philosophy about human existence is made into a presupposition, it is inevitable that not only is there a systematization, but also that a limitation, determined by the age, of the concept "man" is introduced in advance, and in its turn affects the understanding of the gospel. And if by this presupposition is meant no more than "*being* human", even though one works from a *philosophy* of human existence, ambiguity cannot be avoided.

Bultmann's prior understanding of the gospel is the philosophy of existence. It calls a man out of security and points to responsibility, yet it permits man, without a cross for his intellect, to remain in his world that is closed by scientific knowledge, and permits existence to remain in immanence. The *self-consciousness* of modern man is the key-word which Bultmann takes with him into his understanding of the gospel as its prior understanding. This self-consciousness he seeks to unite with the speech of the

[1] *Kerygma und Mythos*, I², pp. 38–39.

gospel, with "the Word of the Cross", and thereby to deepen and explain it.

But does this self-consciousness, of which the content and the goal is man himself, qualify as a prior understanding for a gospel which says that human life has content only as belonging to *God*? Can a philosophy whose leit-motif is man's loneliness in a closed world create concepts and categories capable of interpreting the proclamation of the gospel, in which man is understood exclusively in relation to God? A self-consciousness whose basis is that the course of existence is a closed circle and that heaven is empty—a self-consciousness, whose basic characteristic is, that it knows God, or rather, is known by him? (Gal. 4. 9).

Any basis in existentialist philosophy for understanding the gospel is a borrowing from the gospel itself. Bultmann's own basis for understanding points more to Luther than to Heidegger. That is why there is so strong an evangelical line through the writings of Bultmann, wherever he is primitive and does not work with definitions and logic. In itself existentialist philosophy opens no way. The responsibility which a man *chooses* to take upon himself in order that he may rescue his own humanity from the emptiness of objectification in an existence devoid of meaning and goal is not the same as the responsibility which the gospel proclaims *is* ours towards God in our fellow-man. If a stand is taken on the basis of the self-consciousness of modern man, then, even when dealing with the New Testament, one has surrendered to the science of religion and the multiformity of the history of religions. The self-consciousness of existentialism is no more a prior understanding for the Cross than for Hinduism or for anthroposophy.

The self-consciousness of existentialism has a *self-chosen* validity. But the speech of the gospel is, that God in Christ *gives* us the only valid understanding of self. This latter is also what Bultmann really intends, his evangelical goal.[1] In that case, however, we are outside the self-understanding of the closed world and once more involved in myth, the myth that tells of the God who acts and judges.

[1] See the quotation in *Kerygma und Mythos*, II², p. 90.

In the New Testament, says Bultmann, there are mythical notions and concepts which aim at truths which cannot be expressed in the objective language of science. In mythical language, then, a *provisional* expression is found for something for which there is, as yet, no adequate language.[1] To discover and to mould a language of comprehensibility, in which both the proclamation and faith may speak without misunderstandings, is the task of the new theology.

It has at all times been the hope of devout theologians to create a science of the gospel, a devout department of speculation. This hope, however, is based on a confusion between subject and method. A devout person can theologize, just as he can be an artisan or a biologist; theology itself can never be devout. In part it is due to a failure to recognize this that the problem of demythologizing is so complicated.

With the recognition of a "science of faith" as supporting and regulating the proclamation, the responsibility of theology is exalted to impossible heights. The consequences in the Church's life have never failed to manifest themselves, from the primitive Church to our own day. If theology is a science, its responsibility is a very human one and does not extend beyond the competence of speculation, and it is itself limited by the capacity of speculative thought. By virtue of its biological origin thought is a means of capturing, of hunting in "the struggle for existence". It is the way to material, but not to life. The same is true of theology as a science, and therefore also of the responsibility of theology.

How great an authority is ascribed to theology! It is the gospel which is proclamation, and proclamation has the character of authority. Does the gospel acquire this authority for *us* only after it has been sifted through theology? Does it not thereby become open to debate?

It is far from Bultmann's desire to let his theology be based upon objectifying thinking, or become an expression thereof. He does not aim at an objective science. Objectivity is death. Bultmann, however, means that as truly as there is a language and a science which speak objectively and reduce man to a mere

[1] *Kerygma und Mythos*, II, p. 186.

spectator, so there is also a language in which existence speaks *naïvely*, together with a *corresponding science* which speaks about existence without objectifying it, which are emancipated from every objectifying world picture, whether of myth or that of science.[1] In that language, methodically unfolding itself in comprehensibility and logic, theology must allow the gospel to speak.

It is this very thing, methodical interpretation, which Bultmann brings into close connection with existentialist philosophy.[2] In one way or other, he says, we are inevitably dependent, consciously or unconsciously, on some philosophical outlook as we expound. The question, then, is, which is the *right* philosophy, not, of course, in terms of the finally correct system, but rather "a philosophy with the right starting-point and the right goal".

"The 'right' philosophy is simply one which has worked out an appropriate terminology for the understanding of existence, an understanding involved in human existence itself". But in the explanation it is still not made clear whether this merely means that human existence is something else than *mere* being, "that existence means a form of Being which assumes complete responsibility for itself", and that, therefore, "apart from the resolve to be human, being a person who accepts responsibility for his own Being, not a single word of Scripture is intelligible as a word with existential relevance", or else that the understanding of existence has its own definite content, in other words, a philosophy based on the "contemporary" understanding of man. Its practical utilization indicates the latter. When Bultmann, therefore, admits that "this means subordinating the work of exegesis to that of the philosopher", it is no comfort to be told that "as truly as Scripture and the proclamation speak out of existence and to existence, and as truly as faith is an existential self-consciousness, neither exegesis, proclamation, nor faith need be afraid of becoming subordinate to a science which is alien to their nature", for the science in question is not objectifying science, but consists merely in "systematizing the understanding

[1] *Kerygma und Mythos*, II, pp. 187–189.
[2] See *Kerygma and Myth*, I, pp. 193ff.

of existence involved in existence itself''. It is no comfort; for what gives cause for anxiety is whether it is in *this* sense that ''Scripture speaks out of existence'' and that ''faith is an existential self-consciousness''.

The results of existentialist exegesis show that in the use of existentialist philosophy as an aid to interpretation something else was involved, something more than the mere assertion that it is man who is being spoken to. By virtue of this and the consequent demand for method and logic an alien authority has intruded as an interpreter of the New Testament proclamation. In the course of history it was methodical thinking which created the objective language of science out of the naïve, rough and ready language of daily living. By the very nature of thinking it will continue to be so. It is an old hope and dream of theology to think and speak methodically and scientifically about man in his reality, his existence in the presence of God, but it is no more than a wishful dream. The circumstances for the ''existentialist'' theology of our own day are the same as those of the neo-Platonic theology of antiquity and of the Middle Ages. Where method begins, there does science, and where science begins, there does objectification.

With a theology which on the one side is systematic and faces our own time, and on the other is exegetical and faces the apostolic age, Bultmann undertakes to build a bridge between the New Testament and ourselves. It is one theology with two faces. He is convinced that it is exegesis, the examination of the text, which liberates the gospel from the dress of myth and brings it to us across that bridge. To me it seems clear that it is the systematic side of theology which determines the course of exegesis.

Bultmann maintains that it can be shown exegetically that the acceptance of redemptive events as external realities, e.g. the Resurrection, is *not* ''an essential and constitutive factor in New Testament faith'',[1] but merely functions as a means of expression for the proper intention of the apostles, viz. an existential gospel, and that, at least in the case of Paul and John, this acceptance is pushed aside wherever these events become a hindrance to the

[1] *Kerygma und Mythos*, II, p. 127.

existential proclamation and its appropriation by faith. The existential proclamation is essential, the acceptance of external events of salvation merely accidental.

But it is the prior understanding which determines this view. As a rule such a dichotomy is entirely out of the question. In the case of John it can be maintained only by means of many excisions and reinterpretations, e.g. in the case of 20. 29. In the case of Paul it is inevitably contradicted in innumerable passages, among them the Resurrection Chapter in I Cor. 15, in which the acceptance of external fact by no means is pushed aside, to say nothing of the basis of all apostolic and post-apostolic apologetic and polemics both against Judaism and Gnosticism.

It is at least clear that what Bultmann offers is an exegesis *ad hominem*, an exegesis which carries proclamation rather than an exegesis in an ordinary historical and philological sense. The latter kind would merely demonstrate the great chasm between the apostles and ourselves. Bultmann's exegesis seeks to bring the apostolic proclamation close to us by indicating a tension between that element of it which expresses their world picture, their mythological concepts about Christ, the end of time, and eternity, and that other element which expresses their appropriation by faith and their essential proclamation, their existential understanding. Therefore the expression of faith must be separated from the life of faith, and a bridge must be built for the latter to ourselves with our understanding of nature and of ourselves, so different from that of the apostles.

It is the apostolic proclamation of faith which is our concern and which we are able to receive. It is the goal of the apostolic proclamation, or, to use Bultmann's term, the *intention* of the apostles, which is the object and goal of exegesis.

The word intention, however, introduces much ambiguity. Does it mean what the apostles really wished to say, what an existential interpretation discovers with them, or what God would speak to us through the proclamation? Probably it is the former; but if the former is to be found through the latter, and if the latter is the gospel itself and is God's speech to us—what then?

It is the unity of Bultmann's exegetical and systematic theology which produces confusion, as well as his conviction that theology can at one and the same time serve science and faith.

Every interpreter must cross-examine the text with which he is engaged in a dialogue, out of a prior understanding, if he has any hope whatever of obtaining an answer to his questions. In this Bultmann, of course, is right. It is impossible not to have presuppositions, and if it were possible the text would be silent and the dialogue fruitless. But since he must ask the questions from his own prior understanding he must be conscious that the text may give different answers to different interrogators. The mere presence of "method" with the interrogator does not guarantee the correctness of the "answer" in itself.

The answer will be affected by the prior understanding, the existentialist understanding of man. The intention of the answer given in the New Testament will have overtones of the questioner's intention, that of the existentialist theologian. When the answers which the reading of the text gradually yields seem to the questioner to be marked by great comprehensibility, clarity and evangelical strength, the consequence may well be that not only does the prior understanding condition the answers of the text, but also that the text itself will be bowdlerized in order that its intention may be presented with greater clarity and force. An instance of this seems to me to be found in Bultmann's treatment of the Gospel of John.

Bultmann is convinced that the prior understanding by which he finds the intention of the proclamation of the New Testament, and the standard whereby he measures it, are not alien to the gospel itself, but may be shown to belong to it—the appropriation of the proclamation of salvation, the self-understanding of faith. Thus he has justification from the gospel itself to disengage this existential message from the mythical form in which it is involved in misunderstandings, even though the New Testament witnesses feel no contradiction between their existential proclamation and their proclamation of external, concrete miracles of salvation whether past or future, such as pre-existence, resurrection, and parousia, a contradiction which we are bound to feel.

Yet it is not that easy to discover the existential intention isolated and clearly expressed in contrast with the accidental phenomena within the New Testament itself. Some passages, however, are pointed out, especially the Thomas story in the Gospel of John (chapter 20) with verse 29, "Blessed are they that have not seen, and yet have believed". I quote: "Is not this view characterized as the attitude of unbelief, in the story of Thomas? The point of this story is, surely, that the faith to which salvation is promised must be independent of the miraculous event of the Resurrection. The encounter of faith with Christ, to which the beatitude (John 20. 29) applies, must under no circumstances have the event or the supposed truth of the miraculous happening of the Resurrection as an indispensable condition. The Genuine Easter faith does not depend on bodily appearances of the Risen One. They are not essential to it. . . . With this daring word (John 20. 29) which liberates from all historical scruples the gospel reaches its climax."[1]

Is this exegesis? Had it been the intention of John to say so, would it not have been simpler either not to mention any bodily resurrection of Jesus at all, or, if it was felt as a way to unbelief, directly to deny it? Yet now, apart from the whole context of Mary Magdalene, Peter, and John, the story *is* in the gospel with its drastic emphasis on corporeity. The very saying, "Blessed are they that have not seen, and yet have believed", is connected with this story, a saying which itself presupposes that there are those who *have* seen.[2] If this is a polemic against the tradition of an external resurrection event, it is as complete a failure as possible. No, the intention of John is not an existentialist message which disengages itself from the mythical form. The words do not mean that the disciples really ought to have attained the resurrection faith apart from any irrelevant resurrection appearances, for then John would have understood the bodily resurrection as an aid to faith supplied by God, yet one quite superfluous and even harmful to that faith. In that case John obligingly makes a

[1] Hartlich, Sachs in *Kerygma und Mythos*, II, p. 145, footnote, quoting Strathmann's commentary on John *ad loc.*

[2] Purely grammatically the sentence makes no sense if the object of "believed" is not identical with that of "seen", viz. him who has risen in the body.

great deal of it throughout the whole chapter, only to overthrow it all at the end with a "daring word".

Such an interpretation of the Evangelist's intention is meaningless.

The aim of John is conditioned both by the situation of the story and by that of his contemporaries. It is very simple and straightforward—the Risen One has revealed himself to the Ten; Thomas was not there the first time. John now tells us that the conditions for Thomas' faith after the first appearance were no different from those of the whole Christian community after that, in the days of John's old age and in our own as well; one must come to faith through the testimony of others, through the testimony of the first disciples, to which God gives the power of truth in those who believe. In his terrible doubt Thomas was unwilling to accept faith on the conditions of the community, hence the reproof. Yet the Risen Lord wished to have all his eleven apostles as witnesses, therefore he revealed himself to Thomas as well. Thus it has stood for the disciples from the very first times. Paul, too, claimed the name of apostle with the words, "Am I not an apostle? Have I not seen the Lord?" As witnesses the apostles have a special position,[1] but precisely none as believers ("Blessed are they . . ."). It is actually as simple and naïve for our understanding as the whole apostolic and post-apostolic speaking of witnesses and faith.[2] Those disciples of John who, after his death, added chapter 21 to the gospel may have erred in their use of materials, but they did not misinterpret his intention. It was simple and naïve. There was nothing subtle about it.

It is not, of course, to speak about the Resurrection, but to say something about prior understanding and reading, that I have delayed so long over this matter. As certainly as prior understanding is necessary, just as certainly the system must overcome exegesis in a theology which has its own prior understanding of the nature of the gospel, yet remains bound to Scripture. However curious it may sound, it is because the new theology is

[1] Cf. Paul's statements in I Cor. 9. 1 and 15. 8.
[2] E.g., Romans 10. 13ff.

too closely bound to Scripture that the apostles are made to proclaim existential faith. Thus this interpretation of passages such as John 20. 29 travels from one country to the other, and people are pleased with John!

In the same way they are pleased with Paul where he, too, seems to be susceptible to a similar interpretation of his intention, until they are brutally checked, e.g. by 1 Cor. 15. 12—"How say some among you that there is no resurrection of the dead?" Here Paul engages in the most violent polemic against the belief of "some among you" that the gospel remains valid even when, or precisely when, it is not united with the concept of a resurrection in an external sense. If faith, faith for this life (cf. verse 19) without a resurrection myth, without reference to external miracles of salvation, without support in an external "faith" which is but a counterfeit of true, existential faith—if this was the real intention of the apostolic proclamation, then Paul must at least have been able to recognize that faith when he encountered it.[1] Instead he makes an all-out effort to brand it as devoid of content and as unfruitful. For Paul the resurrection faith is as far removed as possible from being an expression of something else, an expression of faith in the Cross. On the contrary, his demonstration begins from that which is wholly external, the resurrection of men in general, which he relates to Christ's resurrection, the remission of sins, and the content of life: "How can you say 'the dead are not raised'?" "If there be no resurrection, then Christ is not risen: and if Christ be not risen, then is our preaching vain, and your faith is also vain . . . ye are yet in your sins . . . we are found false witnesses of God; because we have testified of God that he raised up Christ, whom he raised not up, if so be that the dead rise not." Paul had here the best opportunity possible of recognizing the nature of existential faith. But so utterly foreign is that thought to him that he can go so far as to say: "If in this life only we have hope in Christ, we are of all men most miserable. . . . Why stand we in jeopardy every hour? If the dead rise not, 'let us eat and drink, for to-morrow we die'."

[1] In II Tim. 2. 18 a similar belief appears to receive a similar treatment.

It is not according to the impulse of the moment that he is speaking here. He drives his point home by repetition. In between he argues along other lines. He explains the biblical and theological necessity of the Resurrection in God's whole plan of salvation. He speaks about the order of the resurrections; he speaks at length about the "how" of the Resurrection. But before all arguments he posits the Resurrection of Christ as the beginning of the gospel and its foundation. It is the days and months after Easter of which he thinks in retrospect. The Resurrection of Christ on the third day, that is what the others, Peter and the circle from Galilee and Jerusalem, had proclaimed as the gospel from the very first, and that which he himself had told them among the first things, "that which you have received . . . and without which your faith is vain", the Resurrection of Christ, firmly based on testimony. He enumerates the series of eye-witnesses by name, from Cephas to himself. This is, indeed, "fatal", whether for Paul or for those who seek to disentangle the real intention of Paul and the other apostles from that which is "incidental".

We may dissociate ourselves from this, but we cannot explain it away. Concreteness is not a mere incidental of the apostolic proclamation, but basic to it. We must allow 1 Cor. 15 to be what it is: not an exception, a fatal example of objectivity in the midst of that which Paul intended to be existential, but a starting point which explains, which shows us Paul's proclamation in its primitiveness and at the same time deprives an existential proclamation of its Scriptural basis. Intention is a dangerous word to use when it is a question of exegesis.

And how do we know that by separating it from the myth, that which was existential for the apostles becomes that existential element which *we* are seeking? We desire to make their aim our own, so that we may receive from them that part of their message which we do not wish to lose. But is what *our* generation is seeking, for instance, in the remission of sins ("this was the central core for Luther"), the same thing which the apostolic gospel proclaims with these words? Our generation has no hope of an eternal kingdom in heaven for a chosen people and no fear of an eternal hell, but we do fear psychological conflict. We know by experience that forgiveness indeed sets free, that it eases psychological pressure and breaks down the barriers between persons so that life may continue in openness and on a straight course. This, then, must be the real intention of the apostles. But no, in the apostolic gospel the remission of sins is a message about what we have been before and what we are now in God's sight, not what we feel ourselves to be. It is a judgement of God and an act of God which point forward; God wills to create a people which he acknowledges to be pure for the coming kingdom. Therefore the remission of sins takes place, according to the apostolic gospel, by the authority of Jesus, the coming Messiah. In the primitive community it is connected with Jesus' death upon the Cross and mediated to us through baptism, the door to membership of the people of God. It is true that for the individual as well it is peace to know that he is not subject to God's wrath, but to his grace. Yet in the apostolic community the remission of sins is proclaimed, not for the sake of personal peace of conscience, but for the sake of the sovereign rule of God, that his kingdom may come, and his will be done. This is how the New Testament speaks. Theology cannot by interpretation add something which in the New Testament is inseparably bound to that which this same theology denies. If speech about the coming kingdom of God, the end of the world, judgement, eternal life, is merely conditioned by a certain age and bound to it, then the speech about the remission of sins has itself no root. A subjective, existential interpretation lies outside the intention of the apostles.

In the New Testament proclamation, the Cross and the Resurrection belong inseparably together, but as two separate events, each with its own effects, interpreted mythologically.

For Bultmann, too, the Cross and Resurrection are inseparable, but as a single event, that of the Cross. For Bultmann the Resurrection is the expression of the Cross in faith,[1] and the

[1] "Faith in the Resurrection is really the same thing as faith in the saving efficacy of the cross", *Kerygma and Myth*, I, p. 41. "The resurrection of Christ is simply an attempt to convey the meaning of the cross", *Kerygma and Myth*, I, p. 38.

Cross is an event of salvation because it is proclaimed as such, because it is proclaimed together with the Resurrection, and proclaimed as resurrection.[1] To believe in the Cross is to appropriate the Cross of Christ for oneself, to let oneself be crucified with Christ. The Cross as a saving event is not an isolated incident, but an event of cosmic importance . . . It is not merely an event of the past which can be contemplated in detachment, but the eschatological event in and beyond time, for as far as its meaning —that is, its meaning for faith[2]—is concerned, it is an ever-present reality.[3] As an event of salvation the Cross of Christ is an historical occurrence originating in the past historical event which is the crucifixion of Jesus of Nazareth. Its significance is the judgement of the world, the judgement of man and his liberation. The preaching of the Cross challenges the hearer to appropriate this significance for himself, to be willing to be crucified with Christ. Only for the first preachers of the gospel, those who had lived in personal fellowship with Jesus and believed in him, can the effectual significance of the Cross be due to the fact that it was the cross of the historical Jesus. For us it is impossible to understand the effectual significance of the Cross on this basis. For us it must mean faith in Christ prior to faith in the saving significance of the Cross. We cannot, however, "return to the historical Jesus", as he for us has become part of history and all its problems. For us there is only the *proclamation of the Cross*, and we can accept this proclamation in its effectual significance.[4] "The saving efficacy of the Cross is not derived from the fact that it is the cross of Christ: it is the cross of Christ because it has this saving efficacy."[5]

In that case, however, we are no longer in the directness of the apostolic gospel, but in an existentialist theology to which the gospel has given rise, a theology which approximates to a philosophy of life. It is a proclamation which is being progressively liberated from the New Testament, in which it originated, and

[1] *Kerygma and Myth*, I, p. 41.
[2] Bultmann's *Bedeutsamkeit* implies, *inter alia*, content, meaning, effect.
[3] *Kerygma and Myth*, I, p. 36.
[4] Ibid., I, pp. 37–38.
[5] Ibid., I, p. 41.

increasingly dependent upon a philosophy. *The* Cross becomes *a* cross.

Bultmann's explanations about the resurrection faith as expressing faith in the Cross are intended as an evangelical theodicy. But it is not in this way that the proclamation of the New Testament can be rescued; it is hopelessly consistent. In it the Resurrection is the basis of faith in the Cross, not the form in which that faith is expressed. Everything which is proclaimed in the New Testament about the Cross is conditioned by faith in the Resurrection. For the apostles, if the Resurrection falls, the Cross falls with it, "and we are still in our sins". In the "scriptures" (e.g. Isa. 53) they found it confirmed and explained.

In existentialist theology the Cross becomes simultaneously a message of death and of victory. Death received from the hand of God *is* victory. Acceptance by faith of the message of the Cross is deliverance from self and thus renewal of life, resurrection to life. This is the gospel of the death upon the Cross.

This is the demythologized form of the Gospel of John the Baptist, of Jesus and Paul, concerning the coming of the kingdom.

Once again we encounter the remarkable fact that when demythologizing seeks to set man free from myth it leads him into mysticism. The gospel becomes the inward understanding of "the Cross". With Paul crucifixion *with* Jesus is not mystical, but mythical language, which joins the community to its Lord who died for it. As an expression of myth-less understanding of the Cross crucifixion with Christ becomes the full significance of the Cross, and we have thus entered into mysticism more rarefied than that of the Middle Ages or of pietism, in which at least the orthodox dogma about the Cross remained a dogma. We are in mysticism, not in the evangelical thought expressed in the lines:

When I on thy Cross am thinking
Under it my seal I find.[1]

That is a word which places the Cross on *God's* side.

[1] "Og naar paa dit kers jeg grunder
ser jeg og mit segl derunder".

Freely quoted by the author from a hymn by Thomas Kingo (1634–1703).

"Not with the myth, but with the Cross, does the Church stand or fall." The question is, which cross? As soon as one seriously undertakes to distinguish between the myth and the cross, the cross becomes psychological; if not, it remains myth. The choice is between the idea of the cross, and the cross itself. For an existentialist proclamation of the cross we have no support from the apostles.

Nor is there any support for distinguishing, by rationalization, between faith in the Cross and faith in Jesus. We cannot, says Bultmann, base our faith in the Cross on faith in Jesus, for we cannot, like the disciples, have a faith in Jesus prior to faith in the Cross. We cannot go back to the historical Jesus, for he has passed into the problematic sphere of history; but we can appropriate faith in the Cross as proclamation, because the Cross is proclaimed as resurrection. But is that proclamation of the Cross then less hidden in history with all its problems and relativity? Has it not happened many times over in history that the Cross has been proclaimed as resurrection? How often have not sacrifice, self-surrender even unto death, both been proclaimed as resurrection and had that effect for the generation or people among whom the sacrifice was offered? It has always been, not the cross by itself, but the cross in the context of him or of those who made the sacrifice of their persons, their wills, their work, their involvement, their effort. Where the pattern, that is, the background and the situation, fades away, the same will happen to the sacrifice, the cross, and its uniqueness. With the apostles the proclamation of the Cross is inseparably connected with the proclamation of Jesus, otherwise the Gospels would never have been written. In a gnosticizing proclamation of the Cross the historical figure inevitably faded away; in an apostolic proclamation, however existential and supra-historical, it never did.[1] The Gospel of

[1] When Paul states that he no longer knows anyone "after the flesh", not even Christ, or when Kierkegaard says, that the whole gospel is contained in the fact that the Deity at such and such a time became man, both are asserting the truth of the gospel. But it is truth with a special emphasis, truth in a special antithetical situation. The contrary assertion is, that one stands in a human relationship to a certain historical person, to Jesus himself. They state that the personal connection of the Twelve with Jesus is no advantage, any more than

John is the clearest example of this. The pattern and the Cross are concomitants. The pattern cannot be allowed to perish in relativity and the Cross to remain absolute. If we confine ourselves to historical research and reasoning, even theological reasoning, then both the pattern and the Cross lapse into relativity. But the apostolic thought is that the proclamation of the pattern and the Resurrection through the Holy Spirit awaken faith in Jesus which makes faith in the Cross possible, real and central.

The New Testament speaks about a *God who acts*, who is the basis of all that happens, while existentialism speaks about a personal attitude towards the meaning and goal of life in a world devoid of meaning and goal, in other words, of a decision with *man* as the basis. Hence the Gospel of the Cross, the Christ-event, if they enter here as proclamation, become *man's* occasion for understanding himself and making a decision. It thus comes to light that the language of existentialism is but a modified form of that secularized language which is incapable of bearing the apostolic proclamation.

Even Bultmann fights in vain against this tendency. The existentialist presuppositions dilute his theology, so that his evangelical goal fades away.

If man himself cannot choose and take the step from inauthenticity to authenticity, there has been no translation. Despite all changes of phraseology we are still in the myth, in the concepts of God's will and work through the Holy Spirit. If we ourselves actually are able to take that step from inauthenticity to authenticity at the instigation of the proclamation of the Cross and of faith, then, despite all changes of phraseology, we have a philosophical, pietistic, or catholic-mystical proclamation of salvation, but not an evangelical one. In that case salvation consists in the *idea* of the Cross, and our appropriation of it in an entrance into the *Cross*, an imitation of Christ, a repetition. The Resurrection

---

the admiration on the part of rationalists for "the noble Jesus". But as the background for the Cross or for the Incarnation, the pattern is equally indispensable for both Paul and Kierkegaard, as appears from their evangelically edifying speech.

becomes *a resurrection of faith through the idea of the Cross*, effective in its own right even where the historical Cross of Jesus fades away. Faith thus becomes an existentialist self-consciousness, however much one points to the event that gave the impulse to it.

In the corresponding language God, salvation, etc., finally become mere concepts, psychological concepts auxiliary to an emotional conception of Christianity, expressions for events in the soul, pietistic mysticism in rational dress.

The theological and ecclesiastical aim of demythologizing is "to assert the essential intention of the biblical writings"[1] by means of criticism. It is to a certain extent possible to speak and write about the intention of the New Testament proclamation, its essential meaning and goal as distinguished from its words. The attempt may also be made to transpose this proclamation of the gospel from a mythical language to a non-mythical one and find an expression of this proclamation which can be adequate for us—at least it is conceivable. It is, however, certain that the existentialist interpretation of the gospel, which is presumed to be the real intention of the New Testament and capable of saving the gospel from perishing, would never have been recognized as a translation by the New Testament witnesses themselves. They would have combated it with all their might as a falsehood (cf. Jesus' conflict with the Sadducees and Paul's against the protagonists of a spiritual resurrection), for them it would have been a proclamation similar to that of the gnostic heresy.

If it is a question of a contemporary view of what the gospel ought to be, the apostolic charge false doctrine would, of course, leave us unmoved. We might well speak of an existentialist interpretation as long as we are fully conscious that by doing so we are severing the link between the apostles and ourselves. But it can never be justified to pass such an interpretation off as an interpretation of the text. To do this would be going beyond the apostolic proclamation. Exegesis can never cease to ask *what* is being proclaimed. If a phrase such as the "intention" or "aim" of the apostles is not to be a source of confusion, it must mean something which is proper to them, in them, for them, not some-

[1] Bultmann, in *Kerygma und Mythos*, II, p. 184.

thing in ourselves or for ourselves. As for what is in them and for them, we have only historical means to discover it. In this matter we have no right by means of our interpretation to mix into their proclamation what it means to us. No more have we the right theologically to construct, out of their proclamation and that which their proclamation means to us, a conception of the nature of Christianity or of the content of the gospel in itself, emancipated from their conceptual forms.

In the discussions of demythologizing one continually encounters expressions such as these—the New Testament proclamation of the Resurrection *means* that with him the new age has dawned, that in him we partake of the grace of God, that God has come to us.

This is, of course, true. Such is its meaning. The proclamation of the Resurrection is naturally more than a mere proclamation that a dead person has returned to life. But what is implied by the verb "*means*"? Does it *mean* this for us or for the apostles? Is it a question of preaching among ourselves, or of interpretation of the text? Is it pastoral discourse, or is it exegesis? Its truth as an interpretation of the text depends upon what is read into the word "means". If its connotation is "it is a metaphor, the best and most natural way in which the disciples could proclaim the decisive event, the inauguration of the new age, in the language of their time . . .", that "the visions, the resurrection appearances, are irrelevant and have but a relative value",[1] then the interpretation is wrong, both as interpretation and as exegesis, regardless of its pastoral value for ourselves, regardless of what the proclamation of the Resurrection may mean to us.

It is at this point and at every other corresponding point in the apostolic proclamation that demythologizing makes the question of the apostolic proclamation and the gospel fade out of sight. I have previously mentioned the theological reason for this, that together with a modern prior understanding a generous quantity of old-fashioned scriptural theology is dragged along. Therefore the contradiction is bound to arise, and the auxiliary word "intention" makes its appearance in an attempt at mediation. By

[1] *Tidehverv*, 1944, pp. 10–11.

means of the ambiguous concept of interpretation the attempt is made to gain a foothold in the New Testament texts for a meaning which is pertinent for ourselves, but not for the apostles.

For the apostles the Resurrection of Jesus means that the new age has dawned, and with it the new relationship to God, the new self-understanding "behold, all things have become new". All this is true, but "means" signifies "effects", "demonstrates". For them the Resurrection of Jesus is not a circumlocution for the dawn of the new age, but its *proof*. If we are really serious about exegesis we must learn to put up with this difference.

In the middle of the past century there was an unwillingness in Protestant circles to admit that there was a strong, rapidly increasing churchly trend in the apostolic age and in the period immediately following. Consequently, in order to gain more time for a slow development, scholars began to scatter the earliest Christian literature over three or four generations, a mistake which it took a couple of theological generations to admit even in part. The apostles were not what we had thought. More recently a prior understanding of the presumed aim of the apostolic preaching has been a factor in rearranging what the tradition of the New Testament indicates as coming first and what followed later. But if the evangelical intention of the apostles is what they themselves indicate in their proclamation, there is no reason whatever, in the question of the Cross and Resurrection, to deviate from what they in their tradition indicate as coming first and as following later. It did not begin with faith in the Cross, but with the women at the Empty Tomb (what happened there is a separate matter). Then came the "visions", and out of these, on the basis of the resurrection faith, there grew the faith in the Cross in connection with the disciples experiences in fellowship with Jesus. This is the account of the oldest generation about this matter, and in such a matter there is no error of memory, certainly no unanimous error. In the details there are enough contradictions. But the essential matter, that it was faith in a concrete Resurrection which opened the way for faith in the Cross, *that* is the common presupposition. That is what after a certain Passover festival in Jerusalem agitated people far and wide, and then lived on for a couple of decades or just under a generation, in daily proclamation and contradiction, before the records known to us were compiled in earnest, while many of the persons who are mentioned as having had a part in it all were still living. The distance of memory is about the same as if a number of people in their fifties or sixties were to record the experiences which they had shared with many others in their twenties and thirties. This is true, quite apart from the great distance, mythologically speaking, between the proclamation of the primitive Palestinian community and that of the Hellenistic missionary community (in which Peter, by the way, quite clearly went the whole way from the one to the other). Neither do the great variations between the accounts of the appearances or their great inconsistencies affect the core of the matter, the common proclamation of the bodily Resurrection. It was only by virtue of the proclamation of the Resurrection as a palpable reality that the Church survived the "eschatological pause" which immediately set in, and which continued, the fact that nothing happened.

The Resurrection is for the apostles the starting point and basis for the proclamation of the new age, and therefore also, if one may use the term, for their existential proclamation. It is not an expression of that proclamation or a paraphrase of it. This is true in the case of the apostles, and of their disciples as well.

We must accept this fact and make up our minds about it. We may not, however, construct a pastoral theology for our times and call it exegesis. What a person with a modern attitude will make of a conception of faith which, since it is based on facts, appears to exclude the true nature of faith, is a separate question. All apostolic preachers, including John, state that the Resurrection appearances created faith. For those who did not see "faith comes by the proclamation", and the proclamation is not our own act, but the act of God through the Holy Spirit. Therefore, "blessed are those who believe" in the Risen Lord through the testimony of others. Faith, too, in the final analysis, is the work of God no less than the saving acts themselves. Behind all this is the thought that God himself creates and gathers to himself a believing people. The preacher is but a herald: believers are chosen by God.

Here, for the apostles, is the category of faith. It is not covered by our mutually exclusive categories of faith in facts and existential faith, two categories of which we are so fond in our theological discussions, but which cause us so much difficulty in actual life, as well as in our dialogue with the apostles.

When we examine this as a problem, we must face the difficulty that the categories of the apostles appear to overlap with our own categories to a sufficient extent as to make misunderstanding unavoidable. Thus the attempt to separate between the apostles' "faith in facts" and their existential faith by introducing the concept of "intention" is understandable, like the energetic struggle against all supra-naturalistic thinking which is intended to be an apologetic for Christianity. If the mythical proclamation of the New Testament concerning, e.g. the advent of the God-Man and his Resurrection are interpreted according to the contemporary conception of truth, and thus as objective, empirical truths, truths of fact, the whole aim of this proclamation is indeed misunderstood. Such mythical statements must not be isolated as assertions of fact in the accepted sense. But the apostolic proclamation does not divide reality into the categories of objective and existential, but into those of the acts of God and acts of the world. According to the New Testament the Risen Lord was seen, not by unbelievers, but only by those who believed; yet he was actually *seen*, and that by many. It is not an expression of objectivity in our sense of the word, nor of subjectivity. "God concealed it from unbelief."

It is not possible by means of exegesis to penetrate behind the conception of reality inherent in the apostolic proclamation and thus disentangle their intention from their actual proclamation. We may objectively perceive their conception of reality, and dissociate ourselves from their proclamation of facts. We may not, however, attribute to them an intention which is detached from their conception of reality and their proclamation of it, however definite it may be, since for them it is both the act of God and faith in it. We could not do so even if ninety-nine per cent of the apostolic proclamation dealt with the faith of the believer, since it would still deal, not with ourselves, but with God.

Hence all the talk about witnesses and faith in the apostolic and post-apostolic periods. According to our form of knowledge it is an expression of two opposite categories, objective and subjective. In the gospel, faith is included in the proclamation; from its very beginning the gospel has been both a message *that* and a message *about*. John the Baptist and Jesus proclaimed: "The reign of God is at hand, repent and be prepared." A few days after the crucifixion the disciples proclaimed: "The reign of God has begun, Christ is the first-fruits of the Resurrection, repent, believe, and enter into life; the Spirit is the pledge of eternal life." And Paul says: "For the hope of Israel and of the resurrection I am being accused." A couple of generations later the closing words of the Gospel of John were written: "These things were written, that ye might *believe* that *Jesus* is the Christ, the Son of God; and that believing[1] ye might have life through *his* name."[2] It is salvation, not by faith, but by *that* faith. The intention of the New Testament is not to proclaim faith, but to proclaim *that* something happened. To this "that" and to its content, faith included, the message of salvation in the New Testament is bound. No *theology* can remedy this.

True, the apostles do not proclaim the Resurrection as a mere brute fact. Such objectification is altogether alien to them. They proclaim it in its meaning, that Christ lives, that the kingdom of God is coming. But this meaning is for them inseparably bound to the Resurrection as an act of God with a character of palpability. From this palpability their witness takes its beginning. This is the case with Paul, with the first three gospels, with the gospel of John as well. 1 Cor. 15 and similar passages exemplify how strongly the external fact can be emphasized. The Gospel of John is an example of how strongly the meaning can be emphasized,

[1] The word "believing" does not imply that the state of faith constitutes life. This is not mysticism.

[2] I.e., by confession of what Jesus is by virtue of being the Christ of God.

but the two cannot be separated. In its struggle against Judaism on the one hand and Gnosticism on the other the apostolic and post-apostolic ages are one great testimony that the subject of the proclamation is the wonderful works of God which had *taken place* under Pontius Pilate, in Jerusalem, and in these the faith which they awakened, not in itself a goal or meaning of life, but an additional testimony that God gathers men into his kingdom. Thus Ignatius, among others, the disciple of the apostles, expresses it: "But as for me my charter is Jesus Christ, the inviolable charter is his cross and his death and his resurrection and faith through him."[1]

The goal of the apostles is not to proclaim faith, but to proclaim Jesus Christ. It is our categories which fail. We have no support from the apostles for the existential proclamation of faith which we seek in their preaching of the Cross, not even if we think that it is the only way to rescue the gospel.

Nor can we isolate or detach the New Testament proclamation of things to come, eschatology, from myth, and thus exploit it for the existentialist proclamation.

The apostolic gospel proclaims the fulfilment of the promises of God, "the Day of the Lord", the coming of Christ to judge the world, the establishment of his eternal kingdom, the resurrection of the dead to eternal life. The way is Christ, in whom converge both judgement and salvation, the Cross and Resurrection. The pledge, the gift by which it is conveyed, is the remission of sins. The truth, the reality of the forgiveness of sins inseparably unites the gospel to the proclamation of the eternal kingdom of the future. God *himself* creates for himself a holy people for his kingdom through the forgiveness of sins. For man grace and the kingdom mean one thing, salvation. Salvation stands and falls with the miracle of the Resurrection. If Christ be not risen, our faith is in vain, we still belong to sin and death, not to God. The Resurrection of Christ is inseparably bound to the Cross of Christ, the Cross of atonement. Christ the Crucified is from all eternity the Son of God and the Judge of the world; he is also

[1] *Philadelphians*, VIII. 2 (Lightfoot's translation).

Jesus, the carpenter from Nazareth, who proclaimed and still proclaims the words of life.

In the gospel the hereafter is inseparably bound to the present life, eschatology to history, the forgiveness of sins to God's eternal kingdom of the future.

If we reinterpret eschatology in order to rescue an existentialist gospel, or hold on to both the God of the gospel and empirical man, we fetter the gospel. Viewed eschatologically it means, not only that death is *our* limit, but also that *our* death is *God's* limit, and that the significance of death is that for God we have ceased to be. This is something which the apostolic gospel cannot be made to say.

Naturally, I cannot discuss this matter in detail, but be content with reminding you that the concept of the resurrection of the dead to eternal life occupies a central position in the proclamation of the earliest community. In this connection it is irrelevant how the concept arose. It is relevant that when the concept of the resurrection enters into late Judaism from outside it, it is brought in by the questionings concerning the fate of the pious and of the wicked, concerning God's justice and faithfulness. It is brought into a nation in which this life, more than for any other nation, was a divine reality, and in which death, more than for any other nation, was a reality and a divine ordinance. It is only in connection with the conception of God that the concept of the Resurrection has significance and meaning. At the time of Jesus its place was assured in the faith of the Jews, except in Sadduceean circles. In the Church it was strengthened and carried forward by the assurance that Christ lives, that where Christ is, there is life, and that where sin is, there is death. This, in turn, is one with the concept that those whom God has chosen, those for whom God has made himself God, *live* unto God. It is this which the fourth gospel tells us in the Lazarus story, "I am the resurrection and the life", with his raising as a sign from God, and which the first three gospels say through the words of Jesus to the Sadducees, "God spake, saying, 'I am the God of Abraham and the God of Isaac and the God of Jacob'; God is not the God of the dead, but of the living". Recently I saw this saying explained as follows,

"God addresses you, the living; Abraham, Isaac, and Jacob are dead and gone". This is, indeed, a striking specimen of the "translated" proclamation of Christianity, but diametrically opposite to what Jesus meant by his words, viz. that God has *not* dispensed with them. The words of Jesus move the patriarchs into the world of the gospel; the modernized proclamation moves the gospel back into the world of the patriarchs and identifies it with ancient Jewish piety, for even then the pious knew the "idea" of the Cross and lived by the grace of God under the condition of death.

I repeat—to attempt to hold together the God of the Gospel and naturalistic man means, not only that death is *our* limit, but also that *our* death is *God's* limit, that for God we have ceased to be. This is what Irenaeus meant when he said that then God has been vanquished and the devil reigns triumphantly in paradise. But the gospel proclaims *God's* victory. Nothing, not even death, can separate a man from the love of God through Jesus Christ.

There the apostles stood; there stands the Church's proclamation of the gospel, even though we can give it no natural significance. On the contrary, every attempt to explain or rationalize it only leads us further into contradictions.

God, here and now. That is the forgiveness of sins. That is the gospel. But a modernized proclamation seeks at the same time to be the gospel and to retain the point of reference of naturalism, man as being here and now, with death as his absolute limit. It seeks to retain this together with what is evangelical, the forgiveness of sins.

In the gospel, however, the significance of the forgiveness of sins is precisely that God does not dispense with us.

The proclamation of the gospel about man is, of course, meaningless to us. So, too, is the proclamation of death as the wages of sin. The devil, too, and death in all its meanings, physical, temporal, spiritual and eternal—their connection has no meaning for us. They acquire meaning only when we insert the natural man and natural death into the context of the proclamation. Then we can begin to discuss the *expediency* of the mortality of organisms in the economy of the world, both from the point of view of nutrition and of development, as some theologians actually do, the appropriateness of man's natural span of life to the progressive transmission of the innermost purposes of existence, social, ethical, and religious, brief enough to secure freshness and renewal, long enough to secure the connection with what already has been attained, with optimism as the principal virtue of the race and pious resignation as that of the individual, in accordance with the law of all organic life. But this is no jest! So it happens, and so it is bound to happen. If the man of naturalism takes the place of man as the gospel represents him, then the God of naturalism, whether conceived in the fashion of humanism or of biochemistry, will soon replace the God of the gospel, however desperate and however long we struggle to preserve the "idea" behind what is evangelical.

The forgiveness of sins, life and salvation; sin, death, and the devil—for the apostolic gospel they are inseparably connected, whether it is the New Testament which speaks, or Irenaeus, Luther, or Grundtvig. Death, naturalistically conceived, cannot enter into the gospel picture. The gospel cannot be proclaimed in that language.

The eschatology of the gospel cannot be isolated for another reason: the proclamation of things to come is not exclusively futurist. A futurist eschatology, in terms of an expectation looking forward to the coming judgement and the kingdom of glory,[1] in the form that the Christian expectation usually takes within the Church, *is* a conspicuous feature in the hope of the apostolic age and in that of the preceding age of Judaism, though not its essence.

Eternity, the reality of the kingdom of God, *is* in the temporal

[1] The use of the words "eschatology" and "eschatological" in more recent theology in an almost opposite sense differs so greatly from the linguistic content of the words, that of "the last things", that I fail to see its usefulness. The meaning is rather, that the content of the gospel is made contemporary, that happens *now*, in time yet "beyond time". It is also clear why this usage has entered. It grasps the eschatology of the gospel with two hands, the hand of naturalism and the hand of the proclamation, in the name of history. But it is not exegesis, but proclamation. Exegetically it has no relation to the content of the New Testament, not even that of the Gospel of John, and it comes perilously near to mysticism.

present. *The Church*, to take one instance, is at one and the same time both eternal and temporal; both from eternity with God, and here, and for eternity. So, too, is *Christ*, both in the Gospel of John and in Paul. So is the *individual soul*, "from eternity inscribed in the books of God". We use the term "pre-existence", but not altogether appropriately.

In itself this is not flight from the world, though it can become a welcome occasion for it. There are many ways of fleeing from the world and an excuse can always be found, in our own times no less than in antiquity. We can conceive of our existence here as something that runs its course but once, whether in a materialistic or humanistic sense, and remain in it in stationary flight. Or else it may oppress us, torment us, and we seek to supplement this existence with something in the future, a social utopia or some other cultural and psychological development, or possibly even with primitive superstition such as spiritism, transmigration of souls, the "eternal evolution" of the individual soul, the long "trail to the stars".

Or else we are being challenged, addressed by eternity, in our life here and now. Our very own life is *subject to eternity*, subject to God.

Undoubtedly there is apocalyptic in a futurist sense in the eschatological thinking and feeling both of the apostles and of the Judaism of their day. Yet the involvement in the present, and with it in all that the New Testament contains of law, ethics, method, and the like, and also the very massive conception of God (as well as of spirit, good and evil spirits, elemental spirits, angels, and principalities) in the apostolic age helped to prevent the eternal and "that which is to come" from leading to escapism.

A purely futurist apocalyptic is a caricature of truly biblical eschatology. But, like so much else, apocalyptic is a language for the gospel, a Jewish and an apostolic language. If we stop short at the language, the result is merely drama or else a pietistic flight from the here and now. The descriptions of the Day of Judgement in the Gospel of Matthew (chapter 25) and the visions of the book of Revelation, to take two instances, might be read as pure apocalyptic, but erroneously so. The involvement in the practical present as given by the God of mercy and accepted and lived in faith, the involvement in the present as belonging to God, as pertaining to eternity, without detriment to the thought of the future, that is the presupposition for a true reading.

Apocalypses existed for centuries, possibly even millennia, both before and after the days of Christ in lands both far and near. Wherever time is divided into phases, each perhaps with its own heavenly ruler as well as its own character, perhaps millennia (as, e.g. in ancient Persia), or is regarded as a continuous flow of a physical and chemical nature (as in our own times), with the consummation projected into a remote future, it becomes science, whether Babylonian astrology or modern geophysics and astronomy. It matters little whether the motive is curiosity, primitive or highly scientific, or whether men are seeking for consolation ("the earth will not perish for some billions of years, and how much may we achieve in that length of time if we keep the peace"). But whenever the end is proclaimed as imminent and present, as in most Jewish and Christian apocalypses, even though a mythological "science" intrudes even there, and when it is proclaimed in the basis of the recognition that we are ripe for condemnation and that there is salvation only at the hands of the merciful God, there we have biblical eschatology, speech about the divine present and the divine eternity. There the language of that proclamation is the only one capable of conveying the apostolic gospel without psychologizing it.

Without doubt there *is* mysticism, in a religious sense, both in the sentiment and thinking of the apostles and of the Jews of that time. It would be strange if it were otherwise, our psyche being what it is. But this mysticism in the New Testament has been greatly exaggerated. It *is* possible to read a great deal, e.g. in the letters to the Colossians and to the Ephesians, as pure mysticism, but that is an erroneous reading.

There is a great difference between mysticism and myth, between mystical, emotional thinking and mythical speech. Mysticism pertains to psychology and is concerned with states of soul and the emotions. Its external form may be contemplative and sensuous, lyrical and visionary, strongly intellectual, even mathematical in character, as occasionally happened in the Middle Ages; yet its nature is speculative and introverted. But much which to us sounds like religious mysticism, as in the case of Paul, is in reality something quite different. It is mythical thinking in terms of the religiously concrete, thinking in personally contemplated realities of ideas which are realities for God and with God, "hypostases". This thinking is found in Jewish wisdom literature before the time of Jesus, and comes out strongly in poetry—the Truth, Wisdom, the Word, the heavenly Man, the Elect One, the Bride of God. Only by way of aesthetics may we perceive something of it, and then but faintly. Even expressions such as "in Christ" are not mysticism. The pre-existent community, God's eternal thought, will, and creature, appears in visible form in time, historically, realized in the flesh, in Christ Jesus, in his Cross and Resurrection. We are "in Christ". Baptism is the visible, historical entrance into the revealed Body of Christ, the revealed community, whose spirit is the Spirit of God. Christ is the way for the elect into the fellowship of the body of the Passion, Death, and Resurrection, the body of the community, the Body of Christ which, being eternal, repeats the flesh of Jesus, the historical coming of Jesus. (Thus "to be crucified with Christ" in Paul means something quite different from what it means in the existentialist proclamation). Since this body is the creation of *God*, it is not a question of our own righteousness, but solely of the righteousness of faith which is God's work, and the holy life is the revelation of the new life in the Spirit. It is the mystery of faith, and mystery is precisely not mystical, but mythical speech, signifying that which was hidden with God and has come has been revealed.

It is not in mystical, but mythical form, that Paul proclaims the gospel concerning salvation.

Religious mysticism is understandable to us. We know it, possibly from our own experience, at any rate both from our contemporaries and from past ages. It flourishes in much of our religious poetry, particularly the pietistic kind. We recognize it, yet as something subjective and without value for the Christian proclamation.

Paul's proclamation, being in terms of hypostasis, is remote from us. It concerns us, however, because they express, not feelings, but divine realities which encounter us; they convey the proclamation. It is part of that mythical thinking by which the apostolic proclamation expresses that the gospel does not happen in the world of our emotions, but confronts us from the reality of *God* in time and behind time. It is a language capable of conveying the reality which comes *to* us, while a psychological paraphrase which *we* understand dissolves the very matter itself. It is alien speech, but speech concerned with reality, or, if we prefer, historical speech concerned with reality. It is sober speech, not mysticism.

For the apostolic proclamation the mythical dress is one with the proclamation itself. The apostles are not aiming at something "authentic" in or behind the myth. The myth of the New Testament is that which is historical for them, the eternal Word, Jesus, the Cross, the Resurrection, the Spirit, faith, the community, the kingdom. For Paul, to take an instance, it makes the very best sense to let the gospel stand or fall with the Resurrection, which is attested by many eye-witnesses still living, from Cephas as the first to Paul himself as the last; and it is entirely mistaken exegesis to attempt to make the Gospel of John (20. 29) state the opposite. From beginning to end the New Testament proclamation is one with its myth of Christ. Were the Christ-myth to fall, then their salvation would fall as well, their new understanding of self as being under grace. With the Resurrection there would likewise fall the Cross, the forgiveness of sins, and the kingdom. It can be expressed no more plainly than in Paul's words, "if in this life only we have hope in Christ, we are of all men most miserable" (1 Cor. 15. 19). *There is nothing behind the myth*. It is as *links* in the coming of the kingdom that the coming of Christ, his Cross and Resurrection, in the apostolic proclamation constitute the saving act of God. Similarly the forgiveness of sins, i.e. the purity of the community; as the liberation of man from "fallenness" to "authenticity" it means nothing.

Therefore the absence of the second Advent, the eschatological pause after Easter and Pentecost, became the terrible frustration which only the time of missionary activity helped to overcome. Thus the Gospel of John was written, not to demythologize the Resurrection, but to state that the kingdom is both present and yet to come, that the time of waiting is but God's pause before the fulfilment of the promises.

By virtue of the Resurrection the hope of the second Advent still retains its place in the proclamation.

The myth is indivisible. It is not in the power of any thinking or of any theology to rescue the gospel from it. Intellectually the myth must be dissolved, but at no point are we able to stop the destruction of the gospel.

If, then, we cling to the myth, it is true that the mythological way of thinking, which brings that which lies beyond on to the plane of the here and now, yet arbitrarily breaks the order of nature, *may* itself produce the same objectifying attitude as modern science and thus have an effect not only irreligious, but contrary to the gospel.

Yet it is true that the mythological way of thinking, in direct contrast to existentialist philosophy, for instance, is able by virtue of its aim to state that the work belongs to God, not to myself, that God is a living, active God, a Saviour.

Myth, narrative myth, *may* appear non-historical and is probably usually intended to be so. But in the apostolic proclamation myth and the mythological form of thought are *bound to history*. The apostolic proclamation itself is not myth,[1] but *utilizes* myth.[2]

The mythical proclamation by the apostles of that which is historical, the coming of Christ, the human life of Jesus, the Cross, the Resurrection, as the saving acts of God, is indissolubly connected with the biblical and prophetic proclamation.

[1] Such as is the case of the Graeco-Oriental mystery myths, e.g. the nature myths about the dying and reviving god, which have been frequently used by specialists in the history of religions as a kind of interpretation of the gospel.

[2] I do not, of course, mean that this is a conscious utilization. The historical events, the history of Jesus, etc., absorb myth as the form of understanding which is obviously appropriate in their case.

It is diametrically opposed to the characteristic dictum of rationalism: "Casual truths of history can never become the proof of eternal verities of reason", i.e. true historical occurrences[1] can never be proofs of eternal, timeless, supra-temporal conceptual truths, a saying, the gist of which is repeated in our own time: "the saving efficacy of the cross is not derived from the fact that it is the cross of Christ: it is the cross of Christ because it has this saving efficacy".[2] A Cross, or the Cross of Christ—this, in a nutshell, contains the difference between a non-historical proclamation of Christianity and one which is prophetic and historical. A cross, or *this* cross, mystical or mythical proclamation.

Mythical or non-mythical form is not, in itself, decisive. It is the relationship of the form to history which is decisive. Gnosticism is full of myths, yet in relation to the apostolic proclamation it is a demythologizing parallel to neo-Platonism and the philosophical element in modern demythologizing. In essence they are non-historical rationalizations of religion, no less than metaphysics was in the Middle Ages.

Discussions of what the apostles would have proclaimed, had they shared the presuppositions of our times, are fruitless. No theology can determine the form of a proclamation which is a true interpretation of the apostolic proclamation while sharing our own intellectual presuppositions and means. Theologically the way is barred.

What God uses the apostles to tell us, is a quite different matter. Here all theologizing ceases, and we speak of the Holy Spirit.

From an existentialist point of view one may perhaps raise the objection against me that I have spoken just as others speak about things or objects, or that I do not realize that God is found only in the *encounter*, that beyond this all is but words. Of this I am aware, but I refuse to enter into theological mysticism; it is

[1] The implication of "casualness" anticipates the triumph of logic.

[2] It is such utterances which become shibboleths of demythologizing. Yet this previously quoted saying of Bultmann does not exhaustively express his intention, nor does it even express it well, though it expresses his theology.

words of which I have been speaking, and I intend to speak about nothing else but words. Nothing else concerns either you or me *in conversation and discussion*. But this is sufficiently important. It is *in the word* that God encounters us in the gospel. It is *in words* that the gospel passes down through the generations. It is in words alone that we are able to speak about the gospel, and that of which we speak becomes a thing, for instance, that thing which we call the apostolic proclamation.

There is a factor with which theologians engaged in these discussions reckon far too little—*the gospel is unconditionally involved in anthropomorphism*, in primitive conceptions of man. It is so and must be so, because the gospel is an address to those who are simple.

Thinking, theology included, has always sought to make the gospel subtle, subtle in its speech about holiness, subtle in its speech about God. Ever since classical antiquity neo-Platonism has been creating theology in the Church, and every form of thought with which the Church, either in the present or in the future, comes into contact will have the same effect. It cannot be otherwise, for it belongs to the very nature of the matter.

But the gospel, and Christ himself, has no other bridge over which to walk among men than the language which we form in daily living, that is, by our social intercourse, and which is kept alive by our social intercourse. It is in human language that we speak of that which is perfect, and in human language we speak of God.

Take the word "goodness" and all that is kindred to it in the gospel, holiness, righteousness, love and many other words. These words live and communicate only because there *is* goodness among men. I mention this because of that truly pernicious pharisaism and self-satisfaction which is always present wherever people are *conscious* of doing what is *right*, by being kind to their fellow-men, by living according to the precepts of morality, etc., and because it has been alleged on that account that our own highly dubious goodness, love, willingness to sacrifice, self-denial, obedience, truthfulness, etc., have no significance. It *has* significance not merely because we have nothing but our own goodness with which to show kindness to our neighbour, which is imperative despite the considerable risk of self-satisfaction which accompanies it, since our left hand knows only too well what our right hand is doing, and our "good" works, viewed evangelically, are thus equated with our evil deeds. That goodness, love, willingness to sacrifice, self-denial, obedience, truthfulness, which as recipients we encounter in converse with our fellow-man, is the only thing capable of keeping alive that language in which we are able to hear the gospel of the goodness of *God*. It is in human language and in human acts that God has spoken to us in Christ. It is in human language and in human acts that we must speak to others. God has given that language power both to bear witness of him and to judge him who speaks it. It belongs to faith in the God who has given to us to live this life in *hope*.

It is in human language that we must speak about God. We must think and speak about God as if he were a human being. For both responsibility and forgiveness, both law and the forgiveness of sins, are words which convey nothing except internal experiences, states of mind, which are the spheres of science and aesthetics—or else they convey to us *God*. But if the words responsibility, guilt, forgiveness of sins, speak of God, then we *are* in the myth, then we think and speak of God as if he were a human person.

The replacement of the anthropomorphic language of the New Testament about God with one which has been theologically and philosophically corrected will lead to no other result than a complete elimination, by etherealization, of the God who is the subject of the proclamation. Conceptual definitions lead directly into a vacuum. History shows this as clearly as could be desired. From the God who walks in the cool of the day in the Garden of Eden the way goes, steadily and directly through gradually increasing theological and philosophical reflection, to the remote, unpredicated Deity of Philo. From the Word (*logos*) of John, personal, primitive, mythical, an unbroken path leads, assisted by the philosophical language of the age, to the impersonal cosmic Reason. From the Father of Jesus Christ a royal highway of theology and philosophy leads, step by step, to the all-embracing Abyss, complete abstraction, *το ὄν*, pure Essence.

The gospel is unconditionally involved in anthropomorphism. It is the primitive language of daily life, without which all proclamation ceases to be, and no bridge can be built to men or between them. "They have taken our God away from us!" was the lament of the ancient monks of Schetis when more enlightened theologians had agreed that God is incorporeal. The theologians may be right a thousand times over, and yet be wrong. Corporeal or incorporeal—as though the gospel were a question of etherealization! We, too, can etherealize matter without its making any difference. It is actually quite possible that what we call matter really ought to be called energy, as many physicists call it, or spirit, as many philosophers have done. From a Christian point of view it is entirely irrelevant, and contains not the slightest comfort in face of mechanism and materialism. When, like John, we call it true proclamation that "God is spirit", it is so, not because it is an ethereal expression as compared with more primitive and gross notions of God. "God is spirit." Either this conveys something more acceptable to philosophy than the story of God walking in the Garden, and is thus without any relevance for the gospel, or else spirit means that we are not in the category of nature, i.e. of process, but of responsibility and grace. "God is spirit" is more an assertion directed to us than concerning God. God is such that *we* must worship "in spirit and in truth", in responsibility and in gratitude.

No one, not even the New Testament, speaks in one language only. We must, however, know when we are on the path of communication and when we are on that of abstract definition.

When we say "God" we are not saying something either philosophical or cosmic, we are not making a statement *about* the world which surrounds us, nor *in* that world. When with the New Testament we say "God", we are conveying revelation which is addressed to us and about us. When we say "God" we say "Jesus Christ"—judgement, obedience, faith, hope, and life.

When we say "faith and hope" we say "the Father of Jesus Christ". Faith and hope are one.

In *faith* we surrender ourselves to him who holds all things in his power, even death and terror. It is true evangelical language when Luther speaks of the "resignation unto hell" (*resignatio ad infernum*) of faith as an expression for completely unconditioned surrender to God. In *hope* we expect all that we expect from him who has life and the future in his hand, from God.

In the Cross is the revelation of the nature of faith, in the Resurrection that of the nature of hope. Yet faith and hope are one, and we have no better word for it than *salvation*. Salvation means, not our will, but God's. But because God is not an abstract Deity, but the Father of Jesus Christ, *confidence* is the world in which faith and hope live. Faith is not fatalism, and hope is no naked expectation.

As little as faith can live and express itself without concepts of faith, which vary according to times and persons, no more can hope live without conceptual forms. The conceptual forms of hope are those of life. And these do not become more true by abstraction.

It is quite true, as Bultmann[1] has recently reminded us, that Luther said that Christian hope knows *that* it hopes, but it does not know *what* it hopes. This is true, for it is the best whether we lay our hope in the hand of God, just as *resignatio ad infernum* is the test of faith. But it is the same Luther who repeatedly and in many ways speaks of eternal blessedness with God after the conquest over death and the devil, and the same Luther who writes to his little Hans about all the loveliness which is to be found in Paradise—apples and cherries, and silver bows, drums and play-mates and little horses with golden harness and silver saddles. A hope which knows nothing, and a hope which knows—there is no contradiction. The one means that hope is in God alone, the other that it is a real person that hopes. Hope—what other garment should it wear than that of desires, the desires of Israel and

[1] In a broadcast dialogue, reprinted with the title, *Die christliche Hoffnung und das Problem der Entmythologisierung*, by Bornkamm, Bultmann, and Schumann, Evangelisches Verlagswerk, Stuttgart, 1954, and in *Glauben und Verstehen*, III, 1960.

the desires of little Hans, joy, happiness, peace, holiness, blessedness with God? What language has our hope than that of life?

Why is the resurrection of the flesh proclaimed, if not in order to assert a living hope? To assert it, not to the wise but to the simple, to say it in such a way that hope does not become a monopoly of those who are experienced in religious abstraction, of those who are subtle in intellect or emotion, for whom the purification of concepts and of emotions goes hand in hand. Such are the currents in the religious world: the purification of concepts begins with the soul. The ego progresses into mere states of consciousness, and the purification of emotions proceeds from primitive feelings of happiness to a liberating annihilation of self, whether under the guise of Christian mysticism, Islamic Sufism, or Buddhistic Yoga. He who is simple lives in flesh and blood, and is not released from his departed ones. Fellowship and faithfulness give content to hope, corporeity gives it shape. Without a shape, hope is a silent word, and the shape of hope is that of life.

Why should we try to persuade ourselves that we can abolish the forms of hope and retain the hope itself? We can etherealize our concepts until they become as remote as Nirvana itself? It will not make our faith more pure or true. He who is simple comes with his prayers; his faith will not become purer or truer by dispensing with prayer. He comes with his ideas and his hopes; without them it is not he himself that comes. All we can do is to hold fast to hope where the gospel itself has bound it, with God. Then it can bear the shape which we give it, and God will fulfil it in his.

It is high time that I recapitulate my main points. It is not because the earth is round, while in the Bible it is flat; not because the age of Christianity is a little flash in the history of all the nations over hundreds of millennia over all the earth, and all theoretical speaking of the truth of Christianity consequently is meaningless—for mankind is itself but a flash in the history of all the teeming life of earth, and the earth itself a flash in the history of the universe—it is not for these reasons that the gospel has no connection with the contemporary view of life. But it is because the basic words of the gospel are giving and *receiving*, while that of our world view is *taking*. With these words we have two worlds which are not even within hailing distance.

The words themselves are capable of translation, but in their new context they become unrecognizable. In the gospel "every good gift comes from above, from the Father of lights". In our contemporary world view all giving is distribution of that which has been taken. In the gospel the greatness of man is the love and the grace of God. In the contemporary world view the greatness of man is his power, his love is his egotism utilized for the common good, his guilt is the limitation imposed upon him by nature. In the gospel good and evil constitutes the sum of all problems. In the contemporary view good and evil is the relativity of all life, a psychological as well as biological relativity. And so it is everywhere.

From the one of these views to the other, from the one language to the other, no path is open. If the attempt is made to preserve the view of the gospel together with the contemporary view, it is possible only by preserving, illegitimately, the inherited pattern of God and man which now, by virtue of our point of view, is reduced to a pattern yet emptied of all its original content. If the attempt is made to reproduce the viewpoint of the gospel in contemporary language without being merely content with new phraseology sufficiently feeble to be adulterated with an alien content and thus be deceptive, it is possible to do so only by an illegitimate appropriation of words and complexes of thought which, when torn out of their total context, freely float between two worlds. This is the case, for example, with some of the words by which the attempt is made to convey to the present the content of the gospel language concerning guilt, forgiveness, and salvation. Without the primitive word "God", conceived as anthropomorphically as the very words "guilt", etc., compel us to do, such re-writings become mere psychology, one without roots at that, since they simply borrow from an alien workshop.[1]

[1] Compare the opposite case of Heidegger, who builds up a non-Christian philosophy with material which has been baptized into Christianity and which

Transposed into the speech of our day, the forgiveness of sins becomes, it is true, contemporary—and surely that is in accord with the intention of the New Testament? At the same time it loses its roots because it is psychologized, *without the forgiver*, since the God who forgives vanishes in a closed universe, vanishes as a Thou, vanishes corporeally, dissolved with the myth; because Christ, and with him the way of thanksgiving has vanished, and vanishes as a thou because it is romanticism and mysticism to address on dead as Thou. The forgiving fellow-man has vanished, dissolved in psychological relativity and comprehension. Wherever guilt does not mean the debt of him that is hopeless in debt, and where the ground of forgiveness is "understanding" (compare Stoicism, and "*tout connaitre c'est tout pardonner*", and also biological humanism), it is not really forgiveness, either for him who pardons or for him whose life depends on obtaining pardon. To be told that we are no longer in debt, that is forgiveness; to be told that we really never were in debt is not forgiveness. To beg for forgiveness and receive the answer, "But I quite understand that you could not help acting like that", is to receive stones instead of bread.

We are helpless in face of the gospel we would seek to rescue. It is only in its anthropomorphic language that it can be heard, only there that it is salvation; otherwise it becomes "understanding", and understanding of self.

It was in myth that the gospel was experienced and proclaimed. Because the gospel was *received*, the myth survived as speech. Of course, as the myth lived on in other times and was surrounded by more distant forms of thought it became *dogma*, since men held on to it as objective speech parallel to scientific speech. But in reality that is an entirely different matter.

In itself, as the expression of an ancient understanding of the world, myth has no evangelical rights. But myth is more than myth. Myth is what it aims at; it is speech that creates responsibility.

---

only under the sign of the Cross retains its significance and its power. It is material arbitrarily selected for an alien use.

We are not helped by a quantitative, partial demythologizing and modernizing. If we yield to the language of the world, the language of the modern world picture, we have no right merely to abolish such things as demons and resurrection. We are compelled similarly to abolish what the gospel says about responsibility, our neighbour, life, sacrifice, and God. For faith they become no more than useless remnants which must change their nature; while for science and philosophy it is no great problem obligingly to keep open a space for that which is no more than a relic of the past.

Whether it is possible to proclaim the gospel in any other language than mythological language, is not the essential point. The essential point is that it cannot be proclaimed in a language conformable to that of science, precisely because that language is methodologically determined and moves in rationalization. It cannot make room for the God of the gospel, the God who acts. The attempt has been made from the presuppositions of a philosophy of personality, existentialism, to make room for the proclamation of the God of the gospel in the language of our world view. But in that case it is either the gospel which is victorious, so that the language is no longer that of our world view and everybody has a right to call it mythical no less than the old; or else the language of the world view is victorious, so that it is no longer the God of the gospel who is proclaimed, but psychology.

Our language, sustained as it is by abstract definitions, is constructed for an entirely different purpose, that of control through analysis. It is not only entirely useless for the task of an evangelical proclamation, but is in direct contradiction to that task, precisely because of its structure, which is that of logic and definition.

Ear and language belong together. If modern language means the language whose structure is determined by *taking*, and if modern men live on a basis of taking moderated by reason, which is our humanistic moral idea, then it is the ear which corresponds to the language. The language to which the ear listens is a hardened language; it is close to the language of the gospel.

Thus the ancient saying about "hearing with the ears, yet not hearing" is still true.

For the sake of our standard of living we are able to grab with hand and mind, creating for ourselves a language corresponding to this purpose, and shaping for ourselves a world picture which corresponds to our purposes and regulates them. At the same time, we are able to *receive* life, and to be bound by those with whom we live life, and speak accordingly.

No one of us acts entirely in the one way or the other; life is too overwhelming for this. But we can clearly recognize that without a consistent language of analysis we cannot make conquests, and that without the sister language of myth, that of blurred and non-logical symbols we cannot live.

We seek to transplant the gospel to our world. Yes—find a language in which a gift is a gift, and deceit is deceit; a language born of self-sacrifice instead of self-assertion, a language of responsibility and debt instead of calculation and demand, a language sustained by faith and hope instead of reason and probability. Find a language which, in a speech that addresses persons and makes them responsible, can express that salvation is not a psychological process within a closed universe, but action, concrete action, from without, from "above", for condemnation to death and for life, which is comprehensible to the only thing in us that is vulnerable and capable of listening and receiving, simplicity. Find such a language with which to replace the biblical language!

Find a language which *contains* the gospel and does not contradict it in every syllable. It is no other than that inadequate, symbolic, quite primitive language which sees the sun rise and set and gives us our measured day to live with those who need us, which knows good as good and evil as evil without psychological relativization; that language which knows responsibility and guilt without a biological doctrine of evolution and differentiation, which knows sorrow and joy without a doctrine of glands and hormones, which distinguishes life and death without the explanatory comfort of the organic economy of the world. It is the language in which we meet one another, live and die with one another, and remember one another. It is the language which has been retained by poetry—not that aesthetic artificiality in which psychical self-analyses are expressed in compositions of colour and tone. It is the language retained by that poetry of life, when Greek and German and European science created for itself a specialized tool for grasping, which, like all techniques, became all-inclusive and all-consuming, in accordance with that terrible law of the *tyranny of the instrument*, under which we make conquests fatal to ourselves.

Every age has its own myth. That of our age is the humbly arrogant myth of man who is both a worm and a god.

The gospel was spoken *in* the language of the age, *against* that age. If the gospel does not act in the same way now, whether or not it has been translated, it is irrelevant. We cannot detach ourselves from the contemporary world picture, and need not do so. If we are to hear the gospel, we must do so as contemporary men, in our own situation. But there is no bridge between the languages, such as can be laboriously constructed by, e.g. theology or philosophy.

The reasons for this are purely practical ones. We human beings of 1954 are by no means all living on the same plane, in the same segment of time. We live in widely different centuries, depending on where we live, our field of activity and our character. Even the individual person lives in widely divergent ages, even in widely divergent languages. For this reason alone demythologizing in the current sense of the word will be far too inflexible a tool when it is a matter of making the speech of the New Testament audible to our generation. It must not be doubted that there is a truly evangelical motive behind it. The gospel is not a codex, but living speech which is recognized by its voice. If the Germans have had difficulties in understanding this and react accordingly, then at least the compatriots of Grundtvig have had excellent opportunity for a century both to hear and understand it. This, too, has *always* been the concern of proclamation, not to give false, but true offence, not to strike at our views, but at ourselves. All this is nothing new. From classical antiquity to the present day all honest preaching has directed the proclamation at the person and made it topical. So diverse, however, is the time for every society and every person, including that which we call, mechanically, 1954, that there is *no* common language in which the content of the apostolic proclamation might be reproduced for *our* age.

The theological use of existentialist philosophy would be a possible language for the gospel only for a minute minority of our contemporaries, apart from the possibility of a fundamental falsification of the gospel by a translation into its thought forms. In addition it contains a special possibility of a *historical* misinterpretation of the tradition and its context. Every person, even a theologian, will be tempted to seek and find concepts which agree with his own in those places, circles, and writings to which he owes his chief inspiration.

It can never be the task of a theology to find *the* language in which the gospel must be perceived or into which it must be "translated".

"But if it is *not* the task of theology to find the new, adequate language to replace myth, but merely renewed mythical expressions, then we should have to continue to demythologize indefinitely!"[1] Precisely so, for true demythologizing or remythologizing can happen only simultaneously with the acceptance of the gospel, when it is being heard and received by the individual in his particular situation, differently by different persons in different nations at different times. The unity of the gospel behind the demythologizing is a matter of faith and cannot be secured by theology.

The question is not one of radicalism or orthodoxy, but of a destructive *stabilization* in the one or the other. What I attack is not radicalism in itself, e.g. in existentialist theology, but a *stabilized* radicalism, a new, valid language.

Theology, and the theologian as a historical scholar and contemporary thinker, are able to present the thought forms of the apostolic age and of our own time. Theology is able, as an

[1] Compare the trend of thought on page 50 in the previously mentioned broadcast discussion.

auxiliary to the Church in the presentation of the totality of the apostolic proclamation, to say, "if this does not concern you personally, then it is all ancient superstition", and to add, "and I can tell you why". No more than that. Here is the limit of theology.

The translation which the gospel must undergo in order to reach a contemporary person cannot be mediated systematically by any theology. In that case it would take upon itself two tasks simultaneously, one of which is our own concern, the other God's concern.

It is our task, by means of honest craftsmanship, to throw light on the tradition of the proclamation, especially on the apostolic process of tradition, to give an account, linguistically and objectively, of "that which is written" and what the Church has said, and also to give an account of the whole connection between the proclamation and the whole manner of thinking of the past, its intellectual life, and its unfolding and scope, as far as our means and ability permit. In other words, it is to find and supply *means* for the translation, in all degrees and of all kinds. In all degrees, for so it happens, whether we do research or re-tell the gospel as fathers and mothers. It happens so, whether we sing a verse of a hymn to a child, or publish many volumes of commentaries and historical works. But the inner basis of language, in which the gospel is heard as gospel by a person, is something that cannot be found, let alone arranged, by any human helper. Where the world of the New Testament and the modern world, both in their historical relativity, are contained by the same mind, there are abundant means of translation. But whether the words of the gospel are *heard* here depends on something else than systematic help for drawing the bounds and determining the gospel. This is true of the scholar; the same is true of the child, if it *hears* the gospel in a verse of a hymn, even though it has studied science during the previous class period.

The two great demythologizing currents in the Middle Ages, the philosophical and metaphysical current of scholasticism, and the psychologizing one of mysticism, were met by Luther with a proclamation of the gospel in a forcefully remythologizing language. The subjective demythologizing of pietism and the rationalistic demythologizing of the Enlightenment were met by Grundtvig's proclamation in forcefully remythologizing language.

The mythical language was capable of conveying the gospel. This was not the case with psychological and philosophical language; they give the wrong emphasis and lead into a blind alley. This is similarly the case in our own day with the language which is determined by natural science. Once again the science of nature has become the contemporary philosophy and psychology, the contemporary view of life. A strong emotional emphasis may give it a certain warmth, but cannot alter its basic character.

The gospel cannot be separated from the narratives of Christ, the narratives of Christ cannot be separated from the proclamation of Christ, and the proclamation of Christ cannot be separated from the New Testament world picture in its widest sense.

This does not imply that the gospel can be heard only if we make a complete surrender to a world picture and a world view which neither is, nor can become, our own. It means, however, that the gospel, as in our hymnody (and who could imagine a demythologized hymnody?), must be conveyed in its own language. In that case, *if* it is being heard in accordance with its own content (otherwise it does not matter), the individual age and the individual person will hear it in the translation which is pertinent and becomes so by bringing to him the Word of God. It is part of our faith in the gospel that its proclamation rests in the hand of God. The gospel, involved in myth, is the Sacrament in words, just as the Lord's Supper is the Sacrament in bread; they are both earth, and both are in the hand of God, food and salvation, Christ. Which were the words which were heard, and how many, and how they were heard, are and remain for alien ears as hidden as the speech of prayer. If the gospel is reality from God, it is not our task to rescue it. No theology, whether it be termed "naïve" or "demythologized" or anything else, is here capable of giving it form and setting bounds, whether narrow or wide, nor of authorizing any language, whether old or new. If the old language cannot convey the gospel it is of no more worth than the new, and *vice versa*.

When evangelical expressions are treated as abstractions they are dissolved in metaphysics or in psychology. Where the Christ-figure is supported by abstract thinking, it is dissolved; and where it is sought to make the Christ-event capable of appropriation by thinking, it ceases to be.

A characteristic law holds good in these matters—there is no external standard for a scientific picture of Jesus; he is entirely in our hands. Nor is there an external standard for the Christ of the Church, of the proclamation; he is entirely in the hands of God. The God of *speculation* is exalted further and further, and vanishes into nothing; the God of the gospel is humbled and becomes as the lowliest among men, and makes our total existence reality. The Jesus of research shrinks and shrinks away into nothingness; the Christ of faith can be like a mustard seed and yet give space and shape to the whole grace of God.

Viewed exegetically and dogmatically, demythologizing is both an exceedingly interesting piece of work, and also one which is fertile in providing perspective, both in history and in principle. If, however, it draws boundaries for the gospel, demythologized language does not, as does the language of the New Testament, set the gospel at liberty, even for ourselves, precisely because of the symbolic character that the language of myth has for us. Demythologizing does not set the gospel free, but fixes its bounds by means of an alien standard. The gospel proclamation of grace and life from God is fixed in an empirically determined concept of life. The present life becomes a boundary; the eternal is psychologized, because our thinking knows no choice, and so forth. In order to receive the gospel we create, beginning from what we already have, a truth by which we may measure the gospel. We sit in judgement upon the gospel no less than did the dogmatism of orthodoxy.

No theology can shape a language which is the correct one for its age. The attempt is bound to be an encroachment on the part of theology, even when it aims at helping to break down a spurious offence at the gospel.

The only thing that we can do is to let the gospel speak to us in its own language, to us who speak a different language. We may point out the relativity of the world pictures and their capability, or lack of it, of making man subject to responsibility. We may show what is the character and aim of the languages which men have spoken and which they still speak in order that they may live life or else conquer it, that they may receive life or take it as spoil.

HEINRICH OTT

OBJECTIFICATION AND EXISTENTIALISM

Bultmann in Switzerland

IN Switzerland the demythologizing controversy can hardly be said to have given rise to a new school of thought, although it has evoked a lively discussion among Swiss theologians.

I

The main contribution has come from the well-established school of Swiss liberalism, which looks chiefly to Albert Schweitzer and Karl Jaspers for its inspiration, with Martin Werner and Fritz Buri as its leading lights at the present time. At first, they were whole-heartedly in favour of Bultmann, but later their attitude crystallized in opposition to him. It is from this party, quantitatively speaking, that the main contribution has come. Here are the landmarks in the controversy: On February 1, 1951, Bultmann read a paper at a conference of Swiss liberal theologians at Aarau. His subject was: "The Christological Confession of the Word Council of Churches".[1] In the Winter Semester of 1951–52 Fritz Buri delivered his inaugural lecture on the theme: "Theology and Philosophy", in which he took issue with Bultmann. This lecture was subsequently published in a revised form under the title "Demythologizing or Dekerygmatizing of Theology" and included in the second volume of *Kerygma und Mythos*. In April 1953 Karl Jaspers read a paper at another conference of the Swiss liberal theologians, which was

[1] Translated in *Essays Philosophical and Theological*, 1955, pp. 273–290.

held that year in Basel. This was entitled "Myth and Religion".[1] Bultmann replied in April 1954 with "The Case for Demythologizing".[2]

What, then, are the issues between Bultmann and the Swiss liberals? First, there is a considerable area of agreement between them. They agree, for instance, as to what the mythical, time-conditioned elements of the New Testament are. But when they come to evaluate those mythical elements they begin to part company. Bultmann thinks that myth should be totally eradicated by means of existentialist interpretation. Jaspers pronounces such a procedure impossible. Like Buri, he would retain all these elements as "ciphers" for Transcendence, not as objective descriptions of reality, but as suggestive symbols.

But there is an even greater difference, one which is quite fundamental. What Bultmann wants is to strip away the mythical symbolism of New Testament religion and get at its existential meaning by removing the adventitious stumbling-block of an antiquated world view which has become untenable for modern man. The Swiss liberals on the other hand deny that myth has to be eliminated in order to make it palatable to modern man. Instead, it must be stripped of its objective validity. All myths, they hold, are potential testimonies to Transcendence. This, of course, eliminates the biblical message of a unique, authoritative, saving act of God, as Buri's watchword, dekerygmatizing, implies. Hence their complaint of Bultmann's orthodoxy, a complaint which Bultmann answers thus:

> Now I have the impression that Jaspers thinks it impossible to have a genuine dialogue with me, on account of what he calls my orthodoxy, or because as a Christian theologian I assert the absoluteness of the Christian revelation. Does Jaspers realize that wherever faith in revelation speaks, it asserts, and must assert, the absoluteness of the revelation, because it regards itself as the true fulfilment of the commandment: "I am the Lord the God. . . . Thou shalt have no other gods before me" (above, p. 190).
>
> For Jaspers, the stumbling-block of the Christian faith is its claim to absoluteness. Perhaps I should be quite satisfied with the effect

[1] Above, pp. 133–180.

[2] Above, pp. 181–194.

my attempt at demythologizing has had on him. After all, the purpose of demythologizing is to make the stumbling-block real.

This puts the difference between Bultmann and the Swiss liberals in a nutshell. It explains why Bultmann can go along with the Christological confession of the World Council of Churches so that "Jesus Christ is Lord and Saviour", not indeed in a metaphysical sense, but existentially—in Christ, and in Christ alone, we are confronted with the claim of God.

In comparison with this, the initial agreement we mentioned would seem to be of secondary importance. In fact, Bultmann himself has said as much. The meaning of myth itself, he has said, is not one of the main issues in demythologizing, and detracts from the primary concern.[1] It would further appear that the debate between the respective parties has reached an impasse. There is little prospect of any profitable continuance of the debate, or of a fruitful synthesis between the two positions.

II

On the other hand, the Bultmann-Barth discussion would seem to be more promising. These two great stars in the theological firmament have their differences, it is true, and the differences are very profound. But they are not divided over the first commandment. In fact, Bultmann's refutation of Jaspers which we have just quoted is remarkably like what Barth said in *Zwischen den Zeiten* which bears the suggestive title, "The First Commandment as a Theological Axiom".

In our analysis of the Barth-Bultmann discussion we shall not confine ourselves to their earliest pronouncements, viz. Barth's excursus on Bultmann in Vol. III/2 of his *Church Dogmatics* and Bultmann's reply, "The Problem of Hermeneutics",[2] in which they make their respective positions perfectly clear. We shall also take note of Barth's more recent observations in "Rudolf Bultmann, an Attempt to Understand him"[3] and in his *Church Dogmatics*, IV/1.

[1] Cf. *Kerygma und Mythos*, II, p. 180.
[2] 1950 Eng. Trans. in *Essays Philosophical and Theological*, 1955.
[3] Above, pp. 83–132.

There was a time when Karl Barth, Rudolf Bultmann and Friedrich Gogarten were associated as younger theologians and spokesmen for dialectical theology, as it was then called. To-day we are witnessing one of the greatest, perhaps the most important of all contemporary debates in Protestant theology, inseparably linked with the name of Rudolf Bultmann. In view of their earlier association with Bultmann, the reactions of Barth and Gogarten to demythologizing, which came in quick succession to one another, are of particular interest. Unlike many other reactions, which are of a more partisan and prejudiced character, these two represent an independent and fresh approach to the debate. So a study of the three essays in question should be unusually rewarding.

Let us turn first to Gogarten.[1] It is a thoroughly systematic treatment, and singularly relevant. His understanding of the issues is remarkably perceptive, and his observations are always to the point. Indeed, his essay will help us to appreciate Barth's vigorous protest in *Church Dogmatics*, III, against some of the features in Bultmann's theology. And it will help us to appreciate the more positive side of Barth's reaction in the most recent volume of the *Church Dogmatics*. It is his combination of criticism with basic positive insights which gives *Demythologizing and History* its distinctive character. Gogarten is an acute controversialist, and his criticism of Bultmann's opponents is remorseless and severe. Yet at the same time he is cautious; he is careful to marshal his arguments with plenty of detail and direct quotation. His essay must have been refreshing and beneficial to all who have at heart the maintenance of sound standards of scholarship in Protestant theology, no matter which side they take. The great advantage of Gogarten's essay is that he lays all his cards on the table and makes his own position crystal clear. He refuses to confine himself to the "critical questions" which are so popular among theologians to-day (and they are really no more than rhetorical questions, intended to refute the opposite side without offering any positive alternative). Our concern here is not with Gogarten's polemics, but with his positive contribution to the debate.

[1] Eng. Trans. *Demythologizing and History*, London, 1955.

III

Gogarten appeals to Luther against contemporary Lutheran theologians. As its German title, *Entmythologisierung und Kirche* ("Demythologizing and Church") suggests, he is seeking to define his position *vis à vis* Bultmann and a particular party within the Church. He is especially critical of the pronouncement of the General Synod of the United Evangelical Lutheran Church in Germany in April 1952, in which Bultmann was condemned. Or, rather, he is critical of the theological presuppositions behind this pronouncement. These presuppositions are to be found in a collection of essays by various Lutheran theologians (Gogarten mentions Ellwein, Kinder, Künneth and Schieder) edited by Ernst Kinder.[1] This polemical occasion of his essay must be borne in mind if we are to be fair to Gogarten. It is not a full-dress critique of Bultmann's opponents. At the same time, however, it contains certain basic insights of its own. It provides the historical background which illuminates the setting of the Bultmann debate and its real aim and importance.

It is to Gogarten's credit that he focuses attention on certain points which had hitherto received only sporadic notice. We have in Bultmann's work not just the theology of an individual scholar nor a welcome solution to certain contemporary problems. Nor is he to be rejected as a danger to the Church's proclamation. Rather, Bultmann is raising the basic question of all theology, though one which is perculiarly pressing to-day owing to the contemporary intellectual situation. This is the question of ontology. It concerns the "*genus* of revelational reality",[2] the "*genus* of the Word of God" (p. 90). It concerns the way in which this ontological *genus* is open to knowledge, its "scientific concept" (cf. p. 85). Gogarten defines it as "historicity; the mode of cognition appropriate to it as historical or existentialist thinking" (p. 17). The crucial question in the demythologizing debate is the correct understanding of history and of historicity. Both sides, Bultmann and the Lutheran theologians, have a "radically different interpretation of history" (p. 10).

[1] See above, p. 9.

[2] *Demythologizing and History*, p. 86.

What does Gogarten mean by history? First, he compares it with its opposite, metaphysics. The metaphysical world view sees man and his history set in the framework of a higher, supra-historical, natural and supernatural order. This order used to be the primary reality, the key to the understanding of man and his history.

> The problem of history in this sense arises from the fact that history is no longer seen as a process within a stationary (i.e. suprahistorical) world (p. 10).

History is here used in an absolutely universal sense. As for man,

> It is not an overstatement to say that his position has become so central that this history is now his own, the history of man. And this idea, the idea that it is his own history, means in its deepest sense that he, man, is responsible for history. . . . This responsibility relates not only to the particular historical decisions of his life, but, at least in intention, to history as a whole, that is to say to history as the history of the world of man. And surely precisely this is the grasping of the actual essential nature of history (*Geschichtlichkeit*) of human existence (p. 19).

What roots has all this in the Christian faith? Is it true to say that "history as a problem, in the sense in which we are here necessarily using the word, arose only with and as a consequence of the Christian faith" (p. 10)? Yes, says Gogarten, in so far as Christian faith is a radical exposure of responsibility as the hall-mark of historicity.

> For if, without prejudice to whatever else may have to be said about history and the character of history, its essential feature is that man bears the responsibility for it as a whole, that is to say for all the events of the world, it is in the concept of sin, as the Christian faith understands it, that the historical nature of human existence finds its explanation. For since man by his sin, namely by worshipping the creature instead of the Creator (Rom. 1. 25), has entirely reversed the true nature of the world and has delivered it up to the bondage and vanity of corruption (Rom. 8. 19ff.), it follows that he is answerable for this as surely as he is answerable for his sin (p. 20).

Here, according to Gogarten, is the quintessence of Christian faith. And this is what he discerns in Bultmann's characteristic insistence on the historicity of human existence. When Bultmann speaks of man as a historical being, he means he is responsible, not only for his actions, but for the essential constitution of his being. Historical responsibility has ontological implications.

For this reason, and for this reason alone, demythologizing is concerned with the history in which man is involved, specifically in redemptive history. This history must be emancipated from its mythological trappings with their historical objectification. Hence the need for existentialist interpretation.

> In the endeavour to achieve an "existential interpretation" there is being prepared an understanding of history which as we have already indicated could be characterized by saying that an attempt is being made to extricate history from the subject-object pattern of thought (p. 57).

Existentialist interpretation is the positive side of demythologizing.

Why this insistence on eliminating the subject-object pattern? Because objectification, in the specifically modern, existentialist sense (which has nothing to do with any phenomonological theory of intentionality, etc.) excludes responsibility, and with it historicity. Here Gogarten goes further than Bultmann. Bultmann rejects only theological objectification, and this is one of the leading motifs of his thought. Gogarten probes the foundations of this rejection with the help of Martin Heidegger's *Sein und Zeit* (section 43)[1] and certain passages in his *Holzwege*.[2] In the earlier work Heidegger tries to show that world views are recent phenomena. Only in modern times has man looked at the world objectively, surveying the universe as a detached observer. In antiquity and the middle ages there is no objectification, no world view in this sense. Only where man emerges out of the world as an isolated subject does the world become an isolated object. It was Descartes who first did this, and in this respect he is the father of all modern thought. Since his day it has been taken for granted that there is a subject-object pattern, both in science

[1] Gogarten, op. cit., pp. 50ff. [2] Pp. 62ff.

and in popular thinking. Now if subject and object confront one another as distinct entities, there can be no responsibility between them, for responsibility presupposes a genuine relationship between man and his world. Man is responsible for his world because his relationship to it is not *a posteriori* or adventitious, but an inherent one. Man's being in the world is an *a priori* datum. This, for Heidegger, is the essential structure of human existence.

The Lutheran theologians insist on the objective historicity of the redemptive event, its historical factuality (cf. Gogarten, pp. 39f.). They are still thinking in terms of the subject-object pattern. This, however, says Gogarten, has unfortunate results. Their theology rests upon a dubious philosophical basis. Their search for a positive position over against Bultmann lands them in inconsistencies and ambiguities, with the result that they completely fail to understand what Bultmann is getting at.

Gogarten has shown—and this is his great achievement—that it is not Bultmann, but his Lutheran critics, who are trapped by their philosophical presuppositions and prejudices. The shoe is on the other foot. For they are tied to the subject-object pattern. Unlike Bultmann, with his use of modern existentialism, they are naïvely unconscious of it all. The tradition they so stoutly uphold "is not so old as they think, for it certainly does not go back as far as Luther and there are grounds for questioning whether it dates from before Descartes" (p. 56). Terms, like "objective event" as used by these theologians, "lose their philosophical meaning, not so much, however, because of their naïve use, for that merely deprives them of their clarity and precision. The real trouble is that those who use their own terms uncritically will treat their opponents' terms in just the same way".[1] In these quotations Gogarten would appear to be giving an accurate description of the respective positions of Bultmann and his Lutheran critics.

By their rigid adherence to the subject-object pattern Bultmann's critics are blinding themselves to the real purport of his theology. Bultmann's attempt to escape from the objectification of redemptive event can mean only one thing, viz. its elimination.

[1] *Entmythologisierung und Kirche* (German text), p. 73.

It becomes a "subjectivistic phenomenon" or an "immanent experience". They will not and cannot see that what Bultmann is trying to eliminate is the subject-object pattern.

The stubborn adherence of Bultmann's opponents to the subject-object pattern inevitably blinds them to the real intention of his theology. His rejection of the objectification of the redemptive event can only imply for them a dissolution of its reality into a phenomenon of subjective experience, an immanent "content of consciousness". This is because they are either unable or unwilling to realize that Bultmann is seeking to banish the complementary terms "subject" and "object" from the theological scene.

As Gogarten sees it, it is this same stubbornness which accounts for the oft-repeated criticism of Bultmann, that his theology does not express that "the mighty acts of God are presented as data prior to all human existence, indestructibly, indissolubly and irrevocably so". But, contends Bultmann, this criticism does not get to the heart of the difference between the contending parties. Bultmann, too, would agree that the mighty acts of God are data prior to human existence. The real point is *how* they are so. The critics say, through "objective factualness"; Bultmann says, kerygmatically.

What is the kerygma? If we accept the radical, *geschichtlich* approach, how can we say that the acts of God are prior to human existence? Kerygma, as defined by the New Testament and the relevant exposition of Luther is the word of Jesus of Nazareth. This word not only *speaks* about God's turning to man, but in the speaking that turning actually occurs. "If we really want to know what the kerygma of the New Testament is all about, we cannot do better than ask what we mean when we say that the Word of Jesus is the Word of God" (op. cit., p. 58). Thus the term kerygma raises the problem of Christology, which, Gogarten agrees, is the crucial problem. The classical theology of the early Church solved that problem "metaphysically by means of the doctrine of the two natures, divine and human, and their unity in the one person of Jesus" (cf. E.T., p. 70). But to-day, argues Gogarten, Christology must be interpreted historically. What does that mean? Gogarten offers an outline of a historical Christology (E.T., pp. 72ff.). The unity between Jesus and God is not one of two natures, but a unity between two types of occurrence. There is an occurrence between the Father and the Son in eternity, and there is an occurrence in time between Jesus Christ and the world. These two types of occurrence are united in the Christ event, which takes place in the kerygma. "And yet these are not two secrets of different kinds or two events of different kinds. They are the one secret of the turning of God toward us in Jesus Christ. This secret is shown to be what it is precisely by the fact that we never can and never may speak of it otherwise than by reference to the way in which each of these events is implied in the other. In the one, the eternal event between the Father and the Son, what is meant is the world, we men, and it is only to this extent that this event concerns us. In the other, the temporal event between Jesus and the world in the earthly life and destiny of Jesus, what is meant is the eternal unity of the Father and the Son, and it is only in this way that there takes place in this event the unity of Jesus and the world and of the world with Him. But this oneness is in both cases a historical oneness" (pp. 72f.). The unity of the temporal and eternal occurrence is constituted by the obedience of the Son of God. Jesus "does nothing of himself", everything through him who sent him (cf. E.T., p. 73).

One of the most notable features in this "historical" Christology, in our view, is that although Gogarten is offering a defence of Bultmann, he unconsciously goes beyond him, and says more than Bultmann has ever said or could say. Where Bultmann speaks of the kerygma he is always speaking of the redemptive act of God which has occurred and continues to occur *pro me*. But the important thing is always the *pro me*. That is what Bultmann focuses his attention on, to the exclusion of everything else. Of course, the redemptive event is a prior *datum*, it is *extra nos*. But it becomes relevant and "historical" only in the moment when it occurs *pro me*. The *extra nos* must of necessity be presupposed, but as such it is neither perceptible nor important. Gogarten's proposed Christology goes palpably beyond this. He does not concentrate exclusively on the *pro me*. *Pari passu* with the occurrence between Jesus and the world there is an occurrence in eternity between the Father and the Son. *Pari passu* with the *pro me* there is a redemptive event, or something like it, occurring *pro se*, with an intrinsic quality of its own. Gogarten does, of course, stress the unity of the two occurrences. The *pro se* is strictly related to the *pro me*. Yet the converse is equally true: the *pro me* is strictly related to the *pro se*, and without it could not be what it is. The kerygma and its implied Christology are determined and constituted by the *pro se*. The implication would appear to be that theology can speak properly of a *pro me* only when it is strictly related in this way to the *pro se*. Does "historical" theology require the two aspects to be held together in an indissoluble structural unity? If so, Bultmann's programme needs to be amplified if his own professed intention is to be properly implemented. These considerations will engage our attention once more in Part V, and once again in connection with Karl Barth's *Dogmatics*.

If, at this point, Gogarten goes further than Bultmann, he is in complete agreement with him over the next point. When he comes to elucidate the central concept of the kerygma he accepts Bultmann's characteristic identification of the Word and act of God. The kerygma, i.e. both the proclamation of Jesus of Nazareth and the Church's preaching of Christ, are not merely witness borne to an act of God in the past. They are themselves that act, the act in which he turns to man. Here is a genuine insight. It is what Luther brought out so clearly in his doctrine of the Word of God. Hence the charge levelled at the official Lutheran critics that they have got Luther wrong. In fact, their adherence to the subject-object pattern has made it impossible for them to understand him. They understand the Word of God "not as his act in the Word, but as communication, communication of something which is not contained directly in the Word itself, or which happens directly in the Word, but communication of something that happened in the past. The Word derives its whole reality from the past event which it communicates. It is the event, according to these Lutherans, which gives it its reality, its objective, factual validity'' (German text, p. 90). Gogarten is quite right when he says that the critics wrongly conceive the Word as communication and blames this on their subject-object pattern of thinking. But supposing the Word does not coalesce with the deed of God, is it therefore only communication, and nothing more? Does such a separation or distinction (a better word here) necessarily involve thinking in the subject-object pattern? Is there not another alternative, viz. to take the kerygma as testimony or witness pointing to something else? To take it thus need not necessarily imply a lapse into objectified knowledge or propositional statements to be manipulated like counters. We just throw these considerations out as questions here, hoping to throw more light on them in Part V. To us it would seem that this theologoumenon of Bultmann (and Gogarten) of which we have been speaking is closely connected with Bultmann's peculiar doctrine of time, an important matter which has been singularly neglected in the Bultmann controversy. We might call it a ''punctilear'' view of time. It lays stress on the present moment, the eschatological now of decision, whether of faith or unbelief, of acceptance or rejection of the kerygma. This is the exclusive horizon of genuine historical occurrence. Granted this view of time, it is impossible to conceive of the act itself and the word which bears witness to it as in any way separate in time (although to make such a separation ought not necessarily to imply that the act is objectified and the Word merely communication). Hence the problem of the Word and the problem of time would seem to be in some way or other identical, a consideration we shall return to in connection with Barth's *Dogmatics*.

What, then, is the upshot of Gogarten's essay? It may be summarized under two headings. First, he shows that if we start out with the subject-object pattern we shall entirely misunderstand what Bultmann is getting at. Secondly, we shall also misunderstand the New Testament. The first point seems to be adequately established in the pertinent arguments against the Lutheran theologians. The second point is still open to discussion. It involves the ontological problem which besets all theology. That is, whether the subject-object pattern provides a suitable ontological framework for an adequate presentation of a real redemptive history.

It certainly will not do to treat this problem in isolation, as though it were just a matter of prolegomena. It can only be discussed concurrently with a consideration of the actual subject matter of theology. The rule must be, *solvitur ambulando*. You cannot separate the method from the subject matter nor *vice versa*. The method must always be adapted to the subject matter. The wider implications of the second point cannot be solved in a single essay, like Gogarten's. All the same, he has taken us quite a long way towards a solution of the wider issue too. He has thrust upon the official Lutheran theologians, who keep harping on objectivity and cling so obstinately to the subject-object pattern, the burden of proof. How surprised they must have been! They will not be able to use that weapon against Bultmann any more. If they want to use it they must first of all prove that it is a suitable weapon, and from the New Testament itself. They will certainly find that very difficult!

Since Gogarten's essay, no one can take the subject-object pattern for granted, for he has made it a relative thing, relative to a particular philosophy. Of course, he is not the only one to do this. Bultmann and others had already done it, but hardly any of them so lucidly as Gogarten. But the chief contribution came from Martin Heidegger, to whom Gogarten is indebted for much of his argument. We have already shown how heavily he leans on Heidegger's essay, *Die Zeit des Weltbildes* ("The Age of the World-view"). There is no question here of Gogarten's prostituting his theology to a particular philosophy. For Heidegger's work is not dogmatic in character but critical, not speculative but phenomenological. It does not provide the theologian with a new vocabulary, but simply helps him to interpret and get rid of a conventional framework—and even the theologian himself was bound sooner or later to discover how unsuitable it really was.

Yet there is one point at which Gogarten and Heidegger are at odds. Gogarten believes there is a certain continuity between historical research and historical thinking. Historical research as pursued to-day forces us in the end to historical thinking by reducing all historicity to relativity and thus laying bare the universal historical environment in which man exists. Thus, for example, Gogarten uses the historical understanding of the origin and transmission of Holy Scripture (i.e. the view that the Bible is not a book fallen from heaven or a metaphysical entity) as a kind of preliminary stage to the historical understanding of its content. (On this see especially chapters II and III of *Demythologizing and History*.) On the other hand, in *Die Zeit des Weltbildes*, Heidegger instances modern historical study as an example of objectifying thought. Historical narration objectifies history, measuring it and charting it with the tools of criticism (source criticism) (cf. *Holzwege*, p. 76). For Gogarten modern historiography is rooted in the original historicity of the Christian faith. For Heidegger it is rooted in the subject-object pattern. We shall not pursue the matter any further here, except to ask whether Gogarten would not have done more for the cause of "historical" theology had he borrowed less liberally from Heidegger. For a critical re-examination of the methods and criteria of historical research would have been to the advantage of a genuine "historical" theology. It would have led to a deepening or even a revision of them. They are so often taken for granted! For after all, this kind of theology is not looking out for objective facts, and therefore refuses to be bound by objective historical results, so called, results which are in themselves quite neutral. Its first aim is to understand the historical content and claim of the testimonies to revelation.

In conclusion, there is one more point to be made. Maybe we must understand Bultmann's critics, who are the objects of Gogarten's highly pertinent charges, better than they understand themselves. It may be that behind their uncertainties, misapprehensions and general vagueness there lurks a very real concern which we cannot afford to neglect. In saying this we are not for a moment detracting from the value of Gogarten's critique of their scientific pretensions.

IV

The character and intention of Barth's *Attempt* is best indicated by his own words: "What follows is simply an account rendered of the way I feel I have been able to understand him so far. I shall then try to come to some sort of provisional attitude towards him and his thesis. For good or ill one cannot avoid doing that. My present purpose is, then, not to speak for him, nor even, strictly speaking, against him, but, if I may put it thus, alongside of or around him. In saying this I would like to emphasize that I am concerned with my own attempt to understand him so far. And I must hasten to add that at best that attempt has proved unsatisfactory, not to say fruitless. I have the impression that many, if not the majority, know the answers no better than I do, but only as though they did'' (p. 84). Barth's essay, therefore, is not a systematic whole. It is not an attempt, though it has an obvious unity of its own, to interpret Bultmann, but is full of spurts, qualifications, conjectures, and seminal thoughts, often thrown out in the form of questions. Our task here is to examine Barth's critique of Bultmann as a whole, both in its principles and in its scope. ''Critique'' however is hardly the right word. It would be truer to speak of the trend or direction of his criticism, for Barth treads very warily. His essay is frankly tentative. Strictly speaking, it offers no definitive exegesis, still less a refutation of Bultmann. We are undoubtedly following his professed intention when we take everything he says, whether for or against Bultmann, with a certain reservation.

The centre of gravity lies in sections III, VI and VIII. Barth raises three objections. First, Bultmann sets out with a rigid *a priori* understanding which makes any real comprehension impossible (VIII). Secondly, the philosophical clue to this *a priori* understanding is relative and insecure, and therefore is not so normative or compelling as Bultmann assumes (VI). Thirdly, as a consequence, Bultmann has abandoned the New Testament's direct speaking about God and speaks of him only indirectly: he speaks directly only of man, of man's self-understanding (III and VI). Since the clue is in no way normative it must be rejected on New Testament grounds. The same applies to Bultmann's style of exposition. He attaches ''an exclusive importance to his use of existentialism'' (ibid.). This brief summary should make it clear that there is a real connection between all three of Barth's objections.

1. Objection number one, i.e. the intrusion of an *a priori* understanding, is in the last resort directed against Bultmann's hermeneutical doctrine (see especially Bultmann's essay, "The Problem of Hermeneutics" in *Essays Philosophical and Theological*). All understanding depends on a prior understanding. Relevant exposition is always determined by the prior questions with which a document is approached. In the case of the New Testament the relevant prior understanding is man's existential question about the meaning of his own existence. It is never consciously or explicitly asked, but it is always implicit. Barth would seem to go too far in rejecting out of hand the whole doctrine of self-understanding. In the last resort it is a theory intended to help the theologian to explain the crucial historic act of understanding and to elucidate its nature. It is particularly relevant to the believing understanding of the New Testament. It will not do to complain of Bultmann's rigid "canon" of understanding, of a "prior decision about the measure and limit of intelligibility". The prior understanding with which we approach the New Testament is always quite general and neutral in character. Just as it is impossible to understand a written document unless one knows the language in which it is written, so anyone who has never pondered the meaning of his own existence is disqualified from understanding the New Testament, which has to do, from beginning to end, with human existence. Or does Barth doubt that the *Deus revelatus* is revealed to men? Can he deny that the scriptural kerygma is always, if not exclusively or primarily, concerned with man? That can hardly be his intention, for he himself has often said just the opposite.

2. As for objection number two, such mistrust of philosophy on the part of the theologian would seem to be without foundation. True, the theologian would, we think, be justified in suspecting, and indeed flatly rejecting the unqualified presuppositions of any particular philosophical system, for that would mean positing a second source of knowledge alongside of Holy Scripture. But there is no reason for distrusting and rejecting the assistance of philosophy or even of a particular philosophy, and for using certain ideas and terms already worked out in a philo-

sophical context for the purpose of theology. Of course, that needs to be done critically and cautiously. It would seem that such misgivings bring their own retribution in the end, for otherwise scientific theology will lose its precision and clarity, while Christian language ceases to be intelligible. Gogarten appears to be quite justified when he says: "Anyone who reflects critically on the terms he uses, whether in theology or physics, is coming close to philosophy and availing himself of its work" (German text, p. 72). As for Bultmann's borrowings from Heidegger, the question is not whether his philosophy is that of Heidegger, but rather, which philosophy is appropriate and suitable to communicate the revelation contained in scripture, elucidating it as an articulated whole, drawing out its true meaning in a relevant manner, and re-stating it intelligibly. Whether we use Heidegger or somebody else, or some as yet non-existent philosophy to be developed out of the Bible, is something we still have to decide. But only scripture can decide it, only the "biblical world" itself. There is no need to remind ourselves that all philosophies are essentially relative.

3. Objection one and two therefore go too far, and are not really pertinent. The roots of both lie in the third objection. Here Barth is perfectly justified. It is not the doctrine of prior understanding as such, but Bultmann's particular prior understanding (self-understanding, authenticity and inauthenticity), which, in effect, turns out to be more than just a prior understanding. For it prejudges the issue. It does not merely avail itself of the help of philosophy, but applies to this particular philosophy, i.e. Heidegger as interpreted by Bultmann, as a result of which Bultmann can no longer speak of God directly, but only indirectly, and directly only of man (cf. on this particularly, Bultmann's essay, *Welchen Sinn hat es, von Gott zu reden?* ["What sense does it make to speak of God?"] in *Glauben und Verstehen*, I). This is to transpose the thought and language of the New Testament into an entirely different key. Here is the main gravamen of Barth's criticism of Bultmann. Barth is always pertinent—and even Bultmann's most ardent disciples must admit it—when he describes the status Bultmann, on his presuppositions ascribes to

the Christ event: "it can take no form outside of this restricted anthropological sense" (pp. 91ff.). In Bultmann the broad New Testament witness to Christ "stand(s) merely as a memorial to the name of Jesus Christ and of the act of God which took place in him" (ibid.). And the history of Jesus Christ is only important as an "act of God. . . . Nothing further can be said about it as the foundation and content both of faith and of the kerygma" (ibid.).

This much is clear: the Bultmann controversy is not about what he stands for or what he means. He means exactly what the New Testament means—that Jesus Christ is God graciously acting upon man. The controversy turns on how to express this intention in our theology and preaching.

Perhaps one might say that it is all a question of language, a question of the functional, theological language relevant for speaking of God and his action. Or, to put it in another way, it all revolves around the problem of time. Barth quotes the New Testament against Bultmann. The Christ event, he says, "is an event with an inherent significance of its own". It does not have to "acquire" this significance for the first time by being understood in faith. Such an event, with an inherent significance of its own, prior to its apprehension, is, from Bultmann's point of view, ruled out by his concept of time. Genuine historical reality exists only in the now of "historical" action, in the now of understanding and decision. Here, already, are good grounds for thinking that the problems of time and of language are closely connected.

Whether it is both problems together, or each in its turn, Barth's argument against Bultmann's doctrine of understanding is the same throughout. It is "himself", "Christ himself", "God himself", God's *pro se* contrasted with a mere *pro me*. This is no mere objectivity contrasted with Bultmann's subjectivism. And—here is a point for the Bultmannians!—it is no good reading into Barth what he does not actually say. And it would be sheer dogmatism to say that everything that does not square with Bultmann's doctrine of history is *ipso facto* ruled out as false objectification. So Barth is left with no alternative but to bring back myth again into the picture. He does, indeed, understand the redemptive event as "an event with an inherent significance of its own", but never as an "objective fact". Nowhere does he presume the subject-object pattern. The reader should watch out for this in the next section.

V

We will now review Vol. IV/1 of Barth's *Church Dogmatics* ("The Doctrine of Reconciliation"). In doing so, our purpose is a limited one, to see whether it offers any further contribution to the Bultmann debate, more positive than what he had to say in his *Attempt*. So this is not really a review, but merely a few marginal notes, a few concise analyses, and attempt to raise a few questions. But the questions we raise are not imposed arbitrarily upon the work; they arise from what Barth himself actually says. "The present situation in theology and also in the peculiar themes of this book mean that throughout I have found myself in an intensive, although for the most part, quiet, debate with Rudolf Bultmann. But his subject is always present, even in those places where with his methods and results before me I have consciously ignored him" (p. ix).

Section 59, entitled "The Obedience of the Son of God", deals with the history of Jesus Christ and its interpretation in terms of his office as High Priest. It was over the actual history of Jesus Christ and with regard to Jesus himself (i.e. in his attempt to find for Jesus and his history the proper and relevant expression), as we have seen, that Barth came to take issue with Bultmann. So what we must look for in *Church Dogmatics*, IV/1, is how, in Barth's opinion, the history of Jesus Christ is to be understood precisely as history. What kind of historicity does it possess? Historicity in Bultmann's sense of the word? Or objective factualness. Or is there a third sense?

We read in Barth:

> The atonement is history. . . . To speak of it we must tell it as history. To try to grasp it as supra-historical or non-historical is not to grasp it at all. It is indeed truth, but truth actualized in a history and revealed in this history as such—revealed, therefore, as history.

> But the atonement is the very special history of God with man, the very special history of man with God. As such it has a particular character and demands particular attention. As such it underlies and includes, not only in principle and virtually but also actually, the most basic history of man. It is the first and most inward presupposition of his existence, and it reveals itself as such. First of all, there took place and does take place the history of God with man and man with God, and then and for that reason and definitely on that basis man exists, and he can be called to knowledge and his own fully responsible decision and in that way have an actual part in that happening. The atonement takes precedence of all other history. It proves itself in fully responsible attitudes. It cannot be revealed and grasped and known without this proof. But when it is revealed and grasped and known, it is so in its priority, its precedence, its superiority to all other histories, to the existence of all men who take part in it.
>
> The atonement is, noetically, the history about Jesus Christ, and ontically, Jesus Christ's own history. To say atonement is to say Jesus Christ. To speak of it is to speak of His history (pp. 157f.).

This passage, which incidentally is obviously directed against Bultmann, clearly claims that all history is to be interpreted in the light of the history of Jesus Christ, not *vice versa*. His history is not to be interpreted in the light of some philosophy. That can offer no insight into its meaning. Hence we cannot force the history of Jesus Christ into the existentialist scheme of authenticity and inauthenticity. In what sense then can we speak of it as history? Only because it is what it is. Hence, apparently, all Barth can do is to go back to the Easter narratives, to the biblical word as such. Does this mean that they are objective facts? That they are history related in objective terms? To suppose that all verbal narration not orientated towards the existentialist scheme of authenticity and inauthenticity is by implication objective (i.e. from a subjective point of view, as Heidegger would say) is a mere dogma. The critically minded theologian should be cautious about subscribing to that dogma! For it is in the Word, in a narration, that we first encounter the history of Jesus Christ. It is, in the proper sense of the word, a myth, not myth in the sense of a construct of objectifying thought. It may be that Bultmann and his disciples would still call this "objectifying". But then the term would lose its pregnant significance and its epistemological value.

How can we speak of the history of Jesus Christ theologically or scientifically? By taking our terminology from our study and experience of the objective world? No, for the history of Jesus Christ concerns human existence. It provides it with the ground of its being and embraces it. Hence the history of Jesus Christ must be expressed in terms of the "existentialia", i.e. in the forms and structures which emerge from the study of existence, and which are therefore suitable vehicles for it. What is the rationale of these existentialia? Not human existence studied apart from the history of Jesus Christ, but existence interpreted in the light of that history. But does not this involve an undue narrowing of our existentalism? Here Barth would seem to lay himself open to the same charge as Bultmann: can there be any other kind of existentialism? Can ontological knowledge be acquired otherwise than from a phenomenological study of the ontic object? The real issue is whether a restricted Christological existentialism can compete in a genuinely ontological way with a broad, neutral existentialism as Bultmann understands it. If so, it will probably turn out to be broad, rather than narrow, enabling us to understand in existentialist terms what ordinary existentialism can make nothing of. The primary material for such a type of existentialism in this new sense is the existence of Jesus Christ. But we must be careful of returning to objectification in our definitions. We must demonstrate its structural affinity to individual human existence. It is not enough to assert a Christian existentialism merely as a thesis. Its implications must be drawn out so as to show how a genuine *pro me* can be extracted from it.

Here Barth's discussion of the "Son of God" is particularly significant. The term expresses the divine condescension into the far-off country in the obedience of Jesus Christ (pp. 157ff.). Barth rejects the mythological interpretation of the divine sonship as derived from the notion of the sacred marriage and thought of in physical terms. Perhaps he does so because that interpretation leaves no room for any real, concrete, or radical limitation of individual existence, such as is implied by any truly Christian doctrine of reconciliation. What then of Barth's alternative explanation of the divine Sonship? Does it imply such a limitation of existence? Barth believes it does. Jesus Christ is God's kingdom come on earth. At the same time he is its first, true subject, the logical complement to God's sovereign reign. For he lives a life of perfect obedience to the Father, and realizes his kingdom in his own person. He is the Son without whom the Father would not be Father. The kingdom of God, expressing as it does the reality of the divine intervention, requires two facets, the one prior to the other, yet both of them attributed to God. It is this polarity which brings in the *pro me*. In the coming of the kingdom of God something happens to me. God surrounds me on every side. By bringing in his kingdom as an event, God confronts me everywhere not only as one who says "Thou shalt" and who challenges me to a decision, but as one who comes personally to my side. Thus the kingdom of God itself implies a doctrine of atonement. God not only demands, but fulfils his own demand in my place. In the Christ event he comes as the obedient One to stand by my side or even to take my place. My existence is radically limited by the coming of the kingdom of God. The constitution of my being is not left suspended in mid-air, but radically changed. At this point one might bring back an existentialist analysis of faith. But to describe it as a "risk", an "absolute decision" or a "leap into the abyss" would be inadequate, and an oversimplification.[1] The genuine structure of existential decision ought really to come out into the open only on the other side of the "absolute situation of decision". This analysis of the Christological interpretation of the divine Sonship should make it clear how relevant Barth's broadened, Christological existentialism is to human existence.

[1] On this compare Barth in his *Attempt*: "I fail to see how Bultmann can suppress the fact that the New Testament describes the death of Jesus Christ as something which for all its incomprehensibility is still comprehensible, and which for all its hazardous character is meaningful. . . . Bultmann's doctrine of the cross comes perilously near the devil's temptation of Jesus to throw himself down from the pinnacle of the temple to prove his divine Sonship and demonstrate the supreme paradox of his faith, and it disturbs me" (p. 99).

On what principle, then, does he thus broaden his existentialism? (Of course, in speaking of it as a "broadening" we are starting from Barth's own position. But that is justified since Barth is the key figure in this discussion: he was the first to introduce existentialism into it.) Here, again, Barth has something to say which is implicitly directed against Bultmann. In section 59, 2, which is entitled: "The Judge Judged in Our Place", and which deals with the vicarious suffering of God, Barth is posing the question: *Cur Deus homo?* His first answer to this question is that God does it primarily for his own glory (p. 212). He then goes on to elaborate the point:

> We must not be put off from thinking in this direction by the charge that it is mere speculation and far too good to be true. If we will not accept the fact that God is also and primarily *pro se*, we shall find it hard to understand what it means that in being *pro se* He is also *pro nobis*, and therefore *pro me*. It is no accident that in the song of the Christmas angels (Luke 2. 14) the "Glory to God in the Highest" comes first, and the "Peace on earth to the men of the (divine) good pleasure" only second (ibid.).

Part of this is directed against Bultmann, and rejects the alternatives "speculation or existentialism". This is not, of course, true of existentialism as such, but of the way Bultmann defines it. Meanwhile Barth agrees with him about the *pro me*, which is so basic. Thus we continue to use such terms as the "existentialia" and to speak of "existentialist thinking". The second sentence in the above quotation ("If we . . . *pro me*") constitutes and defines the broadened existentialism. Barth makes a good point when he says that we shall hardly understand what God's *pro me* means if we will not accept the priority of his being *pro se*. In other words, everything turns upon the proper and primary meaning of his being *pro me*, of his concern with my existence and his claim upon it. What we want is the right kind of existentialism. God's *pro se* is not an additional or distinct thing from his *pro me*, not an abandonment of existentialism, or an intrusion of speculation or false objectification, but a necessary element in the structure of his *pro me*, rightly understood. Yet Barth would add—and we should surely agree with him—that God's *pro me* is a structural element of his *pro se*, the latter being ontologically prior. In any case God's "proseity" and "promeity" are not mutually exclusive; rather they include each other, with a kind of dialectical ambivalence between them. At first sight it looks as though the *pro me* is, *quoad nos*, primary (*Hoc est Christum cognoscere: beneficia eius cognoscere*). But this is true only to the extent that the *pro se* shines through as the primary aspect. The point is made with even greater precision in another passage in the *Church Dogmatics*, which states that the glory of God is the salvation of the creature. This statement, we might say, provides the foundation for a theological existentialism. The issue at stake is the creature's salvation, in an existentialist (before it is in an existential) sense. How does the New Testament define authentic being? In the sudden leap into another dimension, apparently quite unrelated to the salvation of the creature to the glory of God.

In following the train of Bultmann's thought we have brought the *extra nos* which lies at the frontier of man's self-understanding within the scope of the discussion. It has, however, been postulated rather than thought through. It is an existentialism enlarged so as to include God's *pro se*, God as he is in himself. Now you cannot translate this back into the realm of self-understanding. But to begin with it must be conceived in terms of the self-understanding, as the only appropriate way to understand it. "The glory of God is the salvation of the creature." Where the glory of God, that hard and strange, overwhelming external event, is left out of the account, the salvation of the creature, the concern of the individual, is not rightly understood. Anyone who cannot pray in the words of Ps. 115. 1 (*Non nobis domine*) does not understand his own existence. And where theology is not pursued in the spirit of this prayer it is not genuinely existential. One further point: the issue at stake is genuine existentialism, not existence itself, but an existentialist understanding of existence. In any case even Bultmann himself takes account of "God as he is in himself", God as external to man. But he can only see his way to speak of that side of things by employing his anthropological existentialia combined with the postulate of an extra-subjective reality, an act of God *extra nos*, as the only way to reflect upon that side of the matter.

What is to be the shape of this enlarged existentialism? The implied dialectical relation between the *pro se* and the *pro me* has direct methodological consequences. On the one hand the *pro me* becomes the criterion for every statement about God, and on the other hand the *pro se* becomes the criterion for every statement about human existence. Here Barth has something highly pertinent to say:

> That He (God) does, in fact, will to reconcile it (the world) with himself, and to save it, and therefore to magnify His glory in it and to it, is from every standpoint the sovereign will of His mercy. We cannot deduce it or count on it from any side. We cannot establish in principle from any side that it must be so, that God had to link the revelation and increase of His glory with the maintaining and carrying through to victory of our cause, that He had to cause it to take place as an event in which salvation is given to us. . . . If we can speak of a necessity of any kind here, it can only be the necessity of the decision which God did in fact make and execute . . . *Cur Deus homo?* Because the salvation of the world and of men, we ourselves and our salvation, are in fact included in the self-purposiveness of this divine action. Because the great and self-sufficient God wills to be also the Saviour of the world (pp. 213–14).

In other words: God's revelation of his glory is his sovereign, uncaused act of his mercy towards us. Here we have the three prerequisites which any theological statement has to cover: first, the revelation of the divine glory: secondly, the *pro se*, the saving character of the divine action towards us: and thirdly, its absolute primacy and sovereignty. Absolute primacy is the common element to all these, for it accompanies points one and two as well as three. Absolute primacy belongs to events to which our knowledge cannot attain, and from which our knowledge is always derived (cf. Karl Barth, *Credo*, E.T., 1933, p. 45). A derivative statement, an objectifying one, a mythological one in Bultmann's sense of the word, a speculative one, obliterates the sovereignty of the divine action as well as the seriousness of the existential claim it entails. What God's glory reveals has absolute primacy because no other perspective is conceivable. The divine action *pro me* is absolutely primary because all I can do is to respond to it by my decision. I can never assume an attitude of superiority over it. In this concern for the absolute primacy of God and his action Bultmann's demand for an existentialist interpretation has something in common with Polan's requirement for exegesis (*illa autem interpretatio consentit cum sacra scriptura, quae omnem laudem salutis nostrae aeternae. . . . Deo tribuit*). Take the two together, and you have the quintessence of authentic theological statement.

That which has absolute primacy sets a limit to my existence as well as to my thinking. It is the glory of God and my salvation which do this, or rather, they are the twin determinations which set a limit to my existence, and as such form the subject matter of theology.

When we speak of absolute primacy we do not mean to imply that every scientific proposition has its own particular proof. Rather, each statement is part and parcel of a general argument. Every scientific proposition and, therefore, every theological one is in a certain sense secondary. The only question is in what way this is true in theology. Absolute primacy belongs to a theological statement in the sense indicated, what it says is related to an event limited to existential relevance. Such an event can never be used to deduce new facts, whether subordinate or superordinate. There can be no advance of thought which leaves the event behind it. All there can be is deepening of thought, always starting out from the event and returning to it enriched. Such thought does not swing like a pendulum from side to side, but revolves around a constant centre. Theology can never be anything more than a description of the saving events which are fixed once and for all. It must always end up where it started. Theological thinking is always subject to this qualification because of the absolute primacy of its subject matter. Speculation is the untramelled creativity of the free human subject. Theology is the obedient response, and is therefore phenomenological. Because of this permanent relation to its subject matter theological deduction and argument can only be conducted along these lines. How the linear pattern of speculation is related to the cyclical pattern of theological description is a problem which remains to be investigated in detail.

In what dimension and in what manner does the history of Jesus Christ confront us? Again Barth has an answer, and again it is an answer not expressly directed at Bultmann:

> It (sc. the saving act of God) was done as God became man in Jesus Christ, in order to do that in our place and for us. It took place in Him, in the one man, and therefore there and then, *illic et tunc*, and in significance *hic et nunc*, for us in our modern here and now. To be known and explained and proclaimed with this significance it cannot and must not be ignored or dissolved in favour of its significance, it can and must be taken as that which is significant in its significance, and therefore in and for itself as the history of Jesus Christ as it took place there and then, and as it can be and is recounted. That is how it happens for us. For upon the fact that it happened for us there depends the further fact that it has a significance for us as something that happened there depends on the further fact that it can be seen by us to have this significance. Where there is nothing significant, and seen to be significant, there can be no significance or recognition of it. But the significant thing is what happened in Him, in Jesus Christ, in this one man. It is His history as such (pp. 223f.).
>
> The New Testament distinguishes this happening in relation to its significance by an *ἅπαξ* or *ἐφάπαξ*. This marks it off as an event which has to be considered in its uniqueness and particularity, which cannot be dissolved, or merely commemorated *sotto voce* for the sake of completeness (p. 224).

To bring out the ontological presupposition behind these passages a distinction should perhaps be drawn between dimension of being and dimension of manifestation in the history of Jesus Christ—and it is the history of Jesus Christ that Barth is talking about. The history occurs in the dimension of the *ἐφάπαξ*. It is unique in time. It is manifest to us to-day in the dimension of the Word, which testifies to this unique event. From Barth's observations on the *ἐφάπαξ* we may draw an important inference about his doctrine of time, on contrast to Bultmann's (though Bultmann does not speak about time in so many words). Barth differs from

Bultmann on this subject, and is clearly trying to define his position over against him when he speaks of what is "significant in its significance" in the particular area in which Bultmann's doctrine of time is so crucially important. How could he do this unless he is presupposing a very different doctrine of his own? What this doctrine is can be inferred from his argument. He says that the significant thing is not merged in its significance. In terms of time he means that the *illic et tunc* is not merged into the *hic et nunc*. Yet at the same time the *illic et tunc* has a relevance for our *hic et nunc*. In other words the two belong together *ἀσύγχυτος ἀδιαίρετος*. The *ἀσύχυτος-ἀδιαίρετος* is a structure of being, it constitutes the essence of time. (It is of the essence of the temporal *illic et tunc* that it is revelant for the *hic et nunc*.) According to the doctrine of time here implied, the *illic et tunc* exists for the *hic et nunc*. Uniqueness and finality, the *ἐφάπαξ* is of the essence of time. Time is not just run off like a film, as it is when viewed in objectifying terms, a view which Bultmann is trying to dissociate himself from with his punctilear doctrine of time. That would be to surrender the *ἀδιαίρετος*. It makes time a succession of discontinuous moments, the distance between them being bridged only by historical tradition. But this is not to say that Barth goes along with Bultmann, either. For Bultmann surrenders the *ἀσύγχετος*. Then and now are merged in the *nun* of decision. It is of the essence of historical time that although new moments occur, one moment is constitutive and determinative for the moments that follow. This implies succession and direction. But it does not reduce the successive moments to a common level. It is a qualified succession. It is always the occurrence of significance.

The essence of time is revealed in and by means of language. The word belongs to the structure of time. For the word expresses the continuity of meaning which constitutes time. It expresses the mutual dependence of its successive moments. The biblical word is the prototype for this. The unique and final event which occurred there and which decides our existence confronts us in the word of the gospels.

Time and word are complementary. The word is essentially

related to time. It narrates that which has become an event in time, thus making it live on in time. Its function is that of re-presentation (making present again), which is required by uniqueness and finality. In the word the past comes into being again, and the future heralds its arrival.

The word of the gospels names the name of Jesus Christ and narrates the history of his life, passion and resurrection. The ἐφάπαξ of the Christ event confronts us primarily in the gospel story which can be passed on from mouth to mouth. Only in a secondary sense is its implicit meaning and existential significance drawn out in reflection. The primary function of language is to name the reality which confronts us in time, to relate its history. One of the secondary functions is reflection, which explicates what confronts us in concentrated form when it is named and related.

These glosses on a few selected passages of Karl Barth's *Church Dogmatics* do not show the real purpose behind his words, but perhaps they do show what his premises must be if he speaks as he does. The principles we have extracted, both ontological and methodological, are implied in what he says. For every thought-out subject, if it be strictly carried out, has its own appropriate method, its proper arguments, its unity of thought. Our analyses are not meant to do more than suggest a project and a method. The whole of Barth's doctrine of the atonement, and indeed the whole of his *Church Dogmatics* as it has appeared thus far would offer a more complete existentialist ontology and methodology. Would this be a luxury? Certainly not, at least not as far as the Bultmann debate is concerned. Only such a procedure can bring to light their differences all along the line. But would it be a luxury for theology itself? Probably not in this case either. For the scientific knowledge of the "how" inherent in every "what" can provide help and stimulus to those who bear the ultimate responsibility of theologian and preacher.

Thus, it would seem to us, the discussion between Barth and Bultmann has brought us further and thrown fresh light on the demythologizing problem. The concern of each is on the way to a fruitful synthesis. For they both embark from the same premises.

Both take the first commandment as the axiom of their theology. Barth seeks to maintain Jesus Christ in his intrinsic self-hood and God's sovereignty revealed in him. Bultmann uses existentialist interpretation in order to show the relevance of the living Word of God to man's existence. He does it scientifically, yet always in the service of the Church's proclamation. In my opinion these two concerns are in the last resort not contradictory, but complementary.

RUDOLF SCHNACKENBURG

CHRISTOLOGY AND MYTH

SYNOPSIS

1. Bultmann's existentialist interpretation of the New Testament.
2. The Christology of the New Testament as interpreted by Bultmann.
3. New Testament Christology in the patristic age.
4. The resurrection of Jesus—the key to the New Testament.

IN a lecture delivered at the conference of Swiss liberal theologians[1] Rudolf Bultmann discusses the confession of the World Council of Churches (which acknowledges Jesus Christ as God and Saviour) and its compatibility with the New Testament. He thinks that the formula lacks precision; it is not clearly directed against false doctrine and leaves scope for a variety of interpretations on the positive side. We have no desire to refute Bultmann on this point, particularly in view of the incisive statements of the Chalcedonian formula on this score. But in the course of his lecture Bultmann passes judgement on the Christological affirmations of the New Testament itself, which the Council of Chalcedon took seriously. As Bultmann sees it, the New Testament is poles apart from the later Christological definitions, and indeed quite incompatible with them. In his opinion the early Church saw the problems involved in "very God and very man", but "sought to solve them in an inadequate way by means of Greek thought with its objectivizing nature". The solution devised at Chalcedon "found an expression that is now impossible for our thought" (op. cit., p. 286). First then, what does Bultmann think of the Christology of the New Testament?

[1] "The Christological Confession of the World Council of Churches", reprinted in *Essays Philosophical and Theological*, E.T., 1955.

1. *Bultmann's Existentialist Interpretation of the New Testament*

Bultmann's basic contention may be summarized in his own words. Christ is everything that is asserted of him in the New Testament in so far as he is the "eschatological event . . . which can never be objectivized into an event of the past, nor into an event in a metaphysical sphere, which rather militates against every objectivization" (op. cit., pp. 286f.).

One cannot understand this without some insight into Bultmann's theology as a whole. According to Bultmann, faith in Jesus Christ owes its rise exclusively to the earliest Christian community. Long ago, in 1926, when he wrote his book on Jesus (E.T., *Jesus and Word*, 1934), he believed that we can know almost nothing of the life and personality of Jesus, since the early Christian sources show no particular interest in either (p. 8). He is of the opinion that Jesus did not believe himself to be the Messiah (p. 9). In his *Theology of the New Testament* (E.T., 1951) he demolishes all the arguments commonly adduced against this negative position and gives reasons for thinking that faith in Jesus' Messiahship grew up out of belief in his resurrection (p. 27). Peter's confession at Caesarea Philippi is really a post-resurrection episode projected back by Mark into the earthly life of Jesus, as is also the Transfiguration. The story of Jesus' baptism is a legend (though it has a basis in the historical fact that he was baptized by John), and is intended to portray the consecration of Jesus as Messiah in the interests of faith. The triumphal entry into Jerusalem has been coloured by legend. Since the rise of the Easter faith and the consequent belief in Jesus' Messiahship, everything that preceded it has been seen in a new light (pp. 42f.). The proclaimer became the proclaimed, the One whose advent was the decisive event.

None of this so far is new. Biblical critics had long before Bultmann been saying the same thing. The conclusion seems inevitable that from a historical point of view the faith of the earliest Church was a great illusion, which would mean the *coup de grâce* for the Christian faith. Bultmann does not himself, however, draw this negative conclusion. Rather, he tries to find a new way of presenting the Christian faith as the power which moves human existence.

Bultmann agrees that Jesus himself had a decisive and permanent significance. True, "he only appeared as a prophet and teacher. He does not offer any doctrine of his person: but he says that the fact of his activity is decisive. . . . That he speaks *now*, at the final decisive hour, is the arresting novelty of his preaching".[1] As early as 1953 he tells us what he means by the eschatological event. This is a term he has coined for himself, and implies a peculiar conception of the word "eschatological". To this late Judaism, primitive Christianity, the Protestant theology of the Word and contemporary existentialism have been laid under contribution, but fused in such a way that something entirely new has emerged. It is true that the primitive Christian Church believed that the Messianic promises of the Old Testament had been fulfilled, and understood itself as the "eschatological community" (cf. Acts 2; I Cor. 10. 11; II Cor. 6. 2f., etc.). But at the same time it constructed for itself a new theology of its own. It awaited the parousia and the consummation of salvation. It is the unity of fulfilment and expectation held together in tension which is the distinctive eschatological attitude of the New Testament. Bultmann, however, would lay aside the future element as a vestige of mythology. All that is binding for faith is the eschatological "now". This "now" breaks in with Jesus, or more accurately in his Word (he is simply the "Revealer", and this Word is further extended in the Church's proclamation). In the word of proclamation, and in it alone Christ encounters us and God addresses us. These ideas, whose derivation from the Protestant theology of the Word is unmistakable, Bultmann proceeds to interpret in an existentialist sense. Through this Word every man to-day is addressed in his existential situation and summoned to decision.[2] The existentialist interpretation is

[1] "*Die Christologie des Neuen Testaments*" in *Glauben und Verstehen*, I, 1933, p. 265.

[2] Ibid., p. 267: "In the preaching of this Word the decision is immediately present."

still more obvious in the essay, *New Testament and Mythology* (1941), in which "the point at issue is how we understand the fall. Even the (existentialist) philosophers are agreed about the fact of it. But they think that all man needs is to be shown his plight, and that then he will be able to escape from it. In other words, the corruption resulting from the fall does not extend to the core of the human personality. The New Testament, on the other hand, regards the fall as total" (*Kerygma and Myth I*, pp. 28f.). That only this "fallen" man is set free, free from himself, is for Bultmann the meaning of the Christ event. "This is precisely the meaning of that which is wrought in Christ. At the very point where man can do nothing, God steps in and acts—indeed he has acted already—on man's behalf" (ibid., p. 31).

The Christ event further includes the cross and resurrection. This means, "to make the cross of Christ our own, to undergo crucifixion with him" (p. 36). In the concrete situations of everyday life, the same thing is experienced as participation in the resurrection: "In this resurrection they (sc. Christian believers) enjoy a freedom, albeit a struggling freedom" (p. 40). In this way, according to Bultmann (the matter cannot be pursued any further here) God's action in Christ, translated by the word of proclamation into the present, becomes a power directly affecting our own existence, calling us to decision and redeeming us in our humanity.

Now all this gives the Christological statements of the New Testament a completely different twist. For those who understand them as Bultmann does it does not matter *what* we believe and confess about Christ (that the Son of God becomes man, that he is Messiah, that he the crucified One was raised from the dead, that all these things are objective events or historical facts, and presented as such to faith). The only bearing the Christ event has is on my existential situation, its sole importance is for me and my self-understanding. The message of the New Testament is not that which once was, but that which has meaning for me. Thus I need not ask what Christ was, but only what the preaching says about him. It is as though Bultmann were digging up the previous statements about Christ from the depths of the past (a past which he is so sceptical about!) and putting them in the place where alone they make sense and have meaning, viz. in the proclamation and in their relevance to our own existence. Here is the clue to Bultmann's procedure. He is compelled to detach the kerygma from its basis in history and to maintain an attitude of indifference to its historical factualness. The reason for this is that he regards faith's affirmations about Christ, for all their historical appearance, as mythological, and if they are to be made meaningful for modern man they must be freed from mythology. This, thinks Bultmann, can only be done if the Christ event is interpreted existentially as depicted above. True, the question arises whether Jesus Christ is not thereby reduced to a mere fact of salvation, so that he ceases to be a person, as one of Bultmann's critics has claimed (Günther Bornkamm, in *Mythos und Evangelium*, p. 18).

Yet in adopting the existential understanding as his hermeneutic principle, Bultmann finds himself faced with a dilemma: how to avoid a purely arbitrary interpretation? What right have we to divest the New Testament kerygma, which has come down to us only in its mythological garb, of that garb and expound it existentially? Is this a legitimate understanding of the traditional faith? Bultmann rejoins by claiming that in the last resort this is just how the early Church understood the eschatological Christ event, and that despite its mythological thought and language. The early Church, like us, was groping after a new understanding of man, which it believed to be disclosed in the Christ event. What then of this claim? Let us concentrate on that, for if Bultmann fails to sustain it, his interpretation, however ingenious and well meant, is nothing but a modernization of faith in Christ, and no longer deserves the name of Christian.

2. *The Christological Statements of the New Testament as Interpreted by Bultmann*

In his lecture to the Swiss liberal theologians, Bultmann contends that the Christological titles of the New Testament do not describe Jesus objectively, as he is in himself, but only in his meaning for faith.[1] This is the same suggestion as he had already

[1] "The Christological Confession of the World Council of Churches", *Essays Philosophical and Theological*, E.T., 1955, p. 280.

put forward in his essay on the Christology of the New Testament in 1933. The latter essay in fact provides a commentary on what he had stated more concisely and clearly in his Swiss lecture:

> It (i.e. Christology) is not the theoretical expression of practical piety, it is not speculation and doctrine about the divine being of Christ, but it is proclamation, address. It is the "doctrine" that through Jesus Christ righteousness has been created, that he was crucified and rose for our sake (Rom. 3. 24f.; 4. 25; 10. 9; II Cor. 5. 18f.). By this proclamation the hearer is addressed and asked whether he is willing to believe this, that is to say, whether he is willing to understand himself in the light of this fact, as a sinner before God, to surrender himself with all that he is and possesses in himself, and to take up the cross of Christ, and thus as one who is justified, who has a share in the new life, in the resurrection of Christ (*Glauben und Verstehen*, I, p. 260).

In other words, the Christology of the New Testament, according to Bultmann, is exhausted in its meaning for us. It says nothing about Christ as he is in himself. Wherever the Christological statements of the New Testament deviate from this, and become objectifying statements, they must be interpreted critically.[1]

To argue with Bultmann on this point is difficult for more reasons than one.

First, as the last quotation shows, Bultmann admits that there are objectifying statements even in the New Testament. That is why he stigmatizes anything which does not square with his existential interpretation as "mythological". The real sense of such statements must be extracted by critical deduction.

Secondly, Bultmann discerns even in the New Testament a process of Hellenization, tending towards the exaltation of Jesus to divine status (though never to a level of full equality with God). The climax of this tendency is to be found in Hebrews and in the Johannine writings. Such texts, with their incipient objectification, can therefore be relegated to a later stage of development within Hellenistic Christianity, though, of course, he still looks

[1] *Essays Philosophical and Theological*, p. 281.

for the existential meaning in *all* of the Christological titles of the New Testament, and refuses to take them ontologically.[1]

Thirdly, more important still is the internal difficulty in New Testament Christology. Even where titles of majesty are ascribed to Jesus in a purely ontological sense they always imply for those who use them that he is their personal Succourer and Deliverer. Christology merges into secteriology even where there is a tendency towards objectification. This is illustrated quite simply in the Amsterdam confession (which was surely not intended in a Bultmannian sense), with its acknowledgement of Jesus Christ as God and Saviour. It is obviously based not so much on specific New Testament texts as on the spirit of the New Testament as a whole. Like similar statements, it combines the highest Christological title of majesty—that of God—with one that insists on his meaning for salvation. Given this combination, which is to be found on every page of the New Testament, how are we to know whether the titles, confessions and affirmation about Christ are to be taken objectively, as referring to Christ as a person, or only relatively, as descriptions of his meaning for us?

Bultmann is convinced that he can prove his case from the New Testament.[2] Speaking of the Christological titles, he maintains that they describe Jesus as a divine being in a subordinationist sense. Also, there are naïve statements attributing to Jesus Christ functions which, strictly speaking, belong exclusively to God, e.g. the "grace of Jesus Christ" (II Cor. 8. 9), as elsewhere of the grace of God (Rom. 5. 15), or the substitution of the traditional "if God will" (Rom. 1. 10; 15. 32) by "if the Lord (i.e. Christ) will" (I Cor. 4. 19; 16. 7). God and Christ alternate in synonymous parallelism (I Cor. 7. 17). Bultmann regards all this as a naïve, loose mode of expression which only implies that God encounters us in Christ and in him alone. Now it is certainly true that the New Testament regards Christ as the mediator of

[1] In his lecture to the Swiss liberals Bultmann deals first with the passages which identify Jesus directly with God (see under section II). He then proceeds to ask what the intention behind such statements is (see section III). His answer that they merely seek to indicate the meaning of Jesus for faith would seem to fit all of the titles previously mentioned, including the Johannine ones.

[2] On the following, cf. *Essays Philosophical and Theological*, pp. 281ff.

salvation *par excellence* and that the weight of emphasis rests upon *διὰ 'Ιησοῦ Χριστοῦ* but the question is, Is Bultmann right in taking it to mean that the proclamation of Christ opens up a new, authentic, eschatological encounter with God? Or does the New Testament mean quite concretely the *person* of Christ the exalted One, the incarnate, crucified, and risen Son of God, and that this is what is implied by the phrase *διὰ 'Ιησου Χριστοῦ*. The latter interpretation is substantiated by the frequent addition of *τοῦ κυρίου Ιησοῦ*, and is strongly implied in such passages as Rom. 5. 1f., 17, 21; I Cor. 15. 57; II Cor. 3. 4; 5. 18; Phil. 2. 11; I Thess. 5. 9; Tit. 3. 6, etc., in which the redemptive *work* of Christ is presumed. But for Bultmann this proves nothing, since these expressions are only mythological trappings, like the session of Christ at the right hand of God and his pleading for us to the Father as an advocate (Rom. 8. 34). If, however, we take the mediatorial work of Jesus in a concrete, ontological sense, the naïve statements which ascribe to him similar functions to those of the Father have more meaning than Bultmann allows. The triadic texts which mention the Spirit as well (I Cor. 12. 4–6: II Cor. 13. 13) should be a warning against taking these phrases and terms as a loose and inexact mode of speech. For Christ, the exalted Lord, works through the Spirit quite literally in the believers and in the Church. The same applies to God's effecting our salvation through Christ. In other words, these naïve statements all acquire a meaning and an even better meaning than they do on Bultmann's interpretation. Christ exercises his office of mediator as *person*.

Bultmann attaches especial importance to the texts which oscillate between God and Christ as the future judge.[1] From this oscillation (God as judge in I Thess. 3. 13; Rom. 3. 5, Christ in I Thess. 2. 19; I Cor. 4. 5). Bultmann argues that this is only a mythological way of saying that our salvation or damnation depend on our response to Jesus and his Word, as in Mark 8. 38. Acts 17. 31, he thinks, tries to strike a balance between the two. But what Bultmann calls a balance may turn out to be the key to what Paul is really saying in these various turns of phrase. Since

[1] On the following, cf. op. cit., pp. 282f.

God has actually handed over his judicial functions to Christ, one may indeed say that we are judged by the Lord: Christ is the personal agent of the divine judgement. God himself can also be called judge. His tribunal (Rom. 14. 10) is administered by Christ (Rom. 14. 9). Lietzmann's exegesis is correct when he says, "Christ will sit as judge on the tribunal (*βῆμα*) and administer judgement as God's commissary . . . God, who subsequently metes out the rewards (I Cor. 4. 5) can also be called directly the judge".[1] Bultmann misconstrues the whole picture in the interests of his own case when he says: "The judgement is effected in the proclamation of the Word; for this Word, the preaching, spreads life and death" (II Cor. 2. 15, 16). Actually this text with its rhetoric (some pass from death to death and others from life to life) points to the *future* judgement. Even in the Gospel of John, where the judgement on unbelief is transferred to the present (John 3. 18) does not rule out the notion of a future judgement which the Father has committed to the Son (John 5. 22). The connecting link appears at John 12. 48, where, of course, Bultmann eliminates "at the last day" as a gloss from the hand of his ecclesiastical redactor.[2]

The same criticism applies to Bultmann's second point, that the kingly rule of God is sometimes called the kingly rule of Christ (Col. 1. 13; II Tim. 4. 18; II Pet. 1. 11; both combined in Eph. 5. 5). Bultmann is convinced that both sets of passages refer to the identical kingdom.[3] He then goes on to argue that the term *Βασιλεία τοῦ Θεοῦ*, which was originally part of the apocalyptic mythology, has been demythologized in the earliest passages

[1] Hans Lietzmann, *An die Korinther*, I and II (Handbuch zum N.T. 9; Tübingen, 1949, 4th ed.), excursus, p. 122.

[2] Rudolf Bultmann, *Das Evangelium des Johannes* (Kritisch-exegetisches Kommentar über das N.T., Göttingen, 1950, 11th ed.), p. 262, n. 7.

[3] Other commentators see a distinction between the two kingdoms, e.g. M. J. Lagrange, *L'Evangile selon S. Matthieu* (Paris, 1927, 3rd ed.), pp. 161f. and on Matt. 13. 41; O. Cullmann, "The Kingship of Christ and the Church in the New Testament" in *The Early Church*, Ed. A. J. B. Higgins, S.C.M. Press, 1956. Opposed to this exegesis is W. G. Kümmel "*Das Urchristentum*", *Theologische Rundschau*, VII, p. 122f., and in his appendix to Lietzmann's commentary on I Cor. 15. 24ff.; also W. Meinertz, *Theologie des Neuen Testaments* (Bonn, 1950), Vol. I, p. 38; Vol. II, pp. 228–9.

which refer to the *βασιλεία* of Christ. In I Cor. 15. 23–28 we do, it is true, find traces of the late Jewish doctrine of the millenium, but here it is historicized, or, as Bultmann would put it, demythologized, and refers to the present age in which Christ exercises his kingly rule through the proclamation. But this interpretation is very uncertain. The passage does indeed speak of Christ as presently reigning, but the main point it is making is that God's purpose is to put all things in subjection to Christ, his Christ who is the first fruits of them that slept and has already in principle triumphed over the powers of evil. Then, after his victory is complete, the Son surrenders his kingly rule to the Father, that God may be "all in all". There is here a real surrender of his divine rule and authority on the part of the Father to the Son, who after his resurrection is exalted to be the heavenly Lord; and at the End there is just as real a surrender of his rule and authority to the Father. The Kingdom of God in the full sense does not begin until the destruction of the last enemy, death. If Paul shows a certain shift of emphasis from the final kingdom of God to salvation as a present fact (I Cor. 4. 20; Rom. 14. 17) and in Col. 1. 13; Eph. 2. 6 (also in 5. 5?): II Tim. 4. 18 (cf. also Phil. 1. 23) a quite different conception (transcendental presence),[1] this does not mean a demythologizing of the whole idea, or that he is speaking only in a loose, improper sense of the kingdom of God or of Christ.

The consequence, therefore, which Bultmann draws is that "the divinity or deity of Christ is revealed in the occurrence in which we are given a place by the fact that the message of the gospel, which proclaims him as the grace of God to us, rings out",[2] results only when the relevant texts are interpretated in the light of Bultmann's prior understanding. For embarrassing texts like the doxologies or prayers addressed to Christ, Bultmann adopts a different way of removing their sting. They represent a natural, but somewhat later development.

[1] Cf. A. Wikenhauser, *Die Kirche als der mystische Leib Christi nach dem Apostel Paulus* (Münster, 1940, 2nd ed.), 41–7; L. Cerfaux, *La théologie de l'Eglise suivant S. Paul* (Paris, 1948, 2nd ed.), 294–8.

[2] *Essays*, p. 284.

3. *New Testament Christology in the Patristic Age*

With Bultmann you can only argue about his fundamental understanding of the New Testament texts. This does not affect the question whether the earliest Church developed its faith in Christ out of its own resources or from the claims of Jesus himself. Given Bultmann's insistence on anthropology as the hermeneutic principle, and the rigid perspective it entails, all we can do is to demonstrate the improbability of his view. What then is the immediately obvious meaning of the New Testament affirmations about Christ and the earliest recoverable Christology of the primitive Church? Although we shall not convince Bultmann's followers in respect of their prior understanding, it is probably desirable at this point to throw together a few positive observations on the subject.

The two opposing positions are once again succinctly stated in Bultmann's pointed question, "How far is a Christological pronouncement about him also a pronouncement about me? Does he help me because he is God's Son, or is he the Son of God because he helps me?" Those of us who accept the Chalcedonian formula certainly believe that Christ helps us—or, more precisely, saves us, because he is the Son of God. Can we suppose that the earliest Church thought otherwise?

1. The original apostolic kerygma, as preserved in Peter's speeches in Acts, has a common basic structure. It moves from the situation in hand to a brief summary of the Christian message. This generally begins with Jesus' works (his miracles and healings) and goes on to lay particular emphasis on his death as contrived by his human enemies and his resurrection as the act of God (including his exaltation). Then it is said that all these things took place in fulfilment of the Old Testament prophecies. Immediately after this, there is generally a corroborative statement to the effect that the apostles are witnesses of the resurrection, and the whole concludes with an appeal for repentance, faith and baptism.[1] First, then, the mighty acts of redemption are

[1] Acts 2. 22–36; 3. 13–19; 4. 10–12; 5. 30–2; 10. 37–43. The missionary sermon of Paul in Pisidian Antioch (13. 23–41) exhibits essentially the same

set before the hearers, then comes the appeal for a response. First, an unfolding of the redemptive significance and dignity of Jesus, often in terms of a primitive Christology, and then, on the basis of that, the demand for faith and conversion. Is there not a reason for this constant pattern? Since God has so acted, since Jesus enjoys this exalted state as the mediator of salvation, since God has exalted him as Lord and glorified him as the Christ, the Deliverer who will later return to judge both the quick and the dead—*therefore*, because of all this, men must abandon the hardness of their hearts and believe on his name. The objective data—though, admittedly there is here less emphasis on the inherent dignity of Jesus, and more on God's action upon him—are placed before the prospective converts. Never are they challenged to a faith which will only then enable them to experience the redemptive significance of Jesus.

2. Paul is a further witness for this pattern of preaching, despite the fact that justification and the personal appropriation of salvation are so much in the foreground of his thought, which makes him so much more congenial than the Bultmann's approach. Here we would refer to Rom. 1. 3f. (on I Cor. 15. 3–8 see below, under section IV). There is no emphasis here on the redemptive significance of Christ *pro nobis* (cf. Rom. 4. 25). This brief, but packed theological exposé, so striking because of its pre-Pauline flavour[1] confines itself to a description of the dignity of the Son of God and, placed as it is at the opening of the epistle, is evidently meant to underline the dignity of the apostle, as the one who proclaims the gospel of this same Son of God. It seems that for Paul, no less than for his predecessors, the saving significance of the exalted Lord is the consequence of what he is, or of what he has become since God raised him from the dead. Other passages also, such as Rom. 10. 9; Gal. 1. 14, 4. 4ff.; Phil. 2. 6ff.; Col. 1. 15ff., 2. 9ff., suggest that Paul himself shared this basic understanding. The confession of the Son of God

scheme. Cf. on the whole subject, C. H. Dodd, *The Apostolic Preaching and its Developments* (London, 1944, 2nd ed., reprinted 1950), pp. 20ff.

[1] Cf. J. Gewiess, *Die urapostolische Heilsverkündigung nach der Apostelgeschichte*, Breslau, 1939, 12–70.

and the assessment of his universal, cosmic significance have an intrinsic importance of their own. First, his rôle in redemptive history or his cosmic majesty is described and then, only after that, comes his significance for the salvation of the hearers. The parallel between Adam and Christ, so central to Pauline theology (Rom. 5. 12ff.; I Cor. 15. 22) cannot be constructed out of the experience of the brethren who have grafted on to him who is the first fruits of the new humanity (Rom. 8. 29; Col. 1. 18). Paul's thought moves in the reverse direction—from the redemptive history, from the cosmic status of Christ, to the personal quest for salvation through Christ, with Christ, and in Christ.

3. It has not been proven by any means that the Christ cult was developed out of the experience of salvation in him. The texts seem rather to suggest that theological reflection followed upon the redemptive act of God in history. It is God who raised Jesus from the dead, a fact which is repeatedly emphasized as the primary datum for the faith of primitive Christendom. The proclamation of the act of God as an objective fact and the liturgical celebration of the work of God (cf. such an early passage as Acts 4. 24–30) may also have contributed to a clearer understanding of the person of Christ, the Anointed One and servant of God. Why should not the early Christians, as the Messianic titles multiplied, transfer to Christ other high-sounding titles from their Hellenistic environment? The only important thing is that whether this brought any actual accretion to the Church's faith. On this point Bultmann is certainly too radical, like so many of his colleagues in the History of Religions school. For example, moderate scholars reject the theory that the title Kyrios is of exclusively Hellenistic origin, as Bultmann thinks, reviving Bousset's theory.[1] Acts 2. 36 and the invocation *Maranatha* (I Cor. 16. 22; cf. Rev. 22. 20), a liturgical formula which undoubtedly derives from the earliest Aramaic-speaking Church,[2]

[1] R. Bultmann, *Theology of the New Testament*, I, pp. 51ff. Cf. the refutations of W. Foerster in TWNT III, 1093–4; C. H. Dodd, *Apostolic Preaching*, p. 15; O. Cullmann, *The Christology of the New Testament*, pp. 205ff.

[2] K. G. Kuhn, s.v. in TWNT IV, 470ff.; G. Bornkamm, "*Das Anathema in der urchristlichen Abendmahlsliturgie*", in *Theologische Literatur-Zeitung*, LXXV (1950), pp. 227ff.

prove that both the title and the invocation of Jesus in terms of it are rooted in the Palestinian Church, though they may not have acquired their full depth of meaning until they were taken over into the Hellenistic churches. The doctrine of Christ's exaltation to the right hand of God (cf. Acts 2. 33f., 5. 31, 7. 55f.; Rom. 8. 34; Col. 3. 1, etc.) and the parousia hope must have stimulated the worship of Christ quite early on. Hence it is not surprising to find primitive hymns actually addressed to Christ (cf. Phil. 2. 6ff.; Col. 1. 15ff., 2. 9ff.; I Tim. 3. 16), although doxologies in the strictest sense of the word were for a long time directed preferably to God. The distinguishing mark of the Christians is they "call upon the name of the Lord (Jesus Christ)" (I Cor. 1. 2; Acts 9. 14, 21; II Tim. 2. 22). Paul prays for himself personally to the Lord (II Cor. 12. 8) like Stephen in the hour of his martyrdom (Acts 7. 59); but the apostle to the Gentiles prays to the Lord for his churches as well (I Thess. 3. 12; II Thess. 3. 5, 16).

We may, therefore, see the hand of providence slowly guiding the Church in the path of legitimate development. This was a process of clarification and sifting, which eventually led to the Chalcedonian formula.[1] The Church's motive in attributing divinity and divine titles to Jesus in New Testament times was not to "give expression to how the world and men have been called into a new situation by the appearance of Jesus, and so have been called to a decision for or against God, that is, therefore, for or against the world" (Bultmann, *Essays*, p. 285). Rather, the development rose from its faith in the resurrection of Jesus as an act of God. These titles, therefore, are intended as real affirmations about Christ's person. They are all attempts to describe and explain his status in redemptive history and in the cosmos as the mediator of salvation.

4. *The Resurrection of Jesus*

Here we come to the heart of the matter. What did the resurrection mean for the earliest Christians? The apostolic preaching

[1] Cf. further A. Grillmeier in *Chalkedon*, 1, 5/202.

(including that of Paul) starts out from this redemptive fact, and it is the foundation of their whole Christology. But the question still is whether their Easter message is not the product of faith, a faith which Bultmann is perfectly free to interpret as he wants to. It is a fact that Bultmann does believe that the earliest Church arrived at its interpretation of Christ as the eschatological event in the light of Easter morning. "Can the resurrection narratives and every other mention of the resurrection in the New Testament be understood simply as an attempt to convey the meaning of the cross?" (*Kerygma and Myth*, I, p. 38). This meaning lies for Bultmann, who denies the atoning significance of Christ's death along with his demythologizing, lies in the fact that the cross and resurrection make possible the new (eschatological) self-understanding of man. This is, that man should understand himself as crucified and risen with Christ. By attributing to the earliest preachers a conception of the Christ event similar to his own, Bultmann lays the foundation for his interpretation of the rest of the New Testament. There is then nothing to stop him from interpreting even those passages which at first sight seem to oppose it (see under section III) in the same way, for everything must be interpreted in the light of the resurrection. He even takes the Johannine statements about Jesus' divine sonship and unity with God to mean that historical Jesus becomes present in the proclamation, thus taking them as expressions of the paradox of revelation. "The contradictions which pervade the whole gospel are altogether incomprehensible, if its pronouncements are taken as objectifying statements of fact. Alongside the sentences which say that Jesus has dignity and equal privilege with the Father . . . there stand other pronouncements which say that Jesus says and does nothing of himself—that he acts only in obedience to the Father, that he only accomplishes the work which his Father has laid upon him" (*Essays*, p. 290). Such an interpretation can only hold water if the cross and resurrection of Jesus are understood in the faith of the disciples are the (paradoxically) eschatological event, challenging us to accept a similarly paradoxical understanding of existence for ourselves.

Now, of course, Bultmann is perfectly aware that many New

Testament passages take a different view of the resurrection. It is sometimes adduced as a miraculous proof: "Take for instance Acts 17. 31. Here we are actually told that God substantiated the claims of Christ by raising him from the dead. Then, again, the resurrection narratives: both the legend of the empty tomb and the appearances insist on the physical risen body of the Lord (see especially Luke 24. 39–43)" (*Kerygma and Myth*, I, p. 39). Bultmann's reply is that such features are undoubtedly later embellishments of the tradition, of which St Paul is entirely ignorant, though even he had one lapse, when he tried to prove the historicity of the resurrection by adducing a list of eye-witnesses to the appearances (I Cor. 15. 3–8). But this, he contends, is a dangerous procedure, for the resurrection of Jesus cannot be a miraculous proof. Nor can its objective historicity be established, no matter how many witnesses are adduced, for it is itself an objective of faith. There may be a grain of truth in this (see below). But the crucial question remains, how did the earliest Church think of the resurrection of Jesus? The first witnesses were, of course, believers. Was not the resurrection in their eyes, which were the eyes of faith, a historical fact, and therefore really a miraculous proof? Of course they might have been deceived. And it may not prove anything for the sceptic. But that is quite another matter, and is irrelevant here. There is, however, an even deeper reason why Bultmann is shocked at the testimony of the disciples, as he shows when he says that a mythical event like the resuscitation of a corpse is incredible (ibid., p. 39).

The weakness in Bultmann's case has been clearly perceived on the Protestant side. Walther Künneth has written about it in his *Theologie der Auferstehung* ("Theology of the Resurrection", Munich, 1954, 4th ed.). Instead of concentrating on a defence of the historicity of the resurrection, Künneth stresses the supra-historical element in it (ibid., p. 24). This leads him to a number of different conclusions. Historical research is irrelevant for the epistemological side of the problem (ibid., p. 25). This knocks the bottom out of all attempts to explain the resurrection (ibid.). But that is not all. All attempts on the part of orthodoxy to prove the historicity of the resurrection are beside the point (ibid., pp. 17ff.). Catholic theologians will hardly agree with this, at any rate when stated so sharply, though, of course, we should agree that it is only the faith of the witnesses which is susceptible of direct proof, and that it is harder to accept their witness than any other historical evidence. Yet at the same time the apostles' statement of their faith includes a historical element, in intention at any rate, and while this element is not open to objective proof, the subjective reliability of the witnesses is at least open to investigation, and we can form some impression as to the credibility of their testimony. There is no need for us to go more deeply into the theological aspect of the question. We will content ourselves by taking issue with Bultmann over the nature of the Easter faith of the first disciples. Here Künneth insists with refreshing clarity that this faith included the acceptance of the historical factualness of the resurrection, and these under three aspects. It is a real, concrete event, it is a *perfectum*, and it is unique (ibid., pp. 17f.). Künneth takes serious objection to the dismissal of Paul's argument in I Cor. 15 (ibid., p. 23) on the ground that it is dangerous. "The New Testament is undoubtedly concerned with the historical element in the resurrection. The issue at stake is the uniqueness of the event, and that is quite independent of all human consciousness or assessment of it. The centre of gravity in the Easter stories lies, therefore, inevitably in the evidence of the eye-witnesses" (ibid., p. 23).

In a more strictly exegetical study, Karl H. Rengstorf goes still further.[1] For him the appearances of the Risen Christ are emphatically *not* a suspension of history. "They do not narrow history down to the relation of the individual to God. . . . They are not simply the expression of a new self-understanding, commensurate with the redemptive event, and set in motion by it. Quite the contrary. The appearances are presented as an extension of the history of Jesus, and like that history, which stretches from the cradle to the grave, as a personal history acted out in the realm of creation, and must be regarded and accepted as genuine history" (op. cit., p. 74).

[1] K. H. Rengstorf, *Die Auferstehung Jesu*, Witten, 1953.

With this insistence on the historical aspect of the resurrection, Rengstorf never forgets that it also has a far-reaching theological significance. Recent Catholic studies make the same emphasis.[1] "The Easter message is more than an assertion of a historical fact. For the apostles it reaches its climax in the proclamation of religious truth. Raised again, Jesus is confirmed in his Messianic attributes. Glorified, he enjoys divine status" (Schmitt, op. cit., p. 175). "The early Church will not shrink from working out this Christology in more precise terms. In the glorified Jesus it will perceive One who is identical with God" (ibid., p. 189).

Yet these Catholic scholars insist emphatically that this Christology rests upon a real historical foundation. The resurrection is itself an historical event. J. R. Geiselmann has examined the apostles as eye-witnesses, and comes to this conclusion: "The very fact that the first witnesses to Jesus as the Christ claim to be eye-witnesses affords the clearest proof that the primary and most profound issue in their kerygma is a history which they have personally experienced. *Martyrion* and history go together. *Martyrion* is the way history is communicated, the natural corollary of the historical basis of the apostles' proclamation.[2] From the side of speculative and dogmatic theology Karl Adam takes issue with Bultmann on the subject of the Easter message,[3] seeking to prove the reality of the resurrection, and to find out "what kind of reality is to be attributed to the appearances narrated in the Bible."[4] He appeals to the possibility of a supernatural reality existing side by side with an empirical reality. Anything conceivable to thought should not be dismissed without qualification as unhistorical or mythological (op. cit., p. 400). The scriptural evidence leads him to the conclusion which Catholic theologians have always maintained, that while credi-

[1] J. Schmitt, *Jésus réssuscité dans la prédication apostolique* (Paris, 1949); F. X. Durrwell, *La resurrection de Jésus, mystère de salut* (Paris, 1950).

[2] J. R. Geiselmann, *Jesus der Christus* (Stuttgart, 1951), p. 31. Cf. the whole section, 31–48.

[3] Karl Adam, "*Das Problem der Entmythologisierung und die Auferstehung des Christus*" in *Theologische Quartalschrift*, 1952, pp. 285–410.

[4] Op. cit., p. 394.

bility can be demonstrated, nothing can be actually proven (p. 410).

As for the actual evidence, I Cor. 15. 3–8 is usually regarded as the earliest account of the post-resurrection appearances and for the Easter testimony of the primitive Church.[1] Paul is quoting a tradition which he received, probably from the Church of Jerusalem, which has passed on to others (verses 3–5). This is what both he and the original apostles preach (verse 11). Paul is clearly offering this tradition as supporting evidence for the fact of resurrection proclaimed in the original apostolic kerygma. To the traditional formula, which extends to the end of verse 5, he tacks on other appearances known to him, concluding (verse 8) with his own conversion on the road to Damascus. This tendency to seek confirmation for the historical fact results from the theme of the chapter, that anyone who believes in Christ cannot deny the resurrection of the dead, and the proof is adduced by the apostle in verses 12ff.[2] The appearances of the Risen Lord including his own on the road to Damascus are not just a series of visions, but objective occurrences. This is shown by the language he uses to describe them (ὤφθη).[3] If, then, I Cor. 15. 3–8 is the earliest evidence for the primitive Christian Easter faith available to us, the reliability of which is enhanced rather than diminished by the undeniable, though not irreconcilable differences with the resurrection narratives in the gospels, it is more than a little suspicious that Bultmann should stigmatize

[1] M. Goguel, *La naissance du christianisme* (Paris, 1946), p. 54ff. E. Lichtenstein, "*Die älteste christliche Glaubensformel*" in *Zeitschrift für Kirchengeschichte*, LXIII (1950), pp. 1–74, esp. 3–9; Geiselmann, op. cit., p. 73ff.; Rengstorf, op. cit., p. 33ff.

[2] The divergent view of Karl Barth was refuted by Bultmann himself as early as 1926 "for good or evil", out of his own exegetical sense of responsibility: "I can only understand the text as an attempt to make the resurrection of Christ credible as an objective historical fact" (*Glauben und Verstehen*, I, p. 54). As to its actual meaning, Bultmann would go a long way with Barth. He asserts that "Paul lands himself into an inconsistency through his apologetic motive" (ibid., p. 54f.). Cf. further E. B. Allo, *Premiere épître aux Corinthiens* (Paris, 1934, 3rd ed.), excursus, XVII, pp. 394–8; J. R. Geiselmann, op. cit., p. 44ff.

[3] Cf. W. Michaelis, *Die Ersch einungen des Auferstandenen* (Basel, 1944), p. 103ff. TWNT V, pp. 255–62. Rengstorf, op. cit., pp. 38–9, 83–8.

them as dangerous. Actually, he is driven to this by his totally different understanding of the cross and resurrection, an understanding to which the Pauline doctrine of dying and rising again with Christ appears to be more congenial (though, of course, it is not so really). Is it not natural that we should suspect Bultmann of giving a false interpretation to that doctrine, as he does to all the other Christological statements of the New Testament, which are equally based on the original kerygma of I Cor. 15. 3ff.?

Bultmann refuses to accept the traditional sense of the earliest Church's testimony to its faith "that Christ died for our sins in accordance with the scriptures, that he was buried, that he was raised on the third day in accordance with the scriptures, and that he appeared to Cephas, then to the twelve". In the last resort, this refusal to accept the text at its face value must, as we have already said, be attributed to his scepticism as a historian and exegete, and to his rejection as a modern thinker of the mythological language in which the earliest Church expressed its faith. But can such scepticism rescue the Christian faith? Künneth warns us that "the progressive detachment of revelation from its historical moorings . . . leads to the triumph of a new, unhistorical gnosis".[1] We, at any rate, cannot regard Bultmann's existentialist interpretation as a way out of the blind alley into which he is driven by his New Testament criticism and his rejection of the mythological elements in the creed. But is it really impossible for modern man to accept the Chalcedonian formula?[2] Even the early Church, as I Cor. 15 shows (whatever view we take of those at Corinth who denied the resurrection) was not free from difficulties in belief. But it knows that its confession of Christ was founded upon the Easter faith, and that faith in turn upon its faith in God who calls the dead to life.

[1] Op. cit., p. 39.

[2] On this question cf. further O. Simmel, *Mythos und Evangelium* in Std. Z. (1951–52), pp. 33–46; E. Przywara, "*Mythos, Offenbarung, Weisheit, Wissenschaft*" in the *Frankfurter Allgemeine Zeitung*, 4 Nov. 1952; the essays of Karl Adam, F. Mussner and A. Kolping mentioned above; F. Hofmann, "*Theologie der Entmythologisierung—Ausgang oder Irrweg?*" in Theol. Gl. XLIII (1953), pp. 321–47; E. Buess (Prot.), *Die Geschichte des mythischen Erkennens* (Munich, 1953).

BIBLIOGRAPHY

A Bibliography covering publications down to 1953 will be found in *Kerygma and Myth*, I. The present Bibliography covers the years 1954–61.

1. *Works of Rudolf Bultmann available in English*

a. ARTICLES

"The Christian Hope and the Problem of Demythologizing", *The Expository Times*, LXV, 1954, pp. 228–30, 276–80.

"History and Eschatology in the New Testament", *New Testament Studies*, I, 1954, pp. 5–16.

"The Transformation of the Idea of the Church in the History of Early Christianity", *Canadian Journal of Theology*, I, 1955, pp. 73–81.

"The Problem of Miracle", *Religion in Life*, XXVII, 1957, pp. 63–75.

"Demythologizing the Bible", *Current Religious Thought*, N.S. II, 1, 1958, pp. 7–9.

"Theology for Freedom and Responsibility", *The Christian Century*, LXXV, 1958, pp. 967–9.

"What Sense is there to speak of God?", *The Christian Scholar*, XLIII, 3, 1960, pp. 213–22.

b. BOOKS

Essays Philosophical and Theological. Tr. by J. C. G. Greig. S.C.M. Press, London, 1954.

Theology of the New Testament. Vol. II. Tr. by Kendrick Grobel. S.C.M. Press, London, 1954.

Primitive Christianity in Its Contemporary Setting. Tr. by R. H. Fuller. Thames and Hudson, London, 1956.

History and Eschatology (American title: *The Presence of Eternity*). The Gifford Lectures 1955. Edinburgh, The University Press, 1957; Harper, New York, 1957.

Jesus Christ and Mythology. Scribner, New York, 1958.

Existence and Faith. Shorter Writings of Rudolf Bultmann. Meridian Books, New York, 1960.

This World and Beyond. Marburg Sermons. Tr. by Harold Knight. Lutterworth, London, 1960.

2. *Discussions of Bultmann's Demythologizing available in English*

Barth, K. *Church Dogmatics*, III. 2, "The Doctrine of Creation", pp. 442–7, 451–4. Tr. by R. H. Fuller. T. & T. Clark, Edinburgh, 1960.

IV. 1, "The Doctrine of Reconciliation", pp. 767f. Tr. by G. W. Bromiley. T. & T. Clark, Edinburgh, 1956.

Cairns, D. *A Gospel without Myth ? Bultmann's Challenge to the Preacher*. S.C.M. Press, London, 1960.

Davis, G. W. *Existentialism and Theology. An Investigation of the Contribution of Rudolf Bultmann to Theological Thought*. Philosophical Library, New York, 1957.

Hepburn, R. W. *New Essays in Philosophical Theology*, No. 12, "Demythologizing and the Problem of Validity". S.C.M. Press, London, 1955.

Gogarten, F. *Demythologizing and History*. Tr. by N. H. Smith. S.C.M. Press, London, 1955.

Johnson, S. E. "Bultmann and the Mythology" in *Anglican Theological Review*, XXXVII, 1954, pp. 29ff.

Jones, G. V. *Christology and Myth in the New Testament*. Allen & Unwin, London, 1956.

MacQuarrie, J. "Bultmann's Existential Approach to Theology" in *Union Seminary Quarterly Review*, May 1957.

An Existentialist Theology: A Comparison of Heidegger and Bultmann. S.C.M. Press, London, 1958.

The Scope of Demythologizing. S.C.M. Press, London, 1960.

Malevez, L. *The Christian Message and Myth*. Tr. by O. Wyon. S.C.M. Press, London, 1957.

Miegge, G. *Gospel and Myth in the Thought of Rudolf Bultmann*. Tr. by S. C. Neill. Lutterworth, London, 1960.

Owen, H. P. *Revelation and Existence; a Study in the Theology of Rudolf Bultmann*. University of Wales Press, Cardiff, 1957.

Throckmorton, B. *The New Testament and Mythology*. Westminster Press, Philadelphia, 1959.

Wingren, G. *Theology in Conflict*. Tr. by E. H. Wahlstrom. Muhlenberg Press, Philadelphia, 1958.

INDEX